DISCARD

THE GEORGE GUND FOUNDATION
IMPRINT IN AFRICAN AMERICAN STUDIES

The George Gund Foundation has endowed
this imprint to advance understanding of
the history, culture, and current issues
of African Americans.

The publisher gratefully acknowledges the generous contribution to this book provided by the African American Studies Endowment Fund of the University of California Press Associates, which is supported by a major gift from the George Gund Foundation.

ATONEMENT AND FORGIVENESS

ATONEMENT AND FORGIVENESS

A New Model for Black Reparations

Roy L. Brooks

University of California Press   Berkeley Los Angeles London

University of California Press
Berkeley and Los Angeles, California

University of California Press, Ltd.
London, England

© 2004 by the Regents of the University
of California

Library of Congress Cataloging-in-Publication Data

Brooks, Roy L. (Roy Lavon), 1950–.
   Atonement and forgiveness : a new model for
Black reparations / Roy L. Brooks.
      p.   cm.
   "George Gund Foundation imprint in African
American studies."
   Includes bibliographical references and index.
   ISBN 0–520-23941-5 (alk. paper)
      1. African Americans—Reparations.
   2. Atonement.   3. Government liability—United
   States.   I. Title.

E185.89.R45B76   2004
973'.049673—dc22   2004041239

Manufactured in the United States of America
13   12   11   10   09   08   07   06   05   04
10   9   8   7   6   5   4   3   2   1

The paper used in this publication meets the
minimum requirements of ANSI/NISO Z39.48–1992
(R 1997) (*Permanence of Paper*).

*To Watson Branch, a friend, a scholar,
and a beautiful person*

CONTENTS

> Every truth passes through three stages before it is
> recognized. In the first stage it is ridiculed, in the second
> it is opposed, in the third it is regarded as self-evident.
>
> SAYING ATTRIBUTED TO THE GERMAN PHILOSOPHER
> ARTHUR SCHOPENHAUER *(1788–1860)*

When a government commits an atrocity against an innocent people, it has, at the very least, a moral obligation to apologize and to make that apology believable by doing something tangible called a "reparation." The government of the United States committed atrocities against black Americans for two and one-quarter centuries in the form of chattel slavery and for an additional one hundred years in the form of Jim Crow—what Supreme Court Justices Ruth Bader Ginsburg and Stephen Breyer refer to as "a law-enforced racial caste system"[1]—and it has not even tendered an apology for either. The U.S. government should, in fact, atone—that is, both apologize *and* provide reparations—for racial slavery and apartheid. Saying "I'm sorry" just isn't enough.[2]

Atonement would give our government moral credibility and direction through the fog that often engulfs contemporary racial matters. Black Americans, like any self-respecting people, can never forgive or fully trust our government on racial matters until it signals a clear understanding of the magnitude of the atrocities it committed against an innocent people. The past *is* the future. Atonement places the matter of forgiveness on the table. Forgiveness is black America's (the victim's) side of racial reconciliation. Atonement is served on the victim as a kind of civic subpoena. Acceptance is required to seal the deal, to make racial reconciliation possible.[3] *Atonement (apology plus reparations) and forgiveness are thus the key ingredients of racial reconciliation.*

The current debate on reparations, or more precisely, "slave redress" (by which I mean redress for both slavery and Jim Crow), misses an opportunity to move our nation forward with respect to the race problem. Unfortunately, the debate is mostly about "the money," or "compensation," and sometimes about punishment, or "getting even." While I understand the motivation behind this approach to slave redress—which I discuss as the "tort model" in chapter 4—I believe that the debate, if it is to be beneficial to all Americans, particularly black Americans, must be less about the victim and more about the perpetrator.[4] The discussion must be "forward-looking,"[5] by which I mean self-consciously directed toward racial reconciliation. It must begin with and stay focused on the perpetrator's atonement—what I call the "atonement model" (chapter 5). Thus, for me, the atonement syllogism set forth above—to wit, a government has a moral obligation to atone for its past atrocities; our government has not atoned for slavery or Jim Crow; ergo, our government is morally obligated to tender such atonement—states the logic and morality of slave redress. It is a logic I find particularly unanswerable; a logic whose truth I hope the reader will find self-evident.

Like all syllogisms, the atonement syllogism operates apart from matters outside its premises. Its logic is entirely internal, deductive. Yet the consequences of slavery and Jim Crow cannot be ignored when discussing the details of racial reconciliation. Slavery and Jim Crow forced slaves and free blacks, who had few or no resources to begin with, as well as their descendants, into the worst jobs, the worst housing, the worst educational systems, and, in general, the worst plight imaginable in a liberal democratic society. It seems a bit perverse for some to say to blacks now, just thirty years after the death of Jim Crow, that "something is wrong with your culture because you have the worst jobs, the worst housing, and you can't score well on the SAT." The fair thing would be to provide restitution for stolen resources and denied opportunities, many of which are discussed in chapters 1 through 3.

This argument is not as radical as it might seem. Slave redress is, in fact, a racially moderate idea when viewed alongside the once-revolutionary idea of racial equality. It is difficult for those who did not live through the civil rights movement to fathom how dangerous an idea racial equality was for most whites, particularly those in the South. If one believed in racial equality, then one believed in a fundamental restructuring of a social order that had been in place in one form or another since about the time of Plymouth Rock. Most of the hard work and personal sacrifices needed to achieve racial equality have been accomplished thanks to those who came before us. Redress for slavery—the black redress movement—simply picks up the relatively small pieces that did not get swept away during the civil rights movement. Compared to the hard work of ending Jim Crow, providing slave redress in the form of a museum of slavery, an atonement trust fund, or other forms of community rehabilitation—that is, asset-building reparations—as proposed in chapter 5 would be an easy burden for the government to bear.

That burden should be easier for Americans to understand after 9/11. The government came forward in short order with $3 billion for the 3,016 people who died in the attacks on the World Trade Center and the Pentagon. Although it was not responsible for these terrorist acts, our government provided "compensation" and also proposed memorials to honor the victims, both dead and alive. There was an outpouring of compassion, as well there should have been, for the innocent dead and their families. Why can't the government demonstrate similar empathy for the victims, both dead and alive, of its own past atrocities? Why can't the government understand what David Broder refers to as "the strange and powerful ways in which the legacies of the past impinge on the choices and emotions of the present"? This is a question that many black Americans have been asking since 9/11, and one that takes on added significance today, because, as discussed in chapter 6, it comes at a time when demonstrated virtue is a necessary asset in the war on terror.

But perhaps the government is merely following the opinion polls, which show little support for slave redress by white Americans. White opposition to slave redress seems to come from two sources. In the first place, it comes from those who fear that they or their children would be racially disadvantaged if genuine or measurable equality of opportunity were bestowed on blacks. If someone has to be on the bottom in our society, the thinking goes, better that it be blacks than whites. Those who subscribe to this line of thought are not necessarily old-fashioned racists. Most are educated, hard-working middle-class whites who simply have difficulty seeing beyond their own self-interest. They fear that they or their children might become the sacrificial lambs on the altar of racial equality. A second source of opposition comes from whites who are more high-minded. They are imbued with an unbending individualism—the kind that traces back to the ideals of President Reagan, the mythical "frontier thesis" espoused by Frederick Jackson Turner, and the spirit of civic republicanism most prominently embraced during the Age of Jackson (1820–50).[6] These whites deeply believe that our government should not indulge privilege, or, in modern parlance, "special interests."

Our political leaders should not, however, be deterred by such opposition. Most whites are reacting to the existing paradigm for slave redress—the tort model—and know little, if anything, about the atonement model. In focusing on the moral merits of slave redress, the atonement model offers a very different perspective on slave redress. It advances the belief that slave redress serves the moral interests of our government and, in so doing, operates to the benefit of all Americans, not just black Americans. What our political leaders must understand is that the "people" are not always right, that their will can be at odds with moral governance, as in the case of slavery and Jim Crow, and that it is precisely to temper the passions of the majority that we have opted to live under a representative rather than a direct democracy.

I do not discuss the political implications of the atonement model at great lengths in this book, because I have no illusions about reaching those who think only in terms of raw political power—the ox-goring crowd. Reverend Martin Luther King taught us that persistent protest marches and demonstrations, although often met with violent reaction, are the most effective weapons in fighting that type of battle. Perhaps the atonement model will eventually have to be used in conjunction with these political weapons. My hope, however, is that the government and the descendants of slaves can reach racial reconciliation through moral reflection rather than political confrontation.[7]

Our government, in fact, is not far removed from the place where this book seeks to take it. At least in principle, the federal government has already accepted the idea that it, like other governments, should provide redress for past atrocities committed against an innocent people. Native Hawaiians, for example, received an apology from President Clinton a hundred years after the United States overthrew their sovereign nation. Although no president or Congress has apologized to Native Americans for the "ancient atrocities" committed against them, the federal government has given various tribes millions of dollars and, in some cases, returned their land. Japanese Americans and Aleuts received apologies from President Ford and Congress, plus a variety of reparations, both monetary and nonmonetary, from President Reagan and Congress for their forcible removal and internment during World War II. This redress came more than forty years after the fact. Demonstrating, once again, a willingness to confront its past atrocities, Congress in 2000 authorized a government study of the Roosevelt administration's treatment of Italian Americans during World War II. The results of this study, made available in 2001, revealed that Italian Americans suffered some of the same World War II mistreatment as Japanese Americans.[8]

In similar fashion, Congress has passed resolutions calling on other governments to provide redress for acts of injustice in their histories. In 1997, for example, Congress passed the "Lipinski Resolution" calling on the government of Japan to "formally issue a clear and unambiguous apology for the atrocious war crimes committed by the Japanese military during World War II." The crimes to which the Lipinski Resolution expressly referred included the sexual enslavement of "hundreds of thousands of women," Korean, Chinese, Malaysian, Dutch, and other non-Japanese women as young as twelve (documented in dozens of books);[9] and the brutal and systematic "slaughter [of] more than 300,000 Chinese men, women, and children and [the rape of] more than 20,000 women" in the city of Nanjing, China.[10] Significantly, the Lipinski Resolution did not stop with the request for an apology. It went on to ask Japan to *immediately pay reparations to the victims of those crimes*" (emphasis added).[11]

Many governments have joined our government in setting precedents for redressing past atrocities, and they have done so *sua sponte* (i.e., of their own free will). Apology has been the most common way in which governments have sought to provide such redress. The myriad apologies expressed in the past few years include Britain's Queen Elizabeth's apology to the Maori people; Australia's to the stolen Aboriginal children; Canada's to the Canadian-Ukrainians; South Africa's former President F. W. de Klerk's to the victims of apartheid; and Polish, French, and Czech officials' to the victims of atrocities they perpetrated during World War II.[12] In an attempt to explain this phenomenon, this "Age of Apology," I observed on another occasion: "What is happening is more complex than 'contrition chic,' or the canonization of sentimentality. The apologies being offered today are . . . 'a matrix of guilt and mourning, atonement and national revival.' Remorse improves the national spirit and health. It raises the moral threshold of a society."[13]

Although the idea of redressing past injustices—be it in the form of atonement or a monetary payment or social program without a prefatory apology—is now a self-evident truth in many corners of the world, including the United States, this has not always been the case. In fact, the idea of redress consisting of reparations was roundly denounced in the years following World War I. The punitive nature of the regime of reparations the Allies visited upon Germany under the Treaty of Versailles made this form of redress the scorn of the international community. Even during the Paris peace talks, some, such as the British general Henry Wilson, believed that war reparations were a mistake. But it was John Maynard Keynes's devastating indictment of the treaty's reparation clauses, advanced most prominently in *The Economic Consequences of the Peace*,[14] that brought many around to the view that reparations were a mistake. That opinion contrasts sharply with the current view that reparations under the Treaty of Versailles were not especially draconian, given the atrocities committed by the Central Powers, and, hence, cannot be blamed for the rise of Hitler.[15] Quite apart from this revisionist view, the idea of reparations has undergone a conceptual reconstruction. The concept has, in short, been purged of its punitive aura.

It is not difficult to identify the time and place where reparations and other forms of redress for past injustice gained respectability. That transformation took place after the Holocaust. Allied forces played a significant role in this conversion. They not only recorded the Holocaust on film for the entire world to see, but, following orders from Allied commanders, they also made sure the German civilians living in the vicinity of the concentration camps witnessed firsthand this shocking display of inhumanity. German civilians who claimed to have no prior knowledge of Hitler's genocidal operations were paraded through the death camps before the victims were removed. (My good friend and colleague Carl Auerbach witnessed some of these events, because he visited several camps while on special assignment for U.S. military intelligence.) The German people themselves, whether they actually knew about the gas chambers or not, could bear witness to their government's unspeakable crimes against humanity.

There was no way of adequately compensating the victims of this atrocity, no way of returning them to the status quo ante. But the political leaders of postwar Germany felt impelled to do something, even though this genocidal act had not technically occurred on their watch. Speaking for the German government and its people, Konrad Adenauer, the first chancellor of the Federal Republic of Germany, uttered this immortal sentence, which captures the heart and soul of modern redress movements around the world: "*In our name, unspeakable crimes have been committed and demand compensation and restitution, both moral and material, for the persons and properties of the Jews who have been so seriously harmed.*"[16] Adenauer may not have held this moral position at the beginning of his new government. The statement was, in fact, made a few years after the founding of the Federal Republic in 1949. More significantly, his government initially sought to dismantle the Allied program of purges and reeducation of former Nazis and Nazi supporters, including judges, political officials, and teachers, as well as soldiers. Those implicated in Nazi crimes could lose their government jobs or their property as well as face imprisonment. Adenauer thought it more politically expedient to forgive and move on, rather than pursue denazification. Whether he came around willingly to his subsequent position of moral accountability is a matter of some debate among historians.[17] But that is quite beside the point for present purposes. As Justice Felix Frankfurter once noted, "Wisdom too often never comes, and so one ought not to reject it merely because it comes late."

If heartfelt, Adenauer's contrition captures the essence of the post-Holocaust spirit of heightened morality, victim-perpetrator identity, egalitarianism, and restorative justice. It is a model, a moral blueprint of how governments today, including the government of the United States, should respond to redress claims. Indeed, the United Nations regards Germany's redress program, which also provided funds for the new state of Israel, as "the most comprehensive and systematic precedent of reparations by a Government to groups of victims for the redress of wrongs suffered."[18]

The Holocaust, in short, marks the beginning of the modern redress movement. It has emboldened victims of other atrocities to demand redress from their perpetrator governments. The Holocaust has even given nonvictims the right to speak on behalf of victims. Thus, it is no accident that the Lipinski Resolution makes explicit reference to the Holocaust and to the German redress model.

Attesting to its power and magnitude, the Holocaust has not only given voice to new redress claims but also breathed new life into old ones. Nell Jessup Newton links Congress's attempt in 1946 to resolve "*ancient* Indian claims for all time" with "the spirit of post-war egalitarianism and visions of restorative justice," noting:

> The Holocaust in particular impelled policymakers to consider the human rights dimensions of [their] treatment of Native Americans. . . . The Indian Claims Commission Act [enacted in 1946] granted tribes access to the Court of Claim for any future claims, including property claims, redressible by private parties in that Court. The act also created a commission to investigate and settle any and all claims arising *before* 1946 that tribes wished to bring forward.[19]

And as shown above, Congress has attempted to settle past claims of other victim groups as well.

It is only black Americans who have been denied such solicitude. All the civil rights victories—*Brown v. Board of Education* (1954), its progeny, the civil rights legislation of the 1960s and 1970s, and recent Supreme Court rulings upholding affirmative action[20]—do not provide the type of redress for slavery and Jim Crow that is needed to mend the broken relationship between blacks and the federal government. Nor does the defeat of slavery in the Civil War cut it either. While certainly necessary for racial reconciliation, these historic events are not sufficient, as I explain in chapter 6.

My ambition is to make the case for the inclusion of black Americans in this post-Holocaust vision of heightened morality, identity, and egalitarianism and of restorative justice. Although, as discussed in chapter 1, claims for slave redress predate the Holocaust, they have taken on a new significance in the human rights environment that grew out of World War II. There is a poetry and necessity to slave-redress claims when they are viewed in this context that is, unfortunately, missed by both sides of the current debate on slave redress. When slave redress is understood through the atonement model, the black redress movement becomes part of the larger, post-Holocaust international redress movement. Black Americans, thus, ride in partnership, not only with the victims of the Holocaust, but also with the victims of South African apartheid, of the Japanese Imperial Army's infamous World War II system of sexual enslavement (the so-called

Comfort Women), and of similarly large atrocities. Just as the Comfort Women have refused money from the Japanese Diet because of the absence of an accompanying apology, so too should blacks refuse *any* slave redress from the federal government without a prefatory apology. The Comfort Women have demanded not welfare, not a handout, but "atonement money"—there is a difference between being a victim and embracing victimology—and so too should blacks.

The first four chapters set the stage for my argument. Chapter 1 provides a discussion of the purpose and history of the black redress movement, including common threads linking the tort and atonement models, as well as the distinctions between the two. Chapter 2 delineates the ways in which slavery harmed slaves and free blacks alike. Focusing on higher education, chapter 3, the most important and, hence, longest of the ground-laying chapters, attempts to show how today's blacks, the descendants of slaves and free blacks, are the current victims of slavery and Jim Crow. The last of the foundational chapters, chapter 4, provides a critical analysis of the tort model in its litigation mode, which is its predominant expression. Chapter 5 discusses the anatomy of the atonement model—apology plus reparations—and the victim's forgiveness, an issue rarely considered in the current debate. Again, atonement and forgiveness are the key features of racial reconciliation. Finally, looking through the atonement prism, chapter 6 attempts to answer arguments frequently made against slave redress. The Epilogue ends the book with some final observations, including a juxtaposition of the black redress movement with the civil rights movement.

It has taken several years and an army of research assistants to complete this book. I am deeply indebted to them all: Lori S. Batra, Prairie A. Bly, Charity A. Fowler, Naveen S. Gurudevan, Bethany Bogart, Charlotte L. Hasse, Denny Y. Kim, Penina B. Michlin, Shauna N. Roitenberg, Melanie Snyder, Jennifer Spain, and Hillery M. Stones. As always, my assistant, Roanne Shamsky, provided excellent service, for which I am truly grateful. My editors at the University of California Press—Naomi Schneider, Marilyn Schwartz, and Peter Dreyer—were simply superb.

Chapter I | THE PURPOSE AND HISTORY OF THE BLACK REDRESS MOVEMENT

The orchestrated aspiration to obtain slave redress—redress for slavery and Jim Crow collectively—is referred to here as the "black redress movement." Although this orchestration has yet to soar to the symphonic heights of the civil rights movement, and although gigantic conductors of the stature of Martin Luther King and Thurgood Marshall have yet to emerge (but are on the way), it would be wrong to dismiss the black redress movement as a ragtag collection of racial malcontents marching to the beat of their own drum. The movement is growing in strength and acceptance as it becomes better understood. Better understanding is the key to its growth.

Part of this understanding is the realization that, not unlike the pre-1963 civil rights movement (see the Epilogue), the modern black redress movement is in its nascent stage. The modern movement, in fact, began in 1989 with the introduction of a slave redress bill in Congress by Representative John Conyers (D–Mich.). Since 1989, dozens of books, articles, and commentaries have been written about the movement. Similarly, several cities and states have addressed the question of slave redress in various ways. What, then, is the purpose of the modern movement? What, in addition, is its history?

PURPOSE

Whether centered on compensation through the tort model or apology under the atonement model, the black redress movement is an attempt by black Americans and others to secure redress from the federal or state governments for stolen capital on behalf of the slaves, free blacks, and their descendants. By capital, I do not simply mean financial capital (labor and property), but also human capital (education and skills), social capital (social esteem and empowerment), and basic capital (life, liberty, and human dignity). These forms of capital are discussed in greater detail in chapters 2 and 3.

It is equally important to understand that the redress claim against the government encompasses not only the institutions, policies, laws, and procedures of the bifurcated government formed under the Constitution of 1787, but also those of its predecessor regimes. The Continental Congress formed under the Articles of Confederation and the British colonies themselves sanctioned and protected slavery. Slavery remained an institution in this country despite changes in governmental structure and personnel. Various forms of capital were stolen from blacks during a period of approximately two and one-quarter centuries of human bondage (ca. 1638–1865).

The slave redress claim also recognizes the fact that when slavery ended in 1865, it was not replaced with a system of racial equality, except for a few years of Reconstruction. It folded into a system of separate-but-equal Jim Crow laws that lasted approximately one hundred years (ca. 1877–1972).[1] This separate-but-equal regime was much more the former than the latter. Jim Crow was, in fact, a government-mandated or -sanctioned program of racial hegemony and racial preferences for whites, whether rich or poor, male or female, native-born or immigrant. Even though most whites and our political leaders, including the justices of the Supreme Court, claimed that this was not the case, they knew it was.[2] In his years of retirement, President Ulysses Grant wrote with uncommon candor about the true objectives of southern whites in the aftermath of slavery. Southern whites "by force and terror [intended] to . . . deprive colored citizens of the right to . . . a free ballot; to suppress schools in which colored children were taught, and to reduce the colored people to a condition closely akin to that of slavery."[3] The system of racial hegemony ended only thirty years ago with the passage of a federal law, the Equal Employment Opportunity Act of 1972, prohibiting racial discrimination and segregation in state and local employment markets.[4]

The black redress movement, then, makes a twofold argument. First, slavery and the slavelike conditions under which free blacks lived denied these blacks life and liberty (basic capital), plus an estate (financial, human, and social capital) to bequeath to their heirs. Second, Jim Crow forced their descendants, who had little capital to begin with, into the worst jobs, the worst housing, and the worst educational systems, the effects of which are very much in evidence today.

While both the tort model and the atonement model seek redress from the government for the harms slavery and Jim Crow have caused to the slaves, free blacks, and their descendants, the tort model has a secondary purpose, which falls beyond the scope of the atonement model. This is the attempt to seek nonapologetic redress through litigation from private parties who profited from slavery directly. Corporations that have profited from slave labor and wealthy white families whose fortunes were built on the backs of blacks are the main targets of this pursuit. Many blacks today can, in fact, trace their roots back to specific plantation families whose descendants are alive today. Alex Haley's seminal work *Roots* (1976) and, on the other side of the color line, Edward Ball's national bestseller *Slaves in the Family* (1998) illustrate these intergenerational, cross-racial connections. Gwendolyn Hall, a private historian, has gone Haley and Ball one better. She has created a database detailing 161 years of slavery in Louisiana. Everything from slave names, genders, ages, occupations, family relations, and illnesses to the prices paid by slave owners and emancipation records is documented on a CD-ROM located at Louisiana State University.[5]

The major difference between the primary and secondary objectives of the black redress movement may be more than just a matter of emphasis. It may also be one of legitimacy. Because it identifies individual perpetrators, the secondary goal of the movement could be viewed as more legitimate than the primary one, which focuses on governments. On the other hand, the primary objective could be viewed as equally legitimate, if not more legitimate than the secondary objective, because it targets the entities most responsible for slavery and Jim Crow. In addition, the primary purpose, unlike the secondary purpose, spreads the cost of slavery and Jim Crow among all Americans, including whites who benefited the most from these prior systems of racial subordination.

Taken together, these purposes—governmental and private redress—reflect a view of the slave redress issue that the average citizen rarely considers. It is the belief that governmental or private action that "ignores the discriminatory past is just as culpable" as governmental or private action that embraces that past. "No nation," as one pioneer of the tort model has observed, "can enslave a race of people for hundreds of years, set them free bedraggled and penniless, pit them, without assistance in a hostile environment, against privileged victimizers, and then reasonably expect the gap between the heirs of the two groups to narrow."[6] On this point, I am in total agreement with proponents of the tort model.

HISTORICAL BACKGROUND

Though it has a modern dimension, the black redress movement is not a movement of recent vintage. It has deep historical roots in this country. Claims for redress were, in fact, made decades before the end of slavery. And since slavery, each generation of black Americans has reasserted the claim. Black leaders as diverse as Marcus Garvey (a racial separatist) and Martin Luther King (a racial integrationist) have called for slave redress. Today, proponents of redress include the National Association for the Advancement of Colored People (NAACP) (the nation's oldest civil rights organization), Secretary of State Colin Powell, Jesse Jackson, and Louis Farrakhan.[7] Thus, not only does the idea of slave redress enjoy broad support among blacks, it is a timely claim. It is not being raised for the first time some 137 years after the fact.

In sketching the contours of the movement's history, I shall divide the movement into three eras: slavery; post-slavery; and post-Holocaust. The last, which represents the modern movement, is the most important of the three.

THE SLAVERY ERA

The first recorded effort to seek redress for slavery involved a black American born free in 1759 in Massachusetts. This pioneer of slave redress, Paul Cuffe, viewed repatriation to Africa as a form of slave redress. Cuffe and other successful blacks of his day, including Gustavus Vassa, Benjamin Banneker, Phillis Wheatley, and Jupiter Hammon, were part of the larger American movement "toward intellectual and economic self-sufficiency that was so characteristic of the period."[8] Imbued with this postrevolutionary spirit, Cuffe financed the return of thirty-eight free blacks, including himself, to Africa in 1816. Yet he came to believe the government should repatriate both slaves and free blacks to their homeland. As Robert Johnson states, "resettlement was seen as a means of righting a wrong that had begun two centuries earlier. . . . [T]he return to Africa was understood to be a specific, narrowly tailored form of restitution for slavery."[9]

The federal government did in fact finance the repatriation of a small group of free blacks in 1822. This was accomplished through the American Colonization Society (ACS), which was founded after Cuffe's dramatic repatriation. Justice Bushrod Washington, George Washington's brother, was its first president. Indeed, many politically prominent Americans were members of the ACS, including Thomas Jefferson, James Monroe, Andrew Jackson, Henry Clay, Daniel Webster, and Abraham Lincoln. The ACS did not, however, equate colonization with reparations, as did Cuffe and his followers. The organization simply believed that deportation was in the best interests of both races. As Jefferson explained: "Deep rooted prejudices entertained by the whites; ten thousand recollections, by the blacks, of the injuries they have sustained; new provocations; the real distinctions which nature has made; and many other circumstances, will divide us into parties, and produce convulsions which will probably never end but in the extermination of the one or the other race."[10] The abolitionists, however, believed the ACS was only interested in protecting whites, that it "did not have the best interest of African Americans at heart."[11]

Whatever the intentions of the ACS and in spite of Cuffe's singular effort, repatriation as a form of slave redress went nowhere fast. Repatriation was "doomed," as John Hope Franklin remarks, because "the Negro was as permanent a fixture as there was in America."[12] Even in the early nineteenth century, most blacks had come to regard America as their home. They had too much blood and labor invested in this country not to call it home. Blacks wanted to remain in the United States, but on different terms.[13]

Another important antebellum expression of the redress idea came in 1842 in the form of a scathing commentary on society's treatment of blacks, slave and free black alike. It was written by an English barrister then living in the United States. James Grahame castigated the federal government and its citizens, both North and South, for not "redressing long and enormous injustice without any atoning sacrifice or reparatory expense, [for not] restoring and elevating, . . . without any surrender of interest or convenience, the rights and the dignity of a numerous race of men whom they and their fathers have ruined and degraded."[14] A precursor of the atonement model, this early and elegant articulation of slave redress gave way to a more earthly demand for it in the years following the Civil War.

THE POST-SLAVERY ERA

Penniless and defenseless, former slaves pressed for redress during the postbellum period. They did so more out of necessity than as a demand for restorative justice. Ex-slave claims came in two forms. The first consisted of individual claims lodged by former slaves against their former masters. Typical was a letter dated August 7, 1865, written by Jourdon Anderson to his former owner, Colonel P. H. Anderson. The letter said in part: "I served you faithfully for thirty-two years, and Mandy [his wife] twenty years. At twenty-five dollars a month for me, and two dollars a week for Mandy, our earnings would amount to eleven thousand six hundred and eighty dollars."[15] Private redress claims continue to some extent today in the form of lawsuits filed against families and corporations that benefited from slavery.

A second set of claims for redress was based on a federal promise of "forty acres and a mule." Section 4 of the Freedmen's Bureau Act of 1865 authorized the commissioner of the Freedmen's Bureau "to lease not more than forty acres of land within the Confederate states to each freedman or refugee for a period of three years; during or after the lease period, each occupant would be given the option to purchase the land for its value."[16] Section 4 was designed to codify Major General William T. Sherman's Special Field Order No. 15, issued on January 16, 1865, three months before Section 4 was enacted.[17] The promise of "forty acres and a mule" was never fulfilled. In a recent lawsuit, a federal district court judge, Paul L. Friedman, explained what happened:

> Forty acres and a mule. As the Civil War drew to a close, the United States government created the Freedmen's Bureau to provide assistance to former slaves. The government promised to sell or lease to farmers parcels of unoccupied land and land that had been confiscated by the Union during the

war, and it promised the loan of a federal government mule to plow that land. Some African Americans took advantage of these programs and either bought or leased parcels of land. During Reconstruction, however, President Andrew Johnson vetoed a bill to enlarge the powers and activities of the Freedmen's Bureau, and he reversed many of the policies of the Bureau. Much of the promised land that had been leased to African American farmers [approximately 400,000 acres to about 40,000 ex-slaves] was taken away and returned to Confederate loyalists. For most African Americans, the promise of forty acres and a mule was never kept.[18]

Judge Friedman then discusses important evidence that links the current plight of the plaintiffs in the case, black farmers suing the Department of Agriculture for discrimination, with the government's broken promise of "forty acres and a mule." The significance of this discussion warrants an extended quotation:

Despite the government's failure to live up to its promise, African American farmers persevered. By 1910, they had acquired approximately 16 million acres of farmland. By 1920, there were 925,000 African American farms in the United States.

On May 15, 1862, as Congress was debating the issue of providing land for freed former slaves, the United States Department of Agriculture was created. The statute creating the Department charged it with acquiring and preserving "all information concerning agriculture" and collecting "new and valuable seeds and plants; to test, by cultivation, the value of such of them as may require such tests; to propagate such as may be worthy of propagation, and to distribute them among agriculturists.". . . In 1889, the Department of Agriculture achieved full cabinet department status. Today, it has an annual budget of $67.5 billion and administers farm loans and guarantees worth $2.8 billion.

As the Department of Agriculture has grown, the number of African American farmers has declined dramatically. Today, there are fewer than 18,000 African American farms in the United States, and African American farmers now own less then 3 million acres of land. The United States Department of Agriculture and the county commissioners to whom it has delegated so much power *bear much of the responsibility for this dramatic decline* [emphasis in original]. The Department itself has recognized that there has always been a disconnect between what President Lincoln envisioned as "the people's department," serving all of the people, and the widespread belief that the Department is "the last plantation," a department "perceived as playing a key role in what some see as a conspiracy to force minority and disadvantaged farmers off their land through discriminatory loan practices.". . . "Civil Rights at the United States Department of Agriculture: A Report by the Civil Rights Action Team" (Feb. 1997) at 2.

For decades, despite its promise that "no person in the United States shall, on the ground of race, color, or national origin, be excluded from participation in, be denied the benefits of, or be otherwise subjected to discrimination under any program or activity of an applicant or recipient receiving Federal financial assistance from the Department of Agriculture, ". . . the Department of Agriculture and the county commissioners discriminated against African American farmers when they denied, delayed or otherwise frustrated the applications of those farmers for farm loans and other credit and benefit programs. Further compounding the problem, in 1983 the Department of Agriculture disbanded its Office of Civil Rights and stopped responding to claims of discrimination. These events were the culmination of a string of broken promises that had been made to African American farmers for well over a century.

It is difficult to resist the impulse to try to undo all the broken promises and years of discrimination that have led to the precipitous decline in the number of African American farmers in the United States. The Court has before it a proposed settlement of a class action lawsuit that will not undo all that has been done [but is] a good first step towards assuring that the kind of discrimination that has been visited on African American farmers since Reconstruction will not continue into the next century.[19]

The legacy of the past impinges on the present.

Notwithstanding the broken promise of "forty acres and a mule," some blacks did receive land under the Southern Homestead Act of 1866. Unlike the "forty-acres-and-a-mule" promise made a year earlier, the Homestead Act was available to persons of all races. Its purpose was to encourage people to disperse from congested southern population centers. Eighty acres were given to the head of each family under the act, and blacks received hundreds of thousands of acres in this way, but fewer black families received homestead land than the number of black families that would have received "forty acres and a mule" under Special Field Order No. 15.[20]

In 1890, an "Ex-slave Pension and Bounty Bill" was introduced in Congress by Republicans. The idea of the son of an Alabama slaveholder named Walter Vaughan, who had developed "a passion for the welfare of the former slaves," the bill would have provided a maximum payment of $15 per month and a maximum bounty of $500 for each ex-slave. Unfortunately, the bill was never enacted into law. Supporting James Grahame's charge that whites would not give justice to blacks if it meant the "surrender of interest or convenience," Congress rejected the bill on the grounds that, inter alia, "ex-slave pensions would be too large a burden on taxpayers." Some members of Congress also believed that "only education could help the freedmen." The bill was not even supported by the three blacks serving in Congress at the time.[21]

Vaughan continued his fight for ex-slave pensions. His struggle was energized by the growing number of blacks who joined his crusade. "Between 1890 and 1917, over 600,000 of the 4 million emancipated Africans lobbied our government for pensions because they believed their uncompensated labor subsidized the building of the nation's wealth for two and a half centuries."[22] Through the establishment of "Ex-Slave Pension Clubs," including the National Ex-Slave Mutual Relief Bounty and Pension Association, blacks took the forefront in the unsuccessful campaign for a federal slave pension bill. Some white southerners supported the bill because they saw it as an economic benefit for their region.

This round of the legislative effort ended unsuccessfully in 1916. The idea of an ex-slave pension bill never received the support of mainstream black civil rights organizations like the National Negro Business League or the NAACP. The cruelest fate of all befell some of the leaders of the pension movement, many of whom the federal government "pursued, prosecuted, and convicted" on questionable charges, such as "acting fraudulently by collecting money to fund a lobbying effort that instilled the false hope in the hearts of the ex-slaves that the government would give them a pension."[23]

In 1916, in the Federal District Court of the District of Columbia, four blacks reported to have had some affiliation with the ex-slave pension cause filed what may be the first reparations lawsuit ever, alleging that the Treasury Department owed blacks "$68,073,388.99, which was the amount of taxes collected on cotton between 1862 and 1868."[24] According to David Blight, "the records for that period could apparently be recovered and traced," and based on them, this figure "was arrived at as the compensation owed blacks for their labor in production."[25] Like so many redress lawsuits filed today, this lawsuit was dismissed without a decision on the merits.[26]

The final attempt to secure pensions for the ex-slaves came in 1934. It was a last-ditch effort engineered by some of the former slaves themselves. A group wrote to President Franklin Roosevelt asking, "Is there any way to consider the old slaves?" They wanted to know, in particular, if anything was being done about the idea of "giving us pensions in payment for our long days of servitude?"[27] Of course, nothing was done. The idea of constructing a memorial in Washington, D.C., to commemorate the slaves was, however, mentioned as an alternative. But, this idea, which had been kicked around Washington for a number of years, went the way of the ex-slave pension bill.

It is worth mentioning that a memorial commemorating black Civil War veterans, although not quite a slave-redress measure, was the subject of a protest rally in 1915. The demonstration was staged by black veterans in Washington, D.C. Something similar to the black veterans' slave memorial became a distinct possibility in 2003 when President George W. Bush signed legislation that authorized the construction of a museum called the "National Museum of African American History and Culture." Though backed by a 409-to-9 vote in the House and unanimously passed in the Senate, the legislation has a different focus than what the black veterans had in mind when they gathered on the Mall in 1915 to press Congress for the construction of a Civil War memorial. It also has some major defects, which would have displeased the black patriots. There are no assurances that the museum will be built on the Mall, "which sends the message that the story of black Americans is ancillary to the central narrative of American history," and the government is obligated to pay only 50 percent of the cost, with the balance coming from private donations. Most important, from the perspective of atonement, there is no apology for slavery attached to the legislation.[28]

THE POST-HOLOCAUST ERA

The Holocaust shamed the community of civilized nations into taking human rights seriously. It awakened a rare spirit of human understanding, institutionalized in the new United Nations. What the Holocaust taught, perhaps more than any other lesson, is that atrocities can only occur when the perpetrator does not identity with his victim. When the German politician does not identify with the Jewish schoolteacher—when he does not see a common humanity—we have the makings of the Holocaust. But when he does identify with her humanity, when he understands that people of different religious and racial backgrounds have equal moral and legal standing, he is not likely to treat her in barbaric ways. A common morality provides a basis for mutual identification between victim and perpetrator. If this common bond is breached by the commission of an atrocity, the wrongdoer has at the very least a moral obligation to atone for his acts. It is through the process of atonement that the common bond of humanity is restored. The perpetrator reclaims his position in the community of moral beings through apology and reparations.

This post-Holocaust vision of heightened morality, identification, egalitarianism, and restorative justice was certainly not pressed as hard as it should have been in the black redress movement during the 1960s. The most active proponent of slave redress at this time was not Dr. Martin Luther King or the Nation of Islam, even though both were staunch supporters of slave redress. It was the civil rights activist James Forman. Visualize if you will Sunday church service at the all-white and very wealthy Riverside Church in New York City. The year is 1969. King had been assassinated in the preceding year. Forman marches in, interrupting church service, and stands at the front of the congregation holding his "Black Manifesto," a treatise on slave redress. Forman delivers an appeal for redress in the form of what he called "reparations." His appeal is addressed to the "white Christian Churches and Jewish Synagogues in the United States of America and All Other Racist Institutions." Forman's demand, like the "Black Manifesto" itself, outlined in detail many ambitious economic demands, including "the creation of banks, presses, universities, and training centers for African Americans, all to be established as repayment for centuries of racist degradation and exploitation." These demands were, of course, largely ignored. That was 1969.[29]

Nothing of consequence happened in the black redress movement for twenty years. Then, in 1989, and in each year thereafter, Congressman John Conyers submitted a slave redress bill in Congress. Given the name H.R.

40 in recognition of the government's broken promise of "forty acres and a mule," this bill calls for the creation of a commission to study the question of slave redress. It does not request any particular form of redress, but merely asks that the commission study the redress issue. This commission would operate in a manner similar to the commissions established for Japanese and Italian Americans. It would not, however, be as powerful as the Indian Claims Commission, which had authority to decide Native Americans redress claims. Despite these reasonable requests, the bill has never even been voted out of its congressional subcommittee. Consequently, Congress, never having had the redress bill brought before it for formal action, has never voted on it.[30]

H.R. 40 began what I call the modern phase of the black redress movement. It rekindled the redress spirit, which had lay dormant for two decades, among black Americans. More than that, it potentially put a new face on slave redress—an international face. Congressman Conyers has said that the Civil Liberties Act of 1988 inspired him to introduce H.R. 40. In that 1988 redress legislation, Congress apologized to Japanese Americans for their removal and internment during World War II and made its apology believable by legislating a host of reparations, including $20,000 for each victim. The similarities between the redress movement leading up to the Civil Liberties Act and redress movements in other parts of the world, including South Africa, Japan, and Australia, plus other domestic redress movements, such as movements by Native Americans and Hawaiians, are too important to overlook. These movements are less about money than about atonement—apology plus reparations. My ambition is to redefine the black redress movement in light of this international, cross-cultural push for atonement.

Whether I succeed or not, there is no question that the black redress movement has been infused with new vigor since the introduction of H.R. 40. The arguments have gotten more sophisticated and more diverse, the proponents more determined, and the number of believers grows each year. A case in point is the National Coalition of Blacks for Reparations in America, more commonly known as N'COBRA, a grassroots organization created in the early 1990s that enjoys wide support among poor and working-class blacks, which is more responsible than any other group for placing the issue of slave redress on the national agenda.

Now based in Washington, D.C., N'COBRA seeks, inter alia, slave redress primarily in the form of monetary compensation for individual blacks. One of its board members, Taiwo Kujichagulia-Seitu, writes:

> Self-determination, or the ability to determine our own destiny, is the key to reparations, or repairing Black people. . . . The second of a list of six down payment demands for the National Coalition of Blacks for Reparations in America (NCOBRA) is "$25,000 per Black family or the modern day equivalent of 40 acres and a mule." A simple plan for the distribution of such funds would be a requirement for each family (both children and adults) to attend a financial planning seminar prior to receiving the money. At the end of the seminar, they should leave with a plan in hand of how to put the funds to best use in their situation. The use of these funds can also partially serve as a deciding factor in eligibility for business or land grants—the granting boards for which would be elected by members of Black communities across the country. These are just a few ideas.[31]

Portrayed in the media as a "radical" organization, N'COBRA's web site is replete with a diversity of views on the slave redress question. The web site includes links to articles written by mainstream black scholars as well as discussions about such sensitive issues as whether African nations that participated in the slave trade owe black Americans anything.[32]

During the 1990s, other groups and individuals joined N'COBRA in pushing for slave redress. Some of these groups and individuals were pre–H.R. 40 supporters who went on to other issues after 1969. One group that became more active after H.R. 40 was the Nation of Islam. In 1994, the Nation petitioned a UN human rights commission to investigate the issue of slave redress on behalf of black Americans. The petition asked the United Nations to "intervene based on international laws protecting the rights of minorities." The United Nations has yet to respond.

Congressman Tony Hall (D–Ohio) introduced a bill in Congress in 1997 calling for a congressional resolution apologizing for slavery. Unlike H.R. 40, there was no mentioning of a commission to study the question. It merely asked for an apology. The resolution picked up sixteen co-sponsors but was never adopted.[33]

Following a suggestion that appeared in *Essence,* a number of blacks filed "black tax" claims with the Internal Revenue Service during the 1990s. The "black tax" was the estimated current value of "forty acres and a mule."

Blacks claiming this tax reported it on their returns as a tax credit for "slave reparations," or, more technically, as an overpayment of taxes on "undistributed long-term capital gains." One black taxpayer reported annual income of only $3,429 but claimed a refund of $500,000 for the "black tax," which the IRS promptly paid. After paying millions of dollars in "black tax" refunds, the IRS brought lawsuits against accountants who were preparing these returns. An accountant who had filed "at least 13" of these tax returns, Robert L. Foster, was one of the first to be sued. In October 2002, a federal judge in Richmond, Virginia, order him to stop claiming "nonexistent slavery reparations for his African-Americans clients." The IRS has worked out a schedule of repayment for all those who spent their "black tax" refund.[34]

On August 17, 2002, a coalition of black nationalist groups convened a "Millions for Reparations" rally at the National Mall in Washington, D.C. During the demonstration, Minister Louis Farrakhan of the Nation of Islam presented slave redress as a means of empowering young blacks, who, he remarked, were "deserving of a better future." The demonstration could hardly be called a success. The turnout was disappointing and did not begin to approach anything near a million. In addition, only a few of the major figures in the black redress movement, such as Charles Ogletree, Randall Robinson, and Johnnie Cochrane, spoke at the demonstration. Black Americans basically ignored it, perhaps because of its black nationalist bent.

Although the black redress movement has experienced setbacks, it has also achieved some notable successes, particularly in recent years. These victories have come mainly at the state level and within the private sector. In 1994, for example, the Florida legislature enacted the Rosewood Compensation Act to compensate blacks who lost property as a result of a race riot that demolished the all-black town of Rosewood in 1921. No apology was issued, however.[35]

In many respects, California has led the way at the state level. In 2000, California passed legislation that made headline news. It required the state insurance commissioner to obtain from insurance companies doing business in California any records of slaveholder insurance policies issued by any predecessor corporation during the time of slavery.[36] These insurance policies helped to finance the institution of slavery by compensating slaveholders for damage or death to their slaves. The insurance legislation also required the commissioner of insurance to determine whether current law provides a basis for compensating slave descendants and, if not, whether changes in the law should be made. The legislative history behind this new law took note of the related fact that the fortunes of many slaveholders have gone into utility companies located in southern states. Thus, these utilities were in effect built with the blood and sweat of black slaves.[37]

In 2001, California passed additional legislation in support of slave redress. The legislature issued a joint resolution on June 19, 2001, backing both H.R. 40 and Congressman Hall's resolution, discussed earlier. The joint resolution also called on Congress to erect a memorial honoring the slaves.

One of the largest life insurance companies in the United States, Aetna, based in Hartford, Connecticut, which traces its roots to 1853 and once wrote life insurance policies on slaves, naming slave owners as beneficiaries, made two significant moves toward slave redress in 2000. First, it issued a formal apology to black Americans for its participation in sustaining the institution of slavery. Second, it voluntarily created a minority internship program and established a diversity scholarship fund as forms of reparation for its financial support of slavery.[38]

Another Connecticut company made a positive contribution to the slave redress movement in 2000. Connecticut's largest daily newspaper, the *Hartford Courant,* issued a front-page apology for running advertisements for slave auctions and for committing other acts in support of slavery.[39] Unlike Aetna, the newspaper has not been named as a defendant in any of the slave redress lawsuits discussed in chapter 4.

Most of the action on reparations seems to be occurring at the municipal level. Quite a number of cities have passed ordinances supporting the redress movement in one way or another. In 2001, Chicago, Dallas, Detroit, Cleveland, and Washington, D.C., passed resolutions asking Congress to apologize for slavery or, in some cases, to provide redress without apologizing. Chicago's resolution also called on the state of Illinois to deal with its role in slavery. In October 2002, the Chicago City Council approved another ordinance, this one requiring any company wishing to do business with Chicago to investigate and disclose any profits derived from the American slave trade. The Los Angeles City Council unanimously approved a similar ordinance in June 2003. Neither ordinance carries any penalties, but each could provide proponents of slave redress with information that could lead to fresh demands for redress from banks, railroads, insurance, shipping, and other companies. "There can never be any real justice until we discover this information," a Los Angeles councilman, Nate Holden, explained. Detroit, Cleveland, and New York City are considering similar measures.[40]

The Vatican has also supported slave redress. In August 2001, it issued a statement that reads in part: "the evil which has been done must be acknowledged and, as far as possible, corrected."[41] This statement was perhaps timed to coincide with an important international human rights conference scheduled for that month.

From August 31, 2001, to September 8, 2001, government officials, NGOs (Non-Government Organizations), celebrities, and average citizens met at the World Conference against Racism, Racial Discrimination, Xenophobia and Related Intolerance held in Durban, South Africa. Although this United Nations–sponsored conference had the potential to give the black redress movement an important boost, it has been largely relegated to the footnotes of history. Not only was it overshadowed by the terrorist attacks on the World Trade Center and the Pentagon on September 11, 2001, but it failed to achieve anything of real substance for the black redress movement. Still, a study of the conference may provide valuable lessons for the black redress movement.

The primary purpose of this conference was to produce a global blueprint for fighting racism and related offenses on an international basis. I was one of several scholars, political leaders, and activists who came together in April 2001 at the Danish Institute for Human Rights in Copenhagen in the hope of producing a document supportive of the reparations idea that the conference could expressively adopt in its final resolutions. Other groups meeting in other countries, including the United States, had a similar objective. These efforts were doomed even before the conference was called to order.

Circumstances seemed to conspire to prevent the conference from considering the reparations issue. Some of these events were internal; others were external. For example, months before the conference convened, proposed resolutions condemning Israel as a racist country and equating Zionism with racism were announced. The conference consumed much of its time and expended all of its moral capital dealing with these accusatory resolutions. This confrontation gave ammunition to external forces bent on discrediting the conference ab initio. In a disingenuous act that is difficult to forgive, the Bush administration, over the strong objections of its secretary of state, Colin Powell, succeeded in linking the issue of slave redress in the United States with proposed anti-Israel and anti-Zionist resolutions. No friend of slave redress, President Bush's national security advisor, Condoleeza Rice, went along with this nonexistent linkage. In a postconference appearance on NBC's *Meet the Press,* she explained that while the administration had supported the goals of the conference initially, it could not support a gathering that seemed preoccupied with finding ways to condemn Israel. Yet Secretary Powell, who also disagreed with the proposed resolutions targeting Israel, felt that the conference was more than the sum of these misguided efforts and much too important for the United States to pass up. The split between the two highest-ranking blacks in his administration made it that much more easy for President Bush to withdraw from the conference before it began.[42]

A year later, the issue of Durban came before the United Nation for action. "Deeply concerned about persisting and growing racial discrimination, related intolerance and acts of violence," a committee of the UN General Assembly approved a draft resolution on November 25, 2002, that called for "comprehensive implementation of and follow-up to the Durban Declaration and Programme of Action." Even though the Durban Declaration had not adopted language expressly supporting reparations, the United States and Israel felt that they could not support the draft resolution, which passed 153 to 2, with Canada, Australia, and the Marshall Islands abstaining. The U.S. representative agreed with the representative from Israel that, "[t]he highjacking of the Conference did a great disservice to those who would have benefitted from efforts to eradicate racism," and he also cited the "demonstrations outside [the conference] inciting racial hatred" as further reason for the U.S. decision not to support the draft resolution.[43]

Commentators on the right and left have weighed in on the conference, mostly with negative opinions. The *Wall Street Journal,* for example, described the conference as an "orgy of hate and self-denial," charging that "Sub-Saharan Africa wants to talk about slave reparations, but you better not mention Uganda's treatment of the Indians after decolonization or Zimbabwe's treatment of white farmers now."[44] Some observers pointed to the lack of solidarity among the various victim groups on key issues other than the language regarding Israel and Zionism. As an example of what he called "The Solidarity of Self-Interest," the black author and *Newsweek* columnist Ellis Cose, who attended the conference, cited a disturbing development involving black Africans and black Americans. Although both came to the conference advocating reparations for slavery and colonialism, self-interest eventually drove them apart. African nations were interested in debt relief, foreign aid, and investments (called the "New African Initiative") and abandoned the call for reparations to close the deal. "During intense backstage negotiations over world-conference documents, African governments found it relatively easy to drop demands for reparations in return for assurances of support for their own initiatives," Cose notes. "The Africans' willingness to negotiate away the issue prompted one Afro-Latino delegate to quietly suggest that the Africans were abandoning their brothers in the New World. 'They sold us once, and now they're doing it again,' she quipped."[45]

What should the black redress movement take from the Durban experience? At least two lessons, I would say. First, choose your friends wisely. The anti-Israel language was as irrelevant to the issue of slave redress as it was unnecessary for the Durban Conference to accomplish its mission. But by associating with the anti-Israel forces, the supporters of slave redress walked into a windstorm that blew them off course. Perhaps it would have been better to withdraw from the conference after the anti-Israel language became known so as to protect the integrity of the black redress movement. But then again, perhaps the proponents of slave redress felt that it would be hypocritical for them to sit out what at the time appeared to be an important international conference against racism. Second, choose your friends wisely. Political coalitions with other victim groups are likely to founder on the shoals of self-interest. It was not just the Africans who were prepared to sell out their "friends" for selfish reasons; it was other groups as well. As the *Wall Street Journal* pointed out, "The Indians [were willing] to support the U.S.'s attempt to remove the language about Zionism, provided that India's skeleton in the closet, the caste system, [wasn't] mentioned."[46]

Whether black Americans can expect support from foreign governments or other victim groups, such as Japanese Americans and Jewish Americans, is an open question. Certainly, Japanese Americans pretty much flew solo in their fight for reparations from the United States government. They neither built political coalitions nor sought international assistance. They simply drew upon the post-Holocaust vision of heightened morality, identification, egalitarianism, and restorative justice—in other words, the rhetoric of atonement. Japanese Americans were less than 1 percent of the United States population, and they were not politically active as a group when they secured reparations. They prevailed in large part because they captured the moral high ground and, in no small concession to political necessity, were able to garner the support of a few key congressional leaders at the time, such as Senator Bob Dole, whose own World War II wounds enabled him to *identify* with the victims.

Chapter 2 | HARMS TO SLAVES AND FREE BLACKS

Although the use of human beings as domesticated animals reaches back to ancient Mesopotamia,[1] the Atlantic slave trade was not slavery as usual. Initiated by the Portuguese in the fifteenth century, the Atlantic slave trade was a new form of slavery—far more diabolical than that which existed since ancient times, and far more appalling than the intertribal slavery that existed in Africa prior to the European influence. Slavery in the Americas introduced the troubling element of race into the master/slave relationship. For the first time in history, dark skin became the social marker of chattel slavery. And, as a means of justifying this new face—a black face—given to an ancient practice, the slavers and their supporters created a race-specific ideology of condemnation. As I discuss in greater detail in chapter 6, this false rhetoric not only erased the interchangeability of slave and master—the real possibility that a captive might be transformed into kin through marriage or adoption or even become his master's master—from the realm of cultural and political possibility; it also outlasted slavery itself.

The status of the twenty blacks who were put ashore at Jamestown, Virginia, in 1619 by the captain of a Dutch frigate was unclear. Most were indentured servants and were listed as such in the census counts of 1623 and 1624. After their period of service had expired, they were "assigned land in much the same way that it was being assigned to whites who had completed their indenture."[2] But what about the others? Although they were not indentured, they were not slaves; nor were they treated as such by the colonists.

In time, however, racial slavery became institutionalized in the North American colonies—first by custom in the New England colonies (1638) and then by law in Massachusetts (1641).[3] As an institution, slavery thrived in this country until 1865, despite changes in the structure and personnel of our government. Slavery was mandated or sanctioned, not only by the institutions, policies, laws, and procedures of the bifurcated government formed under the Constitution in 1787, but also by those of its predecessor regimes.

The U.S. government was not simply a passive receiver of an illicit tradition. Founded upon the principle of liberty, the government of Washington and Jefferson denied liberty in a most blatant way. More than that, the central government perpetuated a practice that was clearly in decline. "By the eve of the American Revolution," David Brion Davis observes, "there was a remarkable convergence of culture and intellectual developments which at once undercut traditional rationalizations for slavery and offered new ways of identifying with its victims."[4] The founding fathers ignored this convergence of thought and, as a consequence, breathed new life into a morally moribund institution.[5]

Two and one-quarter centuries of human debasement and degradation denied slaves, not only their basic humanity, but also the opportunity to develop resources that could be used for their own empowerment and later bequeathed to future generations of blacks. Slavery harmed the slaves by creating capital deficiencies—developmental encumbrances—within the slave community. These capital deficiencies can be delineated as follows: "basic capital," meaning the denial of life, liberty, and human dignity; "financial capital," consisting of labor, property, and investments; "human capital," denoting formal education, skills, and talent; and "social capital," referring to the way in which a group is viewed by other groups within the society.[6] This, in a nutshell, is the atrocity that the U.S. government and its predecessor regimes forced upon an *innocent* people between 1638 and 1865. Thus, in my view, the peculiar institution stands as the U.S. government's greatest atrocity.

Slavery imposed capital deficiencies on all blacks, not just the slaves.

Both the magnitude and details of these deficiencies can be gleaned from a quick look at the legal status and life experiences of slaves and free blacks ("quasi-slaves") alike.

THE LEGAL STATUS OF SLAVES
AND FREE BLACKS

Surveying the sociolegal status of slaves and free blacks in colonial America, the Supreme Court, in arguably its most infamous case, *Dred Scott v. Sanford* (1857), determined that blacks were "regarded as beings of an inferior order . . . unfit to associate with the white race" and, as such, "they had no rights which the white man was bound to respect." Accordingly, the Court ruled, "the negro might justly and lawfully be reduced to slavery for his benefit."[7] Chief Justice Roger Brooke Taney, who authored the Court's opinion, was primarily referring to the *lex scripto* (the written law) rather than the *lex non scripto* (the common law) of the colonial era, referring, for example, to a 1705 Massachusetts law that forbade the marriage of whites and blacks. Taney, as the ex-slave Frederick Douglass noted in a revised edition of his autobiography, *The Life and Times of Frederick Douglass,* was purporting to describe the sociolegal status of blacks as "historical fact."[8] Yet, as Judge A. Leon Higginbotham makes clear in his seminal treatise *In the Matter of Color,* slaves and free blacks were granted some rights under the written law of colonial America.[9] But to state these rights is almost to deny their existence or, indeed, the existence of any rights sufficient to ensure meaningful capital development.

Virginia is a case in point. By 1705, Virginia law had granted a limited range of rights to blacks as a by-product of a larger endeavor—to wit, the move to proscribe blacks from exercising basic human rights. Whether enslaved or free, blacks were legally excluded from much of the economic, educational, and social life of the state. The 1705 slave code became increasingly repressive with each revision, in 1710, 1723, 1726, 1727, 1732, 1744, 1748, 1753, 1765, 1769, 1778, 1782, 1785, 1787, 1789, and 1792.[10] Under the 1723 revision, for example, free blacks "living at any frontier plantation [were] permitted to keep and use guns," but they were otherwise denied this right.[11] A 1769 revision outlawed the dismemberment of blacks on the grounds that it was "disproportioned to the offense and contrary to the principles of humanity."[12] Yet this same edition of the slave code authorized the castration of any slave who merely attempted to sexually assault a white women. No such penalty was provided for a white man who sexually assaulted a black women, slave or free black.[13] Usually, the penalty for dismembering a slave or free black was merely a fine.[14]

Even in the more "progressive" New England colonies, the ownership of slaves and the concomitant subordination of free blacks were sanctioned by the positive law. Again, Judge Higgenbotham observes:

> It is difficult to discern why, given the relatively small number of blacks in the New England colonies, slavery developed at all. . . .
>
> Yet, New England colonists showed a market preference for black slaves as opposed to white indentured servants. As early as 1645, Edward Downing, Governor Winthrop's brother-in-law, was arguing that blacks were essential to the growth of the colony; . . .
>
> By the end of the 1600s some blacks in New England were perpetual slaves and that status was transmitted to their children. . . .
>
> Perhaps, as some historians have suggested, Massachusetts colonists spoke out in moral outrage against the institution of slavery in 1636. Yet, ownership of human property was endorsed by the power structure, for throughout the colonial period statutes sanctioned the ownership of human beings and the colonial courts protected the masters' ownership interests. Merchants from Massachusetts, the most vigorous slave traders in the New World, made enormous profits from the slave trade. Judicial records are scarce, but those available reveal the prevalence of slavery in the colony.
>
> The institution of slavery remained ambivalently defined in colonial Massachusetts, however. The earliest cases and statutes suggest that at first slavery was viewed as punishment for criminal conduct. Slaves, who were sometimes white, were generally not thought to be perpetually bound to serve. But with succeeding decades, enslavement became perpetual for nonwhites. By 1700 slavery had evolved into a racially identifiable institution. Blacks were imported into the colony as perpetual chattel slaves; Indians were captured and made perpetual slaves. Color itself began to indicate a separate, and lower, social class; free nonwhites were statutorily limited in their movements and in the occupations they could pursue. Despite these deprivations, one factor was crucial and must not be omitted; the nonwhite population in Massachusetts never lost the right and ability to seek judicial determination of the legitimacy of their individual enslavement.[15]

Colonial policies protecting slavery were subsequently incorporated into the founding document of the new republic in 1787. Some have argued that the Constitution as written in 1787 is neutral as to the issue of slavery simply because the word "slave" or "slavery" is nowhere to be found in the text of the document.[16] This argument, at best, is based on a superficial reading of the Constitution. Even the delegates to the Constitutional Convention in Philadelphia saw slavery in the document. They read the Constitution in juxtaposition with its predecessor text, the Articles of Confederation. William Paterson of New Jersey, for example, noted that "under the Articles of Confederation, Congress 'had been ashamed to use the term 'Slaves' & had substituted description.'"[17] Another delegate, James Iredell of North Carolina, agreed that the country's first constitution, the Articles of Confederation, had laid the foundation for the second constitution: "The word *slave* is not mentioned [because] the northern delegates, owing to their particular scruples on the subject of slavery, did not choose the word *slave* to be mentioned."[18] Paul Finkelman suggests that this omission was acceptable to the southern delegates "[a]s long as they were assured of protection for their institution."[19]

The Constitution of 1787 did, indeed, provide ample protection for this evil institution without directly referring to the word "slave" or "slavery." One could quite easily come to the conclusion that the Constitution, in fact, went beyond the Articles of Confederation in its treatment of slavery. Although the latter neither endorsed nor condemned slavery—it simply permitted slavery to exist as it always had, which, of course, is a kind of tacit endorsement[20]—the former affirmatively embraced the peculiar institution. No fewer than five provisions of the Constitution directly accept and protect slavery. *Article I, Section 2, Paragraph 3* (the "three-fifths clause") counted only three-fifths of a slave in determining a state's population for purposes of congressional representation and any "direct taxes." *Article I, Section 9, Paragraph 1* (the "slave-trade clause") prevented Congress from ending the slave trade before the year 1808, but did not require Congress to ban it after that date. *Article I, Section 9, Paragraph 4* ensured that a slave would be counted three-fifths of a white person if a head tax were ever levied. *Article V, Section 2, Paragraph 3* (the "fugitive-slave clause") required the return of fugitive slaves to their owners "on demand." And, finally, *Article V* prohibited Congress from amending the slave-trade clause before 1808.

These constitutional directives, plus about a dozen others that indirectly support slavery,[21] made the Constitution of 1787 *a slaveholder's Constitution.* The nineteenth-century abolitionist William Lloyd Garrison was not exaggerating when he referred to the Constitution as "a covenant with death," "an agreement with Hell," "a pro-slavery" Constitution.[22] Modern historians are in agreement with this view. The late Don Fehrenbacher, for example, asserted that "prior to 1860, the United States was a slaveholding republic."[23] Similarly, the ever-cautious Davis argues: "The U.S. Constitution was designed to protect the rights and security of slaveholders, and between 1792 and 1845 the American political system encouraged and rewarded the expansion of slavery into nine new states."[24]

This foreboding sense that the founding fathers were riding with a few corpses in their cargo was a common feeling at the time. Using Madison's papers, Wendell Phillips, a nineteenth-century Garrisonian, came to the conclusion that "the Nation at large were fully aware of this bargain at the time, and entered into it willingly and with open eyes."[25] Under the slogan "No Union with Slaveholders," Garrison and his followers "refused to participate in American electoral politics, because to do so they would have had to support 'the pro-slavery, war sanctioning Constitution of the United States.'" The Garrisonians, in fact, "repeatedly argued for a dissolution of the Union."[26]

THE LIFE OF A SLAVE

If we were to listen only to slaveholders, we would be compelled to conclude that slavery was a benevolent enterprise. Jefferson Davis, the president of the Confederacy, certainly saw slavery in this fashion. Unlike most of his fellow slaveholders, Davis spoke from experience. Apparently, neither he nor his older brother, the patriarch of the family, mistreated slaves under their control. As one scholar has observed, "The slaves judged and punished themselves. Families were kept together." And, as one of Davis's slaves stated, "We had good grub and good clothes and nobody worked hard." Similarly, Davis treated his black body-servant "with exquisite courtesy and put him in charge of his plantation when he was away."[27]

The slave narratives, on the other hand, paint a very different picture of slavery. These testimonies of ex-slaves give us a vivid view of the hor-

rors of human bondage regardless of the manner in which it was practiced. They tell us without equivocation or hesitation that slavery had no
redeeming value, that the typical slave experience was nightmarish and
demeaning, and that it took a tremendous personal toll on the victims and
their families. The narratives presented here provide a glimpse into the
slave's world, where appalling living conditions and psychological, emotional, and physical persecution were the norm. Under these conditions,
capital development—financial, human, and social—comparable to whites'
was simply not possible. Americans today must come to terms with this
indisputable fact.

One narrative in particular, that of Frederick Douglass, an escaped slave
turned abolitionist and the leading black spokesperson of his day, spoke
ex cathedra for the vast majority of the slaves. It came in the form of a
speech Douglass gave in Rochester, New York, in 1852, courageously condemning, rather than commemorating, Independence Day.

> What, to the American slave, is your Fourth of July? I answer: a day that
> reveals to him, more than all other days in the year, the gross injustice
> and cruelty to which he is the constant victim. To him, your celebration
> is a sham; your boasted liberty, an unholy license; your national greatness,
> swelling vanity; your sounds of rejoicing are empty and heartless; your
> denunciation of tyrants, brass-fronted impudence; your shouts of liberty
> and equality, hollow mockery; your prayers and hymns, your sermons and
> thanksgivings, with all your religious parade and solemnity, are, to Him,
> mere bombast, fraud, deception, impiety, and hypocrisy—a thin veil to cover
> up crimes which would disgrace a nation of savages. There is not a nation of
> savages, there is not a nation on the earth guilty of practices more shocking
> and bloody than are the people of the United States at this very hour.[28]

This narrative is atypical in one important respect, however: it was
penned by the narrator himself, in this case Douglass. Most slave narratives were recorded by others. In addition, most slave narratives were collected either during the first half of the nineteenth century or during the
1930s. These two collections, separated by generations, differ from one another in that the former was taken down by white abolitionists who rewrote
the interviews to conform to the literary standards of the day, whereas the
latter were transcribed word for word by the Federal Writers' Project

(FWP), a federally funded program whose main objectives were to preserve the ex-slaves' language and speech pattern, as well as gather information about slavery. Slave narratives give us an inside view of slavery, from capture in Africa through emancipation in America.

Africans were taken into slavery through several methods. Kidnapping and tribal wars were the most common contexts. Some tribal wars were staged for the sole purpose of capturing slaves. The victorious African chief would trade his prisoners to white slave traders for guns, ammunition, tobacco, liquor, and the like, perhaps believing that slaves in America were treated the same as slaves in Africa.[29]

We were alarmed one morning, just at the break of day, by the horrible uproar caused by mingled shouts of men, and blows given with heavy sticks, upon large wooden drums. The village was surrounded by enemies, who attacked us with clubs, long wooden spears, and bows and arrows. After fighting for more than an hour, those who were not fortunate enough to run away were made prisoners. It was not the object of our enemies to kill; they wished to take us alive and sell us as slaves. I was knocked down by a heavy blow of a club, and when I recovered from the stupor that followed, I found myself tied fast with the long rope I had brought from the desert. . . .

We were immediately led away from this village, through the forest, and were compelled to travel all day as fast as we could walk. . . . We traveled three weeks in the woods—sometimes without any path at all—and arrived one day at a large river with a rapid current. Here we were forced to help our conquerors to roll a great number of dead trees into the water from a vast pile that had been thrown together by high floods.

These trees, being dry and light, floated high out of the water; and when several of them were fastened together with the tough branches of young trees, [they] formed a raft, upon which we all placed ourselves, and descended the river for three days, when we came in sight of what appeared to me the most wonderful object in the world; this was a large ship at anchor in the river. When our raft came near the ship, the white people— for such they were on board—assisted to take us on the deck, and the logs were suffered to float down the river.

I had never seen white people before and they appeared to me the ugliest creatures in the world. The persons who brought us down the river received payment for us of the people in the ship, in various articles, of which I remember that a keg of liquor, and some yards of blue and red cotton cloth were the principal. (Charles Ball)[30]

Although impossible to confirm, it is estimated that from fourteen to twenty-one million Africans were pressed into slavery in the New World over a 350-year period, and that as many as one-third of them died resisting capture or struggling to survive the "middle passage," as the voyage to the Americas was commonly called. The middle passage was a "veritable nightmare." Slaves were packed in ships like sardines, disease was epidemic, and food was scarce and little more than garbage. Many committed suicide rather than endure the middle passage or live as a slave.[31]

> [The ship's doctor] made the most of the room, and *wedged them in.* They had not so much room *as a man in his coffin,* either in length or breadth. It was impossible for them to turn or shift with any degree of ease. He had often occasion to go from one side of their room to the other, in which case he always *took off his shoes,* but could not avoid pinching them; he has the marks on his feet where they bit and scratched him. In every voyage when the ship was full they complained of heat and want of air. Confinement in this situation was so injurious that he has known them *go down apparently in good health at night and [be] found dead in the morning.* On his last voyage he opened a stout man who so died. He found the contents of the thorax and abdomen healthy, and therefore concludes *he died of suffocation in the night.* (Name Unknown)[32]

At the time we came into this ship, she was full of black people, who were all confined in a dark and low place, in irons. The women were in irons as well as the men.

About twenty persons were seized in our village at the time I was; and amongst these were three children so young that they were not able to walk or to eat any hard substance. The mothers of these children had brought them all the way with them and had them in their arms when we were taken on board this ship.

When they put us in irons to be sent to our place of confinement in the ship, the men who fastened the irons on these mothers took the children out of their hands and threw them over the side of the ship into the water. When this was done, two of the women leaped overboard after the children—the third was already confined by a chain to another woman and could not get into the water, but in struggling to disengage herself, she broke her arm and died a few days after of a fever. One of the two women who were in the river was carried down by the weight of her irons before she could be rescued; but the other was taken up by some men in a boat and brought on board. This woman threw herself overboard one night when we were at sea. . . .

We had nothing to eat but yams, which were thrown amongst us at random—and of these we had scarcely enough to support life. More than one third of us died on the passage and when we arrived at Charleston, I was not able to stand. It was more than a week after I left the ship before I could straighten my limbs. I was bought by a trader with several others, brought up the country and sold to my present master. I have been here five years. (Charles Ball)[33]

Having survived the middle passage, the slave faced the auction block and the certainty of being sold to the highest bidder. During his life, a slave could expect to be sold at least twice, and many more times if his owners were in the slave-breeding business. Slaves were inspected like chattel by prospective buyers and even curious onlookers. Perhaps the most atrocious and crushing aspect of the slave market, whether the auction block or a less formal venue, was the breakup of families.

Every first Tuesday slaves were brought in from Virginia and sold on the block. The auctioneer was Cap'n Dorsey. E. M. Cobb was the slave-bringer. They would stand the slaves up on the block and talk about what a fine-looking specimen of black manhood or womanhood they was, tell how healthy they was, look in their mouth and examine their teeth just like they was a horse, and talk about the kind of work they would be fit for and could do. (Morris Hillyer)[34]

Never knew who massa done sold. I remember one morning ol' white man rode up in a buggy and stop by a gal name Lucy that was working in the yard. He say, "Come on. Get in this buggy. I bought you this morning." Then she beg him to let her go tell her baby and husband goodbye, but he say, "Naw! Get in this buggy! Ain't got no time for crying and carrying on." I started crying myself, 'cause I was so scared he was gonna take me, too. But ol' Aunt Cissy, whose child it was, went to massa and told him he was a mean dirty nigger-trader. Ol' massa was sore, but he ain't never said nothin' to Aunt Cissy. Then Hendley what was next to the youngest of her seven children got sick and died. Aunt Cissy ain't sorrowed much. She went straight up to ol' massa and shouted in his face, "Praise God! Praise God!

My little child is gone to Jesus. That's one child of mine you never gonna sell." (Nancy Williams)[35]

I said to him, "For God's sake! Have you bought my wife?" He said he had. When I asked him what she had done, he said she had done nothing, but that her master wanted money. He drew out a pistol and said that if I went near the wagon on which she was, he would shoot me. I asked for leave to shake hands with her which he refused, but said I might stand at a distance and talk with her. My heart was so full that I could say very little. . . . I have never seen or heard from her from that day to this. I loved her as I love my life. (Moses Grandy)[36]

For the great majority of slaves, life on the plantation was far removed from Jefferson Davis's idyllic portrait. Even among Davis's "kindly treated" slaves, to be a slave was to be "owned by another person, as a car, house, or table is owned, . . . to live as a piece of property that could be sold—a child sold from its mother, a wife from her husband, . . . [and to be a] 'thing' whose sole function was determined by the one who owns you.'"[37]

We didn't know nothing like young folks do now. We hardly knowed our names. We was cussed for so many bitches and sons of bitches and bloody bitches and blood of bitches. We never heard our names scarcely at all. First young man I went with wanted to know my initials! What did I know 'bout initials? You ask 'em ten years old now and they'll tell you. That was after the war. (Sallie Crane)[38]

Slaves were not only dehumanized but were typically treated with vicious brutality—worked from dawn to dusk, whipped at the whim of the overseer.

One day while my mammy was washing her back my sister noticed ugly disfiguring scars on it. Inquiring about them, we found, much to our amazement, that they were Mammy's relics of the now gone, if not forgotten, slave days. This was her first reference to her "misery days" that she had made in my presence. Of course we all thought she was telling us a big story and we made fun of her. With eyes flashing, she stopped bathing, dried her back and reached for the smelly ol' black whip that hung behind the kitchen door. Bidding us to strip down to our waists, my little mammy with the boney bent-over back, struck each of us as hard as ever she could with that black-snake whip. Each stroke of the whip drew blood from our backs. "Now," she said to us, "you have a taste of slavery days." (Frank Cooper)[39]

My master used to throw me in a buck and whip me. He would put my hands together and tie them. Then he would strip me naked. Then would make me squat down. Then he would run a stick through behind my knees and in front of my elbows. My knee was up against my chest. My hands was tied together just in front of my shins. The stick between my arms and my knees held me in a squat. That's what they call a buck. You couldn't stand up and you couldn't get your feet out. You couldn't do nothing but just squat there and take what he put on. You couldn't move no way at all. Just try to. You just fall over on one side and have to stay there till you were turned over by him. He could whip me on one side till that was sore and full of blood and then he would whip me on the other side till that was all tore up. I got a scar big as the place my ol' mistress hit me. She took a bull whip once. The bull whip had a piece of iron in the handle of it—and she got mad. She was so mad she took the whip and hit me over the head with the butt end of it and the blood flew. It ran all down my back and dripped off my heels. (Ella Wilson)[40]

Blackshear had them take their babies with them to the field and it was two or three miles from the house to the field. He didn't want them to lose time walking backward and forward nursing. They built a long trough like a great long old cradle and put all these babies in it every morning when the mother come out to the field. It was set at the end of the rows under a big cotton-wood tree. When they were at the other end of the row, all at once a cloud no bigger than a small spot came up and it grew fast, and it thundered and lightened as if the world were coming to an end, and the rain just came down in great sheets. And when it got so they could go to the other end of the field, the trough was filled with water and every baby in it was floating round in the water, drowned. They never got nary a lick of labor and nary a red penny for any of them babies. (Ida Hutchinson)[41]

That slavery was misery for blacks cannot be gainsaid. It not only denied generation after generation of blacks basic capital (life, liberty, and human dignity), but it also denied them the means to develop and accumulate capital—financial capital certainly, but human and social capital as well. Free blacks had a life that was little better. Opportunities for capital development were not substantially different from that of a slave.

Free blacks lived in uneasy coexistence with the peculiar institution. Even a free black living in the North was not really "free." His freedom was relative—he was freer than a slave but considerably less free than a white person. "Because Northern black communities were embedded in a nation that presumed black people to be slaves, black communities cannot be included in free society," Ira Berlin writes. "Instead, they assumed many of the characteristics of *quilombos* or enclaves of fugitive slaves, . . . black Northerners might be considered maroons. . . . The threat of enslavement shocked and terrified black Northerners, sending many into exile. . . . The long shadow of slavery trailed black Northerners, and united them with those who remained enslaved."[42]

Free blacks were excluded from much of the political, economic, educational, and social life of the North. The irony is that this was a region where slavery over time became less profitable than in the South, and where the white population relative to the black population was numerous and rapidly increasing. Northern whites seemed to agonize over the peculiarity of slavery in the land of liberty more so than southern whites. The North was also the breeding ground for the American Revolution and the abolition movement. Yet, as Berlin points out:

> [W]hite northerners introduced new constraints on black life—depriving black men and women . . . [of] the rights most Americans equated with freedom. Various Northern states prohibited free blacks from sitting on juries, testifying in court, carrying guns, attending public schools, and traveling freely. Other proscriptions threatened to transform the state itself into a surrogate master. As part of the national government, northern congressmen joined with southern ones in excluding black people from some of the fundamental rights of citizens. In 1792, the first Congress refused to naturalize Africans and denied black men the right to serve in the national militia or carry the mail, one of the few sources of employment controlled by the federal government. Northern state legislators needed no encouragement from their southern counterparts to extend proscriptions on free blacks. During the 1820's and 1830's, when state constitutional conventions expanded democracy for white men by eliminating property qualifications for voting and holding office, Northern lawmakers simultaneously stripped black men of the suffrage.

Where legislative enactments dared not tread, informal practice—newly established, but anointed with the force of custom—served the same proscriptive function. By general consent, white employers barred free blacks from trades they had practiced openly as slaves, driving them deep into poverty. Unable to gain employment except as . . . day laborers and domestics, black people then found themselves ridiculed for their lack of ambition and irregular work habits. Respectable white men and women shunned them, denying people of color entry to public places and excluding them from churches, schools, and fraternal orders. Older communities "warned out" free blacks, and newer ones barred their entry. When black men and women refused to leave or continued to immigrate, they were assaulted, physically as well as verbally. Their continued presence spurred a movement to colonize or "repatriate" people of African descent, with Africa being the chosen destination. In liquidating slavery, white Northerners tried to rid themselves of black people as well.[43]

The North was thus drenched with racial hatred for blacks even as it fought for the abolition of slavery. An address that appeared in a pamphlet published by the Colonization Society of Connecticut boldly proclaimed: "The habits, the feelings, all the prejudices of society—prejudices which neither refinement, nor argument, nor education, *nor even religion itself* can subdue—mark the people of colour, whether bond or free, as the subjects of a degradation *inevitable and incurable.*" Alexis de Tocqueville noted that even in Quaker Pennsylvania, "no free man of colour dare present himself to vote at an election. Nominally enfranchised by the laws of the State, they are actually disfranchised by the more powerful manners of the people." Similarly, the marquis de Lafayette, the French hero of the Revolutionary War, "after his last visit to America, protested with grief and surprise that the achievement of American Independence had brought only increased misery and oppression on the African race. . . . Africa indeed has had reason to curse the Independence of North America."[44]

Matters were worse in the South. State laws restricted the authority of slaveholders to free their slaves, so as not to create a large population of free blacks—"walking contradictions"—who provided "evil examples" to slaves and, "much worse, [whose] presence imposed a question on the rationale of slavery."[45] These laws not only helped to swell the slave population; they also made life more difficult for free blacks, as each was presumed to be a slave. Free blacks were subjected to such privations and indignities as to make their lives seem unattractive even to a slave. In some respects (not many) free blacks were accorded *less* respect than slaves. Although subsequently discredited, the 1840 census illustrates the white mind-set at the time. As Clayton Cramer explains: "Free blacks were much more often found in . . . [the category of 'insane & idiots'] than were slaves, and as one went north, the frequency of 'insane & idiot' free blacks increased 'with virtual mathematical precision.' To the defenders of slavery, this was clear evidence that blacks were not suited to freedom, and that slavery was a fundamentally humane system."[46]

The overwhelming majority of free blacks in the South, like their brethren in the North, were denied the opportunity to create or develop financial, human, or social capital. They faced racial subordination at every turn, "sternly excluded from all social equality with the whites, from all political franchises and most civil rights. . . . [T]he right of free people of colour even to breathe nature's air in America [was] disputed."[47] As in the North, free blacks in the South were viewed as a "poisonous product" that contaminated the American soil. They were "subjected to the vilest indignities," on which many visitors to the United States commented with surprise. One visitor, a British solicitor, summed up the views of many of his fellow visitors when he observed that, "With close (though perhaps unconscious) copy of the policy of ancient Egypt towards the children of Israel, America denies to free men of colour every liberal motive and every generous style, solace, and recompense of industry; and then insults them with the calumnious reproach 'Ye are idle, ye are idle.'"[48]

While state and local governments in the North and South were responsible for the day-to-day persecution of slaves and free blacks alike, the federal government was far from blameless. By making the conscious decision in 1787 to constitutionalize slavery, the federal government became a front-line perpetrator of an atrocity. By adopting the three-fifths clause, the fugitive slave clause, and other provisions that recognized and protected the peculiar institution, the Constitution was instantly transformed into a slaveholder's charter. In denying slaves and free blacks the opportunity for capital development—including basic life, liberty, and human dignity—the laws of the United States did not recognize the humanity of blacks.

Indeed, this lack of identity between perpetrator and victim gave whites the psychological wherewithal to snatch babies from their mothers' arms and toss them overboard from the slave ships, to wedge slaves into spaces no bigger than a coffin for the long voyage across the Atlantic, to break up families at the auction block or on the plantation, and to brutalize slaves from dawn to dusk until they died. The absence of identity is the common thread that ties slavery to the Holocaust, South African apartheid, and other atrocities. It is the essential delictum of an atrocity.

Slavery has a presence in contemporary society. Many of the capital deficiencies wrought by slavery continue to play an ominous role in the lives of black Americans. These racial disadvantages follow their original arc in broad outline. Only the details have changed.

Chapter 3 | HARMS TO DESCENDANTS

Two persons—one white, the other black—are playing a game of poker. The game has been in progress for almost four hundred years. One player—the white one—has been cheating during much of this time, but now announces: "From this day forward, there will be a new game with new players and no more cheating." Hopeful but somewhat suspicious, the black player responds, "That's great. I've been waiting to hear you say that for four hundred years. Let me ask you, what are you going to do with all those poker chips that you have stacked up on your side of the table all these years?" "Well," says the white player, somewhat bewildered by the question, "I'm going to keep them for the next generation of white players, of course."[1]

Some thirty years after the cheating stopped with the passage of civil rights legislation, the racialized distribution of the poker chips—power, wealth, and privilege—continues to limit opportunities for black Americans.[2] These assets, often invisible, are passed down intergenerationally. Indeed, some economists estimate that "up to 80 percent of lifetime wealth accumulation results from gifts from earlier generations, ranging from the down payment on a home to a bequest by a parent."[3] Thus, power, wealth, and privilege are more than just comforts or indulgences. They create the starting point for the next generation. When power, wealth, and privilege are racialized, the starting point for each succeeding generation is necessarily racialized. It is no wonder that "[t]he typical white family enjoys a net worth that is more than eight times that of its black counterpart."[4]

This is not to say there has been no racial progress over the decades. The point is significant racial disadvantage—capital deficiencies—persists despite such progress. These capital deficiencies are, in addition, rooted in slavery and Jim Crow. True, some racial disadvantage, even if it began during slavery, may be caused by internal, cultural, or behavioral factors. But, as I shall argue in due course, a good deal is caused by external, social, or structural conditions, many of which are themselves products of slavery. Similarly, some external factors influence self-defeating behavior. Nowhere is this more evident than in higher education.

Black high school graduates have significantly less access to elite colleges and significantly less opportunity to complete their college education at less selective colleges than their white counterparts. These disadvantages are not new, nor are their causes, whether external or internal. They were developed during slavery and nurtured during Jim Crow. That, in a nutshell, is the demonstration I wish to make in this chapter.[5]

RECEIVED TRADITIONS

Before making a long, detailed, and context-specific argument regarding the lingering effects of slavery and Jim Crow, I should like to begin with a general critique of the important extant scholarship on the subject, or at least a sampling of it. Scholarship dealing with the question of whether current victims of slavery exist typically proceeds along two parallel lines. Some scholars focus on what can be called the *psychology of slavery,* while others are more concerned with the *socioeconomics* of slavery. Many scholars focus on both. Not surprisingly, conservatives and liberals do not see eye to eye on either matter. I am not in total agreement with either camp.

The Psychology of Slavery

By "the psychology of slavery," I mean attitudes associated with racist rhetoric used to justify the peculiar institution. Harry Ashmore describes this psychology in his observations regarding racial attitudes during the Jim Crow era: "No savant anywhere in the western world arose to challenge the conclusion of the famous 1910 edition of *Encyclopedia Britannica,* assembled under the supervision of the faculties of Oxford and Cambridge: ' . . . the negro would appear to stand on a lower evolutionary plane than the white man, and to be more closely related to the highest anthropoids.' "[6] Ashmore continues: "The concept of white supremacy had been exalted in the South in defense of slavery, but it was by no means confined to the region. Belief that whites were inherently superior to colored people was embedded in the precepts of the European nations that provided the original American settlers, and the immigrants who came later."[7] Conservatives and liberals disagree about the lingering effects of this psychology. Let's begin with the former.

Stephen Thernstrom, Abigail Thernstrom, and Dinesh D'Souza are perhaps the best contemporary conservative scholars on the psychology of slavery. Like many Americans, they see dramatically less racial antipathy toward blacks since the end of the civil rights movement in the early 1970s. Old-fashioned racism, while not dead, is out of style these days. Consequently, conservatives like the Thernstroms and D'Souza do not see blacks in any way limited by the psychology of slavery.[8] As D'Souza writes in recounting a debate he had with the Reverend Jesse Jackson: "I did not deny that racism exists, and conceded that in a big country like the United States one could find many examples of it. But I asked Jackson to prove to me that racism today was potent enough and widespread enough that it could prevent me or him, or my daughter, or his children, from achieving their basic aspirations? Where is that kind of racism, I said—show it to me."[9]

Proof of what the conservatives are arguing can be seen in the American mainstream response to remarks made by Senator Trent Lott (Rep. Mississippi) at the hundredth birthday celebration of retiring Senator Strom Thurmond (R–S.C.). Many conservatives (including the *Wall Street Journal* and the talk show host Rush Limbaugh) and Republican politicians joined liberals and democrats in criticizing Lott's pro-segregationist remarks. The ABC News web site reported the incident, which caused Senator Lott to lose his leadership of the Senate, as follows:

> At Thurmond's 100th birthday party last Thursday [December 5, 2002], Lott boasted that his state of Mississippi backed Thurmond for president 54 years ago. "When Strom Thurmond ran for president, we voted for him," Lott told those gathered at the Capitol Hill celebration. "We are proud of it." To that, the jovial invitation-only crowd of Republican supporters applauded and

laughed. Then Lott continued, "If the rest of the country followed our lead we wouldn't have had all these problems." The room went virtually silent and some in the audience gasped. In 1948, Thurmond ran as a self-described "Dixiecrat" on a segregationist platform. In his campaign, Thurmond vowed that "all the laws of Washington and the bayonets of the Army cannot force the Negro into our homes, our schools, our churches. . . ." Thurmond garnered the 39 electoral votes of South Carolina, Alabama, Louisiana, and Mississippi. He later recanted his segregationist views. . . . [L]ast week was not the first time Lott has spoken out in favor of Thurmond's 1948 campaign in just those words. In November 1980, the *[New York] Times* reported, Lott said virtually the same thing at a campaign rally for Ronald Reagan in Jackson, Miss. After a speech by Thurmond at the rally, Lott said: "You know, if we had elected this man 30 years ago, we wouldn't be in the mess we are in today."[10]

The collective response at both ends of the political spectrum, including the immediate response of conservative commentators, clearly placed Lott's racist remarks outside the mainstream of contemporary American thinking about race.

Liberal scholars do not deny the decline of old-fashioned racism in this post–civil rights movement era. They concede that point. Many, however, argue that there are still enough whites in positions of power who dislike blacks but know enough to keep their opinions private. How many Trent Lotts are there in positions of authority in our society? How is it that he was able to function for so many years at the highest reaches of our government? As Andrew Hacker observes, "there [are] white Americans who continue [to be] convinced of their genetic superiority. . . . [T]his bias [does not] linger only in the rural South; it is also not far from the surface in fashionable suburbs."[11] Justices Ginsburg and Breyer agree, emphatically stating, "It is well documented that conscious and unconscious race bias, even rank discrimination based on race, remain alive in our land, impeding realization of our highest values and ideals."[12]

Other liberals also agree with conservatives about the decline of racial hatred. They argue, however, that a more sinister form of racism exists today. This type of racism operates unintentionally. It functions unconsciously or subconsciously within individuals and systemically within institutions. It is cousin to the old-fashioned style of racism. Both are part of "a very deeply rooted anti-black bias [that has existed] in this country [since slavery]."[13] Indeed, liberals point to recent studies that have identified "newer forms of unintentional racial biases . . . exhibited by many whites who, on a conscious level, endorse egalitarian values and believe themselves to be nonprejudiced. These biases persist inconspicuously but can have grave effects on social perceptions, attitudes, and behaviors."[14]

On the psychology of slavery, I come down on the side of the liberals. Hating blacks and embracing white hegemony, in one way or another, are not one and the same. Although there is still plenty of racial hatred around today, that is not the present issue. For me, the issue today is about racial subordination.

The issue, in other words, is the power, wealth, and privilege—a sense of position—many whites instinctively assert or attempt to maintain over blacks. It is about racism that is cognitive rather than motivational; it is about how whites *perceive* blacks; it is about the use of race as a proxy for "evidence" of criminal behavior in racial profiling, not only by the police, but also by sales clerks in department stores;[15] it is about the dozens of high schools across the South that permit white students to display the confederate flag on their clothing, book covers, lunch boxes, and cars and see nothing wrong with that; it is about negative stereotyping of blacks, a stereotype defined here as "a statistical generalization about some class of person regarding what is taken with reason to be true about them as a class, but cannot be readily determined as true or false for a given member of the class";[16] it is about the little white freckled-faced girl who tells an ABC news reporter that the only thing blacks do better than whites is their hair;[17] it is about the fact that when white children see blacks disproportionately represented in remedial educational classes or being disciplined in school far more often than whites, they take that as strong evidence that blacks are not as smart as whites and misbehave more often than whites; it is about the fact that when whites see a disproportionate percentage of blacks living in dilapidated housing or in poor neighborhoods, they see that as the natural order of things; and, finally, it is about the fact that whites still have difficulty seeing blacks in positions of power, authority, or responsibility, outside of a few exceptional cases like Colin Powell. Indeed, the image of an all-black U.S. Supreme Court would not only create cognitive dissonance among most whites but also put many of them in a froth of anger. To that extent, it is still true that the black American "is 'that shadow which lies athwart our national life,' not as a threat or a curse but as a constant reminder of the injustice and inequality that belie the American Dream and the promise of the nation's foundational ideals."[18]

Some liberals may have moved the psychology-of-slavery argument onto thin ice. In studying the suicide rates of blacks, Alvin Poussaint argues that "a culture of oppression" rooted in slavery has taken a tremendous toll on the minds and bodies of blacks living in contemporary American society "that is virtually unknown to whites." Poussaint, a famous academic psychologist, has been joined by black psychologists outside academia. Omar Reid, Sekou Mims, and Larry Higginbottom are writing a book about what they call "post-traumatic slavery disorder," a derivative of post-traumatic stress disorder. "PTSD," as it is called, is "a general anger and nervousness" about racial matters, which can be experienced in a number of ways, including "a sudden psychotic breakdown," "a series of delusions" (such as that "white strangers on a train [are] staring at [the victim] menacingly"), or an episode of "hyperventilating while walking down the street." Although black people as a whole are suffering from PTSD, the argument continues, the victims are typically adolescent black males, who are showing up "in droves" at hospitals and requiring psychiatric hospitalization lasting at least one month.[19]

Conservatives have been slow to criticize this new wrinkle to the liberal psychology-of-slavery argument. Ward Connerly, a black conservative, is one of the few critics of PTSD. He argues, in classic conservative style, that PTSD perpetuates black victimology. "Some people are just looking for reasons to fail, and this notion of a post-slavery syndrome falls into that category. There is great harm done with something like this." Connerly continues, "We don't want young black kids to grow up thinking they are weak and can't look after themselves." Thus, for Connerly, PTSD is less a medical condition than a policy issue.[20] Of course, neither Connerly nor I have a license to practice medicine.

The Socioeconomics of Slavery

By "the socioeconomics of slavery," I mean socioeconomic patterns created during slavery that are reproduced in contemporary American life. The conservative position on the socioeconomics of slavery is primarily a reaction to the liberal argument. It therefore makes sense to begin with the liberal position.

Glenn Loury, a one-time well-known conservative who has recently drifted toward the liberal position on the socioeconomics question, looks at it from the perspective of capital deficiency theory discussed in chapter 2. In broad fashion, Loury ties capital deficiencies blacks developed during slavery to present conditions. He also suggests that deficiencies in social capital (e.g., being the object of negative group stereotyping) can bring about human capital deficiencies (e.g., poor education owing to low teacher expectations) which in turn can create financial capital deficiencies (e.g., low income owing to poor education or skills).[21]

The key deficiency, in Loury's view, is the deficiency regarding social capital. This deficiency refers to the kinds of social relationships that allow members of a group to take collective action in overcoming problems and "get things done." It is the store of norms and networks a group has at its disposal to influence political, economic, and educational institutions and to participate in public life effectively.[22] Loury argues that blacks today suffer a discernible social capital deficiency, manifested primarily by stigmatization, and that this capital deficiency is related to the low regard in which society has held blacks since slavery.[23]

Stuart Henry and Dragan Milovanovic suggest a different way to discern the socioeconomic connection between slavery and the plight of blacks in contemporary society. This theory, what can be called "social harms" theory, divides social harms into "harms of repression" and "harms of reduction." A harm of repression "occur[s] when an offended party experiences a limitation or restriction preventing [him] from achieving a desired position or standing," and a harm of reduction occurs "when an offended party experiences a loss of some quality relative to [her] present standing."[24] Thus, harms of repression deny opportunities (e.g., overreliance on the SAT limits black access to prestigious colleges and high-paying jobs) and harms of reduction stigmatize (e.g., racial profiling and forms of racial stereotyping that belittle or ridicule blacks). Both sets of social harms began during slavery and linger on in today's society.[25]

Joe Feagin provides the most comprehensive and detailed liberal analysis of the socioeconomics of slavery to date. Through his "social reproduction," or "systemic racism," theory, Feagin attempts to demonstrate how conditions created during slavery have over the years unjustly enriched whites at the expense of blacks. The reproduction of certain socioeconomic conditions transforms prior wealth and privilege obtained through racial oppression into current wealth and privilege. Such systemic racism includes white control of major economic resources (such as corporations and financial institutions), ideological processes (such as the news media and entertainment industry), the administration of justice (the rules by which cases are processed and decided, as well as who decides), and other government institutions. As Feagin explains:

> The perpetuation of systemic racism requires an *intertemporal* reproducing of a variety of organizational structures and institutional and ideological processes. These structures and processes are critical to sustaining racial equalities. Reproduced over time are racially structured institutions, such as the economic institutions that embed the exploitation of black labor and the legal and economic institutions that protect that exploitation and extend oppression into other arenas of societal life. Each new generation inherits the organizational structures that protect unjust enrichment and unjust impoverishment.[26]

Most conservatives do not deny the fact that black Americans experience greater difficulties than whites or even other racial minorities in twenty-first century America. Indeed, the Thernstroms and D'Souza recognize that blacks are near the bottom of almost every measure of socioeconomic success in our society. But they attribute that unpleasant fact to what they regard as a dysfunctional black culture. When they look at black behavior, values, and attitudes, they see such self-defeating traits as crime, victimology, out-of-wedlock babies, and the failure to take education seriously.[27] Black conservatives, including Armstrong Williams,[28] John McWhorter,[29] and Shelby Steele,[30] agree with this argument. Conservatives believe that black victimology, more than any other factor, explains why socioeconomic conditions in black society are so dismal. The conservative critique of the socioeconomics of slavery is not meant to be a putdown of black culture. Rather, it is mostly a genuine attempt to describe socioeconomic reality, which they believe has little, if anything, to do with slavery.

I see several serious flaws in the conservative critique, some of which, quite interestingly, highlight equally grave flaws in positions liberals have taken on related issues. Take, for example, the notion that black students do not take education seriously. This is an old argument that was even made during slavery and Jim Crow to explain the dearth of black college students on white college campuses.[31] Many conservatives and liberals take the position that black students are uninterested in education—"I failed all my classes, it's cool." Conservatives link this to culture, while some liberals see a connection to slavery through PTSD—"slaves were punished if they knew how to read."[32] The problem, of course, is that many slaves still tried very hard to learn how to read, often risking punishment or worse. Frederick Douglass is perhaps the best known of these education-loving slaves. But, more to the point, the high school graduation rate for blacks has been increasing since 1977, while the high school graduation rate for whites has remained relatively stable during the same period.[33] This would strongly suggest that conservatives as well as liberals have misperceived the deep educational desires scores of black students exhibit day in, day out.[34]

The most serious flaw in the conservative critique of the socioeconomics of slavery is their tendency to ignore or discount the force and effect of Jim Crow. Except for a brief period of Reconstruction, blacks faced "harms of repression" and "harms of reduction," to quote Henry and Milovanovic, at every turn from the end of the Civil War to the end of the Second Reconstruction. Although blacks improved their economic well-being during the labor shortages of World Wars I and II, socioeconomic disadvantage, often buttressed by lynchings and other forms of racial violence, was the order of the day. Whole industries and categories of the best-paying jobs were reserved for whites. These apartheid conditions were summarized as follows on the White House's web site during the Clinton Administration: "In grocery and department stores, clerks were white and janitors and elevator operators were black. Generations of African Americans swept the floors in factories while denied the opportunity to become higher paid operatives on the machines. . . . African Americans, even if they were college-educated, worked as bellboys, porters and domestics, unless they could manage to get a scarce teaching position in the all-black school[s]."[35] Thus, in the aftermath of the Civil War, Jim Crow forced the former slaves and their descendants, who had few or no resources to begin with, into the worst jobs, the worst housing, the worst educational systems, and more. Many blacks have not been able to overcome the lingering effects of Jim Crow. This simply cannot be denied or ignored.

Finally, if conservatives are correct in their belief that black culture is inherently dysfunctional, how then do they explain the rise of a genuine black middle class since the death of Jim Crow? We would not have the solid black middle class we now have if black culture was so "junky."[36] But does the existence of a solid black middle class cut the other way as well?[37] Does it not demonstrate that the chains of slavery have in fact been broken for the descendants of slaves? Does it not, thereby, undercut the argument for slave redress? These questions figured prominently in a recent study by a Dartmouth economist.

Bruce Sacerdote makes the argument that the socioeconomic effects of slavery lasted just two generations following emancipation. This much-discussed study, entitled "Slavery and the Intergenerational Transmission of Human Capital," compares the literacy, school attendance, family structure (traditional versus female-headed family), and adult occupational status of the children and grandchildren of former slaves with that of the descendants of free blacks, using data from the 1880 and 1920 censuses. Sacerdote found convergence between the grandchildren of slaves and the descendants of free blacks by 1920 in every category except the prevalence of female-headed households among the former. This suggests to Sacerdote and others that female-headed-household disadvantage is the only measurable lingering socioeconomic effect of slavery.[38]

In my view, Sacerdote's study has limited value in the slave redress debate. The study has several major methodological flaws. First, it fails to factor in the full measure of Jim Crow, which is a big part of the claim for slave redress. Whatever capital deficiencies the slaves suffered, and there were many, as I delineated in chapter 2, their descendants suffered their own set of capital deficiencies under a one-hundred-year regime of racial apartheid. Jim Crow presents claims that, although slavelike, are actionable in themselves.

Second, Sacerdote commits a serious methodological error that is often made by non–civil rights scholars who comment on civil rights questions. The significance of this error warrants some extended discussion. Sacerdote's study and the rise of a genuine black middle class raise a fundamental question in civil rights—namely, how do we measure racial progress? How one calculates racial progress is crucial in discerning a connection between slavery and contemporary life. Many conservative commentators calculate racial progress by comparing an earlier generation of blacks to a later generation of blacks. Thus, for example, Jason Riley, a senior editorial page writer at the *Wall Street Journal,* has written recently: "Black incomes have never been higher, while unemployment and poverty rates rest at all-time lows."[39] Sacerdote's study follows the same pattern. He compares two groups of subordinated blacks over two generations. This type of information fails to measure racial progress adequately, however, because it says nothing about how blacks are doing in relation to whites, who represent the racial norm in our society.

An analogy can be drawn to the antebellum and postbellum periods. Although tremendous intraracial progress from one period to the next was clearly demonstrated by the fact that over four million blacks were released from slavery as a result of the Civil War, blacks still had a long way to go to achieve racial equality measured by what whites had. Free and freed blacks alike had less financial, human, or social capital than whites. They were subordinated at every turn, mired in overt racism and random lynchings. Hence, America *still* had a race problem on its hands notwithstanding significant *intraracial* progress made by blacks resulting from the abolition of slavery.

If Sacerdote's study tells us anything meaningful, it is that free blacks enjoyed very little in the way of socioeconomic opportunities during slavery, that their chances for worldly success were little better than those of the slaves. But this we have known for a long time. Indeed, this is the import of my discussion (in chapter 2) of the life of a free black. Sacerdote's research merely confirms uncontested facts.

Because the opportunities experienced by free black and slave alike were not very different, opponents of slave redress have asserted the alternative-life argument. This curious argument states that if blacks are to be compensated for the life slaves would have had in America but for slavery, they are not entitled to much, because the alternative life of a slave was the life of a free black, which was a life of quasi-slavery. Sacerdote's study supports this argument, although clearly that was not his purpose.

Although the description of the free black's life experiences found in the alternative-life argument is factually correct, the argument is flawed. Like Sacerdote's study, the alternative-life argument is based on an intraracial comparison, slaves versus free blacks. The intent and effect here, however, is to limit the expectations of the slaves, even though slaves were not asking to be liberated into a life "closely akin to that of slavery." They, as well as free blacks, wanted to be treated the same as whites—they wanted equal treatment. Congress, in fact, saw it that way, when in 1866, just one year after the Civil War, it passed a civil rights act that provided, "All persons within the jurisdiction of the United States shall have the same right . . . to make and enforce contracts . . . as is enjoyed by white citizens."[40]

Hence, the grave error committed here, as well as in the Sacerdote study, is that blacks are being compared to themselves. Two subordinated groups are being used as the basis for measuring meaningful racial progress. This is not only absurd but insulting to blacks; for it relegates blacks to a perpetual position of racial inferiority in American society.

Rather than drawing upon intraracial comparisons to chart racial progress, the proper method, in my view, is to make *interracial* comparisons. Blacks should be measured against whites, because whites control the positions of power, wealth, and privilege in our society. They represent the mainstream (or "par value") in American society. Without this comparison—this focus on racial differentials—blacks could easily be relegated to a position of racial inferiority. For, if the test of racial progress were intraracial and if blacks continued to make such progress intergenerationally, no one would care about racial differentials, however enormous, in important areas of American life. No one would have a basis for complaining if blacks moved from the doghouse to the boathouse while whites still lived in the big house.

An interracial perspective, in contrast, helps us to see racial inequality more clearly. It enables us to see slavery's trajectory, the fact that human bondage set in motion a negative set of circumstances that we as a nation have yet to fully redress. Three and a quarter centuries of slavery and Jim Crow created racial fault lines that continue to erupt in twenty-first century America. There is hardly a major segment of American life in which the influence of slavery and Jim Crow cannot be felt. What Justice William O. Douglas said late in the civil rights era rings true today: "Some badges of slavery remain today. While the institution has been outlawed, it has remained in the minds and hearts of many white men" and in many mainstream institutions. There is in contemporary American life, "a spectacle of slavery unwilling to die."[41] The test for *true* racial progress must be equality between the races.

Sacerdote's study is not totally devoid of methodological merit. Indeed, Sacerdote is to be commended for his attempt to bring the discussion of slavery's lingering effects from the level of generality to the level of specificity. Details are what is lacking in most analyses of the lingering-effects issue. The balance of this chapter attempts to add more details to the discussion by focusing on a single context—higher education—and tracing how blacks have fared in that context from colonial times to the present. My goal is to establish the fact that slave descendants (by which I also mean the descendants of free blacks) are current victims of slavery and Jim Crow, at least in the context of higher education.

The argument advanced can be summarized as follows. Slavery created human capital deficiencies in higher education for blacks. These deficiencies—which consist of a low percentage of blacks enrolled in and graduating from mainstream colleges and universities, especially elite schools—have never gone out of existence since slavery, except for one brief period in the 1970s. The fact that these human capital deficiencies have been constant during and since slavery ipso facto establishes a connection to slavery. But there is more. Many of the social forces that gave rise to these capital deficiencies during slavery have also stayed around. Poor public schooling, net family income, racial stereotyping, and other racial harms have sustained black deficiencies in higher education generationally—that is, through Jim Crow and into contemporary society. Thus, like the enrollment and graduation deficiencies themselves, many of their causes have *never ceased to exist.*

FROM THE COLONIAL ERA
TO THE CIVIL WAR

Martin Delany was one of the most accomplished and assertive black Americans of his day. As an editor of the Pittsburgh *Mystery* and co-editor of the Rochester *North Star,* he waged a tireless attack against slavery and segregated education in antebellum America. With impressive letters of recommendation from his private instructors, Dr. Joseph Gazzman and Dr. Julius Le Moyne, Delany applied for admission to Harvard Medical School in 1850. His application, along with those of two other talented blacks, Daniel Laing and Isaac Snowden, ignited a firestorm of protest from the all-white, all-male student body. Among the concerns voiced by the students to both the faculty and Dean Oliver Wendell Holmes, the father of the great Supreme Court justice, Oliver Wendell Holmes Jr., was the belief that the presence of blacks in the lecture rooms at Harvard would lower the medical school's "reputation" and hence "lessen the value of a diploma from it." There was also "concern over additional, and specialized competition." To be sure, there were students favoring the admission of blacks; but the faculty ignored their counterprotest and wasted little time in denying the applications.[42]

Even before slavery took root in America, many blacks exhibited a strong desire for education at the highest intellectual reaches of human endeavor. Indeed, most blacks who came through the middle passage were from West African societies in which education was highly valued. From the fourteenth through the early sixteenth centuries, West Africa was "a great commercial center and one of the world's earliest centers of scholarly knowledge."[43] One such center was the city of Timbuktu in the empire of Mali. Founded in 1307 by King Mansa Kankan Musa, Timbuktu "provid[ed] scholarly learning for all of Africa and the whole of the Middle East."[44] It became home to the University of Sankore. Most of the university's scholars were theologians "well versed in Koranic theology and law."[45] Intellectual centers also developed in Gao, Walata, Jenne, and other cities.

In 1468, Timbuktu became part of the Senghi empire as a result of its capture by Sonni Ali. Many of the city's scholars fled to Walata and other cities, spreading a culture of learning into more African communities. Under the rule of Askia the Great, the University of Sankore developed into "one of the world's greatest seats of learning."[46] Black and white students studied grammar, geography, literature, law, and medicine. One visitor to Timbuktu in 1519, the Moor and noted scholar Leo Africanus, is reported to have seen "numerous doctors, judges, priests, and other learned men who were bountifully maintained at the king's expense."[47]

This embrace of higher learning was undoubtedly transported to America by slaves who survived the middle passage. A slave by the name of Omar ibn Seid reported that:

My birthplace was Fur Tur between the two rivers [the Senegal and Bounoun rivers, 250 miles from Dakar]. I sought knowledge under the instruction of a Sheikh called Mohammed Seid, my own brother and Sheikh Soleiman Kembeh, and Sheikh Gabriel Abdah. I continued my studies twenty-five years, and then returned to my home where I remained six years. Then, there came to our place a large army, who killed many men, and took me, and brought me to the great sea, and sold me into the hands of the Christians. . . . When I left my country I was thirty-seven years old; I have been in the country of the Christians twenty-four years.[48]

Blinded by language, religion, and other cultural differences, not to mention racist ideology used to rationalize human bondage, white Americans could not (and would not) identify with blacks as their intellectual or moral equals. Instead, they saw blacks, in the words of the Supreme Court in the *Dred Scott* case, as "beings of an inferior order, and altogether unfit to associate with the white race, either in social or political relations; and so far inferior that they had no rights which the white man was bound to respect."

Despite such racism, free blacks managed to garner a sliver of higher education in the colonial and antebellum years. Two historically black private colleges were established just prior to the Civil War, Lincoln University in Pennsylvania, founded by Presbyterians in 1854, and Wilberforce University in Ohio. Daniel Alexander Payne, a bishop in the African Methodist Episcopal (A.M.E.) Church, purchased Wilberforce University from a white church group (the Cincinnati Conference of the Methodist Episcopal Church) that had founded it. In 1863, Payne raised enough money from donations ($10,000) to buy Wilberforce University, and he began to set it up as a black institution.[49] These colleges are still in existence. Neither school, however, could claim the distinction of granting the first college degree to a black American or of providing the bulk of college degrees to blacks prior to the Civil War. Those laurels were claimed by white institutions.

As early as 1795, a black by the name of John Chavis attended Princeton, but there is no record of his having graduated. Two African American students were in attendance at Dartmouth as well, but, again, there is no evidence that either actually graduated. John Brown Russwurm, who graduated from Bowdoin College in Brunswick, Maine, on September 6, 1826, is often mentioned as the nation's first black college graduate. Another black, Edward Jones, however, graduated weeks earlier on August 23, 1826, from Amherst. Blacks also graduated from Dartmouth (1828), Ohio University (1828), and Oberlin (which also graduated the first black woman, Mary Jane Patterson, in 1862).[50]

Established in 1833, Oberlin College was one of the first white colleges openly to accept black students. "In its first 50 years, 1,000 African Americans attended Oberlin College and studied the same curriculum as white students in racially integrated classes."[51] Oberlin officials at one time claimed that their college granted half of all the college degrees awarded to blacks in the nineteenth century.[52] Carter G. Woodson, the great black historian, concurred with this self-assessment, writing in 1919 that Oberlin "did so much for the education of Negroes before the Civil War that it was often spoken of as an institution for the education of the people of color."[53] Although Berea College in Berea, Kentucky, founded in 1854, is viewed along with Oberlin as the leading institution of higher education for blacks in the nineteenth century, there is no record of any black graduating from Berea during the antebellum period.[54]

Despite the paucity of higher education, free blacks made advancements during the pre–Civil War period. They became doctors, lawyers, poets, playwrights, historians, and newspaper editors during the antebellum years. Three (Charles L. Reason, William G. Allen, and George B. Vashon) held appointments to the faculty of a white college, Central College in McGraw-ville, New York.[55] Simply looking at the achievements of African Americans from the colonial period through the antebellum period would suggest racial progress. Even John Hope Franklin notes, "Negroes became much more articulate in ante-bellum years than they had been during the previous century."[56] But a broader look at the statistical record tells a very different story.

Human Capital Deficiencies

Statistical data on the number of black Americans in institutions of higher education prior to the Civil War paint a picture of human capital deficiencies in this vital area of American life. Graduation data are more readily available than enrollment data. Most accounts put the number of black college graduates for the colonial and antebellum periods at a mere twenty-eight.[57] The correct figure might actually be higher or lower, but not by much. In fact, one study based primarily on magazines, newsletters, and other material associated with Oberlin College, reports that Oberlin *alone* graduated twenty-eight black students between 1844 and 1865. This study seems reliable, because it gives the names of each graduate, his or her occupation after graduation, and, finally, the occupation of each graduate's father, if known.[58]

That there is uncertainty regarding the number of black college graduates is not entirely surprising. The federal government, which is constitutionally required to conduct a decennial census, the first being in

1790, did not collect detailed data on the racial composition of college graduates during this time. Also, none of the thirty-eight different population counts conducted by some of the colonies before 1790 provide such information.[59] Beyond the failure to collect this specific type of information lies a deeper set of problems, which relate to free blacks and slaves alike.

The decennial census systemically undercounted black Americans. Runaway slaves were understandably reluctant to make their presence known to the census counters even before the Fugitive Slave Act of 1850. The same is true of free blacks. Ira Berlin, Don Fehrenbacher, Paul Finkelman, and other prominent historians have concluded that "prior to 1860, the United States was a slaveholding republic."[60] In this environment, "blacks who were born free, or whose masters had lawfully freed them, were at risk of being kidnaped and enslaved by slave catchers."[61] For various reasons, slaveholders sometimes freed some or all of their slaves, despite laws limiting the master's authority to free his slaves. This created a population of "quasi-free" blacks who, because of their illegal status and fear of being returned to bondage, did their best to avoid census takers.[62] Ira Berlin writes that "it is my belief that the census underestimates the Southern free Negro population by at least 20 percent."[63]

Finally, the absence of a uniform definition of the term *black*, or *Negro*, also distorted the racial statistics. In some states, a "Negro" was defined as a person with "one eighth part or more of Negro blood," while in other states she was defined as a person with "one African ancestor in the previous two generations." But some states, like South Carolina, treated as white "a person of mixed race [who] appeared to be white, and . . . was socially accepted as white."[64] These discrepancies certainly undercut the integrity of pre–Civil War statistics. On the other hand, sophisticated statistical analysis is not needed to establish the dearth of black college graduates in antebellum America.

Causes of Deficiencies

Black Americans suffered two major deficiencies in higher education during the period ending with the Civil War: the dearth of black enrollees and black graduates from mainstream American colleges and universities. Statistics on the number of black enrollees were not complied, but one can deduce the existence of a human capital deficiency in this area from the paltry number of black graduates during this time. Indeed, one can safely say that enrollment was the major deficiency among blacks in this era—there simply were not enough blacks attending college. For this reason, the ensuing discussion of causation will only focus on the enrollment deficiency. Some causes of the enrollment deficiency were internal (or cultural) while others were external (or structural).

Internal. Insufficient secondary education is an obvious internal cause of the shortage of black enrollees in institutions of higher education. As Marilyn Ross points out, "90 percent of blacks remained illiterate" during the antebellum period.[65] But this picture is incomplete, because black illiteracy, an undeniably internal matter, was connected to a powerful external antecedent. Over four million blacks were enslaved by 1860, up from fewer than 700,000 in 1790![66] In some states, free blacks, like slaves, were kept illiterate by law. Those who were permitted to be educated were forced to attend inferior public schools, rendering many of them unprepared for higher education. Thus, the internal cause—insufficient college preparation—was mainly conditioned by two looming external forces—slavery and poor public schooling. This interplay between the internal and external is a recurring racial dynamic in our society.

The level of self-motivation among some free blacks can be counted as another internal factor that negatively influenced black enrollment in higher education. Undoubtedly, some quasi-slaves were discouraged from seeking higher education because they believed that such an ambitious undertaking would only set them up for failure. Given the socioeconomic restrictions to which free blacks were subjected, the idea of studying literature, music, or law certainly would seem fatuous to a rational person. To this extent, an external condition—specifically a harm of repression in the form of discriminatory laws and customs—smothered the desire for higher education among free blacks. This syndrome of not-getting-one's-hopes-up-too-high repeats itself in subsequent years.

Despite that dismal, albeit understandable, outlook, "There is little doubt that free Negroes were eager to secure an education" from which a "more intelligent free Negro citizenry [would] emerge."[67] Indeed, the desire to excel intellectually was shared by the slaves as well. Slaves produced literature, the purpose of which was to "rail against the *arbitrary* and *in-*

humane learning that masters foisted on slaves in order to reinforce a perverse fiction of the 'natural' order of things. The slave wrote not only to demonstrate humane letters but also to demonstrate his or her own membership in the human community."[68]

External. There is little doubt that slavery was the primary external cause of the black enrollment deficiency in higher education in the period ending with the Civil War. Free blacks, as well as slaves, were severely limited by the institution of slavery and the racist rhetoric used to justify its existence. Blacks were persistently stereotyped and belittled in both prerevolutionary and antebellum America, as the Supreme Court's racist discourse in *Dred Scott,* discussed earlier in this chapter, well illustrates. Winthrop D. Jordan, in his classic book, *White over Black: American Attitudes toward the Negro, 1550–1812*, delves into the sources of this racist ideology.[69] In answering the question, "What were the attitudes of white men toward Negroes during the first two centuries of European and African settlement in what became the United States of America," Jordan posits that racist "'attitudes' toward Negroes . . . [arose] from highly articulated ideas about the church or natural rights or the structure of the *cutis vera* [the deeper layer of the skin], . . . [from] off-hand notions and traditional beliefs about climate or savages or the duties of Christian ministers, . . . [from] myths about Africa or Noah or the properties of chimpanzees, . . . [and, finally, from] expressions of the most profound human urges—[in other words] . . . [from] the coded languages of our strivings for death and life and self-identification."[70]

In some respects free blacks, for whom higher education was at least a theoretical possibility, were accorded *less* respect than slaves. The 1840 census, discussed in chapter 2, is a case in point. Free blacks were "much more often" than slaves classified among the "insane & idiots" in nineteenth-century census surveys.[71]

Unremitting and ubiquitous, these racist attitudes certainly affected the quality of college preparation free blacks received in primary and secondary schools. Prior to the ratification of the Fourteenth Amendment in 1868, states had plenary power to "arrange, classify, and distribute pupils." Most states permitted free blacks to be educated, but required them to attend segregated schools. These schools were educationally inferior to white schools—less learning, fewer books, and lower expectations. In response to these discriminatory conditions, blacks began a protracted legal campaign in state courts. Although the struggle for equal educational opportunity began long before the Civil War, victory did not come until after the Civil War, first with a few state court decisions and ultimately in federal court with the Supreme Court's 1954 desegregation ruling in *Brown v. Board of Education.* Poor public schooling, as we shall see, continues to contribute to the black enrollment deficiency a half-century after *Brown.*[72]

Racial discrimination in admissions was another external condition that severely restricted the number of black college enrollees during this period. With few exceptions, blacks were barred from enrolling in institutions of higher education. Thus, even blacks who did in fact have adequate college preparation and who were sufficiently motivated to attend college had few places to go.[73] They were barred by law in most southern states and by social custom in most northern states.[74] Ironically, these restrictions came at a time when "Americans were coming to think of education as a device of great power and as one of the chief means of uplifting the republic."[75] But most whites "felt that . . . [blacks] permanently attached to this country should be kept in ignorance; for if they were enlightened, they would either be freed or exterminated. . . . [Consequently,] the elevation of the race was discouraged in the North and prohibited in most parts of the South."[76]

Some white Americans did in fact challenge racial restrictions placed on college enrollment. Abolitionists were, of course, the most vocal and persistent. They encouraged free blacks "to get as much education as possible for themselves and their offspring." Indeed, at the Convention for the Improvement of the Free People of Color, held in Philadelphia in 1830, William Lloyd Garrison, perhaps the most famous abolitionist aside from Frederick Douglass, advised the congregation that "an ignorant people can never occupy any other than a degraded place in society; they can never be truly free until they are intelligent."[77]

In addition to abolitionists, Quakers and the American Colonization Society (ACS) helped to found black colleges or fund the education of promising blacks at white institutions. One of the most courageous efforts was made by Myrtilla Miner who, along with a Quaker friend and Quaker funds, made several attempts, some more successful than others, to establish an institution of higher education for black girls in Washington, D.C., in the decade prior to the Civil War. Not as innocently, the ACS, of which

Lincoln was a member, supported higher education of black individuals for what many black and white abolitionists considered to be sinister reasons—they wanted free blacks to emigrate back to Africa. The idea was to educate young black men in "mechanic arts, agriculture, science, and Biblical literature," and then repatriate them. "Exceptionally bright youths were to be given special training as catechists, teachers, preachers, and physicians" to prepare them for "civil offices in Liberia and Hayti."[78] Several schools, including the Pittsfield Medical School and the Berkshire Medical School, made it a point to train blacks sponsored by the ACS.[79]

While some free blacks and white supporters believed the best strategy for resolving the college enrollment deficiency consisted of placing as many blacks as possible in white institutions, other free blacks and abolitionists took a different stance. They argued instead that better opportunities for blacks lay in the creation of black colleges—colleges designed specifically for them. Advocates of black colleges insisted that white racism rendered any attempt to educate blacks in white institutions nothing more than an exercise in racial futility.[80] Yet, it was not until after the war between the states that black colleges began to emerge in significant numbers, joining the senior black colleges, Lincoln and Wilberforce, in educating black Americans.

FROM THE POSTBELLUM ERA (1865–95) TO *BROWN V. BOARD OF EDUCATION* (1954)

When Anita Florence Hemmings applied to Vassar College in 1893, there was nothing in her record to suggest that she would be any different from the 103 other girls who were entering the class of 1897. But by August 1897, the world as well as the college had discovered her secret: Anita Hemmings was black [passing for white]. It would be 40 years before Vassar would open its doors to another African-American student.[81]

In 1921, he entered ninth grade at a segregated school in his hometown of Baltimore. A two-story, sixteen-room building, the Colored High and Training School had opened 38 years earlier as the first public high school for blacks in Baltimore. Encouraged by a sterling recommendation from his high school principal, who judged him a student with "very good ability," and by the high expectations of his working-class family, he entered the all-black Lincoln University in September 1925. There, he joined Alpha Phi Alpha, an elite black fraternity, voted with the majority of students in his sociology class to keep the faculty all white, and was later described by a classmate, the great poet Langston Hughes, as "rough and ready, loud and wrong, good natured and uncouth." Upon graduating from Lincoln University, he decided to go to law school. Denied admission to the all-white University of Maryland Law School, he attended Howard University Law School. There he studied under its legendary dean, Charles Hamilton Houston, and graduated first in his class in June 1933. Over the next four decades, this great-grandson of a slave and the son of a country club steward would become the century's most important civil rights lawyer and the first black justice of the United States Supreme Court. His name was Thurgood Marshall.[82]

As a condition of his admission to the University of Oklahoma Graduate School, George McLaurin "was required to sit apart at a designated desk in an anteroom adjoining the classroom; to sit at a designated desk on the mezzanine floor of the library, but not to use the desks in the regular reading room; and to sit at a designated table and to eat a different time from the other students in the school cafeteria." After filing a civil rights lawsuit against the University, but prior to the Supreme Court's ruling on the matter, McLaurin was moved into the classroom, but was "assigned to a seat in the classroom in a row specified for colored students." The only "colored" student in the class, McLaurin was "surrounded by a rail on which there was a sign stating, 'Reserved For Colored.'"[83]

During the postbellum period, the vast majority of the 4.4 million freed slaves remained in the South. Most of the half million free blacks lived there as well. The decennial census of 1860 shows, in fact, that approximately 92 percent of all blacks then resided in the South. Slightly fewer, 90 percent, continued to reside there in 1890.[84] Even after the great northern migrations that took place during the two world wars of the next century, however, the great majority of blacks continued to live in the South.[85]

At the beginning of the postbellum period, the conditions for higher education in the South seemed quite promising for blacks. With their new status as citizens and voters established by the ratification of the Fourteenth and Fifteenth Amendments to the Constitution, respectively, and with the protection of the Union Army, blacks were for the first time in a position to pursue the passion for higher education that slavery had so long frustrated. Blacks applied, and some were admitted, to historically white colleges and universities (or "HWCUs") in the South. Among these educated blacks, some were even hired as faculty at HWCUs. T. McCantis Stewart, on whom the University of South Carolina conferred LL.B. and A.B. degrees in the same year, 1875, is one of the best-known black graduates of an HWCU. More spectacularly, Joseph E. Jones was appointed professor of homiletics and Greek at the Richmond Theological Seminary in 1876. Another black, Richard T. Greener, was appointed professor of metaphysics and logic at the University of South Carolina in 1873. Later, in 1876, Greener received his LL.B. degree from the same institution.[86] There are, however, no reliable records of the total number of black enrollees or graduates from HWCUs in the South during the postbellum period.

Despite evidence of educational attainment at HWCUs in the South, HWCUs in the North continued to offer blacks greater educational opportunities. Between 1865 and 1895, approximately 194 blacks graduated from HWCUs in the North. This calculates to about 6.5 students per year during the thirty-year postbellum period. Most of these graduates, 75 in particular, were from Oberlin College.[87] Thus, the antebellum pattern of black higher education held firm throughout the postbellum period and, indeed, the entire Jim Crow era (ca. 1877–1972), as we shall see. But even though HWCUs in the North continued to provide greater educational opportunities for blacks than those in the South, all HWCUs, whether in the South or the North, limited the number of blacks admitted. This set the stage for the creation of one of black America's most important institutions—the historically black college and university (or "HBCU").

Fearful that most qualified blacks would not be admitted to HWCUs, and would thus be denied a college education, black leaders and white abolitionists, as we have seen, pushed for the creation of black colleges and universities even before the Civil War.[88] This sentiment grew after the Civil War as northern missionary groups, who had followed behind Union forces during the war, establishing "literally thousands of elementary schools for Negroes, . . . became convinced of the Negro's academic potential."[89] In line with this thinking, President Lincoln signed legislation on March 3, 1865, that created the Freedmen's Bureau, a federal agency charged with providing educational opportunities and other forms of relief for the newly freed slaves. Howard University, named for the first commissioner of the Freedman's Bureau, General O. O. Howard, one of the first and still the most famous of the HBCUs, was established during this period.

Most HBCUs were, in fact, founded after the Civil War. Joining Lincoln and Wilberforce, these schools made a largely unsuccessful attempt to meet the higher educational needs of black Americans, both free and freed. Although race-specific in their mission and enrollment, HBCUs, which would be joined in later years by other predominantly black colleges or traditionally black institutions ("PBC" and "TBI," herein also referred to as "HBCUs"),[90] could not, as we shall see, compensate for the dearth of black college enrollees and graduates of mainstream American institutions of higher education from the end of the Civil War to *Brown v. Board of Education.*[91]

Human Capital Deficiencies

Though HBCUs were the primary institutions of higher education for black Americans between 1865 and 1954, the government did not keep reliable enrollment figures in the early years. We do, however, have fairly good graduation data for the entire period. These figures show that the number of black graduates grew steadily during this period. From 1868 to 1952, for example, the number of black graduates went from a total of approximately 400 students for the 1868–84 (sixteen-year) interval, averaging 33.3 students per year, to a total of about 69,500 students for the 1939–52 (thirteen-year) interval, averaging 5,346 students per year on the eve of *Brown.*[92]

Although the number of degrees from HBCUs increased over the decades, these schools could hardly meet the postsecondary educational needs of blacks. The degrees they granted carried little educational value. Insufficiently financed and unevenly governed, HBCUs produced in the main "Jim Crow degrees." Most of these schools provided little more than elementary and secondary education to the thousands of hopeful students who passed through their portals each year.

The main problems lay in the schools' uneven funding and governance. Some schools received federal or state funds and were governed by independent boards of trustees or by blacks themselves. Others were funded and controlled by black churches (such as the African Methodist Episcopal Church) or funded and controlled by white northern religious groups. Most private schools were funded and governed by northern white religious and missionary philanthropists.[93] Regardless of financial or organizational structure, the majority of HBCUs did not have sufficient funding or governance to ensure that students would receive some semblance of a college education. Limited curricular offerings, discouragingly low teacher salaries, and poor staffing, equipment, and facilities were the order of the day at most of these schools. Indeed, the first comprehensive study of HBCUs, which was conducted by the federal government in 1916, concluded with an alarming statistic: "only 33 of the 653 existing . . . private and state schools were teaching any subjects of college grade."[94] This was by design.

Most religious and missionary philanthropists who supported HBCUs held limited views regarding the proper purpose of black higher education. They mainly envisioned higher education as a vehicle for producing black teachers and preachers. In the words of one philanthropist, the primary mission of HBCUs was "to educate . . . a number of blacks and send them forth to regenerate their own."[95] In other words, the idea was "that Negro Higher Education should accept willingly those provisions however begrudgingly awarded by white supporting boards and philanthropy. . . . [T]he evolving Negro college, in turn, dispersed the notion that the Negro, after all, *was* inferior to the white man."[96]

This diminished vision of black higher education was not, however, limited to religious and missionary philanthropists. Most white supporters of HBCUs envisioned blacks learning the "moral and social values of thrift, industry, frugality, and sobriety, all of which were necessary to live a sustained Christian life" and exist in racial harmony with whites in the New South.[97] Most "shied away from questions of racial integration and were probably convinced that blacks' cultural and religious values were inferior to those of middle-class whites."[98]

Despite these obstacles, some HBCUs managed to produce college-level curriculums. Some, in fact, did well early on. Howard, Fisk, Lincoln, Wilberforce, Leland, Atlanta, and Shaw "began collegiate departments by or before 1872."[99] Due primarily to the influence of accrediting associations, the quality of education at many HBCUs saw "significant improvement [by 1954] with respect to administration and organization; preparation of faculty; endowment and other sources of income; supporting instructional services such as library holdings and science laboratories; and other physical expansion."[100]

Even though the quality of HBCUs steadily improved over the years, HBCUs could not carry the full educational load for the entire black population. A 1929 federal study of HBCUs seemed to say as much when it concluded that the black American's "immediate need is more education, better education, and higher education."[101] This study also provided enrollment data comparing whites attending HWCUs with blacks attending HBCUs:

> It was estimated for January 1, 1926, that the population of the United States was 117,136,000, of whom 105,539,000 were white and 11,597,000 were colored. At the same time there were enrolled in colleges, universities, teachers' colleges, and normal schools attended primarily by whites, 942,443, and in colleges, universities, teachers' colleges, and normal schools attended by negroes, 17,506. Accordingly, for every 10,000 whites, 90 white students were attending college; and for every 10,000 negroes, 15 students were attending college.[102]

A subsequent federal study found that no HBCU awarded a doctoral degree in 1947. In that year, blacks earned 8 doctorates from HWCUs, compared with some 3,775 granted to whites. A year earlier, 154 blacks received medical degrees, only twenty of which came from HBCUs (actually, just two: Howard University and Meharry Medical School).[103] The 1950 census reported that in the South, where most backs continued to live, only 4.1 percent of the black adult population had attended college, compared to 13.6 percent of whites, and only 1.9 percent of the black adult population received a bachelor's degree, compared to 6.0 percent of the white adult population.[104]

Clearly, blacks needed educational opportunities beyond those offered by HBCUs. Referring to HBCUs, the President's Commission on Higher Education concluded in 1950 that "America cannot afford to let any of its potential human resources go undiscovered and undeveloped."[105]

Causes of Deficiencies

Between the years 1865 and 1954, black Americans encountered the same human capital deficiencies in higher educational they faced during slavery—insufficient enrollment and graduation from HWCUs. Attendance was the major problem. There simply were not enough blacks enrolled in institutions of higher education to produce healthy graduation numbers. For that reason, it makes sense to focus, once again, on the enrollment deficiency in discussing causation. Both internal (or cultural) and external (or structural) factors will be considered.

Internal. One possible internal cause of the enrollment deficiency was the then-widespread belief that black applicants were simply unqualified to study at HWCUs. Looking at the black literacy rate during the period, one might, at first glance, agree with this explanation. In 1890, the percentage of literate blacks was only 41 percent, compared to a white literacy rate of 68.8 percent. But by as early as 1930, the percentage of literate blacks had increased to 81 percent (an increase of 93.8 percent), compared to 90.8 percent (or a 32 percent increase) for whites.[106] More important, many blacks, certainly more than the paltry number admitted, were sufficiently educated, even in the South, "to undertake a college program in 1865 or shortly thereafter."[107]

The rapid improvement in black literacy undercuts another "racially neutral" justification given for black educational deficiency. That argument asserted that blacks were not interested in seeking higher education. Most blacks, especially in the South, idealized Booker T. Washington, who, as the most famous black leader in America at the turn of the century, preached a philosophy of self-reliance through manual labor: "Our greatest danger is that in the great leap from slavery to freedom we may overlook the fact that the masses of us are to live by the production of our hands, and fail to keep in mind that we shall prosper in proportion as we learn to dignify and glorify common labour and put brains and skill into the common occupations of life."[108] Even W. E. B. Du Bois, Washington's black nemesis, advocated sending "the majority [of blacks] through vocational training, and allowing the remaining 10 percent (the Talented Tenth) to go on to higher education and eventual leadership in the community."[109] The problem with that argument is that not even the top 10 percent of blacks were being admitted to HWCUs. Moreover, by the 1930s, when the black literacy rate had reached 81 percent, blacks were no longer listening to Washington (who died in 1915) or Du Bois (who had become a black separatist). Instead, blacks were largely supportive of the NAACP's campaign of equal educational opportunity. Du Bois, a co-founder of the NAACP, broke with the organization in 1934.[110]

This shift in black attitude was recorded in the pages of the many black monthly periodicals of the era. Higher education received prominent treatment in the *Colored American Magazine,* the *Voice of the Negro, Alexander's Magazine, The Crisis,* and many other black magazines. The coverage grew increasingly assertive between 1900 and 1930, moving from mere profiles of illustrious abolitionist founders or early presidents of HBCUs to discussions of "the value and meaning of a doctoral degree." Whether these magazines were truly representative of black thinking on the value of higher education is open to debate. But I tend to agree with Michael Fultz who asserts: "Without question, these journals were the means through which the black middle class and professional group defined their vision and disseminated their views."[111]

The extracurricular activities of black students at HBCUs offer additional evidence of the desire for higher education among blacks. These activities, which have received little scholarly attention, show black students initiating intellectual activities beyond the classroom. Literary and debate clubs, designed to create a well-rounded, highly educated person, were the primary intellectual endeavors of black students outside the classroom. With faculty support, students at Fisk University in 1868 formed the Union Literary Club, the first and one of the longest-running literary clubs of its kind in the history of HBCUs. In 1881, students at Fisk formed another literary club, Beta Kappa Beta, and no fewer than seven more by the end of the century, including the Dunbar, Extempore, and English debating clubs. Howard, Morehouse, Atlanta, and other black colleges formed similar extracurricular clubs during this time. By 1940, "there was hardly a black school that did not have at least one literary society" in which students discussed or debated such issues as "Was Henry VIII's reign 'productive of more good than evil in England?'" "[Are] pensions for Union and Confederate Civil War Veterans [justified]?" "Was Phyllis Wheatley 'the greatest of African poets?'" Students even grappled with the insightful question "Does higher education meet the demands of the time?"[112]

Despite these impressive demonstrations, it cannot be gainsaid that internal forces in some sense militated against the higher educational aspirations of blacks, whether at HWCUs or HBCUs. Not unlike in the antebellum period, the earthly need to supplement family income caused many black teenagers to end their formal education prematurely. Poor academic preparation put college beyond the reach of others. This cultural picture would, however, be seriously incomplete without a consideration of the external climate of the day.

External. More than anything else, racial discrimination and segregation adversely affected the internal drive for higher education among blacks. Many blacks "felt no enthusiasm for the cause of education as they plowed through books and subjects that told them little about themselves and merely whetted their appetites for a world which they could not hope to enter."[113] Prospective college students could readily see that "college-bred Afro-Americans [were] unable to obtain jobs."[114] Quite naturally, frustration set in. This was particularly so in the towns and cities, as blacks began to leave the farmlands in pursuit of urban opportunities. At times, pent-up racial disappointment would lead to delinquency and crime.[115]

There is no question that blacks were subordinated at every turn between 1865 and 1954. Immediately after the Civil War, southern legislatures enacted local laws, known as Black Codes, that denied blacks the basic rights of citizenship guaranteed by the Constitution. Buttressed by violence and terror, the Black Codes sought to reduce blacks to a condition resembling that of slavery.[116] To be sure, blacks were given some rights, such as the rights to sue and to testify in court. But in the main, blacks were a subordinated people. They could, for instance, be denied employment and housing simply because of the color of their skin. Worse, idle blacks could be arrested under local vagrancy and peonage laws, and then hired out by the sheriff.[117] The connection to slavery is too obvious to miss.

Jim Crow—government-mandated or -sanctioned discrimination and segregation of blacks—began to appear as early as the late 1870s, but mainly in the 1890s. In the South, the Black Codes were mostly replaced by rigid, racially repressive Jim Crow laws. In the North, social norms resembling Jim Crow laws, which actually predated the Civil War, denied opportunities to blacks. These looser, yet vigorously enforced, racial traditions were often just as effective in denying opportunities to blacks as were the Jim Crow laws.[118] Describing his first visit to the North in the 1930s, one white southerner observed: "Proudly cosmopolitan New York was in most respects more thoroughly segregated than any Southern city: with the exception of a small coterie of intellectuals, musicians, and entertainers there was little traffic between the white world and the black enclave in upper Manhattan called Harlem."[119]

Following the Supreme Court's adoption of the "separate but equal" doctrine in 1896 in *Plessy v. Ferguson,* southern states enacted school segregation laws that explicitly precluded blacks from attending HWCUs so long as separate educational institutions were available. In fact, Berea College, which opened its doors to blacks before the Civil War, was convicted under a Kentucky law, which the Supreme Court subsequently upheld, that made it a crime for "any person, corporation or association of persons to maintain or operate any college, school, or institution where persons of the white and negro races are both received as pupils for instruction."[120] Federal school law was often just as discriminatory as state law. A prime example is the Morrill Act of July 2, 1862 (the first Morrill Act), which established a nationwide system of land grant colleges. Congress specified that "the establishment and maintenance of such colleges separately for white and colored students will be held to be in compliance with the provisions of this act if the funds received in such State or Territory be equally divided as hereinafter set forth."[121]

In the North, where there were few segregation statutes governing higher education, HWCUs adopted racially discriminatory admissions policies or practices to regulate the admission of black applicants. At Harvard University, for example, students in the 1930s "were sorted by academic rank and grouped into five categories. The first four were by schools; the fifth was by race."[122] Like Yale and Princeton, Harvard enrolled about five or six blacks each year during this time. Simultaneously, Jewish students were subjected to a 10–15 percent admissions quota.[123]

The few blacks admitted to HWCUs walked into a racial climate that mirrored that of the larger society. Marcia Synnott describes the housing situation at Harvard, which very much reflected the tenor of the times:

When Harvard opened three Freshman Halls in 1914, College officials handled dormitory and roommate assignments carefully to avoid parental and student objections. By intermingling most freshmen in these units, except those permitted to live off-campus, President Lowell hoped to prevent the formation of cliques based upon schools and economic or geographical distinctions. But he believed that black students should be *persuaded* to seek other accommodations, since it would be *unreasonable* to "compel" whites to live in the same halls with them. In 1922, he personally turned down the application of Roscoe Conkling Bruce on behalf of his son, a student at Phillips Academy Exeter. (Bruce himself was a Phi Beta Kappa and magna cum laude graduate of the Class of 1902 and the son of a former United States Senator, Blanche K. Bruce of Mississippi.) Under pressure— a petition signed by 143 alumni opposing the exclusion of black freshmen from the Halls—Lowell and the Harvard Corporation reversed their stand. But if a black student could not afford the cheapest single nor find a black roommate, he would be unable to live in any one of the Freshmen Halls.[124]

In 1954, the Supreme Court's opinion in *Brown v. Board of Education* sounded the death knell to this dual system of higher education, bringing forth the promise that the dearth of black enrollees and graduates of HWCUs would eventually end.

FROM *BROWN* (1954) TO THE POST–CIVIL RIGHTS ERA (1980)

In May 1955, three qualified black students applied to the University [of North Carolina] as undergraduates. . . . The University was forced to choose between admitting the students—thus giving up segregation—or refusing to let them in, which would lead to a NAACP lawsuit that threatened to make it all the way to the Supreme Court. The University decided to admit the students. . . .

On March 3, 1960, after a sit-in in a Greensboro Woolworth, students from five area colleges, including UNC, held a "sit-down strike" at the Howard Johnson's on 15–501 between Durham and Chapel Hill. This occurred the day after Joe Powell, a black graduate student, sat down to eat with three of his white friends. The police came, warning him of an arrest for trespassing if he didn't leave. . . .

. . . Joel Williamson has been at UNC since 1960. He currently teaches White Culture and Race Relations in the American South.

In 1963, Williamson taught his first black student, one of the 140 students he had that year. He recalled the sentiment on campus by both the students and faculty toward this student. "He was treated very well by the other students," Williamson said. "Some professors were intolerant. One in particular gave him a hard time. [He] didn't like him sitting next to the girls."

Williamson also remembered how almost every black student during that time was viewed as a token black student, one who was forced to represent his race. He viewed this as discrimination on campus. . . . [White students believed black students] were admitted to fill a quota. . . .

In 1974, only 40 blacks served on the faculty. Records also indicate that while the enrollment of women increased to 44.6 percent that

fall, the blacks represented only 6.6 percent of the student body—
there were only 165 more black students than the previous year.[125]

In 1954, the Supreme Court in *Brown I* held that the concept of "separate
but equal" has no place in the field of primary and secondary public education.[126] The Court followed this holding a year later with the disappointing ruling in *Brown II* that states had an affirmative duty to dis-
establish de jure segregation in K-12 schools, not immediately, but rather
"with all deliberate speed."[127] That was the first time the Court had deferred the implementation of constitutional rights. Neither case, however,
expressly overruled *Plessy v. Ferguson*. *Plessy* dealt with a different issue—
the constitutionality of separate railroad cars for the whites and non-
whites—but it was widely believed that *Brown I* had tacitly *(sub silentio)*
overturned *Plessy*. *Plessy* was expressly overruled in 1956 in the case of *Gayle
v. Browder*.[128] Thus, by the mid-1950s, the Supreme Court had established
a firm federal policy of a unitary system of primary and secondary education, still limited, however, by the "with all deliberate speed" edict announced in *Brown II*.

The unitary school policy was, however, extended to postsecondary education in 1956 without restrictions. In *State of Florida, ex rel Hawkins v.
Board of Control*, the Supreme Court held that the "with all deliberate
speed" standard did not apply to institutions of higher education, and that,
consequently, blacks had to be admitted immediately "under the rules and
regulations applicable to other qualified candidates."[129] Indeed, higher education presented a host of considerations not present in elementary or
secondary education, which made desegregation at this level easier in some
ways and harder in other ways. There were, for example, no school district lines or residency requirements for attending colleges and universities. Students exercised freedom of choice. On the other hand, there was
one phenomenon of postsecondary education that made desegregation extraordinarily difficult in this setting—HBCUs.

Although relics of a segregated way of life, HBCUs could not easily be
jettisoned. Pressure to preserve these schools came from the fact that they
served important student needs that HWCUs simply could not meet.
HBCUs "fill[ed] a unique niche in our educational system . . . [by pro-
viding] African-American students who have, to that point, been 'shel-
tered' in the African-American community" with a choice between an ed-

ucationally supportive environment and a hostile environment.[130] Despite these benefits, proponents of integration saw these institutions as blemishes on a new racial order and thus sought to dismantle them.[131]

It was not until 1992, well after the *Brown* opinions and *State of Florida, ex rel Hawkins,* that the Supreme Court finally clarified the desegregation standards applicable to all institutions of higher education, whether HWCUs or HBCUs. In *United States v. Fordice,* the Court held that current policies traceable to de jure segregation and that had a discriminatory effect "must be removed to the extent practicable and consistent with sound educational practices." This standard of "racial identifiability" attributable to de jure segregation would seem fatal to HBCUs, but the lone black justice on the Court, conservative Justice Clarence Thomas, did not see it that way and observed in a concurring opinion that the justices "do not foreclose the possibility that there exists 'sound educational justification' for maintaining historically black colleges *as such.*"[132] Justice Thomas noted that HBCUs are important institutions in the black community and serve the educational needs of many black students. His opinion sounded a cautionary note, made clearer in a 1995 case involving elementary and secondary education, in which he remarked: "It never ceases to amaze me that the courts are so willing to assume that anything that is predominantly black must be inferior."[133]

Despite Justice Thomas's favorable reading of *Fordice,* attempts have been made to "desegregate" HBCUs. Indeed, on remand in *Fordice,* the lower court mandated equal admission standards for HBCUs and HWCUs in the state of Mississippi. This ruling was made over the vehement objection of blacks who argued through their attorneys that the new standards would cut black enrollment in half at Mississippi's three HBCUs. The Supreme Court denied an appeal in the case and hence refused to block the lower court's ruling.[134]

Even though the standards for desegregation were uncertain until *Fordice,* colleges and universities on both sides of the color line felt pressure to desegregate soon after *Brown I.* But it was not just the *Brown* opinions that spurred desegregation in higher education. World War II had softened the racial attitudes of many whites—"the war . . . had driven home to us in the United States that we are subject to attack on the ground of inconsistency and insincerity if we, as a democracy, make any requirements for voting or office-holding that do not treat white men and colored men exactly on the same objective basis"—just as it had hardened the racial resolve of many blacks; having fought abroad to save the world for democracy, blacks "were unwilling to accept the denial of their democratic rights at home."[135] Additional desegregative momentum came from the Cold War. American policymakers realized that racial apartheid damaged "the reputation of the United States abroad."[136] Indeed, the government's *amicus curia* brief in *Brown I* referred to former Secretary of State Dean Acheson's comment that racial segregation jeopardized the government's ability to persuade other nations, especially Third World nations, that democracy was morally and geopolitically superior to communism.[137] Finally, the civil rights movement of the 1950s and 1960s, with its sit-ins, marches, boycotts, and the courageous eloquence of leaders like Martin Luther King, Roy Wilkens, and Whitney Young, generated tremendous moral momentum toward desegregation.[138]

In response to these multiple pressures, colleges and universities across the South thus began a slow but unmistakable process of desegregation. In one of the first decisive moves in this direction, the board of trustees of the University of North Carolina medical school voted on April 6, 1954, to evaluate medical school applicants "without regard to color or race."[139] Desegregation was clearly evident across the South by 1958, when the chairman of the Department of Social Sciences at Fisk University, Preston Valien, issued a detailed report on the matter that concluded:

> of approximately 200 tax-supported formerly all-white colleges and universities in the 17 southern states and the District of Columbia, well over half, distributed in 12 states and the District of Columbia, will now accept Negro students. In addition, there is an undetermined but significant number of formerly all-white private and church-affiliated colleges which will now accept students without regard to race. It is worth noting that at least one of these desegregated private colleges is to be found in each of the 17 states. These private colleges are for the most part church-affiliated schools, and all the major religious denominations are represented among their sponsors.[140]

Given this momentum, one would have expected to see the end of the historic problems blacks have faced in higher education. For a short while, it appeared that blacks could claim victory.

North and South, the country was consumed with desegregation and anti-discrimination in the 1960s and 1970s. In this environment, great strides were made in desegregating colleges and universities, more than at any other time in the nation's history. The proportion of blacks attending HWCUs "quadrupled between 1960 and 1980, rising from 1.8 percent to 7.7 percent."[141] Most of these gains came in the 1970s. In that decade, the number of black students enrolled in HWCUs exceeded the number enrolled in HBCUs for the very first time.[142]

By 1976, the racial enrollment gap in undergraduate education literally disappeared. Roughly the same percentage of black and white high school graduates between the ages of eighteen and twenty-four were enrolled in institutions of higher education. In fact, the black rate (33.5 percent) was slightly *higher* than the white rate (33 percent).[143] Significantly, black enrollment also increased at the nation's most prestigious colleges and universities during the civil rights era. According to one study, the percentage of blacks at Harvard, Yale, and Princeton rose from about 2 percent in the early 1960s to 7 percent by 1969.[144] Another study shows black enrollment in the Ivy League colleges overall rising from an average of 2.3 percent in 1967 to 6.3 percent in 1976, and the percentage at other elite institutions rising from an average of 1.7 percent to 4.8 percent during this period.[145]

Causes of Improvement

The most important driving force behind the integration of HWCUs was external. It came as part of the most comprehensive civil rights legislation since Reconstruction. Congress enacted Title VI of the Civil Rights Act of 1964. Title VI is in effect a federal bribe, but an outstanding one. It uses federal funds to induce institutions to act morally. From a legal standpoint, Title VI proscribes discrimination on the basis of race or color in any program that receives federal funding. The government's use of its spending power in this fashion was quite significant, not only because it demonstrated character in the deployment of the taxpayer's money, but also because it enabled the government to extend its reach to private colleges and universities, which are beyond the reach of the Fourteenth Amendment's prohibition against racial discrimination. So important was Title VI that it became a catalyst for legislation prohibiting discrimination in various other forms; such as sex (Title IX of the Education Amendments of 1972) and disability (the Rehabilitation Act of 1973).

Anti-discrimination laws such as Title VI could not by themselves explain the overall racial parity in college enrollment in 1976. Other factors were at work, among which were a larger population of black high school students eligible for college, more active recruitment of black students, and generous financial aid packages.[146] But one factor in particular—affirmative action—undoubtedly had the greatest impact on black enrollment at HWCUs. Affirmative action, meaning racial preferences, goals, and even quotas, reached its zenith during the pre-*Bakke* 1970s.

Regents of the University of California v. Bakke (1978) arose from the fact that the Medical School of the University of California at Davis had set aside a certain number of seats for blacks in each entering class. These set-asides could operate as goals (something to shoot for each year) or as quotas (something that had to be fulfilled each year). Other schools, such as Harvard, used race as a "plus factor" rather than as a goal or quota. Justice Lewis F. Powell Jr.'s controlling opinion in *Bakke* made it clear that reserving a specific number of seats on the basis of color (whether such a system operated as a goal or quota) violated the Constitution. Justice Powell nonetheless found that the use of racial preferences to achieve educational diversity was constitutionally permissible.[147] Without some form of affirmative action, substantially fewer blacks would have been admitted to HWCUs, and, as a consequence, the racial enrollment gap that traces back to slavery would not have been closed in 1976.

Human Capital Deficiency in Graduation

Enrollment is only one part of the equation for determining postsecondary educational attainment. The other and more important part is graduation. Although the racial differential in the college enrollment rate had largely disappeared by the end of the civil rights era, that was not the case for the college graduation, or completion, rate. For instance, in 1965, the graduation rate for cohorts between the ages of 25 and 29 was 6.3 percent for blacks, compared to 13 percent for whites. In 1975, the completion rates were 10.7 percent and 22.8 percent, respectively. Finally, in 1980, which roughly correlates with the college graduation year of the high school class of 1976 (the year in which the black college participation rate slightly exceeded the white rate), the college completion rates were 11.7 percent for blacks and 23.7 percent for whites.[148] Thus, the racial differential increased from 6.7 percentage points in 1965 to about 12 percent in 1975 and 1980.

Causes of Graduation Deficiency

Student attrition is, of course, the most important factor affecting the graduation rate. Obviously, the black attrition rate was higher than the white attrition rate during the civil rights era. Yet that may not have always been the case. A study published in 1963 reported a "significant[ly] lower dropout rate (33.4 percent) among 1,519 Negro students attending Northern integrated colleges as compared to a dropout rate of 40 percent among the larger group of white college students."[149] The researchers, one of whom was the famed civil rights scholar Kenneth Clark, theorized that blacks were especially motivated to finish their education on time. Black students wanted to prove they belonged in HWCUs, and that if integration did not work, it would not be because of them. Clark's study has, however, been criticized by some as methodologically flawed.[150] In any event, by 1973, researchers had gotten so use to seeing a relatively high black attrition rate that they were not only referring to it as "problem," but as "an old one."

There were both internal and external factors that affected the black dropout rate and, ultimately, the black graduation rate.

Internal. One internal consideration concerns cognitive ability. Racial breakdowns of SAT scores became available in 1976.[151] A racial gap in test performance of about 200 points has existed in each year since 1976. Studies show a correlation, albeit moderate, between SAT scores and college performance.[152] Stephan and Abigail Thernstrom see this as evidence that the affirmative action admission policies of the 1960s and 1970s were misguided. Under such admission policies, blacks "are jumping into a competition for which their academic achievements do not qualify them, and many find it hard to keep up."[153]

The reasons for the black dropout rate during the civil rights era were, however, more complex than what the Thernstroms would have us believe. While some studies have shown that "persisters have significantly higher SAT and ACT scores than nonpersisters," other studies "have found high school and college grade performance to be better predictors of college retention than standardized test measures and among the strongest predictors of college retention."[154] Indeed, "[a]dmissions deans say that AP [Advanced Placement] exam is a better predictor of college success than the SAT."[155] Furthermore, black retention rates were higher at private colleges than at public colleges. This may be owing not only to a more rigorous admissions process but also to greater interaction between blacks and teachers in smaller classes. Some studies have reported "a significant influence" of family background on retention rates, while other studies have suggested that family background exerts very little influence. The racial composition of the college (HWCUs v. HBCUs) also affects dropout rates, but not as much as a generous financial aid package. Indeed, after reviewing studies dealing with each of the variables listed above, one researcher concluded that the amount of loan and grant aid allocated to a student and college grade performance had the most significant impacts on blacks (and whites) graduating on time. Finally, the "net" dropout rate declines sharply if readmission at other institutions or the same one is factored in. There are, in short, myriad internal influences on black attrition. Cognitive strength is simply one, and not necessarily the strongest one.[156]

External. Any discussion of a cognitive reason for the black dropout rate must consider external conditions. It could be argued that the cognitive factor, whether measured by test scores or grades, is inextricably tied to the low quality of elementary and secondary education available to blacks during the civil rights era. "Data show that a significant proportion of black high school students [thought] that they [were] enrolled in college preparatory programs when they [were] not."[157] Moreover, as one researcher wrote at the time:

> Black children are educationally . . . [impeded] because the public schools they are required to attend are polluted by racism. Their low scores reflect the racial segregation and inferiority of those schools. These children are perceived and treated as if they were uneducable. From the earliest grades, they are programmed for failure. Throughout their lives, they are classic examples of the validity of the concept of victimization by self-fulfilling prophecy.[158]

Alvin Poussaint, a black psychologist, made a similar point in 1968, arguing that blacks have the motivation for achievement but have not learned the behaviors necessary to give effect to the motivation because of poor education.[159]

Finally, some scholars have suggested that black test and grade performances are tied to a deeper externality—a difference in cognitive styles between blacks and whites. This may sound like an internal condition, but the argument is that the cognitive approach reflected in standardized tests and classroom instruction is "analytic" and thus incompatible with the largely "non-Western" "holistic" learning style of blacks. As a result, blacks coming into HWCUs must bear the additional burden of cognitive adjustment to a "Western" cultural setting.[160] Although this theory, and the related advocacy of Ebonics, was prevalent during the 1970s, it has not been taken seriously with the passage of time.

Focusing on the most likely causes of black attrition during the civil rights era, which arguably are the lack of funds to stay in school and poor academic preparation, I see the footprints of slavery and Jim Crow. These atrocities left blacks with less power, wealth, and privilege to hand down intergenerationally. Consequently, blacks in the 1960s and 1970s had less financial capital than whites to finance higher education. Black students were heavily dependent on scholarships, grants, and loans to stay in school. Families had little money to cushion mistakes, to allow for educational flexibility, or to help out in tight situations. Also, many black students, like their parents, were educated in low-performing public schools. They were stuck in the same Jim Crow rut as their parents and their parents' parents. They were inadequately prepared for the rigors of college academics. These links to slavery and Jim Crow continued into the next era as well.

THE POST–CIVIL RIGHTS ERA (1980–PRESENT)

Cedric Jennings, a self-described "ghetto kid" from D.C., graduated from Brown University. He was among the 6.5 percent of black students in the University's undergraduate student body of 5,559 students. Despite arriving with a combined SAT score of 960 (400 points below Brown's mean), Cedric graduated from Brown with a 3.3 GPA in education and just one class short of a double major in applied math. In many ways, Cedric fits the profile of the successful black-affirmative-action graduate of an Ivy League college discussed by Bowen and Bok (see below). Yet his story also speaks just as powerfully to the existence of human capital deficiencies—such as the dearth of black students admitted to elite colleges—and their causes—such as poor public schooling and inadequate family resources—that have dogged blacks since slavery. No amount of affirmative action can camouflage these continuing racial disadvantages.[161]

The post–civil rights era presents much of the same: black deficiencies in college enrollment and graduation created during slavery and sustained through the postslavery years by external forces rooted in slavery and Jim Crow. This is not to say that college enrollment and completion rates for blacks at elite and other mainstream institutions of higher education have not increased since the end of the 1970s. Clearly, they have. But the age-old racial gap in admissions and graduation still exists. It is this racial differential—an interracial comparison—rather than the increase in black college participation and graduation rates from one generation to the next—an intraracial comparison—that is the most meaningful indicator of a human capital deficiency in higher education among black Americans.

Human Capital Deficiency in Enrollment

With the removal of legal restrictions on enrollment at HWCUs during the civil rights era, one would expect the black enrollment rate at these schools to continue to climb during the post–civil rights era, and, indeed, it has. The vast majority of black students enrolled in institutions of higher education now attend mainstream American colleges and universities. Fewer black students are attending HBCUs, which is somewhat of a mixed blessing given the educational benefits these institutions provide, as mentioned in the preceding section. In 1991, a full 80 percent of the approximately 1.3 million black college students were attending HWCUs.[162] This gigantic shift continues even as black enrollment at HBCUs has steadily increased (although obviously not as much as enrollment at HWCUs) during the post–civil rights era.[163] Many black students during this period have not only attended HWCUs but also enrolled in the most selective of these schools. The percentage of blacks enrolled at Harvard, Yale, and

Princeton, for example, went from an average of about 6.5 percent in 1976 to an average of about 7.9 percent (7.9 for Harvard, 8.4 for Yale, and 7.5 for Princeton) in 2000.[164]

That's the good news. The bad news is that the racial differential in college enrollment has grown since the civil rights era. While the enrollment rate (the percentage of 18- to 24-year-old high school graduates enrolled in college) for black students at HWCUs has risen since the 1970s, minus a few years of setbacks, it has still not reached parity with the white enrollment rate as it had in the 1970s. After reaching a high of 33.5 percent for blacks in 1976 (again, slightly exceeding the 33 percent rate for whites), the black enrollment rate fell during the 1980s, reaching a low of 26.1 percent in 1985 (compared to 34.4 percent for whites in that year). Then, in the 1990s, the black college participation rate began to climb again, reaching a high of 39.8 percent in 1997. But still the black enrollment rate did not regain parity with the white participation rate, as it had in 1976. The white college participation rate in 1997 (45.2 percent) was 5.4 percentage points higher than the black rate for that year. During the twenty-year period between 1977 and 1997, white college enrollment increased by 12.7 percentage points, while black enrollment increased by only 8.3 percentage points; hence the increase in the racial differential since the year of parity, 1976. These figures are particularly alarming when one considers that between 1977 and 1997 the high school graduation rate for white students remained relatively stable, holding at about 81 percent, while the high school completion rate for black students rose from approximately 68 percent to 74 percent, an increase of 6 percentage points.[165] Since 1997, matters have gotten worse. The black enrollment rate fell from 39.8 percent in 1997 to 29.8 percent in 2000 (a 10 percentage point decline in just three years!), while the white rate also fell from 45.2 percent to 36.9 percent (an 8.3 percentage decline). Thus, the racial differential increased from 5.4 percent in 1997 to 7.1 percent in 2000.[166] Using different numbers, other studies report similar results in black and white enrollment during this period.[167]

Causes of Enrollment Deficiency

Internal. One important internal cause of the enrollment deficiency is what can be called "the black gender gap." The overall increase in black enrollment during and since the civil rights era has largely been among black women. The number of black women attending institutions of higher education far surpasses that of black men. In 1965, when figures were first collected, 148,000 black women versus 126,000 black men attended college, a 22,000-student gender gap. Fifteen years later, in 1980, the gender gap increased to 163,000 students, 591,000 versus 428,000 (or by 740 percent). In 1992, over 300,000 more black women than black men attended college, 865,000 versus 537,000. In 1999, black women attending college exceeded black men by 375,000, 923,000 versus 548,000. The black gender gap had grown by 212,000 students (or 130 percent) since 1980.[168]

The black gender gap is apparent not only in undergraduate education but at every other level of education as well—high school, graduate school, and professional school. This suggests that the extremely high number of young black men in jail—more than in college[169]—may not tell the entire story. Indeed, the absence of positive black male role models in the home and in the schools may be a primary cause of the black gender gap. Studies indicate that the lack of positive roles models is "far more acute for black men than for black women." Also, many young black male high school graduates believe that a college or postgraduate degree will not be of much benefit to them. They see themselves facing employment discrimination that is more intense than what black women face, which may not be an unrealistic view. This same study shows "the employment growth for black women in professional positions was double the rate for black men in the 1982-to-1992 period." Currently, black women hold 60 percent of all executive and managerial jobs occupied by blacks. Part of the reason for this is that "black females benefit from the corporate mentality that a black woman is a 'twofer' or 'double minority.'" Explaining what this study means, Bruce Slater concludes that knowledge of such corporate mentality "encourages black women to pursue higher education. However, black men are seen as more threatening to white male–dominated corporate management. For black men, their dim prospects for advancement in corporate America undoubtedly chill their educational aspirations."[170]

Consistent with this study, other studies explain how certain "schooling processes" inhibit black male performance at the elementary and secondary levels. "Teachers consistently give less attention, less praise, and more criticism to Black males."[171] Indeed, black male students are disciplined, suspended, or expelled at a higher rate than that of whites and other groups. During the 1994–95 academic year, for example, nearly half of all black American males enrolled in Colorado's middle schools and high schools were suspended, compared to only one in six white males.[172] When the disciplining of black male students is so out of proportion to the disciplining of white male students year after year, this is not simply a contemporary social phenomenon. Something larger is afoot.

That phenomenon may include the fact that "[a]ssertive behavior by Black males that is encouraged in the home and on the playground usually is seen as negative behavior in the classroom."[173] This, of course, suggests that the gender gap in the college enrollment rate for blacks may have an external antecedent, one related to slavery. White teachers are less forgiving of the behaviors of black male students because they understand little about black culture. There is little empathy or identity between teacher and pupil. Thomas Kochman captures this problem in what he calls "styles in conflict," or white teachers treating black values or behaviors as deviant versions of mainstream ones.[174] This conflict arises, as Alexander Alienikoff has suggested, when whites fail "to recognize and credit self-definition by subordinated groups."[175] What is often present, instead, are fears and prejudices—the very same mind-sets that caused white Americans during the slave era to "cut Africans off from the normal mechanisms of sympathy and identification."[176] Hence, the attitudes visited upon many black male high school students by their teachers are not new. They are a by-product of the mentality and rhetoric used to rationalize the peculiar institution and the subordination of free blacks. I agree here with Valora Washington and Joanna Newman, who have urged, "Perhaps reports of Black boys' more negative attitudes toward school should be viewed as a *consequence* of their mistreatment in school rather than as the *cause* of their low educational attainment."[177]

This is not to say that unruly black students are not to be disciplined. Some values and behaviors of black students need to be changed if these students are to be successful in mainstream society. If a child's behavior is disruptive (such as using profanity in the classroom), the teacher must first try to find its source (such as parents using profanity around their children). This is simply part of a larger process in which the teacher endeavors to understand her students individually—their values and behaviors. Armed with this knowledge and sensitivity, the teacher can now talk to the student about the necessity for changing his behavior. She can explain to him how her suggested or mandatory changes will benefit the student without, by words or deeds, belittling his family, his heritage, or his race. When the teacher does this, she is "teaching to the student." She is connecting with the student, creating an emotionally supportive educational environment. Unfortunately, this type of courtesy and understanding—this type of teaching—seems too often to be missing among teachers and school administrators alike. Consequently, many high school students are left feeling depressed.

External. Affirmative action in the form of racial preferences is an unmistakable external factor that affects the racial differential in college enrollment. The effect is largely positive. Black enrollment rises with the use of racial preferences. Indeed, black enrollment rose sharply in the 1970s, the height of our civil rights consciousness, and then declined in the post-*Bakke* 1980s, even as the black high school completion rate was rising and the white rate held steady. The 1980s were also colored by the Reagan administration's anti–affirmative action stance. During the 1990s, the black enrollment rate begin to climb as the Clinton administration's relatively strong support for affirmative programs and minority scholarships kicked in. Indeed, the Clinton administration reversed a policy prohibiting race-exclusive scholarships established by its predecessor, that of President George Bush Sr. Secretary of Education Richard W. Riley announced the policy reversal on February 17, 1994, stating that "colleges can use financial aid to remedy past discrimination and to promote campus diversity without violating anti-discrimination laws."[178] Then came the white backlash against racial preferences in 1996.

That year, California and Texas invalidated the use of racial preferences in higher education. This was done in California through Proposition 209 (or "Prop 209" as it is commonly called), a voter initiative that amended the state constitution, and in Texas by judicial fiat in *Hopwood v. State of Texas.*[179] Rejecting the diversity rationale that Justice Powell advanced in *Bakke,* and which the Supreme Court subsequently embraced in *Grutter v. Bollinger* (2003), the Fifth Circuit held that the desire to achieve a more diverse student body could not constitutionalize the use of racial preferences in admissions. As a consequence of these anti–affirmative action laws, black enrollment dropped precipitously at elite schools in California and Texas.

The numbers support this conclusion. In 1996, for example, the last year of racial preferences in the University of California (UC) system, 515 black students were admitted to the University of California at Berkeley. Berkeley's admissions records show that approximately 290 blacks were admitted to the fall 2002 entering class, resulting in a 43 percent decrease in black admittees. Likewise, UCLA reports a 32 percent drop in the number of blacks admitted to its campus during this time, and the University of California at San Diego, the number three school in the UC system, shows a 14 percent decrease. Similar results can be seen in Texas. In 1996, the last year of racial preferences in Texas, 501 black students were invited to enroll in the freshman class at the University of Texas at Austin. The next year, only 419 black students were admitted, a drop of 20 percent. Actual enrollment only dropped slightly (2.9 percent in 1996 to 2.5 percent in 1997), because so few blacks decided to attend. The enrollment rate has remained about 3 percent since 1997. At the University of Texas Law School, black enrollment for the entire law school went from 97 blacks in 1996 to 33 blacks in 2000, a drop of 66 percent. At Rice University in Houston, Texas, the entering freshman class was 10 percent black in 1995, but only 5.1 percent black in 2000. Finally, nationwide "[t]here were fewer blacks enrolled in medical schools during 2001 than 10 years earlier. This decline dates back to the mid 1990s."[180]

These statistics are subject to criticism on the grounds that rather than presenting trends they present "snapshots," pictures of years in isolation, in this case 1996 and 2002 or some other year after the demise of affirmative action. Using snapshots to make statistical arguments can be misleading when the years selected for analysis are not representative of the years omitted from the analysis. Thus, the best way to characterize statistical information is to look at average numbers and trends over time.[181] Yet the trends in this instance show the same dismal picture as the snapshots. For example, the average percentage of blacks enrolled at Berkeley's Boalt Hall between 1993 and 1996, pre–Prop 209 years, was 8.7 percent. The average between 1997 and 2002, post–Prop 209 years, was only 3.6 percent. The percentage of the decrease will, of course, vary depending on whether one uses trends or snapshots. For example, blacks constituted 7.6 percent of the student body at Boalt Hall in 1996, 0.4 percent in 1997, and 5.1 percent in 2002. Nonetheless, all the statistics, whether trends or snapshots, show a decline in black enrollment after Prop 209.[182]

Prop 209 and *Hopwood* are linked to slavery in that they perpetuate the enrollment deficiency imposed on blacks during slavery. They help keep alive the vestiges of slavery by reducing the percentage of blacks enrolled at America's elite institutions. Not unlike the now-unlawful poll tax—racially neutral on its face, but extraordinarily discriminatory in its effect on black voters—these anti–affirmative action measures "freeze in" the privilege status of those groups who acquired educational opportunities during slavery and Jim Crow, and "freeze out" blacks who were denied educational opportunities during these periods of discrimination.[183] The Supreme Court seems to have recognized as much when it effectively overturned *Hopwood* in *Grutter* just last year. (Prop 209 still stands because it is a state constitutional rather than a federal constitutional matter.) Indeed, according to the U.S. Department of Education reports, all this anti–affirmative action fervor has had a "dramatic, negative effect" on the prospects of black students. Promising black students are unwilling to waste their time and limited funds applying to schools that have withdrawn the welcome mat. Even those who are accepted are driven away by the knowledge that racial isolation, caused by the dearth of black students on campus, cultivates academic failure. Without a critical mass of blacks on campus, the environment for black academic success is not very promising.[184]

There is, of course, the argument that blacks denied admission to the top colleges and universities enroll in less selective schools, where they belong in the first place. Some scholars have argued that such "cascading" is sound educational policy for blacks and good social policy for the nation. The Thernstroms, for example, believe that black students with lower SAT scores than their white classmates have trouble adjusting to elite institutions and thus would benefit from cascading.[185] Cascading reduces the presence of underqualified black students at elite schools. Everyone wins.

This argument is countered by William G. Bowen and Derek Bok, former presidents of Princeton and Harvard, respectively, who authored an important study on affirmative action.[186] They argue that this "fit" hypothesis is without factual support. Black SAT scores at elite schools are typically at the top end of the spectrum for all test takers, even though they are lower than white SAT scores at elite schools. Also, with an 80 percent graduation rate (compared to an 86 percent graduation rate for white students) during the period of time studied, black students are in fact graduating from elite schools. Indeed, the current black graduation rates at many elite schools is very high; such as 92 percent at Harvard and Amherst, 91 percent at Vassar, 90 percent at Princeton, 88 percent at Brown, and 87 percent at Yale. "[E]ven those black students in the lowest SAT band (those with combined scores under 1000)" are graduating on time.[187] In addition, black graduates of elite institutions go on to earn advanced degrees in law, medicine, and business at a *higher* rate than their white classmates (87 percent versus 83 percent) and at a much higher rate than the national average for black graduates of other four-year institutions (87 percent versus 63 percent). After entering the workforce, black graduates bring scarce legal, medical, and other professional services to black communities. In addition, black graduates, like their white counterparts, overwhelmingly report positive college experiences with diversity. That in itself belies the widely held public belief that blacks feel stigmatized by affirmative action. And, finally, black graduates of elite schools have contributed substantially to the creation of the black middle class that has arisen during the post–civil rights era.[188]

What this suggests, then, is that cascading is not only bad educational policy but also dangerous social policy. It is an unnecessary waste of human capital. More than that, it perpetuates images of an old and discredited racial order—the socioeconomics of slavery—without just cause.

The real culprit in the black enrollment saga, however, is neither cascading nor the absence of affirmative action, but rather overreliance on the SAT and similar standardized tests.[189] Blacks simply do not score as well as whites and other groups on these tests. During the twelve-year period between 1976 and 1988, the black/white racial differential on the SAT declined significantly, going from an average of 240 points to an average of 187 points. But since 1989, the racial differential has actually widened, even though black scores have increased slightly. In 2001, the average point difference was 201 points. Worse, the test gap extends beyond the SAT. As the Thernstroms and others have shown, it appears even before kindergarten and persists into adulthood.[190]

There have been many attempts to explain the racial gap in testing, some more successful than others. One persistent theory is the test bias theory, which is the belief that standardized tests like the SAT are racially biased. Research in the area has, however, shown little or no "content bias." If one takes "a standard vocabulary test and winnows out words with unusually large black-white differences, for example, the black-white gap does not shrink much."[191] Likewise, little "methodological bias" has been shown, although "[t]here is some evidence that describing a test in different ways can affect different groups' relative performance, but we do not yet know how general this is."[192] Finally, researchers have found no "prediction bias." According to Christopher Jencks and Meredith Phillips, "almost all colleges have found that when they compare black and white undergraduates who enter with the same SAT scores, blacks earn *lower* grades than whites, not just in their first year but throughout their college careers."[193]

This does not mean that the SAT has great predictive powers in individual cases, as Cedric Jennings's personal story, which introduces this section, well illustrates. Many students, both black and white, at academically demanding colleges outperform their SAT scores. For example, in one study of such schools, students admitted with an "unacceptable" SAT score of 1,000 "earned grades averaging roughly B," while students admitted with scores at the schoolwide average of 1,289 "earned college grades averaging roughly B+. . . . Anyone who has graded undergraduates knows that this is not a large difference. Indeed, it is the smallest difference that most college grading systems bother to record."[194] Claude Steele reminds us that "even ostensibly significant gaps in scores (300 points on the SAT, for example) can actually represent small differences in the real skills needed to get good college or law school grades."[195] This may be because standardized tests like the SAT are not subject-related. The SAT does not, for example, measure the students' mastery of subjects studied in high school. If it did, the test's predictive power and, hence, its usefulness to colleges, would probably be enhanced. Apparently, the College Board, which administers the SAT, has come to this realization. It will introduce a new SAT beginning in the spring of 2005. The retooled test will include a writing section, new reading questions, and more advanced math, all designed to relate the test "more closely to high school curriculums and more accurately predict a student's performance in college."[196] Given the fact that most black students, including those in the middle class, attend de facto segregated schools that are among the worst schools in the nation, I fear that these reforms are likely to widen the racial differential in SAT scores.[197]

One of the most perplexing sides to the SAT saga is the performance of middle-class blacks versus that of poor whites. The latter outperform the former on the SAT. Most of the recent theories about the black/white test score gap have primarily focused on this phenomenon. One theory, advanced by Richard Hernstein and Charles Murray in 1994, suggests that genetic factors explained the test score gap.[198] There is, however, no evidence indicating that blacks have less innate intellectual ability than whites.[199]

An alternative and more legitimate theory as to why poor whites outperform middle-class blacks on the SAT emphasizes the poor quality of elementary and secondary education most middle-class blacks receive attending de facto segregated schools. Black students receive insufficient educational resources, and they have few teachers who are experienced, rigorous, subject-qualified, and professionally developed routinely. This theory holds, in particular, that the single most important factor in explaining the test score gap is the fact that blacks have a lower level of participation in advanced subjects, particularly AP classes, and little instruction in test preparation, all of which adds up to poor test-taking preparation. The *Journal of Blacks in Higher Education* and the College Board both report that black SAT test takers take a lower percentage of academically demanding subjects in high school than do white test takers. In 2001, for example, 38 percent of black test takers took trigonometry compared to 50 percent of white test takers, and 28 percent of black test takers took honors English versus 39 percent of white test takers.[200] Citing both private and governmental studies, Justices Ruth Bader Ginsburg and Stephen Breyer note:

> [D]ata for the years 2000–2001 show that 71.6% of African-American children and 76.3% of Hispanic children attended a school in which minorities made up a majority of the student body. . . . And schools in predominantly minority communities lag far behind others measured by the educational resources available to them. . . . However strong the public's desire for improved education systems may be, . . . it remains the current reality that many minority students encounter markedly inadequate and unequal educational opportunities.[201]

The connection between poor preparatory education and slavery and Jim Crow seems clear. Although Jim Crow schools have been outlawed, black students, including many middle-class black students, are still receiving a Jim Crow level of education. Blacks today are fighting the same educational battles they fought during slavery. As I said on another occasion:

Public education in America began in schools that were both desegregated and integrated. As early as the 1640s, the Massachusetts and Virginia colonies had no laws segregating African American and white pupils. African American children could attend public schools and were educated alongside white children. For the privilege of attending integrated schools, African American children paid a high price, however. Verbal and physical mistreatment from whites, teachers as well as pupils, were part of the regular curricula throughout colonial America. Under these conditions, African American children could not obtain a quality education.

Emboldened by War of Independence, African Americans began to petition their local governments for separate schools. In 1787, for example, Prince Hall, an African American who fought in the Revolutionary War, petitioned the Massachusetts legislature for an "African" school in Boston. . . .

Finding no legislative redress, African American parents pulled their children out of integrated public schools and placed them in newly created separate private schools.[202]

Another alternative theory, called the "poor parenting practices" theory, holds that it is the absence of "middle-class parenting practices that matters most for the gap."[203] Middle-class parenting practices include reading to young children, having books in the home and making sure they get read, taking trips to museums, and staying in close touch with teachers and administrators to make sure one's children are in fact receiving the most academically demanding courses the school has to offer. Jencks and Phillips suggest that even black families with middle-class incomes lack these middle-class parenting practices. The poor parenting practices theory "suggests that eliminating environmental differences between black and white families could go a long way toward eliminating the test score gap."[204]

As an explanation of why poor white students outperform middle-class black students, the poor parenting theory seems a bit weak. Poor white students would seem to have even less access to middle-class parenting practices and resources than middle-class black students. The theory, however, takes on added explanatory power when considered in junction with the work of John Ogbu.

In *Black American Students in an Affluent Suburb: A Study of Academic Disengagement*,[205] Professor Ogbu, best known for his theory that black students regard striving for good grades to be akin to "acting white," examines the academic performance of black and white students in Shaker Heights, Ohio, an affluent community. Although the community is evenly divided between black and white families, white high school students outperform black high school students on all academic measures—grades, standardized tests scores, and enrollment in AP courses. The reason for this disparity, Ogbu argues, is because black students fail to put forth the effort required for academic achievement. They talk achievement but do not follow it up with the requisite effort. Although their parents are doctors and lawyers, these black students view rappers as their role models and the mean streets of the inner city as a legitimate venue for certifying one's "blackness." These privileged blacks, in other words, are not mimicking the behaviors that helped their parents to succeed. Ogbu blames their parents. Middle-class black parents do not spend enough time monitoring their children's education—the courses they take, their homework assignments, and the teachers who teach them.[206]

It is this lack of educational guidance that gives the poor parenting theory its credibility. What Ogbu seems to be suggesting is that middle-class black parents provide less of this crucial resource to their high school children than do whites, whether rich or poor. There are fewer visits to the school and less nagging of teachers and administrators by middle-class black parents than even by poor white parents. Some middle-class black parents, Ogbu suggests, seem to believe that simply dropping off their children at a good school is quite enough.[207]

The proponents of the poor parenting practices theory have linked the theory to slavery and Jim Crow: "Even when black and white parents have the same test scores, educational attainment, income, wealth and number of children, black parents are more likely to have grown up in less-advantaged households. So part of the explanation for the gap may lay in the widespread discrimination in housing, education and employment that African American children's *grandparents* faced."[208]

Perhaps a more plausible explanation may lie in the real possibility that some middle-class black students are new to middle-class life and attended poor public elementary schools, relics of the Jim Crow past, before moving to places like Shaker Heights.[209] In addition, their parents might possibly be preoccupied with issues of discrimination—such as racial bias on the job or in public places—that middle-class blacks face every day. These recurring encounters tend to drain all but the superstrong, and they ex-act an especially heavy toll from parents struggling to maintain a precarious middle-class lifestyle.[210]

Claude Steele suggests yet another possible link between slavery and the test score gap. This connection arises later in life when students take the SAT, ACT, GRE, LSAT, and other entrance exams. It connects black test-taking skills to the low esteem in which society holds blacks—that is to racial stereotyping and other racial mind-sets rooted in the rhetoric used to justify slavery. Steele and his colleagues call this linking condition "stereotype threat" or "stereotype vulnerability." A student is likely to perform below his abilities in a test situation when he identifies with a group that is the object of negative stereotyping and, in addition, believes others might evaluate him through that stereotype. Thus, blacks perform below their test-taking ability when they turn the standardized test stereotype into a self-fulfilling prophecy.

Steele has conducted various experiments to prove his theory. In one experiment, black students were given two tests. On the first, students were told the test was designed to measure their verbal and reasoning ability. On the second, they were told the test was an unimportant research tool. Black students performed worse on the first test than on the second test. Intellectual paralysis set in on the former, because the students were caught in the grip of stereotype threat. Steele believes the effects of stereotype threat are strongest for high achievers, because they care very much about doing well and may end up trying too hard. Furthermore, high achievers fear that should they not do well, they will have confirmed the negative stereotype associated with black students. Steele conducted similar experiments involving white male and female students, demonstrating they too were vulnerable to stereotype threat in relation to Asian and male students, respectively. So, for example, when white and Asian male students were told the math tests they were about to be given were ones in which Asians do slightly better than whites, the Asian students, predictably, outperformed the white students, even though both groups were strong in math. In a separate experiment, stereotype threat lowered the test scores of strong female math students who were told they were expected to test lower than white males in the subject.[211]

Some scholars question the validity of Steele's stereotype threat theory. They point to studies of black male students suggesting that these students maintain their self-esteem through psychological detachment. That is, they deemphasize the value of grades and test scores as accurate or reliable assessments of their academic abilities. According to these studies, black males actually ignore stereotypes and accumulate high levels of self-esteem, higher than whites, through relationships with friends and family. Bernadette Gray-Little, for example, questions the notion "that if by word or deed you tell kids they are part of a group that cannot succeed, they won't."[212] Although there may be an element of truth to these counterstudies, it is also true that young black males, like other young people, often use boastful talk to mask feelings of insecurity. Furthermore, the stereotype-threat theory seems to make sense when one considers Steele's important observation that the degree of difficulty of a standardized test "makes the negative stereotype about the group [a] relevant . . . interpretation of their performance and of them."[213] In the end, all one can say with certainty is that the link between test performance and self- or racial esteem is a highly complex and controversial subject.[214]

Human Capital Deficiency in Graduation

If there is a more serious human capital deficiency in higher education for blacks than college enrollment, it is college completion. Not enough black college students are graduating. Virtually every study on the subject reports a large and growing racial differential in college completion rates. One study focusing on those from twenty-five to twenty-nine years of age shows a 1980 black graduation rate of 11.7 percent (which is to say that 11.7 percent of blacks in this category completed college), compared to a white graduation rate of 23.7 percent (a racial differential of 12 percentage points) for the same year. Moving forward fifteen years to 1995, this same study shows a 15.3 percent black completion rate, compared to a 26.0 percent white completion rate (a racial differential of 10.7 percentage points). Although the black rate increased more than the white rate (3.6 percentage points versus 2.3 percentage points), the racial gap thus closed by only 1.3 percentage points in fifteen years. By 2000, the black graduation rate decreased to 14 percent, while the white rate increased to 28 percent. Thus, the racial differential actually *increased* from 12 percentage points in 1980 to 14 percentage points in 2000, which is to say, in 2000, the black college completion rate was half of the white college completion rate.[215]

Another study, which focuses on cohorts twenty-five years of age or older who completed four or more years of college, shows similar results. The black graduation rate for 1980 was 7.9 percent, compared to 17.9 percent for whites, a racial differential of 10 percentage points. In 1997, the black completion rate rose to 13.3 percent, while the white completion rate increased to 24.6 percent. Here, not only did the racial gap widen (from 10 percentage points in 1980 to 11.3 percentage points in 1997), but the black completion rate also increased less than the white rate (5.4 percentage points versus 6.7 percentage points). It is noteworthy that the highest black completion rates were recorded at the nation's most academically demanding schools. For the year 2000, for example, the black graduation rate was 92 percent at Harvard and Amherst, 91 percent at Vassar, 90 percent at Princeton, 89 percent at Haverford, 88 percent at Brown, 87 percent at Yale, and 86 percent at Duke, the University of Virginia, and Williams.[216]

Yet another study, using a different definition of the "graduation rate," reveals an even larger current racial differential. The traditional definition measures the percentage of cohorts between the ages of twenty-five and twenty-nine, or twenty-five and older. A new definition, perhaps more informative, is based upon the percentage of all (or a designated group of) enrolled students who earned a degree within six years. Using this definition, one study shows that among freshmen who entered college in the fall of 1995, 38 percent of black students (43 percent of black women and 32 percent of black men) graduated within six years, compared with a white graduation rate of 60 percent—a racial differential of 28 percent! These figures do not cover all college students; only those attending the 324 institutions that make up the National Collegiate Athletic Association's Division I colleges and universities. For all students attending four-year institutions during this same six-year period, the black graduation rate is 45.7 percent and the white rate is 66.8 percent, for a still high 21.1 percent racial differential. These figures reflect the facts that nearly a third of all college students transfer to other institutions before attaining their degree, and that over half of all black students, and approximately a third of all white students, drop out of college never to return.[217]

Causes of Graduation Deficiency

College completion has an inverse relation to attrition—a high attrition rate translates into a low completion rate. My discussion will, therefore, focus primarily on attrition. The black attrition rate is significantly higher than the white attrition rate. The question is why? What role does slavery or Jim Crow play in explaining this racial differential?

Internal. According to the Thernstroms, black academic performance is the primary cause of the racial differential in the college attrition rate. Blacks are ill equipped to do the work, they argue, especially at elite schools. The Thernstroms do not, however, find fault with blacks. Instead, they blame affirmative action, once again:

> When students are given a preference in admissions because of their race or some other extraneous characteristic, it means that they are jumping into a competition for which their academic achievements do not qualify them and many find it hard to keep up. . . . The risk in taking in a high-risk student is that of academic failure. When it does not work out, the loser is not the institution but the individual student who suffers a crushing, humiliating personal defeat that may have lasting results.[218]

Yet there is no evidence that blacks drop out of college mainly for academic reasons. Black grades are lower than whites on average, but still well above the level for academic disqualification. Furthermore, the black attrition rate at the most academically demanding schools, as mentioned earlier, is quite low, such as 8 percent at Harvard, 9 percent at Vassar, and 11 percent at Princeton in 2000. Also, at HBCUs, where affirmative action for blacks does not exist, the attrition rate is higher than the national average of 62 percent. At Texas Southern University, for example, the dropout rate in 1998 was 88 percent. At Alabama State University it was 81 percent, and at no fewer than six other HBCUs, the dropout rate was above 70 percent. Clearly, affirmative action is not the cause of black attrition.[219]

External. There are several more plausible explanations for the high undergraduate dropout rate, many of which are connected to slavery and Jim Crow. One such reason is the financial burden of higher education. The United Negro College Fund and other organizations have reported that "the shift in federal financial aid from direct grants to loans since 1980 has hit blacks especially hard."[220] Black families do not have the financial capital needed to meet the cost of college. Looking at comparative levels of liquid wealth in black and white families, it is clear "that the wealth differential is so huge that it alone can explain the very large college dropout rate for black students."[221] In 2001, the median net worth for all non-Latino white families in the United States was $120,900, compared to a median net worth of $19,000 for all black families, according to the Federal Reserve. "Net worth" is defined as income-producing assets, such as, stocks, bonds, and real estate investments. These are assets on which families can draw, either as income or collateral, to finance a college education.[222]

The level of black net worth is substantially affected by multiple harms of repression that stem from slavery. Many parents of black college students are stuck in low-paying jobs in large part because they were educated in poor-performing, de facto or de jure segregated public schools or were limited by encounters with employment discrimination. These patterns of disadvantage were visited upon their parents and their parents' grandparents and great-grandparents, going all the way back to slavery. During the slavery era, many states made it illegal to educate blacks and legal to discriminate against blacks in employment. Educational inequality and low-paying jobs were extended beyond slavery in new forms under Jim Crow's "separate but equal" doctrine. Hence, because of slavery and Jim Crow, blacks had little education and few employment opportunities, leaving them with little in the way of an estate to bequeath to their children, grandchildren, and future generations. At the point in the inheritance line at which we are today, blacks have not accumulated enough financial resources to pay for college. In our society, as has been noted, as much as "80 percent of lifetime wealth accumulation results from gifts from earlier generations."[223]

A vivid illustration of the nexus between black net worth and prior regimes of racial subordination can be seen in the life story of Reverend George Walker Smith, a local hero in San Diego. In December 2000, Reverend Smith gave an interview on the occasion of his retirement as minister of the Christ United Presbyterian Church in the Golden Hill section of San Diego. Reverend Smith, who had become the leading black figure in San Diego, talked about his background. "I grew up on a backwoods Alabama plantation where African Americans worked the fields [while] the white family in the big house got rich."[224] Elaborating on his life in Alabama, the 71-year-old minister said: "A rabbit had a better chance than black folks. At least there's a season when you can kill rabbits. But for niggers the season was year round."[225] Reverend Smith also spoke of other aspects of his formative years in the South, saying: "If you white folk were coming down the sidewalk and I was meeting you, I had to immediately jump in the street and give you the sidewalk. To me this is humiliating."[226]

What Reverend Smith experienced was the legacy of slavery, even though the institution itself had long since disappeared from the American landscape by the year of his birth, 1929. Sixty-four years after slavery, there were plenty of former slaves still around. But Reverend Smith did not only know former slaves; he felt the lingering effects of slavery. Racial fault lines laid down during slavery and perpetuated during Jim Crow diminished not only Reverend Smith's chances for worldly success and personal happiness, but also the lives of his descendants. Reverend Smith's children and grandchildren inherited a social virus that diminishes their power, wealth, and privileges. Their ancestors contracted the virus during slavery, and through generational transmission, they now have it themselves.

Another possible reason for the high attrition rate among black students is the dearth of black professors on college campuses. The number of black faculty members has remained stagnant for over a decade, even while the number of black students has increased. In 1979, blacks represented 4.3 percent of all college professors; in 1989, they represented 4.5 percent. From 1993 to 1999, the percentage of black professors climbed from 4.8 percent to 6.5 percent, but it dropped to 6.1 percent in 2001. These figures are more egregious in light of the fact that fewer than half of all black professors are employed by predominantly white institutions (most being employed by HBCUs), even though, as mentioned earlier, approximately 80 percent of black students attend predominantly white institutions.[227]

Black professors are important to the academic success of black students. They act not just as mentors and role models, but as Sherpa guides—leaders who take black students through an unknown and often treacherous terrain. Drawing on their personal experiences, black professors are able to mediate racial problems and interpret the often mysterious and arcane rules of campus life for black students.[228] Many black college students feel the same way about college mores as the former *Washington Post* columnist Nathan McCall felt about his prior prison experience: "In many ways, adapting to the white mainstream was a lot like learning to survive in prison: You had to go in and check out the lay of the land. You had to identify the vipers and the cutthroats and play the game by rules that are alien to nature and foreign to any civilized society. Prison primed me just for that challenge."[229]

The dearth of black college professors is linked to slavery and Jim Crow. Many of the same factors that connect black family wealth to slavery also connect the percentage of black professors to the peculiar institution. Racial disadvantages in education and employment visited upon parents, grandparents, and great-grandparents have certainly decreased the supply of black professors. First slavery and then Jim Crow prevented the establishment of a tradition of blacks teaching at HWCUs. Many blacks still cannot imagine themselves doing that type of work. It is not a job children in black communities see their parents, neighbors, or friends of parents pursuing. How could they when everyone in the community is busy with the basics of life? Some needs take precedence over others.

There is another connection between the shortage of black college professors and prior regimes of racial subordination that should not be overlooked: the inertia of discriminatory traditions in the appointment and tenure processes. Although not as prevalent as it was during Jim Crow and slavery, racial discrimination is still a problem in hiring and promotion in higher education. Many white professors seem to apply impossibly high standards in their evaluations of black candidates that they simply do not apply to white candidates, especially during tenure review. Indeed, a 2002 report by the American Council on Education observes that black faculty, as well as black students, face "repeated questioning of their abilities, training, and intelligence" by white faculty and students alike. Racism, this report concludes, is "the heart of many problems" blacks faced at HWCUs.[230]

In response, some deans argue that the dearth of black faculty is explained by the fact that many leave to pursue promising outside offers. But black faculty see it differently. Explaining why she left a prestigious private university, a black professor said: "I left because it is an institution that engages in a pattern of practicing intense bias, which devalues, discourages, and marginalizes." What blacks see too often is "a revolving door" through which black faculty "frequently come and go."[231]

Aware of these daunting problems, many black graduates have no desire to follow in the footsteps of their professors. They are aware of "the energy that systematically dealing with scornful students and office staff can take out of a black faculty." They know that "[i]t wastes and deflects time and energy that could be spent in doing research, writing grants, publishing articles, mentoring other students, serving on college committees, [and] serving local communities."[232] Such experiences do not make the life of a college professor seem particularly attractive to black students.

Racial discord experienced by black students themselves is another factor that has had a direct impact on the rate of attrition among black students. At the annual meeting of the American Sociological Association in August 2002, a panel of scholars argued that racial hostility and a general unwelcoming environment explains not only the black dropout rate but also much of the grade differential between black and white college students. According to Walter Allen, Daniel Solorzano, and Grace Carroll, "undergraduate institutions create a hostile environment for minority students, resulting in their earning lower grades."[233] It's the little things—such as the proclivity of white professors and students to afford black students less intellectual deference than they give to white students—that accumulate to make for a racially hostile environment.[234]

Big things add up as well. Open racial hostility on college campuses has been widely reported since the mid-1980s. For example, the National Institute against Prejudice and Violence has tabulated more than 250 racial incidents at more than 200 colleges in recent years. The Center for Democratic Renewal has reported that racial incidents on college campuses have increased fourfold since 1985.[235] In another recent survey, 64 percent of college newspaper editors at schools enrolling more than 10,000 students and 49 percent of all respondents characterized the state of racial relations on their campuses as "fair" or "poor." Also, 85 percent of the respondents indicated that there had been at least one incident on campus during the past year that could be characterized as racial.[236] In 2000 and 2001, no fewer than 125 incidents of racial hostility were reported on college campuses in every region of the country.[237]

A closer look at the nature of these racial incidents reveals an even bleaker picture. Sometime in the 1990s, white students at Texas A&M University began to hold "Think Ghetto" parties. Students dressed in blackface and Afro wigs and did other things to demean blacks. The parties finally ended in 2002 after the administration intervened.[238] At the University of Michigan in 1988, students spotted posters in classrooms reading: "Support the K.K.K. College Fund. A mind is a terrible thing to waste—especially on a nigger."[239] In 1988, a University of Wisconsin fraternity held a fundraising "slave auction" during which white students performed skits in blackface and Afro wigs, and afterward the audience made bids for the performers' services. At Yale law school, ten African American students received letters reading, "Now do you know why we call you NIGGERS?" A group called the "Yale Students for Racism" signed the letter. At the University of Massachusetts at Amherst, a black residential adviser was beaten up by a white visitor and feces were smeared on the door of his room. Enraged, scores of African American students rampaged through a 22-story dormitory. At Michigan's Olivet College, a racial brawl ignited by a white student's allegations of racial harassment resulted in the hospitalization of two students and the temporary withdrawal of almost all of the school's sixty African American students. And at Chapel Hill, North Carolina, racial tensions erupted over a proposal to build a privately funded, free-standing African American cultural center. Associate Vice Chancellor Edith Wiggins described the controversy's effect on the school: "It has been brutal. . . . There is blood all over this campus."[240] On another occasion, the University of North Carolina provided space for a statue showing a black man twirling a basketball and white students with stacks of books. Black students were, understandably, insulted. Several black male students reported that white students often perceived them to be basketball players simply because they were black and dressed in sweat pants. Even worse was a black female student's shock and dismay when a white student who answered the door at a fraternity house asked her whether she was applying for the cook's position. Many white students look upon black culture, from civil rights heroes to rap music, as "less intelligent" than white culture.[241]

"Racism, as such, is not new," Thomas Sowell reminds us. "What is new are the frequency, the places, and the class of people involved in an unprecedented escalation of overt racial hostility among middle-class young people on predominantly liberal or radical campuses. Painful as these episodes are, they should not be surprising."[242] If it is true that "social support and campus environment affect a variety of outcomes for students,"[243] it is not difficult to understand why so many black students feel the need to leave college before graduation.

•　　•　　•

In soap box racing, engineless miniature cars are started by strong hands that push from behind and release once the cars reach the starting line at the top of a hill. The momentum of the push carries the car forward to the end of the race unless or until something intervenes to interrupt it. Similarly, although slavery ended nearly a century and a half ago, it set in motion a negative set of circumstances for blacks, which were greatly abetted by Jim Crow, and somewhat ameliorated by the civil rights movement, but still remain in motion today. Some regard black culture as an intervening force. Out-of-wedlock babies, a supposed lack of interest in high academic performance, and other socially dysfunctional beliefs and behaviors, real or imagined, have given new and recent momentum to historic racial disadvantage. This charge is very much reflected in D'Souza's analysis of racial disadvantage in higher education. The SAT, he maintains, "is accurately measuring not innate capacity but differences of academic performance. . . . The simple truth is that merit, not racism, is responsible for performance differences on the test."[244] For well-meaning scholars like D'Souza, black culture severs the nexus between prior systems of racial subordination and present-day black disadvantage.

This chapter attempts to disprove that assertion insofar as higher education is concerned. I have argued that black deficiencies in college enrollment and graduation today, consisting of significant racial differentials in both categories, can be traced to slavery. These human capital deficiencies have been dogging blacks since slavery. That fact alone establishes the connection.

In addition, many of the current causes that help sustain these enrollment and graduation deficiencies are themselves rooted in slavery and Jim Crow. One such factor, as I have shown, is racial discrimination in the quality of educational resources deployed at the elementary and secondary school levels, including the assignment of inexperienced or poorly trained teachers to black schools. Indeed, as mentioned earlier, it was the poor quality of education accorded to black students in integrated schools that led to the establishment of the first all-black elementary school after the Revolutionary War. Another cause of the enrollment and graduation deficiency in higher education is the insufficient amount of family resources that can be poured into a child's higher education. This cause arises from the limited educational and employment opportunities afforded to black parents, grandparents, and prior ancestors extending back to slavery. Today's blacks have inherited from their slave ancestors a social virus that diminishes their power, wealth, and privileges.

What this chapter attempts to show, then, is that there are contemporary victims of slavery and Jim Crow. These victims experience the same type of human capital deficiencies their ancestors experienced as slaves, as free blacks, and as victims of racial subordination under Jim Crow. Many victims have, in fact, experienced Jim Crow directly. Although the level of racial deprivation is less intense today than in the past, it still limits educational opportunities for blacks. Yes, internal factors are at work here—they were also at work during slavery—but they are mainly shaped by external conditions that—as during slavery—cannot be ignored.[245]

Chapter 4 | THE TORT MODEL

Whether white or black, opponents as well as proponents of the black redress movement typically conceptualize the question of slave redress
through what can be called the "tort model."[1] Although it can appear in
legislative form,[2] the tort model is primarily a litigation approach to slave
redress. It operates upon a certain set of premises—compensation and, for
some proponents, punishment or even white guilt.[3] Many proponents of
the tort model would be satisfied if the government or a private beneficiary
of slavery were simply to write a check for X amount of dollars to every
slave descendant. In response, some white Americans, such as the neo-
conservative Charles Krauthammer, would gladly have the government
write that check as a means of closing the books on the American race
problem—a kind of justice on the cheap.[4]

While I believe litigation can be a useful tool in the fight for racial justice, and while I have enormous respect for most of the committed and
talented lawyers who are bringing the slave-redress lawsuits, I do not favor the tort model as the *primary* strategy for obtaining redress for slavery. The tort model, like all litigation, is too contentious, too confronta-
tional to provide the kind of racial reconciliation and accord that is needed
for future race relations. It is also too susceptible to lawyer abuse, which
can, in turn, prevent the plaintiffs from receiving genuine relief. Most important, the tort model, whether in the form of litigation or legislation,

is incapable of generating the one ingredient that I believe is or should be the sine qua non of slave redress—namely, atonement and, ultimately, racial reconciliation. I shall elaborate on these deficiencies at the end of this chapter.

My discussion of slave-redress litigation begins with the "precedents." There are two sets of legal paradigms. The first involves the Japanese and Nazi forced labor cases brought against foreign governments (or their successors-in-interest) and foreign corporations (or their successors-in-interest). These defendants are typically sued in U.S. federal court under the Alien Tort Claims Act. The second set of "precedents" is the Japanese American removal and internment cases brought against the federal government, which allege violations under the Constitution and federal statutes.

Both sets of "precedents" are negative (hence they are not strictly legal precedents) in that they demonstrate an unmistakable judicial indisposition toward lawsuits that seek redress for past injustices. In the absence of special legislation or settlement, these lawsuits have been dismissed before the judge has had an opportunity to consider the merits of the claims at trial. Procedural barriers—including questionable subject-matter jurisdiction due to problems of sovereign immunity or the "political question doctrine," the lack of a clear right of action, and violations of applicable statutes of limitations—have resulted in pretrial dismissals of every unsettled case.

Every slave-redress lawsuit that has been decided thus far has met with a similar fate. It may be possible, however, to overcome at least some of these barriers in "private actions"—actions brought against wealthy white families and corporations that have profited from slavery—that have recently been filed. Viable common-law rights of actions based on the incidents of slavery (e.g., the wanton killing of a slave by its corporate master),[5] as well as a frontal attack on slavery itself (under a gains-based theory of restitutionary law) may be possible. Much like the legal theories relied on in *Brown v. Board of Education* (1954), in which the Supreme Court overturned school segregation statutes, these virgin theories are important because they test the moral credibility of contemporary American law. That is, given the morally compelling nature of the slave descendants' claims, there must be a basis in current law for their redress. Our legal system must recognize that current harms stem from a long history of unjust, immoral deprivations imposed upon blacks by the U.S. government. Otherwise, our legal system embodies America's worst atrocity and the corrupt laws that made that atrocity possible.

But, again, I also believe that litigation, or, more broadly, the tort model, may not be the best strategy for redressing slavery and Jim Crow. It has inherent limitations that prevent it from giving us the forward-looking strategy that the black redress movement needs. Without a genuine apology from the perpetrator government, there can be no racial reconciliation. Compensation alone does nothing to restore or establish a broken relationship between victim and perpetrator.

FORCED LABOR LITIGATION

Forced labor litigation consists of dozens of class action lawsuits brought by private citizens and World War II veterans of both the U.S. and Allied armed forces. Named as defendants in these lawsuits are the governments and several corporations of Japan and Germany. Plaintiffs in these lawsuits seek damages for unpaid wages and injuries arising from the labor they were forced to perform under inhumane conditions while being held captive or as POWs during World War II. They assert claims under federal constitutional and statutory law, state constitutional and statutory law, and international common law (or customary international law). These lawsuits have been dismissed on numerous grounds, the primary ones being lack of subject-matter jurisdiction, violation of sovereign immunity, and expiration of the statute of limitations.[6] I shall discuss the forced labor cases involving Japan first.

Japanese Forced Labor Litigation

In re World War II Era Japanese Forced Labor Litigation (2001) is a typical forced labor case, except for the addition of a state statute designed to facilitate the litigation of these cases. The federal judge in this California case consolidated several class action lawsuits brought by plaintiffs of Korean and Chinese descent against the Japanese government. Plaintiffs asserted a number of claims. One set of claims was based, not on statutory or constitutional law, but on judge-made law called the "common law." These claims alleged false imprisonment, assault and battery, conversion, *quantum meruit* (literally, "as much as he deserves"), unjust enrichment, constructive trust, and accounting. *Quantum meruit* and unjust enrichment are recurring claims in redress litigation and hence warrant further comment.

Quantum meruit is a quasi-contract action that seeks to obtain "the reasonable worth or value of services rendered for the benefit of another."[7] *Quantum meruit* will lie for the reasonable value of services rendered "even though there was no contract to do so." In other words, "the law implies an understanding or intent to pay the value of services rendered," unless there is a specific agreement that the services will be performed gratuitously.[8]

Unjust enrichment is a much more complex legal concept than *quantum meruit*. It is generally defined as "the unjust retention of a benefit to the loss of another, or the retention of money or property of another against the fundamental principles of justice or equity and good conscience."[9] Some states require an additional showing of "the absence of law barring the remedy" sought through the unjust enrichment claim, whereas other states require only a showing that "the defendant received a benefit from the plaintiff . . . [and that] it would be inequitable for the defendant to retain such benefit."[10] Most courts seem to require the initial taking of the property to be unlawful, which, of course, would make the doctrine inapplicable to slave-redress litigation because slavery and Jim Crow were legal when they were practiced. But the trend in the law seems to be that the enrichment need only lack "an adequate legal basis" rather than have no legal basis.[11] Perhaps it could be argued that slavery and Jim Crow, although legal, did not provide an "adequate legal basis" for the enrichment.

Unjust enrichment is a necessary element or precondition of the larger claim of restitution. The restitutionary claim affirmatively seeks the return of the benefit for which it would be unconscionable for the defendant to retain.[12] The close relationship between unjust enrichment and restitution is highlighted in *Black's Law Dictionary*'s definition of the former. Unjust enrichment is defined therein as "circumstances which give rise to the obligation of restitution, that is, the receiving and retention of property, money, or benefits which in justice and equity belong to another."[13] Thus, restitution is simply the claim that "[a] person who has been unjustly enriched at the expense of another is required to . . . [provide redress] to the other."[14]

Though traditionally applied only to individual relationships, the concept of unjust enrichment, Joe Feagin argues, should "be extended . . . to the unjust theft of labor or resources by one group, such as white Americans, from another group, such as black Americans. . . . [F]or fourteen generations the exploitation of African Americans has redistributed income and wealth earned by them to generations of white Americans, leaving the former relatively impoverished as a group and the latter relatively privileged and affluent as a group."[15] Similarly, Patricia Williams argues, "If a thief steals so that his children may live in luxury and the law returns his ill-gotten gains to its rightful owner, the children cannot complain that they have been deprived of what they did not own."[16] Feagin notes that Williams, like other legal scholars, including Ian Ayres and Richard Delgado, have also suggested extending the equitable concept of unjust enrichment "to discuss the reality and consequences of racial oppression."[17]

Typically of forced labor cases, the court in *In re World War II Era Japanese Forced Labor Litigation* never reached the merits of these intriguing common law claims. The judge ruled that these claims were barred by the statute of limitations. He reached that decision by applying California's choice of law rules to determine which statute of limitations applied—that of the forum state (California) or that of the place wherein the events took place (China and Japan)—and then noting that it did not matter which forum's law applied "because the statutes of limitations from all three forums are significantly shorter than the age of these claims."[18] The limitation periods were one to three years, depending on the claims, under California law; two years under Chinese law; and ten years under Japan's Civil Code.[19] Thus, in order for the claims to have been seasonal, they would have had to be brought within one to ten years after they occurred.

A second set of claims brought by plaintiffs in *In re World War II Era Japanese Forced Labor Litigation* were based on California constitutional and statutory law, specifically, Article I of the Constitution and Penal Code § 181 (both of which prohibit involuntary servitude); the Unfair Competition Act (UCA), which is part of the California Business & Professional Code; and § 354.6 of the California Code of Civil Procedure. Like the common law claims, the state constitutional and statutory claims were dismissed before the judge could rule on their merits. The judge ruled, for example, that the claims were barred by applicable statutes of limitations, and that he lacked subject-matter jurisdiction (federal constitutional authority to decide the case) because the claims essentially raised political questions in violation of the political question doctrine. First announced by Chief Justice John Marshall in *Marbury v. Madison* (1803), the political question doctrine basically holds, to quote Chief Justice Marshall, that "questions, in their nature political . . . can never be made in this court."[20] An enigma even to constitutional scholars—the Supreme Court routinely decides political matters, from discrimination in elections to the exercise of executive privilege—the political question doctrine basically gives judges discretion to determine which cases are too hot (i.e., too controversial) for the judiciary to handle.

Of special note is the judge's ruling on California's innovative redress law, California Code of Civil Procedure § 354.6. This unique provision was the primary claim on which plaintiffs relied. Section 354.6 was enacted in 1999 to provide a cause of action for any World War II slave or forced labor victim or heir of such victim to "recover compensation for the labor performed . . . from any entity or successor in interest thereof." Procedurally, § 354.6 extends "the applicable statute of limitations to December 31, 2010."[21] Thus, § 354.6 grants both substantive and procedural rights. The judge in *In re World War II Era Japanese Forced Labor Litigation,* however, invalidated § 354.6 on the basis of the political question doctrine, holding that the provision was an unconstitutional infringement on "the exclusive foreign affairs power of the United States."[22] It is noteworthy that the judge did not rule that the 1952 San Francisco Treaty of Peace with Japan, which formally ended World War II in the Pacific, preempted § 354.6. Unlike an earlier case, in which the judge ruled that the Treaty of Peace waived individual forced-labor claims brought by U.S. and Allied veterans against Japan,[23] the case sub judice involved nationals of nations (Korea and China) that were not signatories to the Treaty of Peace.[24]

It should be noted that the questions of whether § 354.6 violates the political doctrine question and is preempted by the Treaty of Peace is on appeal before the California Supreme Court at the time of this writing. The justices are reviewing a 2003 decision by a state court of appeals that agreed with the waiver ruling issued in *In re World War II Era Japanese Forced Labor Litigation* (again, a federal court ruling) but did not agree with that court's ruling on the political question doctrine.[25] It is likely the

California Supreme Court will rule the same way other courts have ruled on the waiver issue—in other words, it will allow nationals of nonsignatories (e.g., Korea and China) to sue Japanese corporations, while denying such a right to nationals of signatories (e.g., the United States). If the California Supreme Court sustains the state appellate court's ruling on the political question doctrine (namely, that § 354.6 does not violate that doctrine), state and federal law will collide, as the federal judge in *In re World War II Era Japanese Forced Labor Litigation* ruled just the opposite. Eventually, the U.S. Supreme Court will have to resolve the matter.

The final claim alleged in *In re World War II Era Japanese Forced Labor Litigation* was asserted under an ancient federal statute—the Alien Tort Claims Act (ATCA). Originally enacted in the Judiciary Act of 1789 to create a right of action against nefarious nations, the ATCA gives a federal court "original jurisdiction of any civil action by an alien for a tort only, committed in violation of the law of nations or a treaty of the United States."[26] The ATCA gives federal district courts subject-matter jurisdiction to entertain suits against state actors or private actors "alleging torts committed anywhere in the world against aliens in violation of the law of nations."[27] Since the ATCA has no statute of limitations, courts are instructed to "borrow" from the most suitable statute of limitations. In this case, the judge borrowed from the ten-year limitation period contained in the Torture Victim Protection Act,[28] which provides a cause of action in federal court to victims of torture around the world. As plaintiffs' claims were not filed within ten years of their occurrence, their ATCA action was dismissed on statute of limitations grounds.[29]

In dismissing the ATCA claim on statute of limitations grounds, the judge made several observations, by way of *obiter dictum* (an incidental, nonbinding opinion), that, taken together, may appear to be useful in the slave-redress cases. The judge cited a line of cases that have included "customary international law," or *jus cogens,* in the definition of "the law of nations."[30] This, then, makes *jus cogens* violations actionable under the ATCA. In addition, the judge ruled that the prohibition against slavery is "specific, universal and obligatory." The prohibition, in other words, is among those "widely held fundamental principles of civilized society that . . . constitute binding norms on the community of nations."[31]

This analysis of international law thus establishes precedents—affirmative *stare decisis*—to the effect that slavery is a violation of customary international law and, hence, the law of nations, that the prohibition against slavery is "implicit in International Law." This law, in addition, predates World War II. That is, it was understood prior to World War II that "to enslave . . . is an international crime."[32] Although slave descendants, like all U.S. citizens, cannot sue under the ATCA, which is only available to aliens, they can bring an international claim under other federal statutes discussed below in the section on private actions.

But while the judge's analysis is critical for the forced labor cases, it has little utility for the slave-redress cases. International law contains doctrines that cut off historical claims going back as far as slavery. One such doctrine is the dominant theory of rights. This doctrine holds governments blameless for acts committed by predecessor regimes—acts they obviously could not control.[33] Slave-redress claims based on the portion of slavery that predated the founding of the United States of America in 1787 would, therefore, not be actionable under international law. A more devastating procedural doctrine for slave-redress litigation is the doctrine of intertemporal law. Recognized by several major international conventions, including the Universal Declaration of Human Rights (1948), the European Convention for the Protection of Human and Fundamental Freedoms (1950), and the International Covenant on Civil and Political Rights (1966),[34] in criminal proceedings, the doctrine of intertemporal law has been adopted in civil proceedings by the International Law Commission (ILC), a distinguished group of international law judges and legal scholars. Article 13 of the ILC's Articles on State Responsibility provides that "an act of a State does not constitute a breach of an international obligation unless the State is bound by the obligation in question at the time the act occurs."[35]

A final blow to slave-redress claims based on international law is the fact that most legal scholars have determined that slavery was not illegal during its practice in the United States. Neither *jus cogens,* treaties, nor conventions outlawed human bondage until sometime during the late nineteenth century. Slavery was not illegal under multilateral treaties or conventions until "somewhere between 1885 (the Treaty of Berlin forbidding slave-trading) and 1926, when the Slavery Convention confirmed that states had jurisdiction to punish slavers wherever they were apprehended."[36] The United States, then, was ahead of international law in banning slavery with the ratification of the Thirteenth Amendment on December 6,

1865. On this ground, it must be said that international law establishes no cognizable claim based upon the historic wrong of slavery.[37]

Before leaving the Japanese forced labor litigation, I should mention the sovereign immunity issue. Although this issue did not arise in *In re World War II Era Japanese Forced Labor Litigation,* it has done so in other cases. Sovereign nations are cloaked with immunity even though they are otherwise subject to federal jurisdiction under the ATCA. A recent illustration of this limitation is a federal class action suit brought by fifteen foreign women who were victims of sexual slavery and torture at the hands of the Japanese Imperial Army in Japanese-occupied Asia before and during World War II (the so-called Comfort Women). The judge suggested that the Foreign Sovereign Immunity Act of 1976 (FSIA), which grants presumptive immunity, with several exceptions, to foreign nations sued in U.S. courts,[38] might apply retroactively to World War II and even before that time. Prior to 1952, foreign sovereigns were granted immunity in U.S. courts only at the discretion of the executive branch. A defendant state may thus be able to claim immunity under the ATCA for acts committed long ago. The judge in the Comfort Women case did not, however, decide the immunity issue before him, including the issue of whether the FSIA applied retroactively, because he did not have to. Instead, he disposed of the lawsuit on another ground; namely, that the Comfort Women claims were nonjusticiable; in other words, the claims violated the political question doctrine discussed earlier.

The fact that the judge chose to dispose of the Comfort Women class action lawsuit on jurisdictional grounds based not on sovereign immunity but on nonjusticiability highlights what will likely be a recurring problem in the slave-redress cases filed against governments. Cases seeking judicial redress against a government for the latter's commission of a past injustice may be too hot for courts to handle—too political. Courts may feel this question is more suited for a legislative rather than a judicial solution. The nonjusticiability, or political question doctrine, may well hang over the slave-redress cases like the sword of Damocles.

Nazi Forced Labor Litigation

Although sovereign immunity was a principal defense in the Japanese forced labor litigation, it was first raised in the most famous of the Nazi forced labor cases, *Princz v. Federal Republic of Germany.*[39] *Princz* occupies a special place in the annals of such cases, not only because it was one of the first, broaching many of the procedural issues that would prove decisive in subsequent cases, but also because of its rather unique factual pattern.

Hugo Princz, a Jewish American, was a Holocaust survivor. At the time the United States entered the war against Germany in 1941, he was living with his parents, his sister, and his two brothers in what is now Slovakia (formerly part of Czechoslovakia). The Slovak police arrested the entire Princz family as enemy aliens, and turned them over to the Nazi SS. Rather than allow the Princz family to return to the United States as part of the civilian prisoner exchange then being conducted by the Red Cross, the SS sent the family to concentration camps. The decision turned solely on the fact that the Princz family was Jewish. Princz's parents and his sister were sent to Treblinka, where they were eventually murdered, while Princz and his two younger brothers were sent to Auschwitz-Birkenau, where they were forced to work at an I. G. Farben chemical plant. After being injured at work, Princz's brothers were starved to death in the "hospital" at Birkenau. Princz was later sent to Dachau, where he was forced to work in a Messerschmitt factory. When U.S. soldiers liberated Dachau at the end of the war, Princz was in a freight car full of concentration camp prisoners en route to another camp for extermination. While other liberated prisoners were sent to displaced persons camps, Princz, because he was an American, was sent to an American military hospital for treatment.[40]

After the war, the government of the new Federal Republic of Germany established a program of redress for Holocaust survivors (unlike Japan, which did not offer to compensate its World War II victims). Germany's redress program was, in fact, a reparations program (apology came first; see the Preface and chapter 5) and thus will be referred to as such in this discussion. More than that, Germany's approach to redress has become the model for all others. According to a recent report by the United Nations, Germany's reparations program, which also provided funds for the new state of Israel, is "the most comprehensive and systematic precedent of reparations by a Government to groups of victims for the redress of wrongs suffered."[41] Despite this exemplary record, the German government denied Princz's 1955 request for reparations because he was neither a German citizen at the time of his imprisonment nor a "refugee," within the meaning of the Geneva Convention, after the war. Princz would have, however, qualified for reparations when the German government changed the criteria for eligibility in 1965 had he applied again before the statute of limitations ran out in 1969.[42]

In 1984, joined by the U.S. Department of State and members of the New Jersey congressional delegation, Princz initiated a series of requests to the German government and the BASF, Hoechst, and Bayer corporations, I. G. Farben's subsidiaries, for redress in the form of ex gratia payments or the establishment of a pension fund. All such requests were denied. With the 1991 Treaty on the Final Settlement with Respect to Germany awaiting ratification by the Senate, the Bush administration renewed its attempt to resolve Princz's claim through diplomatic channels. That effort failed, as did similar attempts made later by the Clinton administration.[43]

In 1992, Princz filed a lawsuit in federal court against Germany alleging both tort and quasi-contract claims, all common law claims. The former were for false imprisonment, assault and battery, negligence, and intentional infliction of emotional distress, while the latter was for *quantum meruit* based on the value of his labor in the I. G. Farben and Messerschmitt plants. Germany moved to dismiss on grounds that it was cloaked with sovereign immunity, which thereby removed the case from within the court's subject-matter jurisdiction. Germany also argued that Princz failed to state a claim upon which relief could be granted due to the expiration of the statute of limitations. The district court ruled that it had jurisdiction on the ground that the FSIA "has no role to play where the claims alleged involve undisputed acts of barbarism committed by a one-time outlaw nation which demonstrated callous disrespect for the humanity of an American citizen, simply because he was Jewish."[44] The court of appeals, however, reversed on the jurisdictional issue. It ruled that Princz was caught in a legal catch-22: "If the FSIA applies retroactively to the terrible events giving rise to this case, then it bars the suit, which comes within no exceptions in the Act. If instead the case is governed by pre-FSIA law of sovereign immunity, then it is not within post-FSIA diversity jurisdiction of the court," because when Congress enacted the FSIA it deleted the grant of diversity jurisdiction over cases brought by a U.S. citizen against a foreign state.[45] Thus, the court, like the court in *In re World War II Era Japanese Forced Labor Litigation,* did not decide the choice of law issue presented by the fact that the FSIA was enacted in 1976, long after the events in question.

Princz, unlike the plaintiffs in *In re World War II Era Japanese Forced Labor Litigation,* brought only common law claims. This path is also taken in some of the slave-redress cases, as we shall see. Rather than relying on federal constitutional or statutory law, both of which upheld the institution of slavery, some plaintiffs in the slave-redress litigation advance traditional tort and quasi-contract claims. These nonfederal claims invoke the federal court's diversity jurisdiction, which, in general, gives the district court subject-matter jurisdiction over nonfederal claims between parties who are citizens of different states. *Princz* lacked such jurisdiction because the FSIA amended a portion of the diversity statute to remove therefrom cases brought by a U.S. citizen against a foreign government. The slave-redress cases face a subject-matter jurisdiction hurdle of a different but equally lethal nature, as we shall see.

In an effort to avoid the subject-matter jurisdiction, or sovereign immunity, problem, lawyers litigating Nazi forced labor cases changed their strategy after *Princz.* Rather than suing Germany (a state actor, or a government), lawyers began to target corporations (private actors) who "employed" or benefited from forced labor. During the 1990s, for example, some fifty-three lawsuits, including forty-two putative class actions, were filed in U.S. federal courts against German companies, mainly banks, insurance companies, and industrial corporations. Significantly, these defendants had corporate subsidiaries and other substantial assets in the United States. This made them not just "deep pockets" but defendants with collectable assets. Eventually, these dozens of actions were consolidated for litigation in a single case, *In re Nazi Era Cases against German Defendants Litigation,* in the Federal District Court of New Jersey, on August 4, 2000. But a funny thing happened on the way to the forum: the cases were settled with court approval on November 13, 2000. Plaintiffs were happy to forgo the uncertainty of litigation for the certainty of monetary relief.

This unusual turn of events was occasioned by the passage of a law in Germany, translated as the "Law on the Creation of a Foundation 'Remembrance, Responsibility and Future'" (commonly referred to as the "Foundation Law") on August 12, 2000. The Foundation Law took effect on October 19, 2000, with the exchange of diplomatic notes between Germany and the United States. Under the terms of the Foundation Law, not only Germany and its corporations, but also the Swiss, Austrian, and French governments and corporations, in exchange for litigation peace, agreed to make substantial contributions to a fund whose initial capitalization would be 10 billion deutsche marks (DM). Under the terms of the settlement, the fund would make payments to various groups of victims of Nazi persecution. The class of victims included slave laborers (defined as workers who were "intended to be literally worked to death") and forced laborers (defined as workers who were "compelled to work against their will, but in somewhat less harsh conditions than slave laborers"). Also included in the victim class were subjects of medical experimentation, children held in a *Kinderheim* (or children's home), and persons whose insurance money and other property were "aryanized" (stolen or damaged). Significantly, not only the direct victims of these acts, but *their immediate descendants* were included among the eligible claimants, provided the victims died after February 16, 1999. This is one of the few times a perpetrator of an atrocity provided redress for persons who were not direct victims. This may provide some precedential value for slave redress.

Madeleine Albright, secretary of state in the Clinton administration when the Foundation Law was enacted, estimated at the time that one million victims across the United States, Europe, and the rest of the world would receive benefits under the Foundation Law. Although the rate of recovery differs depending on the type of victim, the Foundation Law is supposed to pay up to DM 15,000 for each former slave laborer and up to DM 5,000 for each forced laborer. These amounts are obviously more symbolic than compensatory.[46]

There is little doubt that the Foundation Law would not have been enacted without the confluence of several events. Certainly, the burden of having to defend multiple ATCA cases, most of which were class actions, was motivation for settlement. Although plaintiffs did not face the hurdle of sovereign immunity under FSIA, because the lawsuits were being brought against corporations rather than governments, they still faced a statute of limitations problem.[47] Given the fact that the corporate defendants had a good defense, the settlement did not actually buy them peace from the prospect of having to pay damages based upon a finding of liability. What the settlement did do, however, was relieve them of the burden and cost of having to litigate, which was no small matter.

The U.S. Supreme Court has enforced the Foundation Law by invalidating California's Holocaust Victim Insurance Relief Act of 1999

(HVIRA),[48] which required any insurer doing business in the state to disclose information about all insurance policies sold in Europe between 1920 and 1945. This information could have provided Holocaust-era victims with evidence needed to mount lawsuits against insurance companies doing business in California. Insurance companies had a strong incentive to disclose, because failure to do so could have resulted in the revocation of their state business licenses. In a five-to-four decision, the Court agreed with the federal government that the HVIRA interfered with the section of the Foundation Law that established the International Commission on Holocaust Era Insurance Claims (ICHEIC) as the exclusive vehicle for processing unpaid Holocaust-era insurance claims. Justices Ginsburg (who wrote the dissent), Stevens, Scalia, and Thomas dissented.[49]

In addition to securing litigation peace for the corporate defendants, the Foundation settlement made good business sense in two respects. First, it made sense to use corporate money, especially when combined with a government bailout, to make the cases disappear rather than to make the lawyers rich. The former was a better return on investment than the latter. Second, by making the cases disappear, the corporate defendants were able to avoid adverse publicity in American markets. It simply does a foreign corporation no good to have to defend dozens of lawsuits in American courts brought by sympathetic, largely American plaintiffs.

More important than the threat of litigation was the pressure brought to bear by plaintiffs' powerful allies at the highest reaches of government and business. President Clinton appointed Under Secretary of State Stuart Eizenstat as his special representative to apply pressure on the German government and to get personally involved in the negotiations.[50] Investment and commercial bankers on Wall Street who floated German bonds and provided crucial financial capital to German corporations and their U.S. subsidiaries, also applied pressure. Many of these captains of industry had relatives who were Holocaust survivors or former forced or slave laborers, and they could thus identify with the plaintiffs' claims.[51]

Many proponents of the tort model are banking on a similar outcome in the slave-redress lawsuits. They are hoping that the proliferation of lawsuits will force a settlement, and that supporters of the Nazi forced and slave labor litigation will throw their support behind this strategy. Yet I doubt that a settlement is likely unless blacks can exert the kind of political and financial pressure on the federal government and corporations that

Jews were able to muster in the Nazi cases. Unless that happens, slave-redress litigation will suffer the same fate as the Japanese forced labor litigation.

Even if the slave-redress litigation did result in the kind of legislative victory that the Nazi forced and slave labor cases have enjoyed, I would not be happy with that result. My dissatisfaction has far less to do with the fact that any legislative payment is likely to be symbolic rather than compensatory, as the Foundation Law well illustrates, than with the fact that no apology is expected under such a legislative scheme. In my view, atonement should be the sine qua non of redressing past injustices. Atonement is essential when, as here, monetary amounts can only be symbolic. A deep apology fortifies the symbolism. I shall elaborate upon the necessity of an apology after discussing one more set of "precedents" and the slave-redress cases.

JAPANESE AMERICAN REMOVAL AND INTERNMENT

During World War II, the U.S. government forcibly removed approximately 120,000 Japanese Americans from their homes and placed them in internment camps located mainly in the midwestern section of the country. This large-scale operation of removal and internment was conducted under the authority of Executive Order 9066, without prior criminal indictment or conviction. Signed by President Franklin Roosevelt on February 18, 1942, and ratified soon afterward by Congress, Executive Order 9066 ordered the establishment of "military areas" from which any person could be excluded. Executive Order 9066 was followed by other executive orders in quick succession, including Executive Order 9102, issued on March 20, 1942, which created the War Relocation Authority and empowered it "to provide for the removal from designated areas of persons whose removal is necessary in the interest of national security."[52]

Evacuation and internment were cruel and inhumane acts, especially in the context of a free society. Evacuees were given as little as forty-eight hours' advance notice to gather the few belongings they were allowed to take with them. Most evacuees lost their homes, businesses, and personal possessions, sometimes selling them for pennies on the dollar, if lucky.

Living conditions in the internment centers were harsh at best. Armed guards stood watch over the internees from high towers. Imprisoned behind barbed wire fences, the internees could not leave the interment centers except in emergencies, and then only if accompanied by a white escort. The physical facilities consisted of barracks, a mess hall, common baths, showers, toilets, and laundry facilities, and a recreation hall. "Food, shelter, medical care, and education were provided to the evacuees free of charge, but even when their value was added to the low salaries [some internees received for work they performed], the economic hardship imposed by the internment was obvious."[53]

Government officials alleged that Executive Order 9066 and its progeny were issued out of military necessity. General John L. DeWitt issued a report in 1942, for example, stating that in the wake of the Japanese attack on Pearl Harbor on December 7, 1941, more attacks on American shipping and coastal cities were "probable," as were air raids and sabotage of vital command installments along the West Coast. DeWitt's report also claimed that enemy agents within the United States would assist the Japanese attackers, and that the "112,000 individuals of Japanese ancestry living in the area were 'potential enemies' because of their ties to Japan."[54]

DeWitt's security concerns were contradicted at the time by various sources both within and outside the government. Federal Bureau of Investigation Director J. Edgar Hoover, for example, expressly refuted allegations in DeWitt's report that illicit shore-to-ship signaling had occurred in the early days of the war.[55] Moreover, Curtis B. Munson, a Chicago businessman designated special representative of the State Department by President Roosevelt to assess the loyalty of Japanese Americans in California and Hawaii, reported in November 1941: "There is no Japanese 'problem' on the Coast. There will be no armed uprising of Japanese."[56] Munson's conclusion was, however, "impressionistic." Lieutenant Commander Kenneth D. Ringle, an expert on Japanese intelligence, conducted a more detailed study of the "Japanese problem," reporting on January 26, 1942, that "at least 75 percent of the American-born U.S. citizens of Japanese ancestry were loyal to the United States and that a large majority of the alien residents were at least 'passively loyal.'"[57]

Despite these contrary reports, President Roosevelt choose to believe General DeWitt's claim that removal and internment were warranted by military necessity. This is the view the Supreme Court took in the few cases that reached it out of the many lawsuits filed challenging the removal and internment of Japanese Americans.[58] Taking judicial notice of General DeWitt's report (meaning the document was admitted into evidence without cross-examination), the Supreme Court in *Hirabayashi v. United States*,[59] *Yasui v. United States*,[60] and *Korematu v. United States*[61] upheld the criminal convictions of three internees who violated the wartime curfew and exclusion orders. The Court ruled, inter alia, that these orders were legal under the federal government's constitutional power to wage war.

Shortly after the war, Congress enacted the Evacuation Claims Act of 1948, which authorized the attorney general to "adjudicate certain claims resulting from evacuation of certain persons of Japanese ancestry under military orders," but specifically excluded compensation for "loss on account of death or personal injury . . . or mental suffering" and for "loss of anticipated profits . . . or earnings."[62] These limitations created an act that, as some scholars have observed, "resulted in no compensation for most and limited compensation for the others."[63] It could be argued that the act demonstrates the dangers of allowing the perpetrators of an atrocity to dictate the terms of redress.

Against this background, former internees pursued two courses of litigation in the decades after the war. The first was *coram nobis* (Latin for "error before us") litigation brought by three former internees, Gordon Hirabayashi, Minoru Yasui, and Fred Korematsu, to overturn their convictions of violating the wartime curfew and exclusion orders. The second and more important litigation strategy sought redress for all internees, not just those criminally convicted of violating the wartime curfew and exclusion orders. In this litigation, *Hohri v. United States,* the plaintiffs sought monetary relief for violations of their constitutional rights and losses to homes and businesses.[64]

Although abolished in civil cases, the ancient writ of *coram nobis* is still available in criminal cases to correct convictions where other remedies are not available.[65] The *coram nobis* lawsuits were successful in that, although they did not result in monetary relief, which would have been beyond the scope of the writ of *coram nobis,* they did result in the overturning of petitioners' criminal convictions. The courts issuing the writs declared an injustice and sought to redress it by correcting the historical as well as the legal record on which the Supreme Court had relied in its prior decisions.

Henceforth, the record would show that racial prejudice and war hysteria, rather than military necessity, had been the real reasons for the removal and internment of Japanese Americans. Had the Supreme Court known the true facts in 1943 and 1944, had evidence surrounding the DeWitt report not been altered or suppressed, the Court would not have given judicial notice to the DeWitt report, and it would not have upheld petitioners' criminal convictions.[66]

The *coram nobis* litigation suggests two precedents for slave-redress litigation. One precedent is actually criminal and, therefore, does not fit squarely within the parameters of the tort model, which is quintessentially a civil form of redress. No one goes to jail or is fined under the tort model. But the writ of *coram nobis* can theoretically be used as a kind of tort remedy by blacks to overturn convictions obtained through prosecutorial or even judicial misconduct, especially during the days of Jim Crow. Many blacks now in their seventies and eighties bear the scars of criminal convictions in southern courts forty or fifty years ago. Writing in the midst of that era, Leon Friedman observed: "Too many southern officials let their emotions and prejudice sway their decisions in only one direction: against the Negro. The result is not isolated injustice or occasional error. An entire pattern and practice is established that effectively overrules the law in the statute books or the Constitution. A new kind of law owing its allegiance only to the hates and fears of the white community governs the day-to-day existence of the southern Negro."[67]

Friedman was summarizing the accounts of dozens of lawyers who had litigated civil rights cases in the South and subsequently wrote about their experiences in a collection titled *Southern Justice* (1965), which he edited (it is now unfortunately out of print). Each lawyer addressed the questions of "how the legal institutions [in the South] have been used to cripple the struggle for Negro rights and what has been or can be done to protect Negroes from this kind of legal abuse."[68]

Blacks were subject to discriminatory treatment in northern courts as well. But Friedman argued that southern justice was "special"; for example, "northern police [did] not arrest Negroes for distributing handbills or trying to vote. . . . [Southern] judges [had] no difficulty in finding Negroes . . . guilty despite the lack of any evidence of a crime." Southern law was "underlaw." It had "one of the attributes of law—consistency— but it [was] not law that can result in justice. There [was] no equality, desert [deserved reward or punishment], consciousness, dignity, regularity or decency in its operation."[69]

I see the writ of *coram nobis* as an instrument of justice that could be used to overturn dozens of improper convictions meted out to blacks under southern underlaw. Like Hiabayashi, Yasui, and Korematsu, whose convictions were overturned forty years after the fact, blacks who were wrongfully convicted during the Jim Crow era, whether for rape, robbery, burglary, theft or murder, should be permitted to file *coram nobis* petitions to undo those convictions. *Coram nobis* would be appropriate upon a showing of prosecutorial or judicial misconduct in the nature of altering or suppressing evidence. Even though all the sentences will likely already have been served, the prospect of a clean criminal record might bring some relief to the victims of southern underlaw.

The Japanese-American *coram nobis* litigation offers a second precedent that is more in line with slave-redress litigation. This is the use of litigation to correct the historical record of an atrocity. Of the three *coram nobis* petitions filed in the Japanese-American litigation, the *Korematsu* and *Hirabayashi* petitions, filed in San Francisco and Seattle respectively, resulted in judicial opinions correcting the official record created in the prior cases. In fact, the *Hirabayashi* court of appeals did more than correct the record. It "issued a strongly worded opinion that both condemned the government's litigation strategies during the original internment cases and criticized the government's approach to the *coram nobis* litigation itself."[70] In contrast, the *Yasui coram nobis* petition, filed in Portland, Oregon, did not elicit a judicial opinion regarding the facts surrounding the events in question. The judge merely vacated Yasui's criminal conviction without commenting on the issue of prosecutorial misconduct. "I decline to make findings [of fact] forty years after the events took place," Judge Belloni in fact stated. "There is no case nor controversy since both sides are asking for the same relief but for different reasons. The Petitioner would have the court engage in fact-finding which would have no legal consequences. Courts should not engage in that kind of activity."[71] Judge Belloni's failure to revise the factual record in the case prompted Yasui to appeal the judge's otherwise favorable decision. Unfortunately, Yasui died before the appeal was decided.

As I discuss in the next chapter, there is an urgent need in today's society to correct the historical record of slavery and its lingering effects. Ours was a proslavery Constitution prior to 1865; slavery played a central role in the socioeconomic development of our country, the benefits of which are still enjoyed today; and slavery laid down racial fault lines the tremors of which can still be felt today. These lessons need to be taught and incorporated into our lives. Litigation is certainly one means of teaching these lessons, depending on the judge.

As important as the *coram nobis* litigation was, it was not the Japanese Americans' primary litigation strategy, which was rather to seek redress for all internees, not just those convicted of violating the wartime curfew and exclusion orders. To obtain this, a lawsuit was filed against the federal government in 1983 by nineteen former internees and a Japanese-American organization. In this case, *Hohri v. United States,* the plaintiffs sought monetary relief for violations of their constitutional rights, loss of homes, businesses, education, and careers, and for physical and psychological injuries, including destruction of family ties and personal stigma, arising from their wartime removal and internment.[72] The judge in this case never reached the merits of the plaintiffs' claims. Instead, he dismissed the entire case on procedural grounds. Thus, *Hohri,* not unlike the Japanese and German forced labor cases, is a negative precedent for slave-redress litigation. *Hohri,* in fact, dealt with two questions raised in the forced labor litigation: the statute of limitations and sovereign immunity. *Hohri* ruled against the plaintiffs on both issues. But because the *Hohri* plaintiffs were citizens suing their own government, the *Hohri* court's reasoning on the sovereign immunity issue was different than in the other precedents.

Unlike many forced and slave labor cases, no choice of law question was presented with respect to the statute of limitations issue in *Hohri.* There was no question that the applicable statute of limitations for claims brought against the United States, the court ruled, was § 2401(a) of Title 28 of the U.S. Code, which states that, except where specially provided elsewhere, "every civil action commenced against the United States shall be barred unless the complaint is filed within six years after the right of action first accrues."[73] In devising this limitations period, Congress, the court noted, attempted to weigh several competing policy considerations—such as the plaintiff's need for a reasonable time within which to present her claim, the defendant's right to be free of stale claims, and the court's interest in preserving evidence (which might be lost owing to death or disappearance of witnesses, fading memories, or document destruction or disappearance) for the search of justice. Based upon the six-year statute of limitations, the judge ruled that the right of action on which plaintiffs were suing "accrued" (i.e., the clock began ticking) at the time the underlying incidents occurred during World War II. "Once plaintiff is on inquiry that it has a potential claim, the statute can start to run."[74] Given the absence of fraud or any other reason to delay the start of the statute of limitations in this case, plus the fact that the lawsuit was filed on March 16, 1983, thereby "tolling" (or stopping) the statute well beyond the six-year limitations period, the plaintiffs' lawsuit was time-barred.

The court disposed of the sovereign immunity question with equal ease. To the extent plaintiffs were asserting constitutional, implied-in-law contract, or equitable claims, these claims were barred by the doctrine of sovereign immunity, because Congress has not expressly waived the government's immunity regarding such claims. To the extent that the plaintiffs were asserting expressed or implied-in-fact contract claims, these claims fell within the Tucker Act's waiver of sovereign immunity for such claims but were barred by the Tucker Act's six-year statute of limitations.

What about the Federal Tort Claims Act (FTCA)? This act allows individuals injured by federal government officials or employees in the course of performing their official duties to seek money damages against the federal government in the Court of Claims, after the claims have first been presented and denied by the appropriate federal agencies.[75] The court ruled that any claims asserted under the FTCA's waiver of sovereign immunity were barred by that statute's two-year limitations period. In addition, the plaintiffs had failed to exhaust their administrative remedies.[76]

After two technical appeals, one reaching the Supreme Court,[77] the Federal Circuit, an appellate court with exclusive jurisdiction over certain cases brought against the federal government,[78] affirmed the trial judge's dismissal of the internment case.[79] The dismissal came in 1988, the year in which President Ronald Reagan signed the Civil Liberties Act that issued a government apology for removal and internment and backed the apology with reparations consisting of, inter alia, $20,000 for each former internee and a scholarship fund. The act forecloses litigation for those who accept statutory reparations.[80] It is doubtful whether *Hohri* inspired the act in the same way that the dozens of German forced and slave labor cases led to the Foundation Law. Indeed, legislative inquiry into the internment matter began in 1980, well before *Hohri* was filed in 1983. That investigation produced a 1982 report, titled *Personal Justice Denied,* condemning removal and internment. *Personal Justice Denied,* in turn, led to a 1983 report recommending the redress that was eventually authorized under the Civil Liberties Act of 1988.[81]

It is against the backdrop of this litigation—Japanese and Nazi forced and slave labor cases and Japanese-American removal and internment cases—that slave-redress lawsuits have been filed. Most of slave-redress cases were filed during the 1990s and are still being filed today, with more to come in the future. Lawyers filing slave-redress cases have attempted to learn from the "mistakes" of prior redress litigation. They have largely been unsuccessful, however, because the "mistakes" are structural; that is, they arise from the normal operation of our legal system.

SLAVE-REDRESS LITIGATION

Public Actions

The first set of slave-redress lawsuits were filed against the federal government. All have been dismissed before a decision on the merits could be reached. Not unlike the forced labor and internment cases discussed earlier, these public actions have been dismissed mainly on statute of limitations, sovereign immunity, and nonjusticiability (or political question) grounds. Proponents of the tort model, however, often point to *Pigford v. Glickman,*[82] a case in which the plaintiffs and the federal government reached a settlement, as an example of a "successful" slave-redress lawsuit. But this case, which was greatly aided by an unusual event—Congress passed legislation tolling the statute of limitations governing the plaintiffs' claims[83]—does not fit the profile of a typical redress case, slave or otherwise. The claims on which the plaintiffs sued did not take place during slavery or Jim Crow. Yet, as I shall explain in due course, *Pigford* teaches valuable lessons about the potential dangers of class action litigation that could befall "successful" slave-redress litigation.

The first attempt to litigate a slave-redress claim, or the first to result in a judicial opinion, was filed in 1916. This case, *Johnson v. MacAdoo,*[84] was filed against the secretary of the Treasury by four blacks in the Federal District Court of the District of Columbia, a state court. The plaintiffs alleged that they and their ancestors were enslaved from 1859 to 1865 and were forced to pick cotton that was subject to taxation under the Internal Revenue Tax and Raw Cotton Act of 1862. This revenue, totaling over $60 million, belonged to them, the plaintiffs claimed, as unpaid wages. Without addressing the merits of this claim, the trial court dismissed the complaint, and the court of appeals later affirmed that dismissal on grounds of sovereign immunity.

The next public action to reach a judgment was *Berry v. United States*,[85] filed in federal court in 1994. The plaintiff in this case, Mark Berry, sought title to forty acres of U.S. government land in San Francisco or, alternatively, $3 million in damages. This action was filed *pro se* (i.e., the plaintiff represented himself, which is never a good idea, even for a lawyer) and styled as a class action representing the descendants of slaves. Despite the plaintiff's desire to bring this case as a class action, however, the case had to proceed as an individual action, because a *pro se* plaintiff can represent only himself and no one else. Subject-matter jurisdiction was invoked under Article III of the Constitution, the Thirteenth and Fourteenth Amendments, and the Freedmen's Bureau Act of 1865. Section 4 of the Freedmen's Bureau Act authorized the commissioner of the Freedmen's Bureau "to lease not more than forty acres of land within the Confederate states to each freedman or refugee for a period of three years; during or after the lease period, each occupant would be given the option to purchase the land for its value."[86] Section 4, it should be noted, was designed to codify Major General William T. Sherman's Special Field Order No. 15 issued on January 16, 1865, three months before § 4 was enacted. This act gave rise to the federal government's unfulfilled promise of "Forty Acres and a Mule."[87]

The request for redress in the form of a transfer of land was untenable, because it went against the indisposition in the legal systems of the United States and many other Western nations to take land, especially very valuable land, out of the possession of one who has held legal title for a long period of time.[88] Even the German government, which has in many ways been a model provider of reparations, has balked at the thought of returning a valuable piece of German real estate to its rightful Jewish owners sixty years after the theft.[89] On the other hand, the return of land as a form of redress is not unheard of in Western law. South Africa has created an extensive program of land restitution, including the creation of a commission and judicial tribunal with powers to return privately as well as publicly held land to the rightful owners.[90] Although certainly not as extensively as South Africa, the United States has even returned land to Native Americans.[91] But Berry may have gone too far in asking for forty acres of valuable federal land in San Francisco, including the Federal Building, the U.S. Mint Building, and the U.S. Naval Station (Treasure Island). Hedging his bet, he asked for $3 million as an alternative.

The district court dismissed all Berry's claims on procedural grounds, never having reached the merits. Judge Jensen ruled that none of the jurisdictional bases on which the plaintiff relied were in fact jurisdictional. Article III of the Constitution, the Thirteenth and Fourteenth Amendments, and the Freedmen's Bureau Act did not confer subject-matter jurisdiction on the court to hear plaintiffs' property claim. Each, instead, provided a right of action (a legal claim) that required an established jurisdictional base (again, judicial authority to hear a claim) if it was to be heard in federal court. In that regard, Judge Jensen considered two jurisdictional statutes. The first was the Tucker Act,[92] which "confers exclusive subject matter jurisdiction on the Court of Federal Claims for '[a]ny civil action or claim against the United States . . . founded either upon the Constitution, or any Act of Congress' where money damages [do not] exceed $10,000."[93] The phrase "Act of Congress" did not, however, include discontinued statutes like the Freedmen's Bureau Act, which expired on July 17, 1989, after several extensions by Congress. Thus, in addition to the court's lack of subject-matter jurisdiction, the plaintiff did not even have a viable right of action based on that Reconstruction Era statute.[94] Furthermore, even if the plaintiff did have a claim under the Freedmen's Bureau Act, it would be barred by the six-year statute of limitations for civil actions against the federal government.[95] Next, Judge Jensen turned to the Quiet Title Act,[96] which in conjunction with a provision of the Tucker Act,[97] confers jurisdiction on district courts to quiet title to land in which the United States has an interest. The Quiet Title Act was inapplicable in this case, however, because it does not apply to claims that could have been brought under the Tucker Act.[98] And even if the Quiet Title Act were applicable, the plaintiff's claim would be time barred by the act's twelve-year statute of limitations.[99] The six-year statute of limitations accrued, Judge Jensen said, "when plaintiff's ancestors allegedly did not receive land under the Freedmen's Bureau Act, last enforced in 1869. There is no question that more than six years have passed since then."[100]

Basing a slave-redress claim on the Freedmen's Bureau Act was problematic for another reason. Even if the act were still in effect, it only covered claims regarding land "within the insurrectionary states" and the payment of rent or a purchase price. Plaintiff claimed title to land located in California and did not allege the payment of rents or a purchase price.[101]

In all its discussion of the statute of limitations issue, the court did not consider, as perhaps it should have, the question of whether the applicable statutes were subject to equitable tolling based on the conditions of the newly freed slaves and the racial climate from the end of Reconstruction to the end of the civil rights movement. The equitable tolling doctrine permits plaintiffs to file an action after the expiration of the applicable statute of limitations if they were prevented from making a timely filing due to inequitable circumstances. Had the plaintiffs slave ancestors been tricked or induced to forgo filing a lawsuit by any misconduct on the federal government's part? Had the government turned a deaf ear to repeated requests for information about the status of its promise of "forty acres and a mule"?[102] On the other hand, given the expiration of the Freedmen's Bureau Act and the absence of a property right of action under the constitutional provisions alleged in the complaint, one could understand why Judge Jensen did not consider the equitable tolling question.

Having dismissed the lawsuit on jurisdictional grounds, Judge Jensen did not have to reach the question of sovereign immunity. He did, however, comment on the question twice. First, he observed in a footnote: "If either the Quiet Title Act or the Tucker Act is held to confer jurisdiction on the Court, . . . both Acts have been construed as a waiver of sovereign immunity."[103] Second, the judge noted that sovereign immunity was not waived under the *Bivens* doctrine, which creates a constitutional right of action under certain conditions, because that doctrine waives the immunity of federal agents, not the federal government. In fact, the Supreme Court in *Bivens* refused to rule on the question of sovereign immunity.[104]

Finally, Judge Jensen rejected the plaintiffs argument that if Japanese Americans and Indian tribes are entitled to redress, so are blacks. Redress in those cases, the judge observed, "was authorized by existing Congressional statutes specifically addressing those topics."[105] The court, in short, could find no procedural basis on which to permit the case to proceed to its merits.

Berry was followed one year later by another public action filed, once again, in a California federal court. Like *Berry*, *Cato v. United States* was brought *pro se*.[106] But unlike *Berry*, *Cato* reached the federal appellate level, where lawyers took over. The lawyers did no better than their clients, however. Insurmountable procedural barriers overwhelmed the legally adroit and the novice alike.

The plaintiffs' complaint sought "compensation of $100,000,000 for forced ancestral indoctrination into a foreign society; kidnapping of ancestors from Africa; forced labor; breakup of families; removal of traditional values; deprivations of freedom; and imposition of oppression, intimidation, miseducation, and lack of information about various aspects of their indigenous character." The plaintiffs also requested that the court "order an acknowledgment of the injustice of slavery in the United States and in the 13 American colonies between 1619 and 1865, as well as of the existence of discrimination against freed slaves and their descendants from the end of the Civil War to the present." In addition, they sought "an apology from the United States."[107]

Both the trial court and the appellate court threw out the complaint. The former did so on the ground that plaintiffs' allegations did not translate into legally actionable harms or refer to any basis for the exercise of federal jurisdiction. On appeal, counsel for the plaintiffs argued that the Thirteenth Amendment provided a right of action against the United States for the harms enumerated in the complaint. Furthermore, the discrimination alleged in the complaint was fresh, it was "continuing." Finally, counsel argued that sovereign immunity does not bar a Thirteenth Amendment action against the federal government, "otherwise, the Thirteenth Amendment's obligation is meaningless."[108] The appellate court rejected each of these arguments on several grounds.

First, it ruled that the plaintiffs lacked standing to assert their constitutional claim, which the court read as a claim "based on the stigmatizing injury to all African Americans caused by racial discrimination." Under the doctrine of standing, the plaintiff must have a tangible, personal injury traceable to the defendant's conduct. "Without a concrete, personal injury that is not abstract and that is fairly traceable to the government conduct that she challenges as unconstitutional, Cato lacks standing," the court said. This claim was also defective because it "does not trace the presence of discrimination and its harm to the United States."[109] Quite frankly, that was a silly ruling because slavery and legal subordination and stigmatization that followed in its wake would not have been possible without the federal government's complete complicity. Our Constitution created a "slaveholding republic" prior to the Civil War and, thereafter, authorized a regime of racial apartheid under the separate-but-equal doctrine. Federal law, in short, mandated and sanctioned "[racial] discrimination and its harms" in the United States.[110]

Next, the court raised the sovereign immunity question. Its ruling on the question made explicit what Judge Jensen's ruling in *Berry* only implied; namely, the Thirteenth Amendment itself is not a jurisdictional, or "self-enforcing," provision. Unless a Thirteenth Amendment claim can be asserted pursuant to a jurisdictional statute—the grant of jurisdiction carrying with it a waiver of sovereign immunity—the claim is without jurisdiction. The most likely jurisdictional statute for tort actions against the United States, the court noted, is the Federal Tort Claims Act (FTCA). The FTCA vests the Court of Claims with jurisdiction (and hence waives sovereign immunity) for tort claims against the federal government so long as those claims accrue on or after January 1, 1945, and are brought within two years after the occurrence.[111] Constitutional tort claims do not, however, fall within the FTCA, the court ruled.[112] Another statute that waives sovereign immunity, namely, the Administrative Procedures Act, was inapplicable, the court noted, because it only applies to lawsuits seeking "other than money damages," whereas plaintiffs were seeking damages. [113]

Finally, the court rejected plaintiffs' constitutional claim on nonjusticiability grounds. Similar to application of the political question doctrine in forced labor litigation discussed earlier in this chapter, the appellate court, agreeing with the district court, ruled that the "legislature, rather than the judiciary, is the appropriate forum for plaintiff's grievances."[114] It is difficult to take the court's nonjusticiability argument seriously, given the fact that the federal courts have long been thrown into the political thicket by cases like *Brown v. Board of Education.* The question of school desegregation in the era of Jim Crow was as much a political question as it was a legal or moral one.

After *Berry* and *Cato*, federal courts have not hesitated to dispose of public actions seeking slave redress. The opinions have even gotten shorter.[115] One putative slave-redress case has, however, managed to survive pretrial dismissal. This case, *Pigford v. Glickman*,[116] was aided by the passage of a statute by Congress tolling the applicable statute of limitations. While, as I shall argue in a moment, I do not believe this case fits the profile of slave-redress cases, it does expose the dangers of class action litigation, of which anyone considering the soundness of the tort model should be aware.

In 1997, black farmers filed a class action lawsuit in federal court against Dan Glickman, at the time President Clinton's secretary of agriculture. The complaint alleged that the U.S. Department of Agriculture (USDA) systematically discriminated against black farmers in its financial assistance programs for farmers (including awarding farm loans) and failed to process claims of racial discrimination filed by black farmers. The action was brought under the Equal Credit Opportunity Act (ECOA),[117] which provides a statutory right of action for claims of discrimination in credit transactions. Section 1331 of Title 28 of the U.S. Code, the general "federal question" statute, gives federal courts subject-matter jurisdiction over controversies that arise under federal statutes, such as ECOA. Thus, plaintiffs had a right of action and the district court had jurisdiction over the right of action. Plaintiffs, therefore, did not face the right-of-action and sovereign-immunity problems that typify public actions for slave redress.[118] But what about the statute of limitations problem?

Actions brought under ECOA have a two-year statute of limitations.[119] The government was poised to raise the defense of statute of limitations as grounds for barring acts of discrimination that took place more than two years prior to the filing of the federal action. Many black farmers filed complaints of discrimination with the USDA in 1983 for acts of discrimination that allegedly occurred as far back as 1982. A report issued in 1997 by the Office of the Inspector General of the USDA concluded that "the USDA had a backlog of complaints of discrimination that had never been processed, investigated or resolved." Thus, black farmers who had waited since 1983 for the USDA to respond to their complaints learned only in 1997 that the USDA had stopped processing them. Yet, as the court noted, "the government would argue that any claim under ECOA was barred by the statute of limitations."[120]

The Inspector General's report and a 1996 report issued by the USDA's Civil Rights Action Team, which concluded that "minority farmers have lost significant amounts of land and potential farm income as a result of discrimination by [the USDA],"[121] helped to persuade Congress to pass legislation tolling the two-year statute of limitations. Congress has the power to waive an otherwise valid defense to a claim against the United States for any reason, including in recognition of "its obligation to pay a moral debt."[122] On October 21, 1998, President Clinton signed into law a bill that tolled the statute of limitations for all discrimination complaints filed with the USDA before July 1, 1997 (the year in which the *Pigford* complaint was filed) alleging acts of discrimination that took place between January 1, 1981, and December 31, 1996.[123] With right of action, jurisdictional, and statute of limitations questions resolved in their favor, plaintiffs had crossed significant procedural barriers. The case could now proceed to the merits.

But the case never got that far. Two procedural matters ended the case in the plaintiffs' favor. First, the case was certified as a class action, twice in fact: as a "(b)(2)" class action—wherein class remedies are primarily limited to injunctive or declaratory relief—and then, the court vacating the prior certification order, as a "(b)(3)" class action—wherein class remedies can include monetary relief. As a "(b)(3)" class action, the membership was limited to black farmers who farmed or attempted to farm between January 1, 1981, and December 31, 1996; applied to the USDA for farm credit or believed they were the victims of USDA discrimination during this time; and filed a discrimination complaint on or before July 1, 1997.[124] Second, the case was settled. By mid-November of 1997, after the Inspector General's February 1997 report, the government had rethought its original opposition to the lawsuit and began settlement negotiations.[125]

Some proponents of the tort model have embraced *Pigford* as a successful slave-redress lawsuit. Even Judge Freedman, who approved the settlement agreement, saw the case in this light. He concluded his opinion, in rather dramatic fashion, as follows:

> Forty acres and a mule. The government broke that promise to African American farmers. Over one hundred years later, the USDA broke its promise to Mr. James Beverly [one of the original plaintiffs]. It promised him a loan to build farrowing houses so that he could breed hogs. Because he was African American, he never received that loan. He lost his farm because of the loan that never was. Nothing can completely undo the discrimination of the past or restore lost land or lost opportunities to Mr. Beverly or to all of the other African American farmers whose representatives come before this Court. Historical discrimination cannot be undone.[126]

Pigford is not, in my view, a true slave-redress lawsuit, but rather a traditional civil rights lawsuit. Neither the complaint nor the court's approval of the settlement was based on slavery or Jim Crow or even an event that took place during slavery or Jim Crow. The claims sued upon dated back only to 1981, almost a decade after Jim Crow ended. Although the claims relate or connect to slavery and Jim Crow, the plaintiffs did not rely upon that connection, and, indeed, did not have to do so in order to win. The lawsuit targeted present-day discrimination—discrimination that was active rather than passive, fresh rather than old.

In contrast, slave-redress cases target the present-day manifestations of past atrocities. These cases are about the lingering effects of past discrimination. The cause of the discrimination on which the plaintiffs sue is in the past, not the present. They seek a judicial decree based on a connection between the present and slavery or Jim Crow, or they simply target an event that took place during slavery or Jim Crow, usually the latter as in the case of the Tulsa lawsuit, *Alexander v. Governor of the State of Oklahoma,*[127] discussed next. Thus, slave-redress lawsuits are about the past atrocities of slavery and Jim Crow. Acts of current discrimination, or active discrimination, may be at issue as well, but the case is not about those acts. *Slave-redress cases succeed because of their connection to the past, not in spite of that connection.*

It is because of this focus on the past that slave-redress cases acquire their special difficulties. The absence of a well-established claim, the want of subject-matter jurisdiction, the running of applicable statutes of limitations, and the problem of justiciability converge on slave-redress litigation, sometimes all at once. The typical slave-redress lawsuit, in short, faces procedural barriers that are not present in *Pigford*. Indeed, in its procedural posture, *Pigford* is very different from cases like *Berry* and *Cato*, as well as from the forced labor and internment cases.

Yet *Pigford* is not totally irrelevant to the tort model. It offers valuable lessons for the lawyers who are or will be pursuing that strategy for slave redress. These lessons concern the lawyers' conduct after the settlement had been reached. After negotiating what appeared to be a reasonable settlement on behalf of their clients, the lawyers managed to snatch victory away from many members of the class.[128] They persistently failed to meet filing deadlines for obtaining payments and filed no more than "a small fraction of the total petitions requested by the farmers."[129] The sordid details, which prompted one trial judge to describe the lawyers' conduct as "bordering on legal malpractice," are summarized by the court of appeals:

The decree provided for class counsel to receive an advance payment of $1 million in fees to cover decree "implementation." Consent Decree Para 14(b). The decree entitled counsel to seek additional fees under [§ 1691e(d) of] the Equal Credit Opportunity Act, for their work in connection with filing the action and implementing the decree. Consent Decree Para 14(a). One year into the implementation process, the district court "took the extraordinary step of awarding a second advance"—this time for $7 million. . . . The Department [USDA] and class counsel eventually settled all fee claims for $14.9 million. Attorneys and firms sharing the fees were: . . .

Several months after class counsel received their second fee advance and just two weeks prior to the deadline for filing petitions for monitor review for the "vast majority of claimants," class counsel filed an emergency motion seeking an extension of time. . . . Counsel revealed that they had filed only a small fraction of the total petitions requested by the farmers. Concerned that "counsel's failings . . . not be visited on their clients," and relying on "explicit assurances" by counsel as to the work load they could realistically shoulder into the future, . . . the district court permitted counsel to file pro forma petitions by the original deadline and then to either file supporting materials or to withdraw the petitions at the rate of at least 400 petitions per month. . . .

A few months later, the district court observed "a very disturbing trend": class counsel had failed to meet their monthly quota "even once.". . . Worse still, counsel had "drastically cut its staff, bringing Class Counsel's ability to represent the [farmers] into serious question.". . . "Alarmed by Class Counsel's consistent failure" to meet decree timelines, the district court noted counsel's "remarkable admission that they never had a realistic expectation of meeting" agreed-upon or court-ordered deadlines for the monitor review process. . . . The court described counsel's performance as "dismal"—"bordering on legal malpractice"—and "wondered" whether class counsel would have been in such a predicament had they not filed "three new sister class actions" against the Department. . . .

The district court eventually imposed a series of escalating daily fines on class counsel for untimely monitor review filings. . . . Instead of simply submitting materials in support of their clients' petitions in a more timely fashion, however, counsel drastically increased the rate at which they *withdrew* petitions for monitor review—from 19% to 48%—"once again" leading the district court to "question Class Counsel's fidelity to their clients.". . .

Consider the case of Earl Kitchen, a farmer from Arkansas. . . . Kitchen was initially represented by . . . , a member of one of the firms sharing in the fee award. . . . During the course of representing Kitchen, [his attorney] obtained extensions of several paragraph 10 deadlines either with consent or over the Department's objection. Around the time the Department agreed to pay class counsel $14.9 million, [Kitchen's attorney] missed the deadline (already extended by mutual consent) to submit written direct testimony. [The attorney's] failure could have drastic consequences, for absent submission of testimony, Kitchen's claim will "be extinguished.". . . Consent Decree Para 10(g) (putting the burden of proof on the claimant).

In the meantime, the district court, deeply concerned about the decree's viability, asked the American Bar Association Committee on Pro Bono and Public Services to "assemble a team of *pro bono* lawyers to assist Class Counsel on an emergency basis.". . . In response, lawyers from the Pro Bono Committee and the firms of Arnold & Porter and Crowell & Moring recruited some of Washington's largest law firms: Covington & Burling; Sidley, Austin, Brown & Wood; Steptoe & Johnson; Swidler, Berlin, Shereff & Friedman; and Wilmer, Cutler, and Pickering. The district court, recognizing the competing demands on class counsel arising out of their representation of multiple claimants . . . at various stages of the claims resolution process, hoped that this added assistance would lift the "heavy burden of . . . litigation from the shoulders of Class Counsel," enabling them to "focus on the petition [for monitor review] process."[130]

Thus, the court was deeply concerned about what it termed "the farmers' . . . betrayal . . . by their own lawyers."[131] Farmers like James Beverly, one of the original plaintiffs whom District Court Judge Friedman mentioned by name in his opinion, paid a heavy price for their lawyers' lapses. Beverly had been waiting for twenty years for a government loan so that he could refurbish his pig-breeding farm. Dealing with career USDA employees who were part of the original problem of discrimination, and now with greedy or incompetent lawyers, Beverly, like other black farmers, felt he had returned to square one. As regards the quality of the legal representation provided by his lawyers, Beverly said it best: "They beat their chests about 'this is the largest civil-rights settlement in the history of the United States.' That's an outright lie."[132]

Pigford, then, offers valuable lessons for the proponents of the tort model. These lessons have less to do with pointing the way to successful litigation—again, *Pigford* lacks the procedural complications of slave-redress cases—than with highlighting the dangers of unethical or incompetent representation too often associated with class actions.[133] These dangers do not disappear when litigation strategy shifts from public to private actions.

Before turning to the private actions, there is one more public action to discuss: *Alexander v. Governor of the State of Oklahoma*.[134] This action, prepared by the Reparations Coordinating Committee headed by the Harvard law professor Charles Ogletree, is the only public action filed against a state rather than the federal government. Also, it is the only one that targets events that took place during Jim Crow rather than slavery. The complaint was filed on behalf of over two hundred black victims or their descendants of the worse race riot in the history of our country—the Tulsa Race Riot of 1921.

The riot was sparked on May 30, 1921, when a nineteen-year-old black male named Richard Rowland entered the elevator at the Drexel Building in downtown Tulsa to deliver a package. He stumbled against a white female elevator operator named Sara Page, who screamed for help. When Rowland ran from the building, Page screamed attempted rape. Arrested later that day, Rowland protested his innocence, and explained to the authorities that he became frightened and ran when Page screamed, knowing that many blacks had been lynched on false charges of raping white women. Rumors began to fly when the *Tulsa Tribune* published an outrageously inaccurate article titled "Nab Negro for Attacking Girl in an Elevator," which reported that Rowland had torn Page's dress, scratched her face, and touched her hand. A white lynch mob began to gather outside of the jail. News of the lynch mob traveled to the all-black section of Tulsa, called "Greenwood." Fearing for Rowland's safety, a group of some thirty black men armed themselves and proceeded to the jail. Many of them were World War I veterans who had fought in Europe. They were confronted by a white crowd as they arrived at the jail. The riot began when a black World War I veteran refused to surrender his weapon to the white crowd. Fighting escalated in the ensuing hours as more and more residents from both races joined in. As the outnumbered blacks retreated into the Greenwood district, whites began to destroy property as well as lives. In the process, they inflicted between $2 to $3 million in property damage: 18,000 black homes and businesses were burned, and another 304 black homes were looted. When the riot finally subsided, 4,241 blacks were left homeless, and 300 were dead.[135]

The plaintiffs in *Alexander* had resided in Greenwood at the time of the riot. Most now live in other states. They allege that the state of Oklahoma, the city of Tulsa, the office of the chief of police of Tulsa, and other unnamed defendants, acting under local or state authority, had "terrorized" them, denying them liberty and property without due process, equal protection of the laws, the right to petition government, plus several statutory and common law rights, and had, moreover, been responsible for the wrongful death of loved ones. One of the more compelling allegations is that "The City of Tulsa denied restitution claims made by every black resident of Greenwood, but allowed restitution claims made by whites."[136] The plaintiffs claim rights of actions under the First, Thirteenth, and Fourteenth Amendments to the Constitution of the United States, the Civil Rights Act of April 9, 1866 (known as a "§ 1981 cause of action"), and the Civil Rights Act of April 20, 1871, which provides two causes of action, "§§ 1983 and 1985(3)."[137] Common law rights of actions for replevin (recovery of personal property wrongfully taken), forcible entry and detainer, wrongful death, false arrest, and involuntary servitude are also claimed. The allegations of the complaint are certainly cognizable under most if not all of these laws, and jurisdiction seems sustainable pursuant to a number of federal statutes.[138] The only procedural hurdles facing this public action are sovereign immunity with respect to the claim against the state, and the applicable statute of limitations. As to the latter, the complaint does, however, state a number of allegations in support of an equitable tolling of the applicable statute of limitations, including the following quotation from the Oklahoma Commission to Study the Tulsa Race Riot of 1921: "Before there was this commission, much . . . [of the evidence] was buried somewhere, lost somewhere, or somewhere undiscovered."[139]

In the eyes of the court, these considerations were not sufficient to overcome the statute of limitations problem. Judge James Ellison dismissed the case nearly one year after it had been filed because of the long-expired, two-year statute of limitations. Thus, *Alexander* met the same fate as every other public action: dismissal before a decision on the merits could be reached. This is most unfortunate because the merits of *Alexander*, like those of other slave-redress cases, were compelling. As even Judge Ellison noted: "That plaintiffs' claims are barred by the statute of limitations is strictly a legal conclusion and does not speak to the tragedy of the riot or the terrible devastation it caused." The hope of slave-redress litigation rests mainly with private actions.

Rather than face formidable procedural hurdles in suing the government, particularly the federal government, blacks have devised a new litigation strategy in the slave-redress cases—suing private entities, mainly corporations, that have profited from slavery. Corporations named in these dozen or so private actions include commercial banks (such as Fleet Boston Financial Corporation), investment banks (such as J. P. Morgan Chase & Co., Lehman Brothers Holdings, Inc., and Brown Brothers Harriman), tobacco companies (such as R. J. Reynolds Tobacco Holdings, Inc., Brown & Williamson Tobacco Corp., and Liggett Group, which is now indirectly owned by Vector Group Ltd.), insurance companies (such as Aetna, Inc., Lloyds of London, and American International Group), railroads (such as CSX, Union Pacific, and Norfolk Southern Corp.), and textile companies (such as Westpoint Stevens, Inc.). These and other corporate defendants not yet named are alleged to be successors-in-interest to predecessor corporations that profited from slavery by, inter alia, insuring slaveholders against the loss of slave "property" and using slaves to build their railroads or make their products.[140]

Most of the private actions filed thus far have been class actions. In the first of this genre of lawsuit, the named plaintiff, Deadria Farmer-Paellmann, brought the action in federal court in New York City on behalf of herself and all other "African-American slave descendants . . . whose ancestors were enslaved in the agricultural industry."[141] On the other side of the country, Timothy and Chester Hurdle, whose father, Andrew Hurdle, was a slave, filed a slave-redress lawsuit in federal court in San Francisco. Plaintiffs in this case are unique in that they learned of slavery firsthand through their father's personal suffering.[142]

Although the class of plaintiffs and specific claims alleged in most of the private actions are different, they face common procedural complications under existing law. Most important, private actions, like most public actions, do not have clear actionable claims, or rights of action, and may be time-barred by applicable statutes of limitations. Yet private actions do not generally face problems of subject-matter jurisdiction arising from the defense of sovereign immunity. Not being governments, the defendants cannot claim this defense. The federal court's constitutional authority to decide private actions is usually predicated on the diversity of citizenship statute. This statute grants federal courts subject-matter jurisdiction over claims brought by citizens of different states, provided the amount in controversy exceeds $75,000.[143]

The right of action alleged in private law actions is characteristically based on international law and Anglo-American common law—*lex non scripto* (the unwritten law)—rather than on statutory or constitutional law—*lex scripto* (the written law). Violations of international human rights include the right to be free of torture, rape, starvation, physical and mental abuse, summary execution, and forced labor.[144] Common law claims include *quantum meruit,* conversion, and unjust enrichment. Thus, the claim is that even though slavery was legal as a matter of *lex scripto,* slavery, or some aspects of it, was illegal as a matter of *lex non scripto* as well as international law.

This legal strategy may seem questionable, given that slavery was legal under international law (as discussed earlier), and given what is generally believed to have been the legal status of blacks during slavery. Roger Taney, chief justice of the U.S. Supreme Court, purported to summarize the latter when he wrote in 1857 that even emancipated blacks were "beings of an inferior order, and altogether unfit to associate with the white race, either in social or political relations; and so far inferior that they had no rights which the white man was bound to respect."[145] As a generalization about the legal rights of blacks before and after the American Revolution, Taney, as one scholar notes, "offered an illusory picture of certainty about the Negro's status in that earlier age."[146] Quite simply, free blacks and slaves alike had rights at the state level (codified as well as common law) that the white man *was* bound by law to respect.[147] The problem, of course, is to determine what these rights were and whether they provide a right of action. Some scholars suggest that there was enough uncertainty about the legal rights of blacks—"not merely because he was both perishable and expensive but because of uncertainty as to just how much of him was property and how much humanity"[148]—that a judge looking at this body of law today and of a mind to uphold slave redress could find sufficient ground for doing so. It may be, for example, that human bondage was legal under both international law and domestic common law, but not necessarily some of the *incidents* (or excesses) of slavery as practiced on many plantations; such as working slaves to death, torture, rape, or malicious murder.

What we may need today is a judge (or judges) who can exhibit the capacity of Chief Justice John Marshall, whom many rank as our greatest Supreme Court justice ever. Marshall exhibited, some say, the capacity "for giving a veneer of reasoned inevitability to a tortuous logical path" in the interest of justice and fairness.[149] An example of this judicial technique can be seen in the context of slavery in Judge Leonard Henderson, who sat on the North Carolina Supreme Court during the antebellum period, serving as its chief justice from 1829 to 1833. Using some rather dubious legal footwork, along with analysis that augured judicial restraint, Judge Henderson extended the common law of England, which protected the freedom of blacks so long as they remained in England, to sustain the conviction of a slave master for murdering a slave.[150] The crime was actionable under the common law, but not under the state statutory law. To make sure the murderer got his just deserts, Judge Henderson ruled that absent a controlling statute, the common law itself protected the slave, not from slavery, but from his master's excesses: "There is no statute on the subject, it is the Common Law, cut down, it is true, by statute or custom, so as to tolerate slavery, yielding to the owner the services of the slave, and any right incident thereto as necessary for its full enjoyment, but protecting the life and limbs of the human being; and in these particulars, it does not admit that he is without the protection of the law. I think, therefore, that judgment of death should be pronounced against the prisoner."[151]

Just six months later, the North Carolina Supreme Court extended the common law to protect the slave from assault and battery by whites other than his master.[152] Thus, if a private-action plaintiff can show that his slave-laborer ancestor was wantonly killed by a defendant corporation or its predecessor-in-interest, this might form the basis for a wrongful death action, absent statute-of-limitations considerations, of course.

Rather than attacking the mere incidents of slavery, it may be possible to lodge a frontal attack on the institution of slavery itself using common-law doctrine. Some legal scholars in the field of remedies have argued that there is ample space within the palace of justice to accommodate these cases without having to add on additional rooms. Anthony Sebok, for example, argues that the doctrine of unjust enrichment (discussed earlier in the context of the forced labor litigation) is "viable" against corporate defendants. He gives two reasons for this conclusion. First, questions of proof may be easier to resolve in plaintiffs' favor because corporations usually maintain good records (although let us not forget the paper shredding that went on at Enron). This "makes it relatively easy to track how a dollar wrongfully gained 200 years ago was reinvested until today." Second, styled as a lawsuit that seeks redress for the wrongful gains held by the perpetrator—what is called a "gain-based lawsuit" as opposed to a "harm-based lawsuit," which focuses on the harms sustained by the victim as a result of the perpetrator's acts—a private action against a corporate defendant provides a cognizable right of action under the law of restitution.[153]

There are common-law precedents that suggest the existence of a restitutionary claim in private actions. Sebok cites Lord Mansfield's dictum in the 1760 case of *Moses v. MacFarlen,*[154] for example: "Defendants upon the circumstances of the case are obliged by the ties of natural justice in equity to refund the money represented by the intangible thing they took,"[155] and another restitution scholar, Hanoch Dagan, cites others.[156] However, Sebok raises an important moral issue, called the "commodification question." The equitable theory of unjust enrichment, Sebok argues, commodifies the wrongs of slavery, essentially a human rights matter, because it necessarily entails the use of "the quotidian language of property and restitution law." In other words, Sebok believes that "the language of restitution implies . . . that the claim is not about forcing the slaves to labor, but rather about failing to pay for the work they did. . . . Thus, . . . restitution claims commodify the horrors of . . . Slavery by implying that the wrong committed is the retention of property that has been wrongfully taken, rather than the violation of human rights, the destruction of culture, and the oppression of people. . . . [In short,] 'employing a legal tactic that frames the right to freedom in terms of the right to property' may end up degrading the human values at stake and sapping the moral language of the reparations movement."[157] Dagan answers the commodification question, or what some have called the "blood money" issue,[158] in a most creative fashion.

Restitutionary claims do not trivialize slavery by "reducing them to prosaic grievance about unpaid wages," Dagan argues, because these claims are in reality not about the value of the victim's labor to her master; rather, they speak to the value of the victim's labor to herself. Restitution in private law actions vindicates the victim's right to be free from wrongful interference with her inalienable right to control her labor—whom she shall work for and under what conditions. "Denying restitution for the wrongful appropriation of human labor" in the context of slavery, Dagan asserts, "would not elevate human labor above the marketplace, but rather [would] shift the entitlement to its beneficial use [from] the wrongful appropriator."[159]

Moreover, given the correlative relationship between legal rights and legal remedies—what is called the "correlativity thesis"—restitution must be regarded as "the notional equivalent at the remedial stage of the right that has been wrongly infringed."[160] Remedies concretize rights; they make rights meaningful. If the law were to allow the perpetrator of an atrocity to retain his ill-gotten gains, that would not only stand as a "sequel" to the atrocity and, in the case of slavery, the corrupt laws that made the atrocity possible, but it would also stand as their "present embodiment." Thus, finding a recovery in law for slavery provides "a credibility check" on the "integrity and moral significance" of the extant law.

But what about the fact that slave descendants are not the direct victims of slavery, and the fact that the law has a "good faith purchaser doctrine" that cuts off intergenerational claims? As to the first question, Dagan provides an easy answer: "I do not think that this difficulty should block the suit of the slave descendants. The inheritability of the right to gain-based recovery has been recognized . . . in another context that involves an entitlement of the incomplete commodification type, namely: the right of publicity."[161] Similar to the equitable tolling of a statute of limitations, the good faith purchaser doctrine "balances the moral importance of present claims with past injustices."[162] The decision here is one of distributive justice. That is, under the doctrine, the disputed asset remains with the current owner if she had no knowledge of the original owner's (i.e., the slave's) conflicting claim *and* if she can show that her losses, should the asset be taken away from her, are equal to "the losses likely to be suffered by the original owner" (or in the case of slavery, the slave's descendant). The current owner's loss includes the value she put into the purchase of the asset and the value she spent in reliance on her ownership of the asset. Someone who inherits an ill-gotten asset has put less value into the asset than a person who has purchased the asset, even though both may value the asset equally.

Dagan argues that it is easier to balance the competing hardships in favor of slave descendants than corporate defendants in private law actions because the latter are "direct recipient[s] of wrongful gains from slavery." Such privity is based upon the institutional continuity of a corporation— its "fictive legal personality, unlimited life, and successorship in the event of merger or acquisition."[163] In contrast, most owners of slave assets (whether land or the slave-labor benefits) are typically unaware of the fact that they own tainted assets. They, therefore, would likely be able to successfully use the good faith purchaser doctrine. What this means, Dagan suggests, is that "the fine-points of the law of restitution" may have motivated the plaintiffs' attorneys in the private actions to sue corporations and wealthy white families that build their fortunes on slavery rather than to sue any other of the "countless people in the United States today who own land, buildings, and other assets that originally belonged to slave owners." The choice of defendant was not, in short, "opportunistic and morally arbitrary."[164]

Finally, Sebok argues that the statute of limitations, an important procedural barrier in private actions, may be subject to equitable tolling on the ground that new technologies have given plaintiffs a first-time opportunity to discover the defendant corporations' unjust gains.[165] If this argument works in private actions, it is difficult to see why it would not work in public actions as well.

Yet while citing a number of rules that prevent the limitations period from accruing—such as where the gain was fraudulently concealed or, in the absence of such fraud, the plaintiff was ignorant of the pertinent facts due to no fault of his own—or that allow the limitations period to be extended—such as where "justice demands, which usually requires an element of [further] wrongdoing by the defendant"— Dagan concludes: "To the best of my knowledge, there is no case law on the question of whether a statute of limitations can be tolled by the emergence of new evidence previously unknown because of undeveloped technologies."[166]

On the whole, both Sebok and Dagan demonstrate that there are many creative ways in which a court may be able to sustain private actions against corporations. A gain-based claim of unjust enrichment—one that focuses on the wrongful taking of the slave's inalienable right to control his labor rather than the failure to pay wages—could provide a sound legal and moral (noncommodifying) right of action. The emergence of new evidence previously unknown because of undeveloped technology could provide an equitable basis for tolling the statute of limitations for such claims. And the institutional continuity of corporate defendants may both provide evidentiary benefits for the plaintiffs and deny defendants the use of the good faith purchaser defense. If the slave descendants' claims are morally compelling, then they *must* be cognizable under U.S. law. Otherwise, the extant law stands as the "present embodiment" of America's worst atrocity and the corrupt laws that made it possible. This is a credibility check no less important than the Supreme Court's landmark 1954 school desegregation case of *Brown v. Board of Education.*

DEFICIENCIES OF THE TORT MODEL

Although I have argued that our legal system should embrace claims for slave redress as a means of responding to the needs of black citizens, and although, in the aftermath of *Brown* "[i]t is now a commonplace to say that the legal system is an instrument as well as a product of social change,"[167] I do not prefer an adjudicatory approach to slave redress.[168] Adjudication in our legal system is essentially adversarial—discord is built into the process—and lawyers, not judges, are given the primary responsibility for making sure the process works. Too often the adversary process does not function well, and too often the problem lies with lawyers. Sometimes lawyers obfuscate the truth, exaggerate the contentiousness of litigation, or, whether out of greed, laziness, or sheer incompetence, sacrifice the interests of their clients in service of their own interests. For these and other reasons, many legal scholars favor the inquisitorial process prevalent in civil law systems (such as in France) wherein the judge takes a more active role in shaping the case and marshaling the evidence.[169]

There is, however, a more important reason for my ambivalence toward the use of litigation as a first-line strategy for obtaining slave redress. Litigation (and, more generally, the tort model) cannot bring forth what for me is the sine qua non of redress—a genuine apology for slavery from the main perpetrator, the federal government. Such an apology is impossible in private actions, which are not brought against the federal government. In public actions, some of which expressly request a government apology as a form of remedy, any apology would come at the end of a litigation gun. Whether arrived at by judicial fiat or by settlement, such an apology would not be genuine.[170] Indeed, the typical settlement agreement in civil litigation contains an exculpatory clause wherein the defendant expressly denies liability. Accepting personal responsibility lies at the heart of a genuine apology.

Furthermore, the chief characteristic of the tort model is antithetical to racial harmony and reconciliation, which for me is the major social objective or reason for slave redress. The tort model's main objective is to compensate the victim. The desire is for the perpetrator to simply come forward with a check. For some black Americans, the main reason for seeking redress is "to punish white Americans for their ancestors' brutal enslavement of African Americans."[171] Apology and racial reconciliation are not even ranked second in importance.[172] But without the demand for a genuine apology as a condition precedent to receiving money or any other form of redress, and without the desire for racial reconciliation, the tort model undercuts the moral basis for redress and, hence, dishonors the memory of the slaves. Divorced from its moral underpinnings, any form of redress, especially the payment of money, looks, smells, and tastes like a racial shakedown, even though that is not the intent.

Properly speaking, redress received under the tort model is not a true "reparation." This term has a very specific meaning that is inextricably tied to the idea of atonement. A reparation makes an apology believable. It turns the rhetoric of apology into a meaning, material reality. It is for that reason that I speak of the "black redress movement" rather than using the more common term "black reparations movement." The relationship between reparation and atonement is explained in greater detail in the next chapter.

Applied to litigation, the tort model can also result in an insufficient development of the historical record. As discussed in the next chapter, development of the historical record is, in my view, crucial to any attempt to redress slavery or any other past atrocity. With so many lawsuits pending, and many more impending, it is quite probable that one judge may see the facts of slavery, including its effects on contemporary society, differently from another judge. It is quite probable that we may end up with several different versions of the same set of facts, as often happens in complex litigation.[173] Perhaps the larger concern is that there may not be *any* development of the historical record at all. Some judges may feel institutionally constrained to develop the record of an event that took place so long ago, as was the case with Judge Belloni in the *Yasui coram nobis* case discussed earlier. If the case is tried before a jury, there will be no formal finding of facts except a verdict for or against the parties. And, finally, the parties may simply agree to a quick settlement without paying any attention to the historical record, except the usual settlement refrain that the defendant does not admit to a violation of any law.

The final problem with the tort model returns us to square one—its moral deficiency. Whether in litigation or legislation, the tort model clouds the black redress movement's identity with international human rights movements. True, litigation even in the international arena can be an effective strategy in achieving human rights objectives. But the best human rights movements have sought atonement from the perpetrator as a primary goal. Participants in these movements have refused to accept money from the perpetrator unless it was "atonement money." When pursued only through the tort model, the black redress movement loses the opportunity to identify with this morally centered approach—an approach that includes the continuing struggles of the Comfort Women, black South Africans, and Jewish and other victims of Nazi atrocities.[174]

Thus, the best strategy for securing slave redress proceeds along this high moral ground. That strategy is, in my view, the atonement model.

Chapter 5 | THE ATONEMENT MODEL

> We must make sure that their deaths have posthumous
> meaning. We must make sure that from now until the
> end of days all humankind stares this evil in the face.
>
> RONALD REAGAN

Racial reconciliation should be the primary purpose of slave redress. It is what gives the idea of slave redress its forward-looking quality.[1] When Americans embrace the idea of slave redress, they welcome the belief that we must go back in time and place to right a heavy wrong and to make the present and future more racially harmonious. They understand that there is a price to pay for collective amnesia, for that type of erasure.

Some might say that racial reconciliation is unnecessary or that the past should remain buried. These good people miss many points. They miss the point that the federal government committed a horrific racial atrocity for which it has never apologized. They miss the point that the government has little credibility on racial matters with the great majority of its black citizens. They miss the point that black Americans continue to suffer the lingering effects of slavery and Jim Crow. They miss the point that it is all about due respect—as one of the architects of Los Angeles's slavery disclosure ordinance (see chapter 1) has said: "I don't want a check. I just want fairness."[2] And they miss the point that the slaves, whose forced labor was central to our nation's eventual development, deserve to be recognized and honored alongside other American heroes.

The road to racial reconciliation must be paved with the post-Holocaust spirit of heightened morality, identity, egalitarianism, and restorative justice. This journey to racial reconciliation necessarily begins with the government tendering an apology and then solidifying its remorse with repa-rations. This path to slave redress—the atonement model—embraces the core belief that redress should be about apology *first and foremost.* It re-jects the tort model's preoccupation with compensation and punishment. Focusing on compensation before apology is the moral equivalent of plac-ing the cart before the horse. And the attempt at punishment slakes the appetite for revenge but does little to foster racial reconciliation in a soci-ety like ours.

To be sure, redress (including monetary compensation) without a clear, formal apology from the government-perpetrator would still be helpful to slave descendants, even if it does little to commemorate the memory of the slaves. But could we not say the same thing of welfare? Redressing slav-ery and Jim Crow should be about honor, not alms. It should be about black pride and dignity, and, last but not least, it should be about com-memorating and memorializing the slaves. These heroic men, women, and children were denied freedom so that all Americans might live in the freest and most prosperous nation humankind has ever known.

Simply providing slave redress without a prefatory statement of deep re-morse—an act that puts slave redress in its proper historical and interna-tional context—is too inelegant a response to slavery and Jim Crow. Both were atrocities. They were, in the words of the UN Charter, violations of "human rights and fundamental freedoms [guaranteed] for all without dis-tinction as to race, sex, language, or religion."[3] If slavery and Jim Crow were not atrocities but garden-variety forms of discrimination similar to what white ethnic groups have experienced, then perhaps there would be no need for an apology from the government. But blacks did not enter the lion's den voluntarily, and, more to the point, human bondage and government-sanctioned segregation, the latter often buttressed by racial violence, were exceptional acts of human degradation. Given this, simply throwing money or programs in the direction of blacks without an apology is unacceptable to me because it fails to demonstrate "new moral aspirations." Only apol-ogy is sufficiently endowed to perform such heavy moral lifting.

Atonement, however, entails much more than the tender of an apology. It also requires making restitution—that is, providing a reparation or repa-rations commensurate with the atrocity. Reparations are essential to atone-ment, because they make apologies believable. They turn the rhetoric of apology into a meaningful, material reality and, thus, help to repair the damage caused by the atrocity and ensure that the atrocity will not be repeated. Atonement, then, is defined here as apology *plus* reparations.

This chapter, the most important in the book, elaborates on the atonement model. Included in this discussion is the question of forgiveness, the victim's acceptance of the perpetrator's tender of atonement. Forgiveness is essential to the forward-looking, reconciling potential of slave redress. Yet forgiveness is rarely mentioned in the current debate over slave redress. That is to be expected given the debate's focus on the tort model. Without insistence on an apology, the question of forgiveness never comes up.

While I view atonement and forgiveness as the sine qua non of racial reconciliation, I do not treat them as morally equivalent concepts. The perpetrator's duty to atone for a past atrocity is a moral imperative, but in my view, the victim's duty to forgiveness can only be a civic responsibility. This is a matter of considerable debate among scholars, as I shall attempt to make clear, but I take the position that the victim of an atrocity, unlike the perpetrator of the atrocity, has no moral debt to cover. Furthermore, the civic duty to forgive is entirely predicated upon the quality of the atonement tendered. If substantial, reparations will make the apology believable. Then, and only then, does the atonement impose a civic obligation on the victim to forgive. Hence the formula: atonement—apology and reparation—plus forgiveness leads to racial reconciliation. Slave redress benefits the victim, perpetrator, and society as a whole.

THE ANATOMY OF APOLOGY

Reclaiming Moral Character

The image of Holy Roman Emperor Henry IV standing barefoot and repentant in the snow at the castle of Pope Gregory VII at Canossa in 1077 is embedded in Western culture as a symbol of remorse. The excommunicated emperor sought forgiveness from his papal adversary for having defied him over the question of lay investiture. Nine centuries later, West German Chancellor Willy Brandt displayed even more sincere remorse on a visit to the Warsaw Ghetto:

> I had not planned anything, but I had . . . a feeling that I must express the exceptional significance of the ghetto memorial. From the bottom of the

abyss of German history, under the burden of millions of victims of murder, I did what human beings do when speech fails them. Even twenty years later, I cannot say more than the reporter whose account ran: "Then he who does not need to kneel knelt, on behalf of all who do need to kneel but do not—because they dare not, or cannot, or cannot dare to kneel."[4]

A tender of apology is no trivial matter, particularly when made by state officials on behalf of their governments. It is an act fraught with deep meaning and important consequences.

Let us begin with some understanding of what apology is and is not in the context of atonement. Apology, most importantly, is an *acknowledgment* of guilt rather than a punishment for guilt. When a government perpetrates an atrocity and apologizes for it, it does four things: confesses the deed; admits the deed was an injustice; repents; and asks for forgiveness. All four conditions are essential to taking personal responsibility.

Some might add as a fifth condition the requirement that the perpetrator must change its behavior toward the victim. The purpose of this requirement is to ensure, as much as possible, that the atrocity will never be repeated. This, of course, assumes that the behavior giving rise to the atrocity has ended. It makes no sense to consider a tender of apology a true apology while the atrocity is still raging on.

I think it is more logical, however, to treat the behavioral element not as an ingredient of apology (which is essentially rhetoric, albeit essential rhetoric), but as an element of a meaningful reparation. Treating the changed behavior as part of the reparation makes sense in situations where, as in the case of American slavery and the Holocaust, all or most of the direct victims have died by the time the apology is tendered. Many victims of an atrocity do not survive the atrocity. Hence, as to dead victims, it makes no sense to require the perpetrator to change its behavior toward the victim other than by providing a meaningful reparation. Such a reparation could be the construction of a memorial honoring the lives of the dead victims. I shall discuss the forms of reparations in greater detail later in this chapter.

The matter of dead victims raises the difficult question of how far back the duty to apologize goes. Is there a moral statute of limitations on this duty? Does the perpetrator have anything to apologize for if all the victims are dead? The easy answer to these questions is that the matter of apology becomes moot if there are no living victims to receive the apology. Viewed in this way, the living-victims requirement acts as a kind of statute of limitations on redressing past atrocities. But the easy answer is not always the correct answer.

Whether the victim is alive or dead should be irrelevant to the question of how far back the duty to apologize extends. Because we are dealing with a matter of morality rather than a question of legality, the duty to apologize remains until the requisite apology is made. So long as the perpetrator or its successor-in-interest is alive, the atrocity's moral stain does not perish with the victims. The perpetrator still has something for which to apologize. It is only the tender of apology (followed by a meaningful reparation) that retires the moral duty to apologize. For this reason, Polish President Aleksandr Kwasniewski did the morally correct thing a few years back at a ceremony honoring 1,600 Jews murdered by Polish civilians on the eve of World War II. Although all the victims were dead, he offered this apology: "For this crime, we should beg *the souls of the dead* [emphasis added] and their families for forgiveness. Today, as a man, citizen, and president of the Polish republic, I ask for pardon in my own name and in the name of those Polish people whose consciences are shocked by this crime."[5] The imposition of a statute of limitations on the Polish government's duty to apologize would be improperly legalistic.[6]

Two other considerations—one favoring the victim and the other favoring the perpetrator—add further support to my argument that the unfulfilled duty to apologize survives the death of the victims so long as the perpetrator or its successor-in-interest is still alive. First, it would be a cruel irony if the perpetrator could absolve itself of the moral duty to apologize by simply wiping out all its victims. Second, the perpetrator should not be denied the opportunity for redemption if, for example, living victims decided, for one reason or another, not to come forward and make their presence known. Indeed, this happened with many of the Comfort Women during the early stages of their redress movement in Japan, although the Japanese Diet still refuses to issue an apology.[7] This argument speaks to an essential feature of apology, often overlooked in the literature on apology as well as in the black redress movement. I shall take a moment to elaborate.

When the government makes a tender of apology, it is attempting to reclaim its humanity, its moral character, its place in the community of civilized nations in the aftermath of the commission of an unspeakable human injustice. While I would not go so far as to say that apology is for the perpetrator and reparation is for the victim, I would say that, in a real sense, *apology is as much for the perpetrator as it is for the victim.* What this means, of course, is that apology must of necessity be voluntary. It cannot be coerced, such as by court order, judicial settlement, or political deal making. Although the needs of the victim or political considerations might broach the idea of apology, a true apology is freely bestowed. It comes from the heart, and cleanses the perpetrator's character after the commission of an atrocity.

In sum, the presence of the victim is not necessary for the tender of apology, or for that matter, reparations, to take effect. If there are no living victims, that simply means there may be no one to accept the tender of apology and its implementing reparations—in other words, no one to forgive the perpetrator—save perhaps the whole of civilized society. If the victims have living descendants, then they are qualified to forgive as the next-best-class. The living descendants may themselves be victims of the lingering effects of the atrocity, in which case they would also be qualified to forgive on behalf of themselves as indirect victims. But if no qualified person were available to accept a tender of apology and implementing reparations, the *redemptive* effect of the apology should still stand. It would be better, of course, if the victims were able to witness this special occasion, but their absence should not invalidate the redemption—the perpetrator's ability to redress its self-inflicted moral wound.

If an unaccepted apology still brings redemption to the perpetrator, why should the perpetrator be required to seek forgiveness? Why is apology's fourth element necessary? At an earlier stage in my thinking about apology, I did not include forgiveness among its elements precisely because I did not (and still do not) believe that the victims' presence was a necessary precondition for the perpetrator's redemption to take effect. But upon further reflection, I have come to the conclusion that apology must impose an affirmative duty on the perpetrator "to seek forgiveness from the person harmed."[8] I found Elie Wiesel's rabbinical reflections on the matter to be most persuasive. The *New York Times* reported Wiesel's remarks on the subject of the dedication of a Holocaust Remembrance site at the Brandenburg Gate in Berlin as follows: "Mr. Weisel concluded by urging

Parliament to pass a resolution formally requesting, in the name of Germany, the forgiveness of the Jewish people for the crimes of Hitler. 'Do it publicly,' he said. 'Ask the Jewish people to forgive Germany for what the Third Reich had done in Germany's name. Do it, and the significance of this day will acquire a higher level. Do it, for we desperately want to have hope for this new century.'"[9] Seeking forgiveness enriches the moral quality of the apology. It makes the apology more believable and, hence, the prospect that the atrocity will recur more unlikely.

What role does justice play in moral apology? Mark Gibney and Erik Roxstrum argue in their excellent analysis of state apologies that retributive justice should be viewed as an essential feature of apology, or at least in assessing the adequacy of apology. Perpetrators must be held accountable if they are still living.[10] This argument is generally correct except for special occasions when other moral precepts must override retributive justice. A case in point is South Africa. While conceding that the South African Truth and Reconciliation Commission's decision to grant amnesty to apartheid perpetrators who made public confessions presents an intense conflict between retributive justice and other moral precepts—including "truth, reconciliation, peace, [and] the common good"—Wilhelm Verwoerd, a South African philosophy professor, correctly observes that, "in the context of a fragile transition to stable democracy," amnesty combined with "public shaming" and institutional restructuring is the right, morally correct thing to do.[11] Without amnesty, there would be no prospect of racial reconciliation and democratic government in South Africa.

Another reason retributive justice should not be included among the essential ingredients of apology is more typical. It might be more appropriate to view the perpetrator as the government entity itself—focusing on the government's corporateness—rather than as individual members of the government. John J. McCoy, one of the chief architects of the removal and internment of Japanese Americans during World War II, was alive when Congress enacted legislation apologizing to Japanese Americans in 1988. Of what benefit would it have been to place him in jail after the government atoned? Sometimes it is wise to forgo retribution in the interest of urgent social, political, or moral considerations.

Restorative justice, on the other hand, plays an important role not in moral apology itself, but in its solidification. I regard this form of justice as one of the most important reasons for providing reparations. It helps to situate atonement within a post-Holocaust vision that also includes heightened morality, identification, and egalitarianism. I shall return to the matter of reparations in greater detail after considering two more important issues that often arise in the context of apology—clarification of the historical record and innocent whites.

Clarification of the Historical Record

Implicit in the atonement model's process of apology is the condition that the perpetrator set the historical record straight. This requirement is not only a necessary feature of the atonement model, it is an essential one. It provides the factual foundation for apology. Clarification results in a collective judgment regarding the magnitude of the injustice, including its lingering effects, and the extent of the perpetrator's responsibility. Setting the historical record straight can, to borrow from Elazar Barkan, "fuse polarized antagonistic histories into a core of shared history to which both sides can subscribe."[12] It helps a nation, especially a heterogeneous one, to create what Jürgen Habermas calls "discourse ethics," a set of norms on which people with different interests can agree.[13] Donald Shriver describes "a series of meetings between Polish and German teachers and historians for the purpose of revising school textbooks of the two countries so that the story of their twentieth-century relationship would be interpreted to each other's young people in mutually acceptable accounts."[14]

Clarification is desperately needed regarding the historical record on American slavery. The telling of this story has been the mother's milk of white misunderstanding about the peculiar institution and white complacency about its lingering effects. When whites reject reparations on the ground that they had nothing to do with slavery, they fail to understand the centrality of slavery in the socioeconomic development of this great country from which they benefit. When whites reject reparations on the ground that there are plenty of successful black Americans today, including the oft-cited Oprah Winfrey, Tiger Woods, Michael Jordan, and Colin Powell, they fail to see the millions of black Americans who have not been able to overcome the lethal legacy of slavery. When our government refuses to apologize for slavery, it reinforces white ignorance and complacency about slavery. The government makes it clear that it fails to see "racial slavery and its consequences as the basic reality, the grim and irrepressible theme governing both the settlement of the Western hemisphere and the emergence of a government and society in the United States that white people have regarded as 'free.'"[15]

David W. Blight, one of the nation's leading authorities on the Civil War, sounds this note in *Race and Reunion: The Civil War in American Memory*.[16] Our nation achieved a degree of unity after the Civil War at the expense of blacks, he observes. White Americans North and South were able to come together in the aftermath of that sectional struggle by celebrating the bravery and heroism of white soldiers in both the Union and the Confederacy, all the while minimizing the importance of slavery and the significance of its destruction.

David Brion Davis, perhaps our leading historian on the institution of slavery, and the founding director of the Gilder-Lehrman Center for the Study of Slavery, Resistance & Abolition at Yale University, offers a theory as to why so many white Americans continue to discount the enduring legacy of slavery. Davis argues that white indifference about slavery reflects that fact that the South won an ideological victory in the Civil War. What Davis means, according to Mark Alden Branch, who interviewed Davis for the *Yale Alumni Magazine,* is that the South convinced the rest of the nation "that the role of slavery in American history [should] be thoroughly diminished, even somehow as a cause of the [Civil War]." Thus, "while the Union . . . won the Civil War, the country gradually came to accept—or at least not challenge—the Southern version of history in the years after Reconstruction. 'The terrible price of reconciliation and reunion was marginalizing slavery and race.'"[17]

Indeed, for most of the twentieth century, mainstream historians portrayed slavery as a minor event in southern history. Slavery was seen as an event that did not have much impact within the South let alone the country as a whole. The standard work on slavery was written by a southerner with an unapologetically racist point of view. Ulrich Bonnell ("U.B.") Phillips's *American Negro Slavery* (1918) portrayed "southern slavery as a benign and paternalistic institution, 'a training school' and 'civilizing agency' 'for the untutored savage.'"[18] Phillips, whose book appeared on course syllabi at Harvard University and other leading universities well into the 1950s, also painted Reconstruction as a failure. Reconstruction was the twelve-year period after the Civil War (1865–77) in which blacks were given civil rights and the opportunity to exercise political power. Phillips and other white scholars ignored the works of black scholars, such as W. E. B. Du Bois's *The Suppression of the African Slave Trade to the United States of America, 1638–1870* (1896) and *Black Reconstruction* (1935), as well as important primary sources, such as Frederick Douglass's autobiography, *The Life and Times of Frederick Douglass* (1845; revised 1892). It is difficult to overstate the influence these scholars have had on American attitudes toward slavery and Reconstruction. "The writings of Ulrich B. Phillips on slavery and of William S. Dunning on Reconstruction were so rich in scholarly documentation and so closely tuned to the nation's ideological needs—exemplified by popular films from *Birth of a Nation* to *Gone with the Wind*—that their influence on textbooks, fiction, journalism, and other historians would be difficult to exaggerate," Davis observes.[19] One indication of the extent of the South's ideological victory is the fact that Frederick Douglass's autobiography was out of print from the end of the nineteenth century to 1960.[20]

It was not until the mid-to-late 1950s that an "anti-Phillips reaction" took root among historians. Kenneth Stampp's seminal work on slavery, *The Peculiar Institution: Slavery in the Ante-Bellum South* (1956), sometimes called "the historians companion to *Brown v. Board of Education*," depicted slavery as "harsh and brutal." This book along with Stanley Elkin's *Slavery* (1959) and Eric McKitrick's *Andrew Johnson and Reconstruction* (1960) were the first of many attacks on Phillips's southern perspective.

The problem with Davis's thesis is that scholarly repudiation of the southern ideology is nearly fifty years old. One would think that the South's war ideology was null and void. Why, then, do Americans continue to possess a collective amnesia regarding slavery's lingering effects? Why do they not understand slavery's importance to the nation's development as a world power as well as its debilitating effects on black Americans?

Ike Balbus may have the answer.

Balbus offers an interesting psychological explanation. He argues that whites have an emotional interest in denying the fact that an American institution as horrific as slavery could have lingering effects in twenty-first-century America. "Arguments about what should be are rarely a match for the needs that negate them," Balbus writes. The implications of this mind-set on the debate for slave redress is clear to Balbus: "Thus, white Americans are unlikely to be moved by principled arguments in favor of reparations if they have a deep psychological stake in resisting them."[21] There is in whites a "powerful unconscious resistance" to slave reparations because of "[t]he 'depressive' anxiety and guilt that inevitably accompany the awareness that we have harmed . . . [an innocent people]." The effort to reach whites is, therefore, "a *work of mourning* whose importance is matched only by its difficulty" [emphasis in original].[22] Balbus and other psychologists explain that a psychoanalytic case for depressive anxiety and guilt "does not require that any given individual white has actually harmed blacks but rather only that they have . . . harbored demonizing racial [beliefs]," or in other words, "that they have thought about doing so."[23]

If this analysis is correct, white Americans will have to cross a significant psychological barrier to reach a point of clarification regarding slavery and its lingering effects. That effort may be helped along substantially if whites were to understand that they are *not* guilty of instituting, operating, or condoning the peculiar institution. They were not even alive during its existence. So how could they be responsible for slavery? Taking this position places me at odds with many proponents of slave redress whom I respect tremendously. But I believe it is simply wrong to lay guilt on persons who simply had nothing to do with the enslavement of blacks. If Balbus is correct in his assessment of the psychological burden of guilt, then we had better be very careful about laying guilt trips on innocent people.

While today's whites are innocent of the charge of instituting, operating, or condoning slavery, they have, in my judgment, a great deal to be *grateful* for. Whites are the primary contemporary beneficiaries of slavery. My position on the question of innocent whites is, however, rather limited. It does not apply to corporate or individual culpability that can be directly tied to slavery or Jim Crow. I shall take a moment to elaborate on my thinking and, in the process, attempt to distinguish it from that of other scholars who would otherwise subscribe to my atonement model. If my position is correct, admittedly it is not by much.

Innocent Whites

Many, perhaps most, scholars who believe an apology for slavery should be given argue that white Americans by themselves or along with the federal government should apologize for slavery. Three theories are usually advanced in support of this position. The first, which arises at many conferences on slave redress but has not to my knowledge been published, is a politico-philosophical argument that goes something like this: In a representative democracy, the *people* are ultimately held accountable for the laws enacted by their elected officials, because the latter act on their behalf; the *people* are an institution whose identity passes down intergenerationally no less than that of the government; ergo, the *people* of the United States must bear responsibility for slavery and apologize. It would be different, the argument continues, in a dictatorship where the people have no control over the lawmakers. In that case, the people are not part of the government; in other words, there is no *people.*

The second theory is based on equity—the area of law that does justice where justice should be done, sometimes in spite of existing legal rules—in particular, the concept of "unjust enrichment." As discussed in chapter 4, unjust enrichment simply posits that a person who has been unjustly enriched at the expense of another is required to provide restitution to the disadvantaged person. "If a thief steals so that his children may live in luxury and the law returns his ill-gotten gains to its rightful owner, the children cannot complain that they have been deprived of what they did not own," Patricia Williams argues.[24] Joe Feagin would extend the concept of unjust enrichment to incorporate group wrongs as well as individual misconduct.

A final major argument in favor of holding what I would call "faultless" whites accountable for an apology is more civic-minded. Lukas Meyers, for example, argues that "even 'faultless people' may be said to have an obligation, as part of our larger duty to create just societies, to provide reparations to those who have suffered wrongs in the past. . . . Surviving victims of . . . past injustices as well as those currently living people who[,] as a consequence of the lasting impact of the past public evil[,] are disadvantaged today and have to be compensated."[25] I might add that John Torpey regards Meyer's reference to "surviving victims" and "those currently living people" affected by the lingering effects of the past injustice to be effective answers to the "knotty question, often raised as an objection to paying reparations (or even just apologizing), of 'How far back should we go?'"[26]

As envisioned here, the atonement model does not, however, place a direct obligation on faultless whites to apologize for slavery. The current generation of whites had nothing to do with an institution that predates their existence. Unlike the federal government or its predecessor regimes, white Americans cannot take *personal* responsibility for slavery. They cannot, in other words, satisfy the conditions for apology set forth earlier—confess the deed, admit the deed was an atrocity, repent, and ask for forgiveness. White Americans, in short, are not morally culpable for slavery.

Let me also suggest that keeping the apology at the government level, be it federal or state, may make atonement more politically acceptable to politicians than pitching it at the individual level. The Australian experience is instructive. Prime Minister John Howard was reluctant to support a proposal that would have white Australians issue an apology for the government's forced removal of Aboriginal children from their families. This policy was in effect between 1850 and 1967, and resulted in the removal of approximately one hundred thousand Aboriginal children from their homes, many of whom were physically and sexually abused or forced to work as unpaid laborers. Working in partnership with the Catholic Church, the government's aim was to assimilate the Aboriginal children into Australia's mainstream society.

Prime Minister Howard opposed having whites apologize because he did not want them to "embroil themselves in an exercise of shame and guilt."[27] Not everyone agreed with this view. In fact, community groups launched more than 120,000 "Sorry Books" in which some 400,000 whites signed their names and "expressed in their own words their sorrow for the forced removal policies." On National Sorry Day in 1998, sponsored not by the government but by these community groups, the books were given to elders of the "stolen generations" in hundreds of cities, towns, and villages throughout Australia.[28]

Eventually, Prime Minister Howard supported the idea of an apology coming not from the people but from Parliament. Consistent with this restriction, the apology had to simply "acknowledge" that past atrocities were committed in the name of the Australian people. It could not express the sentiment that the Australian people individually or collectively "regret" acts for which they were not directly responsible. In my judgment, this was a fair compromise, so long as Parliament took full responsibility and expressed remorse for its direct role in the forced removal policy.

I would, in fact, apply that form of compromise not just to claims for slavery, but to similar claims brought against the U.S. government. Thus, although Congress has apologized to Japanese American internees, I would not support such an apology as an acknowledgment of collective guilt by Americans living today, except, of course, to the extent that they played an active or passive role in the internment of Japanese Americans during World War II. On the other hand, I would most certainly support a congressional apology as an act of regret for institutional wrongdoing by the federal government (which was responsible for the internment) or as an act of *collective acknowledgment* (as opposed to collective regret) on behalf of today's Americans that past atrocities were committed in the name of the American people. We point with pride to the founding of this great country, although we had nothing to do with it and probably could not recreate our Constitution today even if we tried. Similarly, we must recognize past injustices committed in the name of Americans. It has been said that "national pride" and "national shame" regarding historical events must coexist, that "[w]here there is no room for [both] national pride or national shame about the past, there can be no national soul."[29]

I am not sure how much of this effectively rebuts the arguments supporting white apology—the *people*-as-enduring-institution argument, Feagin's unjust-enrichment argument, and Meyer's civic-responsibility argument. Feagin's argument, in particular, is enhanced by his considerable research on the lingering effects of slavery (see chapter 3). Perhaps white Americans should apologize for the unique benefits slavery has bestowed upon them.

Someday I might come around to that point of view. But for now, I think it is fair to argue that "innocent" whites should be *grateful* rather than *apologetic* to the slaves—that they should collectively acknowledge slavery's contribution to our society and to their privileged position within that society. In addition, they should show their appreciation for the beneficial effects of slavery not only by supporting political measures designed to honor the lives of the slaves, but also by backing political efforts aimed at redressing the lingering negative effects of slavery. Thus, I would agree with Meyer's argument to the extent that he is saying we should all support political measures and shoulder our share of sacrifices to make this a just society or more just than it is already.

THE ANATOMY OF REPARATIONS

Essence of Reparations

Once the perpetrator of an atrocity has apologized, it now has the burden of making its precious words believable. It must solidify its apology. In other words, the perpetrator of an atrocity cannot expiate the sin it has committed against an innocent people until it has undertaken a great and heroic task of redemption. That task of redemption is a reparation. The second element of the atonement model, a reparation can thus be defined as *the revelation and realization of apology.* It is the act that transforms the rhetoric of apology into a meaningful, material reality. Simply saying "I'm sorry" is never enough when righting an atrocity.

A reparation is by nature asymmetrical. Only victims of the atrocity are eligible to receive a reparation. A scholarship program for African Americans as a form of redress for slavery is a reparation. But a scholarship program for "minority and women students" even when presented as a form of redress for slavery is no more a reparation than are Holocaust payments to American gentiles, including blacks. It is important to understand, however, that asymmetrical civil rights policies—reparations—are not intended to displace ongoing civil rights enforcement or other social reforms. On this point, I wholeheartedly agree with Elazar Barkan.[30] I would add that symmetrical human rights measures, such as traditional U.S. civil rights legislation, are designed to be equally accessible to all victims of discrimination. Employment discrimination laws, for example, are open to blacks, other persons of color, women, and whites. Although there may be some duplication, symmetrical and asymmetrical human rights measures are not mutually exclusive. Japanese Americans who have received reparations from the federal government were not excluded from traditional civil rights laws or even precluded from participating in social welfare programs. That is how it should be. Symmetrical and asymmetrical human rights measures serve different purposes.

Forms of Reparations

Reparations can come in many forms. They need not be directed toward the victims personally nor involve cash payments. Indeed, when one looks at the ways in which governments have responded to atrocities committed under their authority, a pattern begins to emerge.[31] A basic distinction is made between what can be called *compensatory* and *rehabilitative* reparations. Compensatory reparations are directed toward the individual victim or the victim's family. They are intended to be compensatory, but only in a symbolic sense; for nothing can undo the past or truly return the victim to the status quo ante. In contrast, rehabilitative reparations are directed toward the victim's group, or community. They are designed to benefit the victim's group, to nurture the group's self-empowerment and, thus, aid in the nation's social and cultural transformation.[32]

Whether compensatory or rehabilitative, reparations can come in monetary or nonmonetary forms. Unrestricted cash payments or restricted cash payments (such as scholarship funds) given directly to the victims or their immediate families are monetary compensatory reparations.[33] In contrast, unrestricted cash payments or restricted cash payments to the victim's group (such as, scholarship funds or an atonement trust fund that provides an estate for educational purposes or venture capital to eligible members of the victim's group) are examples of monetary rehabilitative reparation.[34] Although nonmonetary reparations can be compensatory, such as a statute commemorating a family member, they are more likely to be rehabilitative. Affirmative action for the victim's group and a museum memorializing the slaves and educating the public about slavery's contribution to our nation are all examples of nonmonetary rehabilitative reparations.

The perpetrator of an atrocity ultimately has the responsibility of coming forward with an appropriate form of reparations. In so doing, the perpetrator must give due respect to the victims' needs or desires. This, of course, is a moral responsibility, part of the perpetrator's atonement. What follows are suggestions concerning the types of reparations that may be appropriate for slave redress. My intention is to be illustrative rather than comprehensive, yet to provide enough details so that we have a pretty good idea as to the direction in which the government ought to be moving.

Solidifying the Apology for Slavery and Jim Crow

There are no dearth of ways in which our government could make its apology for slavery and Jim Crow believable. Compensatory reparations in the form of government checks to slave descendants, usually broached in the context of the tort model, have received the most attention in the national debate. In my view, compensatory reparations are inappropriate for slave redress. Rehabilitative reparations are far more appropriate, for two reasons. First, they are structurally designed to reach a greater number of victims. As such, they are likely to be both more effective than compensatory reparations in solidifying the apology for slavery and Jim Crow and more helpful in fostering racial reconciliation. Second, rehabilitation reparations are narrowly tailored to the harms visited upon slaves and slave descendants. Slavery and Jim Crow operated at the group level—blacks were persecuted, not because of who they were individually, but because of who they were collectively. Rehabilitative reparations proceed at this level of generality; they speak more to the group than to the individual.

The two rehabilitative reparations I favor most are a museum of slavery and an atonement trust fund. The former would be a memorial to the slaves, and the latter would be a governmental response to some of the capital deficiencies today's blacks have inherited from their ancestors. As will become clear in a moment, the museum of slavery envisioned here is very different in structure and purpose from the "National Museum of African American History and Culture" President Bush signed into law in 2003 (see chapter 1).

Slavery museums modeled on the Holocaust Museum in Washington, D.C., and the Simon Wiesenthal Center Museum of Tolerance in Los Angeles should be built in Washington, D.C., and every state capital to commemorate the contributions slaves made to our country and educate Americans about them, as well as about the lingering effects slavery has on blacks today. These objectives can be realized through high-tech, interactive experiences. Visitors will be led back in time to witness the horrors of racial slavery, from capture in Africa, to the middle passage, and, finally, to the peculiar institution. Men, women, and children will be able to walk through a recreated slave ship in which hundreds of blacks were packed together for weeks like sardines in incredibly tight spaces as the ship made its way from West Africa to the American colonies (and later to the United States). Visitors will also be able to listen to recordings of slave narratives spoken by the slaves themselves. This experience should give the visitor a close-up view of life on the plantation, including the mind-numbing drudgery of working in the fields under the hot sun from sunup to sundown and the dehumanizing conditions of the slave quarters.

Reenactments of the debates on slavery at the Constitutional Convention in 1787 and in Congress on the eve of southern succession can be presented in a "Point of View Diner" that serves a menu of slave-related topics on video jukeboxes. Was the North's creation of a union with the South a necessary evil or merely a convenience? Was that union ultimately good for the slaves? Did Union soldiers fight to end slavery or to save the Union? Did Confederate soldiers fight to keep slavery or for states' rights? What contributions have slaves made to our nation? How are blacks disadvantaged by slavery? What is racism? Visitors will listen to the debates on these and similar topics, and then input their opinions as to which side of the debate won. After instant tabulation of the results, the visitors might be surprised to learn how little our opinions may have changed over time.

Some might argue that a museum of slavery would be a racially divisive reparation, because it would dwell on the darkest hour in our nation's past. But I believe it would have just the opposite effect. Like the fabulous 1970s TV series *Roots*—at the time, the most watched event in TV history—the museum of slavery will pull a racially divided nation together through a mixture of awareness, understanding, and, in some cases, empathy. The museum of slavery will, in fact, teach many valuable lessons. Among these are:

- Slavery was more than just another everyday tragedy. Millions of innocent lives were sacrificed and families were broken up for personal profit and the socioeconomic development of our country. Human beings were denied liberty at its worst so that other human beings could enjoy liberty at its fullest. We must take into our hearts and minds those who perished at the hands of our country. They were great Americans.

- We need to learn and remember, because none of us was there to see slavery, and because many Americans continue to suffer from the lingering effects of slavery—the psychology and socioeconomics of slavery.

- There is a line drawn in time between those who view human life, liberty, and well-being as expendable in pursuit of personal gain, and those who believe in the dignity of all human beings. We must always look down from time to time to see on which side of the line we stand.

- We must rededicate ourselves to the cause of freedom, tolerance, and human dignity, even when the tide of public opinion flows against us. These are the values that make our nation exceptional. These are the values worth fighting for.
- The emancipation of black slaves redefined our ideas of democracy and freedom. It made America a better nation, truer to her ideals. In this sense, emancipation and slavery transcended skin color.
- By remembering the nation's resolve to end slavery, we gain a positive racial perspective that enables us to move forward with probity and intelligence on racial matters. This racial outlook reminds us that we are on a mission of racial justice, that we must come together to complete this mission, that this is our history's call, which we must answer.

The museum of slavery, in short, will be a national symbol that gives voice to the millions of nameless slaves who made possible the aspirations of others. For the vast majority of Americans, the museum will challenge their thinking about slavery and, it may be hoped, transform them. Certainly, the construction of the museum will cost taxpayers money. But if it was worth constructing memorials to mourn the death of the some 3,000 innocent people who perished in the World Trade Center, the Pentagon, and on a field near Shanksville, Pennsylvania, at the hands of terrorists, then it is surely worth constructing a tribute to the millions of slaves who died in forced service to this country.

My second proposal is the atonement trust fund. As envisioned here, the federal government would finance, and reputable trust administrators selected by prominent black Americans would administer, a trust fund for every newborn black American child born within a certain period of time— five, ten, or more years. The Supreme Court seems to view racial progress in increments of twenty-five years, a generation, but the eligibility period can certainly be negotiated.[35] The purpose of the trust fund is to provide a core group of blacks with one of the most important resources slavery and Jim Crow have denied them—financial capital, family resources, or an estate, handed down from generation to generation. Subject to the restrictions mentioned in a moment, each black child within this group would receive the proceeds from the trust fund annually or upon reaching a certain age. He or she would then have the financial wherewithal to take a meaningful step toward a successful future, including enrolling in and graduating from college. The atonement estate would also be earmarked for elementary and secondary education, allowing parents to take their children out of inferior public schools.

Before sketching the contours of the atonement trust fund, I should like to take a moment to explain why this particular reparation applies only to slave descendants and not to other racial minorities, who, nonetheless, would continue to receive symmetrical social benefits. Slavery created and Jim Crow sustained a racial hierarchy based on color. Under this system of racial favoritism, presumptions of beauty and intelligence and other manifestations of group privilege are determined in large part by the group's proximity to the European (or white) phenotype. Asians, Latinos, or other racial groups whose phenotype is closer to the European model than that of blacks experience less disadvantage than blacks, although more than whites, *owing to slavery and Jim Crow*.[36] This is true even among blacks. For example, in American society, black women who are admired for their beauty—such as Halle Berry, Tanya Banks, and Vanessa Williams—have predominantly European rather than Negroid features. One could argue, however, that because nonblack minorities experience at least some disadvantage from the lingering effects of slavery and Jim Crow—which is to say, the "black-white paradigm," or "black-white binary," which sees the color line only in black and white, is invalid—the atonement trust fund, which after all is designed to redress the lingering effects of slavery, should be made available to all racial minorities. But to do this, we would have to determine the relative degree of disadvantage each racial group actually sustains because of slavery and Jim Crow. We would have to determine, for example, what percentage of the social problems Latinos experience are fueled by the continuous flow of poor and unskilled immigrants into Latino communities, or how much harm slavery and Jim Crow visits on Asians who continue to experience housing discrimination yet have higher incomes and educational levels than even whites.[37] This exercise would simply run the idea of reparations into the ground—it would make a mockery of an otherwise laudable principle. For that reason, a line has to be drawn somewhere.

I draw the line at blacks for several reasons. First, blacks were the *main target* of slavery and Jim Crow. No other American group inhabited the peculiar institution. No other American group sustained more casualties or lengthier suffering from slavery and Jim Crow. No other American group harbors as much ill will against the federal government for slavery and Jim Crow. Second, this gives blacks a connection to slavery and Jim Crow—both familial and psychological—that no other racial minority has. There is a collective memory here that only blacks have, and a collective emotional need that only the government can satisfy. Third, unlike Asians and Latinos, blacks did not volunteer for this tour of duty. Blacks were kidnapped from their homeland and brought to this country by brutal force, the likes of which we have not seen before or since in American history. In short, although blacks, Asians, Latinos, Native Americans, Indians, and other people of color are victims of what Joe Feagin calls "systemic racism" (or the "white-created" paradigm of racial subordination), they do not experience and hence do not react to racial subordination in exactly the same way. Each experiences a different pattern, or syndrome, of white oppression, which sometimes overlaps, and each reacts differently, from despair to disregard, from levels of resistance to total acceptance. White-on-black oppression is just different from other white-oppression syndromes, whether racial or gender.[38] As Patricia Rodriguez has observed, "White means mostly privilege and black means overcoming obstacles, a history of civil rights. As a Latina, I can't try to claim one of these."[39] Black Americans carry the weight of the atrocities—slavery and Jim Crow—for which atonement is being sought. But, again, all racial minorities, including blacks, should continue to receive the protection of symmetrical social measures, including the civil rights laws.

Although the atonement trust fund would apply primarily to blacks, several restrictions would be imposed on the management, transfer, and use of trust funds. Each trust fund would have a life of twenty-five years (the amount of time it would take each child to get through college or many graduate or professional schools) and be maintained by the federal government. A board of commissioners, consisting of reputable citizens selected by blacks, would oversee fund operations in their respective regions of the country. Commissioners and their staff would, for example, help fund recipients make the right choices in schools and business opportunities. All payments from the trust fund would be by electronic transfer. Recipients would never really see or handle the funds.

Money accumulated in the atonement trust fund would only be spent for education or to start or invest in a business. Good primary and secondary education, graduation from a prestigious college or university, and small businesses are important ingredients in building family resources and sustaining their accumulation from one generation to the next. The trust fund would provide resources to help black children escape poor-performing public schools, alleviate the financial burden that causes many black students to leave college before graduating, and finance business opportunities for blacks who do not go to college. Venture capital funds would not, however, be made available until the recipient's twenty-fifth birthday (or later). An eighteen-year-old simply lacks the maturity to know his or her aspirations or to make sound investment decisions. For that reason, vocational education and mandatory consultations with a managerial advisory board, consisting of retired business persons selected by the board of commissioners, would be additional requirements for the receipt of venture capital. Finally, wealthy black families would be excluded from the program. Because wealth is relative—$100,000 in Tupelo, Mississippi, is not the same as $100,000 in New York City—the income level would be set regionally by the board of commissioners.

The amount of money each black recipient should receive for education or business investment could be determined in numerous ways. One way is to base it on projected educational costs. A broader approach is offered by Boris I. Bittker, whose calculation operates upon the relevant assumption that the purpose of monetary relief is to close the considerable net family wealth gap between blacks and whites, discussed in chapter 3. Bittker takes the difference between the average earnings between whites and blacks (let us call this value EG, for earnings gap) and multiplies EG by the number of black Americans (BA) to arrive at the amount of money blacks as a group should receive. This sum (the reparations amount, or RA) is determined annually, and is the amount Congress funds each year until the net family wealth gap is closed.[40] Bittker does not say how long it would take to close the net family wealth gap. I would suggest that the funding period be consistent with the life of the atonement trust fund— twenty-five years for each beneficiary. Bittker's formula, then, is roughly, EG × BA = RA.

Another approach, offered by a former student of mine, the attorney Darrell L. Pugh, takes the racial income gap figure (EG) and capitalizes it to determine the present value of the investment required to realize the income necessary to close the gap. "For example, assume an average income gap of $5,000 a year and an average market rate of return of 10 percent. Under the capitalization approach, it would take $50,000 of investment capital per eligible worker to close the gap—5,000/.10 = $50,000. This figure could then be multiplied by the number of African Americans available in the adult workforce."[41] Pugh's approach would permit funding to be phased in over time, "not only to encourage capacity building but to make the political feasibility of funding more likely."[42]

Bittker and Pugh demonstrate that it is quite possible to calculate a monetary amount to be paid to slave descendants either per capita or through some program of eligibility like the atonement trust fund. Indeed, calculating the value of human life is rather routine in our society. Government agencies, juries, and insurance companies do it everyday. It is also important to note, as one thinks about the reparations calculations, that these calculations are always subject to second guessing. For example, when the Environmental Protection Agency did a cost-benefit analysis of a clean-air proposal that valued the life of a person over seventy years old at $1.4 million less than the life of a younger person—the so-called "senior death discount"—it was criticized by economists on several grounds, including that the calculation was faulty.[43]

I offer the museum of slavery and atonement trust fund as forms of redress for slavery and Jim Crow, not as substitutes for ongoing civil rights reforms. The U.S. government still has an obligation to do what governments are supposed to do—protect its citizens from invidious discrimination. The museum of slavery and atonement trust fund should be viewed as special addenda to the struggle for racial justice in the United States. When viewed in juxtaposition to the milestones of this struggle—the abolition of slavery and Jim Crow—the museum of slavery and the atonement trust fund present easy burdens for our government. The hard question is whether white self-interest or perception of the public good will, once again, impede racial justice.

THE ANATOMY OF FORGIVENESS

Forgiveness is the victim's willingness to respond affirmatively to the perpetrator's tender of atonement; specifically, the latter's expressed request for forgiveness. The focus here is on the victim's side of racial reconciliation. Forgiveness raises several questions. What does it mean to forgive? Is forgiveness the victim's duty or prerogative? If the former, is it religious, moral, or something else—perhaps civic?

In pondering these questions, we should keep in mind that forgiveness is an omnipresent theme in literature, religion, and culture. It is, for the most part, respected and encouraged in every corner of the world. Even a writer with as diverse interests as Shakespeare gave a great deal of attention to the subject of forgiveness. Many of his comedies—particularly *Measure for Measure, All's Well That Ends Well, Much Ado about Nothing,* and *The Two Gentlemen of Verona*—explore the inadequacy of forgiveness.[44] Yet Shakespeare also saw something good and whole about the cognate notion of mercy. In *The Merchant of Venice,* Shakespeare gives Portia these immortal lines: "The quality of mercy is not strained/It droppeth as the gentle rain from heaven/Upon the place beneath."[45] In her eloquent essay "Forgiveness 'Written Within & Without' Law," Jeanne Moskal discusses another great author's treatment of the subject of forgiveness. Moskal argues that "in his later work, Blake came to view forgiveness as a new dispensation, along the lines of an ethics of virtue, almost achieving an independent conceptual status, written successfully 'without' the dispensation of law."[46] An African proverb proclaims, "He who forgives ends the quarrel," and a Shawnee chant goes, "Do not wrong or hate your neighbor; for it is not he that you wrong; you wrong yourself." And a famous Chinese aphorism states, "He who opts for revenge must dig two graves."[47]

Although all people have a general familiarity with the idea of forgiveness, it is actually a rather complex concept. Forgiveness has been defined as, inter alia, "the overcoming of moral hatred," "the overcoming of resentment," "forbearance," and empathy for the perpetrator's humanity. If there is a consensus definition, it is perhaps "the overcoming of resentment." This conception of forgiveness is held by a number of philosophers, including R. S. Downie, Kathleen Dean Moore, A. C. Ewing, and Jeffrie Murphy. Although he was certainly not the originator, Bishop Joseph Butler is generally deemed to be the most important early scholar to have defined forgiveness as the overcoming of resentment. Butler gave sermons on forgiveness some three centuries ago. Paul Newberry, however, argues that Butler's notion of forgiveness centered on "checking revenge or forbearance" rather than the forswearing of resentment.[48]

Another philosopher, Paul Lauritzen, brings much clarity to our understanding of forgiveness. He defines forgiveness as "a two-part response to a situation of injury; negatively, it is the remission of an attitude of resentment evoked by the injury; positively, it is an effort to reestablish a broken relationship."[49] Michael Henderson is in essential agreement with this understanding of forgiveness. He maintains that forgiveness requires the "surrender [of] the desire for revenge." Forgiveness "asks you to reappraise the hurt and its source and to go through a shift in how you think and feel about the offender and yourself. . . . Forgiveness can be a truly transforming experience that allows us to move beyond our selfish desires and needs."[50]

In addition to knowing what forgiveness is, it is equally important to know what forgiveness is not. Forgiveness does not equate with mercy, pardon, or amnesia. The elimination of resentment, which Lauritzen sees as the negative side of forgiveness, distinguishes forgiveness from mercy and pardon. "Forgiveness is essentially restorative; mercy and pardon are essentially palliative."[51] Nor does forgiveness mean the victim is supposed to forget about the atrocity. As Lorna McGregor asserts, "the horrific acts endured by the victim will never be erased from [the victim's] memory."[52] The theme of "forgive but do not forget" was a constant refrain in Archbishop Desmond Tutu's leadership of the South African Truth and Reconciliation Commission.[53]

Some theorists see virtue in "a forgiving disposition" and vice in the withholding of forgiveness. These theorists celebrate people who "have forgiven before they have been injured."[54] One of the leading proponents of this point of view, R. S. Downie, attaches both a secular and a religious duty to the "forgiving disposition." The secular moral duty is based on the Greek term, *agape,* meaning brotherly love. *Agape,* Downie writes, " involves the treatment of other people not just as sentient beings but as beings who are rational and able to obey moral rules and pursue moral values just as the forgiver himself can. The forgiver is required to prevent any barrier remaining permanently between him and the forgivee . . . and to renew trust in him. . . . [Thus,] *agape* becomes the forgiving spirit by extrinsic denomination."[55] Downie also finds a Christian justification for the forgiving disposition, to wit: "Since your Heavenly Father has forgiven you, you ought to forgive others. In other words, forgiveness is justified as being a response to injury fitting in creatures who are themselves liable to error."[56] Hence, Downie seems to suggest that the Christian ethic to forgive is absolutely unconditional, because "that which in a context of injury is called the forgiving spirit is always in itself to be morally approved of."[57]

In contrast, there are those who appear not to believe in forgiveness. These hard-liners seem to argue that a forgiving disposition exhibits weakness. Nietzsche, for example, believed that forgiveness manifests a "slave morality." S. J. Perelman once quipped: "To err is human, to forgive supine."[58]

For those scholars and theologians who stand somewhere between Nietzsche and the forgiving disposition, the question becomes, is forgiveness the victim's duty or prerogative, and what is the nature of that duty or prerogative? Some religious traditions regard forgiveness as a moral duty conditioned upon atonement. Louis Newman makes it clear that "traditional rabbinic authorities regarded the duty of one individual to forgive another as conditional upon the repentance of the offender."[59] Once this condition is met, forgiveness must be granted, because the Judaic view treats forgiveness "as a moral imperative . . . shaped decisively by the beliefs in a compassionate God whom we have a duty to emulate and in the special covenantal relationship established between this God and Israel."[60]

In similar fashion, many secular scholars regard forgiveness as a conditional moral duty. They see in forgiveness a moral quality, but only after the perpetrator demonstrates remorse. Unconditional forgiveness, they maintain, is not a virtue; it is a vice—the "vice of servility." It reveals the victim's lack of self-respect.[61] "Forgiveness is possible only after someone has renounced what he has done wrong, corrected it and compensated for it."[62] Forgiveness, in short, is conditioned upon apology and reparation; or, in other words, atonement.

Even after atonement, some scholars and theologians would not say that forgiveness is immediately forthcoming. They perhaps see forgiveness as the victim's moral duty but believe that it would be premature were it to come at this time. The preconditions for forgiveness go beyond atonement. Indeed, the seeds of forgiveness must be planted and harvested over time in the relationship between victim and perpetrator. Forgiveness grows out of the reestablishment (or establishment) of a healthy relationship between the victim and perpetrator. This can take some time, as David Heim states: "At some point, there will be forgiveness, but it will take place when we [the victims] have a relationship with them, [when we] are working together for a future together."[63]

Other scholars believe that, even when the perpetrator has atoned for his sins or has satisfied additional preconditions, forgiveness can never be a moral imperative. At most, it can only be a moral prerogative. Lauritzen is perhaps the leading scholar on this point. He argues that it can never be the victim's moral duty to preserve or restore a relationship broken by another. This is most obvious, Lauritzen says, in cases involving grave injustices or where the effects of the transgression are irreversible. The example Lauritzen gives is from William Styron's novel *Sophie's Choice:*

> In the incident from which the book has its name, Sophie and her two children arrive at Auschwitz, prisoners of the latest German round-up of Polish resistance members. Upon disembarking from the train which had brought them to this death camp, Sophie encounters the infamous selection process by which SS doctors determined those who were strong enough to work, and thus to live, and those who were to die. In a break with routine procedure, however, the doctor before whom Sophie is brought makes her the victim of a perverse plot to commit an unforgivable crime. He gives Sophie a choice: one, but not both, of her children may live; only she must decide or both shall be killed. Sophie chooses, and the burden of her choice ultimately destroys her, but what I want to bring out here is not the effects but the nature of the crime. Even if, miraculously, Sophie's little girl survived, we would still, I think, want to say that no amount of restitution, no change of heart on the part of the doctor could make forgiveness a requirement in such a case. Indeed, it was precisely the doctor's belief that such a crime was unforgivable that led him to commit it. As Styron portrays it, the doctor, having been pressed into the wretched service of the selection process, and despairing of the godlessness of his existence, plans an offence which he believed only God could forgive. His need for divine forgiveness, he hoped, would restore his faith.[64]

Before expressing my view of forgiveness and applying it to slave redress, it might be useful to summarize the philosophical thicket from which we have just emerged. First, forgiveness is defined as a two-part response to an injury: the remission of an attitude of resentment toward the perpetrator (a negative response) and an effort to reestablish or establish a broken relationship (a positive response). Second, forgiveness does not equate with mercy, pardon, or amnesia. Third, some theorists believe in the forgiving disposition (based on a fundamental religious belief in a common identity with God or a philosophical belief in a common identity with human beings as ends in themselves), whereas others believe forgiveness exhibits a character flaw in the victim. Between these two groups, where the great majority of theorists lie, two additional points can be made. One, the fourth point, is that some theorists believe that the victim has a moral duty to forgive, but only after the perpetrator has met certain preconditions (e.g., atonement or the restoration of a relationship). Finally, other theorists maintain that the duty to forgive simply does not exist. At best, the victim has a moral prerogative to forgive, because otherwise it might be impossible to forge the requisite relationship between victim and former offender. Even when the injury is minor, some would argue, "it is best to treat forgiveness like certain forms of benevolence: praiseworthy but not required."[65]

I do not regard forgiveness as a moral imperative. Indeed, in the absence of atonement, I am prepared to argue that forgiveness is *morally objectionable*. The indiscriminate forgiver disrespects herself. Her forgiveness manifests an unjustifiable abandonment of "the appropriate retributive responses to wrongdoing." The indiscriminate forgiver preserves an unhealthy relationship with her perpetrator. She, the victim, accepts the perpetrator "in his identity as offender." For these reasons, atonement must be an absolute precondition for forgiveness. There must be a tender of atonement by the perpetrator, including a specific request for forgiveness.

While my rejection of the forgiving disposition places me in the company of most forgiveness theorists, my views as to the nature of the duty to forgive makes me a bit of a loner. I do not regard the duty to forgive as raising a question of morality. It is neither a moral imperative nor a moral prerogative. The tender of atonement, insofar as the atonement model is concerned, arrives on the victim's desk not as a religious or moral subpoena, but as a civic subpoena. Atonement imposes no correlative duty of a religious or moral nature on the victim to accept it. The tender of atonement (including a substantial reparation) creates an *unconditional civic* obligation on the part of the victim to participate in a process of reconciliation. Forgiveness acknowledges that the civic relationship is "worthy of respect and restoration." This does not, however, mean that the negative aspect of forgiveness—the forswearing of resentment—is entirely eliminated as an element of forgiveness. On this point, I would disagree with Peter Digeser's intriguing attempt "to separate forgiving from the elimination of resentment." Once atonement takes place, that should automatically cause the cessation of resentment; otherwise the resentment will poison the civic relationship.[66]

Civic forgiveness is crucial for black progress in our society. There is, understandably, deep and long-standing resentment by blacks toward whites and "the system" for racial injustice. Blacks did not come to this country of our own free will, and we cannot return to the place from whence we were stolen. We are here to stay. But if the federal government atones for slavery and Jim Crow, we must fully commit ourselves to a process of racial reconciliation. If the federal government's apology and reparations are substantial, then there is no reason for us to withhold forgiveness. My argument, then, comes down to this: meaningful reparations render the apology believable and produce a redemptive effect; and meaningful reparations induce civic forgiveness and make racial reconciliation possible. Atonement (apology plus reparations) and forgiveness foster racial reconciliation. Viewed in this forward-looking way, slave redress provides Americans on both sides of the color line with a rare opportunity—a third Reconstruction—to finish building the palace of justice that the civil rights movement began.

POLITICAL IMPLICATIONS OF ATONEMENT

The art of politics concerns the allocation of goods and services in a society. Most forms of reparations require a certain amount of reallocation of goods and services. The range of reparations set forth earlier carry political implications to one degree or another. This is perhaps more true of the atonement trust fund than the museum of slavery. In this section of the chapter, I shall attempt to broach several relevant political considerations, although my argument ultimately rests on moral grounds.

I begin with an important lesson about successful political ideas retold by Dick Morris, perhaps the most skillful political analyst in the past dozen years. In *Power Plays: Win or Lose—How History's Great Political Leaders Play the Game,*[67] Morris argues that successful political ideas succeed by appealing to the common good. Political leaders, in other words, must translate personal interests or ideas into universal values. They must repackage individual desire into something that resembles the public's interest. Lincoln was successful in mobilizing the North to fight in a civil war, Morris argues, because he was able to translate his personal abolitionist goals into the universal value of Unionism. In contrast, Woodrow Wilson failed in his bid to launch the League of Nations because he was unable to repackage his personal goals into values most Americans deemed important at the time. The lesson Morris takes from such political experiences is this: the political leader who best serves the people best serves herself.[68]

There are any number of ways in which morally motivated politicians can truthfully connect atonement to the public's interest. The first is a recognition that atonement can heal old wounds that might otherwise be left to fester. Whites tend to underestimate the extent to which slavery and Jim Crow continue to disadvantage blacks. This is to be expected, given the South's ideological victory in the Civil War, discussed earlier. Although I do not recommend a truth commission for slave redress, one of the important lessons we have learned from truth commissions, such as the South African Truth and Reconciliation Commission, is that the simple public acknowledgment of wrongdoing by perpetrators of human injustice can have a remarkable healing effect on victims. When the apology is reinforced with reparations, the healing effect is substantially enhanced. The United States's formal recognition of an injustice that has long been ignored—its acknowledgment in twenty-first-century America of the gravity of slavery and Jim Crow, as well as slavery's centrality in the social and economic development of this country—would go a long way toward closing wounds that have been allowed to fester for too long.[69]

In healing old wounds, reparations can also help our society understand and resolve its damaged political culture—a culture in which whites and blacks deeply disagree on most policy issues involving race. Atonement provides an opportunity for whites and blacks to work together in a sustained effort to help our government redeem its humanity in the long aftermath of the atrocities that slavery and Jim Crow were. Far from being a threat to national unity, atonement can be a vehicle for civic republicanism. Healing old wounds and providing genuine racial opportunities are essential ingredients for social integration. They give blacks reasons to believe the system is fair and worth investing in heart and soul. In this sense, atonement for slavery and Jim Crow can potentially play a political role that is similar to the political role it has played in transitional states. In postapartheid South Africa, for instance, where "the difficulty of mounting political projects with broad appeal to populations tends to favor a politics of legal disputation rather than mass mobilization[,] . . . reparations politics present itself as a useful tactic for progressive politics."[70] Atonement for slavery and Jim Crow can similarly set the stage for genuine racial reconciliation and racial progress in American society.

The reparations component of atonement can possibly generate a backlash. Whites may be resentful of government policies that seem on the surface to benefit only blacks. This could lead to a resurgence of anti-black racism. There are, however, a number of other considerations that, taken together, should lessen our concern about a reparations backlash. First, it bears repeating that reparations are not designed to replace ongoing symmetrical civil rights measures. Other civil rights groups, as well as whites, will continue to receive basic civil rights protections. Second, as John Torpey points out, "The likelihood of a backlash is not necessarily a reason not to pursue [reparations]. . . . Much politics provokes backlash of one sort or another, and, in the absence of a convincing universalist project, the forward-looking aspect of reparations politics may have much to offer in contemporary struggles to enhance equality."[71] Finally, it behooves us to keep in mind the fact that the backlash argument is not new to questions of racial progress in this country. It was most famously used in repeated efforts to thwart school desegregation following *Brown v. Board of Education.*[72] Dealing with a much more serious form of white backlash— namely, racial violence—than will likely occur in anticipated opposition to reparations, a wise Supreme Court once wrote, "Law and order are not here to be preserved by depriving the Negro Children of their constitutional rights."[73] That sentiment applies with equal force to black reparations. Indeed, if backlash were a sufficient reason to halt racial progress, there would have been very little racial progress in our society (see chapter 6 for additional considerations).

THE CONSTITUTIONALITY
OF REPARATIONS

Although the atonement model prescribes a legislative approach to slave redress, the courts will inevitably become involved. There is not a major question in our society on which the federal courts, including the Supreme

Court, have not spoken. Since the museum of slavery will be open to the public, the constitutional question really only involves the atonement trust fund. Does the Constitution permit the federal government to establish and finance a program of reparations whose immediate benefits will go exclusively to blacks? Given their inherent asymmetricality, are black reparations constitutional?

In pondering this matter, let us not forget that law is less a set of rules than a state of mind. As the Supreme Court's attitude toward a matter changes, so do the governing rules. Nowhere is this observation more apparent than in the area of law governing the atonement trust fund. Section 5 of the Fourteenth Amendment authorizes Congress to enact appropriate legislation to enforce the guarantee of equal protection under the laws set forth in Section 1 of that Amendment. Section 1 is a prohibition against state power and is coextensive with the prohibition against federal power promulgated in the Fifth Amendment's guarantee of "due process of law."[74] To discuss one is to discuss the other. Shortly after the ratification of the Fourteenth Amendment, the Supreme Court ruled that the amendment's purpose was exclusively racial: "We doubt very much whether any action of a State not directed by way of discrimination against the negroes as a class, or on account of their race, will ever be held to come within the purview of this provision."[75] Yet today, the Supreme Court reads the amendment with broader purpose, such as prohibiting gender-based discrimination, and has, in fact, applied the amendment *against* blacks, such as in striking down race-based affirmative action programs.[76] Similarly, the Supreme Court in *Brown v. Board of Education* overturned the doctrine of "separate but equal" in primary and secondary education, throwing out decades of prior rules.[77] Thus, were the Supreme Court favorably disposed toward slave redress, and to the idea of an atonement trust fund in particular, it would find a way to uphold its constitutionality. Here are a few suggestions.

The constitutionality of the atonement trust fund could be based on the "nonsubordination principle." In contrast to the color-blind principle, on which much of the Supreme Court's general interpretation of the equal protection clause purports to be based, the nonsubordination principle permits Congress to enact race-conscious legislation so long as the legislation is not invidious, does not stigmatize or otherwise subordinate a racial group. Support for the nonsubordination principle can be found in the Supreme Court's own case law. Three of the most unlikely cases are

Plessy v. Ferguson, Brown v. Board of Education, and *Bolling v. Sharpe.* As I explained on another occasion:

> *Plessy* upheld a statute that separated African American passengers from white passengers in railway cars. The Supreme Court accepted the argument that the statute's racial distinction "has no tendency to destroy the legal equality of the races, or reestablish a state of involuntary servitude." This view of the statute gave birth to the Court's "separate but equal" doctrine. What is so revealing about this opinion is that the Court addressed the contention of the plaintiff that the statute stamped African Americans with a "badge of inferiority." The Court responded that such a suggestion of inferiority did not arise from the statute itself but from its interpretation by African Americans. It is of some moment that the Court felt it necessary to rebut the charges of racial subordination. If the 14th Amendment vindicated only the colorblind principle, there would be no need to discuss the issue of racial subordination. Because the Court did not find racial subordination in *Plessy,* it concluded that the statute was constitutional. . . .
> Proponents of the colorblind principle invariably cite *Brown* as support for the principle. But the opinion does not even so much as mention the word "colorblind" or cite to Justice Harlan's dissent in *Plessy* wherein the term is actually used. The Supreme Court in *Brown* ruled that "separate educational facilities are inherently unequal." At the time of *Brown,* that was certainly true, not only in Topeka, Kansas but in most other Jim Crow school districts across the country. "[T]he policy of separating the races is usually interpreted as denoting the inferiority of the Negro group," the Court noted. Thus, a close reading of *Brown* seems to indicate that the Court only intended to invalidate those racial classifications that subordinate or stigmatize a racial group. The same must be said of *Bolling v. Sharpe,* in which the Court, on the same day that it decided *Brown,* overturned a school segregation law in Washington, D.C. School segregation in the nation's capital was unconstitutional, the Court said, because it was not "reasonably related to any proper governmental objective, and thus it imposes on Negroes a burden." Arguably, neither *Brown* nor *Bolling* stand for the colorblind principle; both vindicate the nonsubordination principle.[78]

Clearly, the nonsubordination principle and the color-blind principle cannot coexist. There is a tension between the two that goes beyond the fact that one is color-conscious and the other is not. Color-blindness is less concerned with social equality—what is sometimes called "measurable equality"—than is nonsubordination. Conversely, nonsubordination is less concerned with legal equality—what is sometimes called "formal equal opportunity"—than is color-blindness. This tension is highlighted in Justice John Harlan's dissent in *Plessy.* Remembered for its bold embrace of the color-blind principle, that famous dissent also expressed Justice Harlan's belief that color-blindness would *not* lead to a restructuring of the racial hierarchy in American society. Instead, Justice Harlan believed that whites would retain their social dominance under a color-blind Constitution. The very paragraph that sets forth the color-blind principle begins as follows: "The white race deems itself to be the dominant race in this country. And so it is, in prestige, in achievements, in education, in wealth and in power. So, I doubt not, it will continue to be for all time, if it remains true to its great heritage and holds fast to the principles of constitutional liberty."[79] But one might legitimately ask, What good is legal equality without social equality?

This is not to suggest that the nonsubordination principle rejects a fundamental tenet of our liberal democratic society—namely, the belief that the state should remain neutral as to matters of race, that it should not favor one racial group over another. The nonsubordination principle accepts this command, but asserts that the lingering effects of slavery and Jim Crow implicate the state in a continuing regime of racial subordination. A government is not neutral as to the matter of race when it ignores the lingering effects of slavery and Jim Crow.

If the Supreme Court employs its current regime for scrutinizing color-conscious legislation rather than the nonsubordination principle, it is still possible that the constitutionality of the atonement trust fund could be upheld. The Court's current approach has been fashioned over the past three decades in a variety of cases (primarily education, employment, and voting)[80] dealing with the issue of affirmative action. Beginning in 1978 with *Regents of the University of California v. Bakke,* continuing in 1995 with *Adarand Constructors, Inc. v. Peña,*[81] and ending most recently with *Grutter v. Bollinger* and *Gratz v. Bollinger,* these cases, all of which deal with constitutional challenges to the voluntary use of racial preferences in the public sphere, operate under a framework that centers on the standards of judicial review employed in equal-protection cases.

The highest, or most exacting, standard of review in these cases is the "strict scrutiny test." Nowhere to be found in the Constitution or in its legislative history, the strict scrutiny test is a legal doctrine made up entirely by judges. It was developed as a means to facilitate close judicial review of Jim Crow and other "suspicious" legislative enactments. The test operates to strike down, as a denial of equal protection of the laws, any governmental activity or legislation that is either predicated upon an explicit racial or other "suspect classification" or is violative of a "fundamental personal interest." The act under scrutiny is saved from judicial strangulation only if the government can meet a twofold burden. First, the classification must be justified by a "compelling governmental interest." Second, the means chosen to achieve that purpose must be the least restrictive, most narrowly tailored means available and substantially related to achieving the compelling governmental interest. Outside the context of higher education, protecting national security and remedying past institutional or individual discrimination are among the few (if not the only) times the government has been able to demonstrate a compelling governmental interest to the Supreme Court's satisfaction.[82] Within the context of higher education, a narrowly tailored use of race to admit a diverse student body is sufficient to satisfy the strict scrutiny test.[83]

Another level of scrutiny relevant to this discussion is less exacting than the strict scrutiny test. It is a "middle tier" or an "intermediate level" of scrutiny. Unlike the strict scrutiny test, which is applied to racial classifications, the intermediate level of scrutiny is applied to explicit gender classifications. The latter are not regarded as suspect classifications by the Supreme Court, because there are often legitimate reasons for a state to use such classifications. Under this standard of judicial review, the classification in question must serve an important governmental objective and must be substantially related to the achievement of that objective.[84]

Prior to 1995, the Supreme Court seemed to suggest that the strict scrutiny test did not apply to race-based affirmative action plans created by Congress. Indeed, in *City of Richmond v. J. A. Croson Co.*,[85] the first case in which a majority of justices held that the strict scrutiny test governed the benign use of race by state or local government, Chief Justice William Rehnquist and Justices Sandra Day O'Connor and Byron White ruled that Congress, as a co-equal branch of government, is entitled to greater deference than cities and states.[86] Agreeing with this view, the Court in a subsequent case,

Metro Broadcasting, Inc. v. FCC,[87] applied the less-exacting intermediate standard of review in upholding the constitutionality of a congressional affirmative action plan favoring racial minorities. Speaking for the Court, Justice William J. Brennan Jr. wrote: "We hold that benign race-conscious measures mandated by Congress—even if those measures are not "remedial" in the sense of being designed to compensate victims of past governmental or societal discrimination—are constitutionally permissible to the extent that they serve important governmental objectives within the power of Congress and are substantially related to the achievement of those objectives."[88] The decision in this case was split by the narrowest of margins, five to four.

Demonstrating a fair amount of indecision, the Supreme Court in 1995, just five years later, and by yet another five to four margin, reversed *Metro Broadcasting.* In *Adarand Constructors, Inc. v. Peña,* the majority accused the *Metro Broadcasting* majority of taking a "surprising turn" in treating benign racial classifications by the federal government "less skeptically than others." Believing that the color-blind principle should be vindicated as a matter of basic democratic theory, the Court wrote:

> The Fifth and Fourteenth Amendments to the Constitution protect persons, not groups. It follows from that principle that all governmental action based on race—a group classification long recognized as "in most circumstances irrelevant and therefore prohibited"—should be subjected to detailed judicial inquiry to ensure that the personal right to equal protection of the laws has not been infringed. These ideas have long been central to this Court's understanding of equal protection, and holding "benign" state and federal racial classifications to different standards does not square with them.[89]

Adarand would seem to sound the death knell for the atonement trust fund, unless it can be tendered as compensation for the federal government's own prior racial discrimination against blacks. A circuit court opinion in *Jacobs v. Barr,*[90] which ruled on a similar piece of reparations legislation, clarifies this point.

Jacobs dealt with the constitutionality of the Civil Liberties Act of 1988.[91] In this unprecedented legislation, Congress, on behalf of the federal government, apologized and provided atonement money of $20,000 each to citizens and permanent resident aliens of Japanese ancestry who were forcibly relocated and placed in internment camps during World War II. The act also apologized and provided reparations awards of $12,000 each to the Aleuts who were forcibly relocated from their homelands in Alaska during the war. The Civil Liberties Act is asymmetrical; no other groups are entitled to compensation under the act. A German American who was detained with his German father during the war challenged this feature of the act on grounds that it denied him equal protection of the laws. Finding that there was ample evidence in the legislative history of the act demonstrating that Japanese American and Aleutian internees were the victims of racial prejudice at the hands of the federal government, while German American internees were not (e.g., no mass exclusion or detention of German or Italian Americans was ordered, and those detained, including the plaintiff and his father, were first given due process hearings to establish their threat to national security),[92] the court ruled that the act passed constitutional muster under both the intermediate scrutiny test, which, based on *Metro Broadcasting,* was the controlling standard of review at the time the case was decided, and the strict scrutiny test. "Congress . . . had clear and sufficient reason to compensate interns of Japanese but not German descent; and the compensation is substantially related (as well as narrowly tailored) to Congress's compelling interest in redressing a shameful example of national discrimination."[93]

A similar discriminatory predicate can certainly be established for the atonement trust fund. As chapters 2 and 3 indicate, slavery and Jim Crow were more than mere acts of everyday societal discrimination. They were mandated and sanctioned by the U.S. government, undeniably "shameful examples of discrimination," to use the language of *Jacobs.* Congress can certainly find ample evidence of this in the historical record should it decide to enact legislation creating the atonement trust fund. Passing H.R. 40, which, as discussed in chapter 1, would establish a national commission to study slavery and its lingering effects, would help greatly in developing this historical record.

Must the beneficiaries of the atonement trust fund, like those of the Civil Liberties Act, be direct victims of the federal discrimination in question? Certainly, there are current victims of slavery and Jim Crow, as discussed in chapter 3. But privity (a close and direct relationship) between beneficiary and perpetrator may not be legally required for at least two reasons. First, as we have seen, the Supreme Court's constitutional regime governing affirmative action upholds race-conscious remedies designed to redress the perpetrator's past discrimination. Because such discrimination can occur (and often occurs) years, even decades, prior to the crafting of the race-conscious remedy, the beneficiary and victim are not necessarily one and the same person. Thus, the absence of privity between the beneficiary and victim seems to be built into the controlling constitutional law.[94]

Second, Congress has enacted legislation that provides relief to non-victims of employment discrimination. Section 706(g) of Title VII of the 1964 Civil Rights Act, the nation's primary employment discrimination law, empowers a court to order, upon a finding of unlawful discrimination, specific forms of relief "or any other equitable relief as the court deems appropriate."[95] This provision was intended, Congress said, "to give the courts wide discretion in exercising their equitable powers to fashion the most complete relief possible."[96] The Supreme Court has held that the last sentence of what is now § 706(g)(2)(A), which prohibits a court from ordering a Title VII defendant to hire, reinstate, promote, or provide payback to an individual for any reason "other than discrimination" in violation of Title VII, does not prohibit a court from awarding (or an employer from granting through a consent decree) preferential, race-conscious remedies that benefit nonvictims.[97] On its face, the Court said, that last sentence does not "state that all prospective remedial orders must be limited so that they only benefit the specific victims of the employer's or union's past discriminatory acts."[98] While it is true that the nonvictims in these cases were incidental beneficiaries of nonmonetary relief, whereas today's blacks, assuming *arguendo* that they are nonvictims, would be targeted beneficiaries of monetary relief under the atonement trust fund, the Supreme Court's reasoning could easily extend beyond the specific facts of the cases. The purpose of such relief, the Court reasoned, was "not to make identified victims whole" but to dismantle the lingering effects of prior discrimination and to prevent discrimination in the future.[99]

Thus, using § 706(g) and the Civil Liberties Act as models, Congress should be able to enact a statute that made a legislative finding of past governmental discrimination against blacks as a group and then proceeded to award atonement money under the atonement trust fund to current blacks. The purpose of the award would be atonement for past sins and not "compensation" for the slaves themselves, the direct victims of slavery. (Rationally, the only way to "compensate" the slaves, all of whom are dead, is by memorializing their legacy through a museum of slavery.) This reasoning, it seems to me, provides a logical basis for benefiting nondirect victims. To borrow the language of the Supreme Court, "Such relief is provided to the class as a whole rather than to individual members; no individual is entitled to relief, and beneficiaries need not show that they were themselves victims of discrimination."[100]

The remarkable symmetry between the constitutional and statutory standards on affirmative action should not go unnoticed. Both focus on the group rather than the individual, notwithstanding language to the contrary in *Adarand,* discussed earlier. More important, both seek to deal with the *residual effects* of prior acts of discrimination. This would seem to provide the necessary legal grounds for deciding the privity issue. But in the end, a judicial resolution of that and other legal questions surrounding the atonement trust fund might well turn on a substantive determination of the merits of slave redress.

Chapter 6 | OPPOSING ARGUMENTS

In this final chapter, I shall address many of the most significant arguments advanced in opposition to slave redress. Some of my answers have already been stated. They are contained in the previous chapters of the book and, thus, require little more than a brief explanation and cross-reference. New responses are discussed more extensively.[1]

1. The whole notion of atonement seems opportunistic and morally arbitrary, because African tribes played a major role in the enslavement of blacks, and no one is asking them to apologize.

There is no moral equivalency here. As one commentator has noted, "it wasn't the [African] locals who instigated the [transatlantic slave] trade, or who supervised the appalling cruelty of the Middle Passage, or who later worked the victims to death. Nor was it really the locals who profited by the business, except in the short term."[2]

Also, some African nations have in fact apologized for their predecessors' participation in racial slavery. For example, the president of Benin, Mathieu Kerekou, sent a delegation to the United States to extend an apology for his country's role in the African slave trade. In a visit in 2000 to the capital of the former Confederacy, Richmond, Virginia, Benin's minister of environment and housing, Luc Gnacadja, stated: "We cry for forgiveness and reconciliation." But even if no African nation apologized for slavery, that would not absolve our government of its own moral duty to apologize for *its* role in slavery. There is enough moral culpability in varying degrees to go around. Each wrongdoer is responsible for its own wrongdoing.

2. There is no rational basis for slave redress, because chattel slavery—the use of human beings in a commodious and bestial manner—was a universally accepted practice during the time the government enslaved blacks.

Slavery has a long presence in Western civilization. From ancient Mesopotamia to 1888, the year Brazil freed its last slave, virtually every Western society condoned slavery, and many, including the pacifist Quakers, practiced it. Human beings were used as a form of currency, even to retire debts, or as items of barter. But if there was a common thread linking all systems of slavery, it was the treatment of human beings like domesticated animals or pets—what Orlando Patterson refers to as the "Sambo" stereotype and David Brion Davis calls the "effort to bestialize human beings."[3] Slavery's long and ubiquitous presence in the Western world does not, however, immunize it from current condemnation and redress.

Not only should we look upon the past with better vision, but there was no dearth of people during the slavery era who had 20–20 vision. I agree with President George W. Bush, who said in a speech given in Africa in 2003 that "some have said we should not judge their failures by the standards of a later time, yet in every time were men and women who clearly saw this sin and called it by name. We can fairly judge the past by the standards of President John Adams, who called slavery 'an evil of colossal magnitude.' We can discern eternal standards in the deeds of William Wilberforce and John Quincy Adams and Harriet Beecher Stowe and Abraham Lincoln."[4] I have never heard the president sound so right.

Also, slavery's wide acceptance in ancient times does not justify or even explain the singular evil of slavery in the Americas. This brand of human bondage, introduced by Portugal as early as 1444, was unprecedented. As Basil Davidson points out, "The trans-Atlantic slave trade vastly devalued human life compared to what existed virtually anywhere on the continent before."[5] This difference in the quality of slavery applies with equal force to Africa prior to transatlantic slavery. "For centuries in Africa," Howard French reminds us, "ethical conventions had governed the taking and use of slaves, who in most cases resembled the serfs of Europe more than the chattel of the Americas."⁶ Thus, although slavery within the continent began long before the arrival of whites, and continued for a good many years after it was abolished in the United States, it was "a very different kind" of slavery.

This difference lay mainly in the emphasis on phenotype and concomitant notions of racial inferiority. Color became the social marker of slavery in the New World. That was not the case in Greece, Rome, or other ancient places—"Among the ancients, the slave belonged to the same race as his master," Alexis de Tocqueville notes.⁷ Among the Africans as well, the slave belonged to the same race as his master. But in America, the slave belonged to a *different* race than his master.

Racial, or color-conscious, slavery appeared in direct response to the unique demands of the plantation system in the Americas. First, the sugar industry in Latin America and later the cotton industry in North America needed dark-skinned workers, without whom they could not have survived. "The grandiose visions of New World wealth—once the Spanish had plundered the Aztecs and Incas—seemed always to require slave labor. Largely because many experiments in enslaving Indians failed, African slaves became an intrinsic part of the American experience."⁸ This led to the eventual importation of somewhere between nine and twenty million Africans to the New World over four centuries.⁹

One of the most important distinguishing features between ancient or African slavery and American slavery was the interchangeability of power and status between master and slave. In ancient slavery, "the roles of master and slave could be reversed: Diogenes [the master] could become the slave and Manes [his slave] . . . could become the master."¹⁰ Indeed, some slaves became well-known community leaders, as I shall discuss in a moment. Similarly, in Africa prior to the slave trade, there were "cases in the Zaire Basin in Africa in which a slaveholder lost his wealth in gambling and then became enslaved to one of his own former slaves."¹¹ No such possibility presented itself to the black slave in America, North or South. No master would ever have conceived of becoming the slave of his black slave-turned-master at anytime in his lifetime. Most slaves, in fact, were not even manumitted.

Marxist scholars have attempted to explain why this ancient practice of interchangeability did not take hold in American society. They argue that interchangeability only worked in societies with primitive or rudimentary markets, that it did not work in societies characterized by advanced markets.[12] Where the slave was purchased as a source of labor, as in the Americas, his commodification created a powerful disincentive to interchangeability. It simply made no economic sense to the master class to accord such freedom to the slave class. On the other hand, in cultures wherein slaves were mainly prisoners captured in war, the line between master and slave was more fluid. These "slaves had symbolic value as proof of a tribe's power and honor."[13] Thus, because of economic imperatives, interchangeability and a kind of "soft" slavery developed in traditional slave systems, but not in American slavery.

Master-slave interchangeability in America was also made impossible by the creation of a race-specific ideology of condemnation, which was itself a departure from the received tradition of slavery. Intended to justify the new look given to an ancient institution, this false rhetoric—namely, racism—not only removed from the realm of cultural and political possibility the interchangeability of slave and master—that is, the ancient prospect that a slave might someday even become his master's master—but it also outlasted slavery itself. Not even the status-conscious Greeks traveled in this nefarious direction. The Greeks first justified slavery not on racist grounds but on a theory that held most men to be naturally inferior due to their inability to govern themselves or others. This thinking was in harmony with the Platonic mind-set regarding the just society. Subsequently, the Greeks, in line with Aristotelian dogma, refined that theory to distinguish between natural and accidental slaves. Slaves by nature were "the barbarians deemed noble only when at home," Aristotle wrote. Slaves by misfortune were those who "regard themselves as noble everywhere," and should not be enslaved, as in internecine wars between Greek city-states:

> There is a slave or slavery by law as well as by nature. The law of which I
> speak is a sort of convention—the law by which whatever is taken in war
> is supposed to belong to the victors. But this right many jurists impeach . . . :
> they detest the notion that, because one man has the power of doing violence
> and is superior in brute strength, another shall be his slave and subject. . . .
> Others . . . assume that slavery in accordance with the custom of war is justified by law, but at the same moment they deny this. For what if the cause of
> the war be unjust? And, again, no one would ever say that he is a slave who
> is unworthy to be a slave. . . . Wherefore Hellenes do not like to call Hellenes
> slaves, but confine the term to barbarians.[14]

Likewise, color did not define the Egyptian, Roman, or Christian notions of slavery. Although there were various methods of enslavement in ancient Egypt—including birth, criminal penalty, and even self-enslavement in satisfaction of personal debts—"[t]he principal and oldest cause of slavery was capture in war."[15] Roman slaves came in all races and colors. Roman law, moreover, came to accept "the Stoic conception of the essential equality of the human race."[16] Christianity, as noted earlier, set in motion moral forces that would eventually sound the death knell for slavery. The Patristic Fathers did, however, defend slavery. "They relied chiefly on Noah's curse upon Canaan for Scriptural authority, but did not apply it specifically to Negroes, who were a small minority among Roman slaves."[17]

The racist rhetoric created to justify the enslavement of blacks not only made interchangeability impossible, but it radically changed the slave's status in other ways as well. Although American slaves, like their brethren in antiquity, could be marginalized, even killed, at the whim of their masters, they enjoyed far fewer privileges and respect than slaves in prior times. Our government did not recognize the *peculium,* or private property of slaves, as did the governments in the Graeco-Roman world.[18] Nor did American society appreciate the talents of the slaves as did ancient societies. "It is known that several of the most celebrated authors of antiquity were or had been slaves: Aesop [ca. 620–560 B.C.] and Terence [ca. 190–159 B.C.] are in this number," Tocqueville notes.[19] Nathaniel Weyl summarizes the social construction of slavery in ancient times:

> [Roman] slaves provided, to a varying degree in different periods, much of the brain power of the Empire. Slaves brought Greek culture to the Roman *nouveaux riches.* Slaves and freedmen dominated most of the free professions. Those who gained their freedom served, especially during the reigns of Caligula, Claudius and Nero, as powerful elements in the managerial elite which ruled the Roman world. This bureaucracy of freedmen and slaves was depicted by Suetonius, Petronius and others as gross, uncouth, degenerate and money-mad, but those who drew the caricature were linked to the envious remnant of a dying aristocracy. . . . Enfranchisement was frequent and, in Cicero's opinion, a hard-working slave could buy his freedom in six years. [20]

No such accommodations were accorded to the American slave. Indeed, had the victims of the peculiar institution been allowed to hold private property, or even a small bundle of financial or intellectual assets, it would have called into question the veracity of the racist rhetoric used to defend slavery. The Supreme Court was largely correct in 1856 when it summarized the status of blacks since the inception of slavery in North America "as beings of an inferior order, and altogether unfit to associate with the white race, either in social or political relations; and so far inferior that they had no rights which the white man was bound to respect."[21]

The use of racist ideology to justify slavery is not only an important point of distinction between traditional slavery and American slavery; it also took on a life of its own, outlasting the institution of slavery itself. This is perhaps the most diabolical feature of American slavery, because it means that former slaves and their descendants can never really be totally free of slavery. After manumission, the American slave in fact entered the netherworld of quasi-slavery. This was a life of repression and reduction, an inevitable by-product of the ideological debasement of the black slave. Color was construed as a social stigma, from which blacks, freed or not, could not escape. This life contrasts sharply with the life of the manumitted slave in antiquity or in Africa before the slave trade. "Freedom alone," Tocqueville observes of ancient slavery, "separated [slave and master]; freedom once granted, they easily intermingled."[22]

American slavery also operated on a much more self-sustaining basis than ancient slavery or African slavery prior to the slave trade. The peculiar institution was a stand-alone operation, one that involved the brutal yet profitable transoceanic transportation of human beings. In contrast, ancient and African slavery generally operated as an appendage or afterthought to some larger endeavor, usually as the spoils of wars. The traditional system of slavery in Africa changed, however, in response to external pressures. Slaves were no longer acquired as captives of African internecine wars. "Negro potentates not only had no scruples about selling their subjects to foreigners, but competed in man-stealing and waged tribal wars motivated solely by greed for vendible slaves."[23]

There is one other very important aspect of American slavery that cannot be ignored when considering the question of apology. The culpability of the founders of the republic is heightened by the very fact that they breathed new life into a morally moribund institution. "By the eve of the American Revolution," David Brion Davis observes, "there was a remarkable convergence of culture and intellectual developments which at once undercut traditional rationalizations for slavery and offered new ways of identifying with its victims."[24]

There is some indication that the global perspective on slavery may have changed directions by the time slavery took hold in the American colonies (ca. 1640), almost a century and a half before the new republic (1787). Most of the Western world no longer viewed slavery as a morally respectable enterprise. Some scholars see signs of this turnaround as early as the Roman Empire.[25] Having accepted the fundamental proposition that all humans are essentially equal, Roman law, it is argued, sought to reduce the harshness of slavery. "From Nero on, the trend of Roman law was to ameliorate the slave's position."[26] The Christian Church, which had always permitted slavery, came to regard the act of freeing slaves as "an act of Christian virtue," and, indeed, this attitude led to the freeing of thousands of slaves by, among others, St. Melania, St. Ovidius of Gaul, and Chromatius, an official who served under Trajan.

So powerful was this sense of morality, Weyl argues, that "[i]n the 13th century, when Christians found it hard to find slaves to free on high church festivals, they brought pigeons and let them fly off."[27] Even though St. Thomas Aquinas and St. Thomas More defended the practice, slavery slowly died out in Europe during the centuries between the death of Justinian, whose legal codifications lasted two centuries after Rome's conversion to Christianity, and the rise of the Renaissance.[28] Weyl adds that in the sixteenth century, the French jurist Jean Bodin declared that slavery had become extinct in his country four centuries earlier, and that "a slave became free merely by touching French soil."[29]

Robert Shell's account is slightly different. He argues that Christianity's change of heart only applied to baptized slaves, and that the issue of whether slaves should be baptized was very contentious as late as 1618 when it was raised at the Synod of Dort (Dordrecht) in Holland, which brought together Protestant theologians from Great Britain and the Continent. Although the delegates could not agree on a single policy, Shell maintains, their writings ended or limited the trade in Christian slaves.[30] Thus, Weyl and Shell are in basic agreement with each other and with Davis's cautious opinion that "by the 1760s and early 1770s . . . the emergence of a widespread conviction that New World slavery was deeply evil and embodied all the forces that threatened the true destiny of the human race."[31]

The American colonists were certainly aware of the changing global perspective on slavery, but they chose to ignore it. Some colonies enacted legislation for the specific purpose of countermanding principles established at the Cape of Good Hope calling for the treatment of baptized slaves in accordance with the customs afforded to other Christians.[32] But there were some dissenting voices that sought to bring the colonies in line with the new-age thinking. The New Englander James Otis, for example, made a famous speech in 1761 calling for the immediate freeing of all slaves. Benjamin Franklin, who at one time not only owned two house slaves, whom he later freed, but also invested heavily in the slave trade, stood almost alone among the founders in "adamantly opposing slavery" in 1776. Thomas Jefferson charged that "'the Christian King of Great Britain' . . . was responsible for the horrors of the slave trade,"[33] but the protector of liberty who penned the soaring declaration "that all Men are created equal, that they are endowed by their Creator with certain unalienable Rights" owned some two hundred slaves. George Washington, Alexander Hamilton, Patrick Henry, John Hancock, and other founders also owned slaves. In all, ten U.S. presidents owned slaves (George Washington, Thomas Jefferson, James Madison, James Monroe, Andrew Jackson, John Tyler, James Polk, Zachary Taylor, Andrew Johnson, and Ulysses Grant).[34] Indeed, when the Declaration of Independence was signed on July 4, 1776—not only on behalf of the Second Continental Congress, but also on behalf of "[t]he unanimous . . . thirteen United States of America"[35]—slavery, David McCullough reminds us, "had long since become an accepted part of life in all of the thirteen colonies."[36]

This hypocrisy was too obvious for even the founders to miss. As discussed in chapter 2, the founders, by not using the words "slave" or "slavery" in the Constitution, made a veiled attempt to hide the fact that they were codifying a morally indefensible practice in that great document. They knew what they were doing, that they were going against the grain of developing opinion in the Western world, and against the views of a moral minority in their own country.

Clearly, then, American slavery was different. It kept alive a moribund institution—one that Western societies had marked for extinction due to its moral bankruptcy. Worst of all, American slavery injected the element of race or color into slavery. For the first time in Western civilization, the slavers took serious note of the fact that master and slave were of different races. More than that, slavers targeted dark-skinned people and, not co-incidentally, developed a racist ideology that sought to justify this prac-tice—a social marker that affected free blacks as well and that continues to outlive slavery itself. The social construction of race that emerged from this protracted transaction in human bondage certainly contributed to the destruction of master-slave interchangeability that had existed in antiq-uity and in Africa before the slave trade. This is reason enough for the gov-ernment to apologize for slavery.

3. Camille Paglia, among others, argues that slave redress would be unfair to present-day white Americans, especially white immigrants, who simply have had nothing to do with slavery. Along with blacks like Armstrong Williams, John McWhorter, and Shelby Steele, Paglia also argues that the claim for re-dress lends itself to the vulgarism of identity politics and victimhood. In other words, making the claim for slave redress leaves blacks enslaved to the past.[37]

My initial response to Paglia's innocent-whites argument is to note its faulty factual predicate. Redress under the atonement model is not about the guilt or innocence of white Americans any more than German repa-rations for the Holocaust were about the guilt or innocence of the German people in 1960, 1980, or, for that matter, today. The atonement model re-quires the *government* rather than the individual citizen, who had noth-ing to do with slavery, to acknowledge wrongdoing.

While I do not believe whites should apologize for slavery or Jim Crow, I do believe they should support slave redress because it is the morally cor-rect thing to do and because of the benefits slavery and Jim Crow have bestowed upon them and this nation. Whether white or a person of color, each American has a reason for supporting slave redress based upon the benefits each has received from slavery.

Whites in General. White ethnic groups benefit more than other American groups from the lingering effects of slavery. They are favored in the color hierarchy created by slavery and preserved by Jim Crow. Whiteness in the main is an asset in this country, not a liability. Those who have it benefit from it, both in terms of the psychology of slavery and the socioeconom-ics of slavery. In short, racial fault lines laid down during slavery continue to give whites racial advantages. Robert Jensen candidly describes the priv-ilege he, as a white male, enjoys in this society:

When I seek admission to a university, apply for a job, or hunt for an apartment, I don't look threatening. Almost all of the people evaluating me for those things look like me—they are white. They see in me a reflection of themselves, and in a racist world that is an advantage. I smile. I am white. I am one of them. I am not dangerous. Even when I voice critical opinions, I am cut some slack. After all, I'm white.[38]

Richard Delgado elaborates on the "drawing power of whiteness":

Not only are whites in this country the most numerous and powerful group—something that could easily change over time—they are also normative, their ideas, hopes, values, holidays, heroes, traditions, language and narratives enshrined deeply in American culture. American children's heroes, like Snow White, are Euro-American. Language imagery associates whiteness with purity, innocence, and virtue. Think of our most sacred ceremonies: white is for weddings, black for funerals. Even many minorities carry these associations and attitudes in their heads. Phrases like "sisterhood is powerful," "brown and black power," "power to the people," and others invoking outgroup solidarity possess an undeniable appeal. But whiteness's rewards, which include acceptance, validation, power, and influence, can plant a seed of doubt in the mind of any but the most dedicated insurgent of color.[39]

Given the power of whiteness in contemporary society, Joe Feagin, among others, makes a strong case for disgorgement. He argues that, as recipients of "stolen" goods, whites have a civic, if not a moral, duty to disgorge their unjust gains.[40] One might also argue that allowing whites to retain their ill-gotten gains stands as a "sequel" to slavery and, in addition, represents the "present embodiment" of that corrupt past. Disgorgement, then, operates as a credibility check on the integrity and morality of the current political order.

Although there is considerable merit to this line of argument, I do not think disgorgement is necessary, or that "innocent" whites should have to apologize for slavery, an atrocity for which they are not personally responsible. But I do believe they should be *grateful* for the bounty and advantages they have received from slavery—that is, they should collectively acknowledge slavery's contribution to our society—and that they should show their appreciation by unequivocally supporting political measures designed to honor the lives of the slaves and to redress the lingering negative effects of slavery (see relevant discussion in chapter 5).

White Southerners. While I do not believe white southerners can be blamed for what their ancestors did in fighting to keep blacks in bondage—both the North and South held slaves, but only the latter fought to retain slavery—they can be blamed for a protracted celebration of a racist heritage. If southern whites wish to be emancipated from the legacy of slavery, they must reject that legacy. They must burn the Confederate flag, that brazen symbol of white hegemony. Thus, in the context of slave redress, white southerners carry additional responsibility. They must, as one southern historian has said, "stop venerating a heritage that was centered on slavery and a flag that came into existence to represent the defense of slavery."[41]

White Immigrants. Newcomers to our shores have a special reason to show appreciation for what the slaves have done for them. Even the most recent arrivals enjoy the lingering beneficial effects of slavery. As Vivian Martin has said, "There would have been no there here [no country] to make immigration seem attractive to your ancestors if there hadn't been slaves here first who built it."[42] White immigrants have another reason to support measures aimed at honoring the slaves and redressing the lingering negative effects of slavery. Immigrants necessarily assume the liabilities as well as the assets—the negative legacies as well as the positive legacies, slavery as well as the Declaration of Independence—of our country or any other country to which they emigrate. A Russian immigrant to the United States will enjoy the freedoms this country has to offer, but she will also spend a good portion of the rest of her life paying off the national debt, even though she had nothing to do with its establishment or accumulation. Whether a recent arrival or a member of an old-line family, an inhabitant of a country cannot pick and choose from among aspects of the country's history. Certainly the nation's largest and longest moral debt, slavery carries over from generation to generation until it is paid off. There is a corporateness to any country that cannot be gainsaid.

Nonblack Persons of Color. Just as black Americans have supported redress for Native Americans and Japanese Americans, these groups owe a debt of gratitude to blacks. But the obligation to support slave redress is deeper and broader than a simple quid pro quo. Like all Americans, Native Americans, Asians (including Pacific Islanders), and Latinos should support slave redress because it is the right thing to do. That is, they should support their government's attempt to right moral wrongs for which it is responsible. In addition, most nonblack racial minorities are part of America's immigrant experience. Like other immigrants, they assume the country's legacies, both negative and positive. Finally, there is a sense in which nonblack persons of color benefit from the lingering effects of slavery more than blacks but less than whites. Indeed, some nonblack persons of color, as Frank Wu reminds us, have traded on their "honorary whiteness"—their closeness to the European ideal—and, in so doing, have "perpetuat[ed] the problem of race."[43] I do not, however, wish to push this line of argument. For the point made here—that nonblack racial minorities should support slave redress—and the one made in chapter 5—that the atonement trust fund should only apply to slave descendants—can be advanced on other grounds.

Blacks. Like all Americans, blacks should support slave redress because in doing so they support morally good government and racial reconciliation. But blacks have a special reason to support slave redress—dignity. No self-respecting black should be satisfied with the racial affront that has dogged black Americans for hundreds of years. How can blacks expect the respect of others if we do not demand respect from those who have disrespected us in the past? Any self-respecting person would demand an apology from someone who accidentally stepped on his foot. Any self-respecting people would demand no less from a government that deliberately stepped on its face for nearly four centuries.

The identity-politics, or victimhood, argument, which is a recurring protest among black conservatives levied against anything that does not smack of black self-help, can be quickly disposed of. Pursued through the atonement model, the claim for slave redress does not reduce itself to identity politics, any more than redress claims advanced over the years by Japanese Americans, Native Americans, black South Africans, Jews, or the Comfort Women. Slave redress under the atonement model is about standing up for one's human dignity. When opponents of slave redress argue that the entire enterprise stigmatizes blacks as hapless victims in need of a governmental rescue, they are wrong, at least with respect to the atonement model. Seeking reparations under the atonement model is an affirmation rather than a negation of self-respect. It is a demand for honor, not an exercise in identity politics. "[T]hough what is remembered may be painful, forgetting is more devastating to the self and destructive to the human spirit."[44]

4. Slave descendants are not direct victims of slavery and, thus, are not entitled to receive anything for that atrocity.

First, there is the link between slavery and slave descendants through Jim Crow (see chapter 3). Second, privity between perpetrator and recipient is not morally necessary, and may not even be legally necessary. Following in the path of traditional civil rights law where, for example, the victims of a private or public entity's past discrimination do not have to be the beneficiaries of the entity's affirmative action program, there is no need to insist on privity in the context of slave redress. The Supreme Court has supplied solid reasoning for this position in justifying certain affirmative action plans. In upholding the constitutionality of involuntary affirmative action programs imposed by judicial decree, the Court reasoned that the purpose of such affirmative action programs is "to provide [relief to] the class as a whole rather than to individual members; no individual is entitled to relief, and beneficiaries need not show that they were themselves victims of discrimination"[45] (see relevant discussion in chapter 5).

5. The debt was paid off through the enactment of civil rights legislation during the 1960s. Coming after that, the demand for slave redress is nothing more than another attempt to obtain racial preferences; it is affirmative action through the back door.

The civil rights legislation of the 1960s ended the atrocity of Jim Crow. It did not atone for Jim Crow or slavery. Atonement comes only after the atrocity has ended. More than that, atonement legislation speaks to the moral enormity of slavery and Jim Crow in a way that traditional civil rights laws and affirmative action simply cannot. Traditional civil rights laws and affirmative action are *symmetrical* measures. That is, they apply to blacks but are equally accessible to other groups as well. A constitutional civil rights provision, the Fourteenth Amendment, for example, provides that "No State shall . . . deprive *any person* of life, liberty, or property, without due process of law; nor deny to *any person* within its jurisdiction the equal protection of the laws."[46] Title VII of the Civil Rights Act of 1964 makes it unlawful for employers to discriminate against "*any individual* . . . because of such individual's race, color, religion, sex, or national origin."[47] The Voting Rights Act of 1965 guarantees the right to vote to "*[a]ll citizens* of the United States who are otherwise qualified by law to vote at any election [under state or local law] . . . without distinction of race, color, or previous condition of servitude."[48] And racial preference law (affirmative action) applies to racial minorities, women, and even veterans.[49] Thus, many groups have access to our anti-discrimination laws. Civil rights legislation does not apply only to blacks.

In contrast, redress for slavery and Jim Crow, like redress for other atrocities, is necessarily *asymmetrical.* It applies only to the victims of slavery and slavery's lingering effects, just as the Civil Liberties Act of 1988 applies only to the victims of internment during World War II. Focusing on the moral enormity of slavery and Jim Crow (with its spectacle of black lynching) under the atonement model separates slave redress from routine civil rights laws, including racial preference law. It provides not only a rational but also a moral basis for singling out blacks for special treatment. It is the only way other protected classes (such as Latinos, Asians, Native Americans, and women), who are accustomed to being treated *pari passu* with blacks, can properly understand and, it may be hoped, accept this departure from standard civil rights treatment.[50] Blacks would be receiving something of value from the government that is not equally available to other traditionally subordinated groups. This large asymmetrical undertaking can only be justified within our liberal democratic state as a one-time response to events of extraordinary proportions.

6. The debt owing to slavery was paid handsomely with the blood of Union and Confederate soldiers during the Civil War.

This argument is misguided for several reasons. The North fought to put down a rebellion so as to preserve the Union. Had the Constitution definitively addressed the question of state secession from the Union, the North would still have had a fight on its hands. The South was not going to allow a piece of paper to stand in its way, which is to say the South fought to preserve its slaveholding way of life. Hence, while the South fought to deny the slave's liberty, the North fought in spite of the slave's liberty, at least at the beginning.

The North's reasons for fighting the war subsequently changed to include the abolition of slavery. This transformation began after the Emancipation Proclamation was issued in January 1863 and was completed by the time of Lincoln's Second Inaugural Address. Public opinion in the North was reshaped in large part by returning soldiers who spoke firsthand of the horrors of chattel slavery. James M. McPherson, our preeminent Civil War historian, makes this point in *For Cause & Comrades: Why Men Fought in the Civil War,* although he also makes it clear that the war did not and could not have begun on that note.[51]

But even if the Civil War had begun with the primary purpose of ending slavery, that would not constitute an apology nor reparations for slavery, to say nothing about Jim Crow. Aside from the brief period of Reconstruction, slavery was not replaced with a system of racial equality. Slavery was replaced with a regime of racially repressive laws in the South and racially repressive social norms in the North. Ending slavery only to impose another, albeit less severe, system of racial subordination on blacks is more akin to a slap in the face than an apology or reparations for slavery.

Finally, as I mentioned earlier, atonement (apology and reparations) cannot logically begin until the atrocity ceases. Ending slavery itself cannot be viewed as a redress for slavery. That undertaking simply brings the injustice to an end, a precondition for atonement, but it does not itself constitute atonement for the injustice. Atonement can only come after the injustice has ended. For example, the act of liberating the Jews from Nazi concentration camps is not a reparation or an apology for the Holocaust.

7. Ward Connerly and Dinesh D'Souza argue that blacks have nothing to complain about because they are "better off as a result of slavery." If it were not for slavery, blacks would be suffering in Africa today rather than living in the freest and most prosperous nation in the world.[52]

With all due respect to both Connerly and D'Souza—and putting aside the fact that neither mentions that we live in the freest and most prosperous nation in large part because of the slaves—they put forth a morally bankrupt distributive argument that can easily be dismissed by posing the following rhetorical question: should American Jews then be thankful for the Holocaust because it caused many of them to leave Germany for the United States and helped to establish the state of Israel in 1948? Good ends—which, of course, is not what the slavers or Hitler intended for their victims—can never justify immoral means. Slave redress is less a question of distributive justice than a question of restorative justice.

8. The atonement model assumes a legislative rather than a litigation approach to slave redress. What happens if legislation fails?

Then we litigate, as happened in Tulsa. There, the Oklahoma legislature did not offer an apology for its role in the Tulsa race riot of 1921, even though its culpability was clearly established by a state commission it had set up to study that tragic event. Furthermore, the Oklahoma legislature adopted the commission's findings and promised to provide rehabilitative reparations, but it failed to follow through. A lawsuit was then instituted to obtain compensation for the victims of the riot (see chapter 4). Redress litigation has yet to bear fruit, not because these cases lack merit—indeed, courts have yet to speak to the merits of these claims—but because they face serious procedural obstacles. But, that said, I wish to reiterate that even successful slave redress litigation has its limitations. Most important, it cannot bring about the type of forward-looking redress our country needs. Without an apology and reparations, the issue of forgiveness is never broached. And without forgiveness, there can be no racial reconciliation (see chapters 4 and 5).

9. Reparations are by definition asymmetrical measures; they are designed to benefit only the victims of the atrocity in question. Wouldn't symmetrical measures, which are accessible to many more people, be a better way to win the legislative battle? Wouldn't Congress be more inclined to pass legislation that was not race-specific?

Giving reparations a symmetrical look would distort the way in which reparations have been conceived in the modern international redress movement, of which the black redress movement is, in my view, a part. The purpose of reparations is to redress the atrocity in question so that both victim and perpetrator can establish or reestablish a healthy relationship. In addition to this historical purpose, asymmetrical measures are more logical and much more meaningful to the victims of the atrocity. Tailoring reparations to the atrocity that begets them heightens our awareness of the atrocity; it places the atrocity above the garden-variety of social wrongs for which symmetrical measures are designed. There is little logic in atoning for the Holocaust by providing general aid to the citizens of Germany, or in atoning for Japanese American internment by strengthening Title VII or opening welfare eligibility. These reforms are distributive rather than restorative and hence miss the point of atonement. Distributive programs should be in place in spite of these atrocities. And so it is with slave redress. Renewing our commitment to racial equality, a hollow gesture at best, or undertaking a new war on poverty is not narrowly tailored to slavery or Jim Crow, the sine qua non of white-on-black oppression. Neither speaks to the moral enormity that these race-specific systems of subordination were. Race-specific harms require race-specific remedies.

True, such an approach may be politically unwise, and hence may exhibit a flaw in the atonement model. But I would argue that the real flaw is in our political system and the will of the American people. The flaw may lie in the character of the American people, in their unwillingness to push their representatives to apologize for slavery and Jim Crow, atrocities for which our government is undeniably responsible.

The argument that symmetrical measures should be used to atone for slavery and Jim Crow may reflect different concerns. It may exhibit a belief that the descendants of slaves are not seriously victimized by slavery or Jim Crow, or that race-specific measures are too racially divisive, that they constitute bad social policy. Chapter 3 is an attempt to demonstrate the debilitating effect slavery and Jim Crow continue to exert on the higher education aspirations of black college students. I stand by that demonstration, which I believe can be replicated in other areas of American life.

The argument that race-specific measures constitute bad social policy is too solicitous of the views of unsympathetic white Americans; it does not give sufficient deference to the views of most black Americans. Not to do anything specific about slavery and Jim Crow is upsetting to most blacks and many whites. Moreover, *any* civil rights policy, whether symmetrical or asymmetrical, is racially divisive in this country. That, indeed, is the history of the struggle for racial justice in this country. Martin Luther King is a national hero today, but when he was alive pushing for civil rights, both symmetrical and asymmetrical, he was vilified by the majority of whites. Had he ceased his efforts so as not to upset whites, the nation's civil rights record would be far worst than it is today.

10. A frequently asked question by white persons goes as follows: "I'm sure there is some black blood in my family. Am I entitled to a reparation?"

The short answer is that this question should be ignored because it is an attempt to trivialize the redress issue. On the other hand, the question does raise a serious matter for consideration—namely, the issue of eligibility—despite the speaker's intent. This issue can also arise in connection with a black immigrant, say from Jamaica or Canada, who seeks reparations under the program.

Let me begin by saying I am in favor of self-identity. People should be allowed to determine their own race. But for purposes of receiving reparations for slavery or Jim Crow, that self-determination should be subjected to two constraints or checks to protect the integrity of the redress mission. One is honesty and the other is history. The recipient should be a person who has always represented himself as a black person. There was a case in Boston where two Italian brothers sought to benefit from an affirmative action program created in the city's fire department by claiming their grandmother was black. The judge convened an evidentiary hearing for the purpose of determining their race sociologically; that is, whether they self-identified as blacks in their private and public lives. The photo they presented of their grandmother looked suspicious, and they could not establish that any of their friends or co-workers or their boss saw them as black. Their claim was a sham, and so it failed.

If the reparations claimant can establish that she or he is sociologically black, then he must satisfy another requirement—namely, a familial connection to slavery or the first fifty years of Jim Crow. Documents or testimony from a minister or other reputable persons who know the family's history would be sufficient to establish the requisite nexus. The family-history requirement would naturally disqualify foreign-born blacks from the redress program for slavery or Jim Crow. They are not, however, left without a remedy. The race-based discrimination they face in America will have to be dealt with through our normal, symmetrical civil rights laws and enforcement.

11. It is impossible to calculate the amount of reparations to which each black American is entitled. Even if calculation were possible, how could something like the atonement trust fund be financed, especially considering the fragile state of our post-9/11 economy?

Some blacks may be able to arrive at a reasonable amount of reparations due to them. This could be done with the assistance of family databases like the one at Louisiana State University discussed in chapter 1. Otherwise, individual reparations could be calculated on the basis of formulas presented in the work of Bittker and Pugh discussed in chapter 5.

Redress does not, however, have to be awarded on an individual basis. Redress can be rehabilitative (community-oriented), which I favor, rather than compensatory (focused on individuals). As discussed in chapter 5, scholarship funds, an atonement trust fund, and a museum of slavery are among the forms of rehabilitative reparations the government could create. None of these forms of redress involves the kind of logistical problems that can arise from the calculation of compensatory reparations.

Whether calculated at the group or individual level, reparations can be financed in a variety of ways, some better than others. As Professors William Darity and Dania Frank explain:

> Public-finance theory suggests that nonblacks could finance [reparations] . . . by paying additional taxes, borrowing (dissaving), or lowering their spending. Alternatively, the United States could borrow by issuing government bonds to finance the reparations program. In general, African-Americans should not bear the tax burden of financing their own reparations payments. Blacks paid local, state, and federal taxes for more than 80 years while being disenfranchised in the U.S. South, a paradigmatic case of "taxation without representation." If, however, taxes are levied universally to finance reparations, guarantees must be put in place that the reparations payment net of the tax is substantial for black taxpayers. Furthermore, reparations income should be tax-free.[53]

The claim that the nation cannot afford to pay for reparations after 9/11 is a canard, and an old one. It is the same reason given to the ex-slaves who pressed for reparations in the years following the Civil War, and to their descendants who continued to seek reparations in subsequent years, both before and after 9/11. Despite this claim of poverty, Congress in short order established a victim compensation fund of $3 billion for the 3,016 people who died in the attacks on the World Trade Center and the Pentagon.

Congress "found" this money, even though, unlike in the cases of slavery and Jim Crow, it lacked moral culpability for these particular tragedies.[54]

12. After 9/11, this is not a good time to point an accusatory finger at our government. In fact, to do so can only be construed as an unpatriotic act.

In the wake of the terrorists' attacks on the World Trade Center and the Pentagon on September 11, 2001, Americans on both sides of the color line have become self-consciously patriotic in ways we have not seen since the days of World War II. This, then, would not seem to be the proper time for African Americans to point an accusatory finger at our government, let alone raise the issue of apology for slavery. What could be more unpatriotic than to raise the ugly specter of slavery at a time when Americans should be pulling together, closing ranks behind our president to fight the deadly threat of terrorism? What could be more socially divisive than to resurrect a national embarrassment that ended some 138 years ago?

Let me begin with what I take to be self-evident: loving one's country is a weaker form of patriotism than loving one's country because it is virtuous. Even conservatives like Dinesh D'Souza would agree with this observation. Indeed, D'Souza, an opponent of reparations, makes the point quite elegantly in *What's Great about America.* Patriotism in its highest form, D'Souza argues, is more than just enthusiastic flag-waving in the days and months following September 11. It is more than joining the armed services to fight bin Laden or al-Qaeda. Patriotism is rallying around our country because its citizens and institutions—its culture—function from high moral ground. America tries to do the right thing, and that is why we love America. D'Souza quotes Edmund Burke's lovely words, "To make us love our country, our country ought to be lovely."[55]

In fact, D'Souza argues, Americans cannot effectively respond to the most sensible Islamic critique of American culture without basing that response on virtue. It is not enough to say our culture is better than Islamic culture because we are more prosperous than Islamic societies. Nor is it sufficient to say we are better because we exercise more freedoms—especially political and religious freedoms—or because we are more tolerant of others—particularly of women and foreigners—than those living under Islamic regimes. In short, American exceptionalism is not a good defense of America these days.

The best Islamic critics do not deny American exceptionalism. But, as D'Souza correctly observes, they demur to it, dismissing our prosperity and freedoms as "worthless triviality." The best and the brightest of Islamic scholars argue that the things that make us exceptional are not the most important values of a society—virtue is. Virtue is the highest value of the good society. Virtue is the will of God, and it is the will of God that the Islamic world is trying to implement. That is what makes the Islamic culture morally superior to America and Western culture in general. Even though we may have fallen short of our goal, the Islamic argument continues, at least we are trying. Yes, "the United States and the West may be materially advanced but they are morally decadent . . . , especially in the sexual domain."[56] Jerry Springer; Howard Stern; Dennis Rodman; Madonna; the Artist Formerly Known as Prince. "Hey! American man! You are a godless rapist of your grandmother's pet goat."[57]

D'Souza believes America must respond to the Islamic critique of the West by acknowledging the fundamental truth of the Islamic premise— in other words, virtue is the highest goal of the good society—but then follow that admission with a brilliant observation: Islamic societies can never be truly virtuous because they lack what the West has in abundant supply—namely, liberty. Freedom is a necessary and essential condition of a virtuous society. The Islamic woman who is *required* to wear a veil is not modest, D'Souza argues, because she is being forced to wear it. A coerced virtue is no virtue at all: "The fundamental difference between the society that the Islamic fundamentalists want and the society that Americans have is that the Islamic activists seek a country where the life of the citizens is *directed by others,* while Americans live in a nation where the life of the citizens is largely *self-directed.* . . . The Islamic fundamentalists presume the moral superiority of the externally directed life on the grounds that it is aimed at virtue. The self-directed life, however, also seeks virtue— virtue realized not through external command but, as it were, 'from within.'"[58] Liberty is what makes the West more likely to achieve virtue than the Islamic world, although decadence is an inescapable possibility of a free society.

With this type of thinking, D'Souza should be an unabashed supporter of a governmental apology for slavery, but he is not. Like most conservatives, D'Souza does not believe "that racism today [is] potent enough and widespread enough that it could prevent [any person of color, including blacks,] from achieving their basic aspirations."[59] These aspirations, according to D'Souza, are "to be in the entering class at Berkeley and Yale," to have "more seats in the boardroom at Microsoft and General Electric," and "greater representation in the Congress."[60]

While I certainly do not agree with D'Souza's argument that race has become a trivial matter for blacks in our society, as it has for certain non-black racial minorities,[61] that argument is quite beside the point, because apology is about the perpetrator's virtue. Apology is the virtuous act of honoring the lives of the millions of dead slaves who contributed to the economic development of this country without so much as receiving a paycheck. If it is virtuous to construct a memorial for the victims of 9/11, then it is surely virtuous to pay similar tribute to the millions of slaves who died in forced service to this country.

My response to the 9/11 argument, then, is simply this: the atonement model is an affirmation rather than a negation of the new American patriotism. This new patriotism, unlike the old patriotism, encourages us to love our country, not simply because it is our country, but because it is "lovely"—that is, virtuous, morally decent. Apologizing for slavery and Jim Crow is an important demonstration of this new patriotism, because no government can commit an atrocity as large as slavery and simply walk away from it, without so much as offering an apology, and call itself "virtuous." The government that turns its back on its moral transgressions cannot expect to have credibility when it criticizes the moral shortcomings of other nations. Apologizing for its own atrocities is something our government, with the support of the American people, should choose to do, because it is the morally correct thing to do. Atonement gives shape and substance to flag-waving. Atonement says to the world that America has not only grown stronger over the years but also grown up.

13. Opinion polls indicate that white Americans simply do not support reparations. No politician will support such a politically unpopular program.

If black Americans had waited for favorable white opinion before pursuing racial justice, the civil rights movement would have never gotten off the ground when it did. Dr. Martin Luther King would have never marched or spoken so eloquently on behalf of racial justice. Indeed, it is *because* of negative white attitudes that blacks had to seek civil rights and, in the process, educate whites. Educating whites about reparations is one of the missions of this book. Much of what Americans on both sides of the color line know about reparations is based on the tort model, not the atonement model. Proponents of reparations, many of whom are white, must fight to shift the focus from the unappealing tort model to the more palatable atonement model and to maintain that focus.

This effort must be directed toward politicians as well, and must include getting them to lead rather than to follow "the people." That, indeed, is the role they are supposed to play under our form of government. As Brian M. Carney has stated, "It is precisely to temper the passions of the people that we resort to representative rather than direct democracy. Such a form of government, in turn, imposes an obligation on our elected leaders—not merely to follow public opinion but to shape it."[62] Joe Feagin and Eileen O'Brien are hopeful that effective leadership on racial matters can come from the current group of political, business, and civil leaders. Their research demonstrates that elite white males, the "baby boomer" generation, are persistently and strongly progressive on racial matters.[63] This certainly works to the benefit of the atonement model.

14. What precisely should blacks do to help repair the broken relationship with America? How should they contribute to racial reconciliation?

With the government's genuine apology for slavery and Jim Crow, with the construction of the museum of slavery, and with the creation of the atonement trust fund, slave descendants will have good reason to embrace America as a country that is worthy of their respect—a country that does not ignore its discriminatory past or the consequences that flow therefrom. Atonement should convince disaffected blacks that it is time to change their behaviors and attitudes toward America. After atonement, it will be difficult to justify the racial chip so many slave descendants wear on their shoulder, in some instances as a badge of honor. In a postatonement America, slave descendants will simply have no right to be angry about centuries of racial exploitation, no reason to feel largely constrained by the past, no logic to act, like Styron's Sophie, in a self-sustained, self-destructive protest against "the man," or "the system." To the rapper's and hip-hop's legitimate charge of racial desperation—"I'm sorry if my language offends you, but it can't offend you any more than the world your generation has left me to deal with"[64]—a postatonement U.S. government can legitimately respond: "Get over it; for you now have the means and, hence, good reason to relinquish racial anger and resentment and, in turn, release yourself from an imprisoning life."

It would, however, be Pollyannaish to expect disaffected slave descendants to adopt, at least initially, the star-spangled view of America that is held by so many immigrants of color, such as the Somali refugee working as a police officer in an inner-city neighborhood who gushes: "I go to work every day, put my life on the line—and it is a pleasure to do that . . . because this country I owe a lot. I owe my life and my family's life. So the most precious thing I can offer to this country is not money, not time, but my life. That is my intent—to . . . be a good citizen. There is no place like the United States, when it comes to immigrants."[65] It will take a period of demonstrated success before postatonement slave descendants can be expected to imbibe the immigrant's uncritical love of America. Slave descendants are casualties of America's history of race relations; new immigrants of color are not. Even second- and third-generation immigrants of color, whose people were not enslaved by *this* government, have racial sensibilities that are quite different from those of slave descendants. As discussed in chapter 5, what is problematic about America for slave descendants is not necessarily problematic for other persons of color.

Thus, unlike other racial minorities, slave descendants have, at best, mixed feelings about this country. There is the desire for worldly success, *but not* on the terms set by "the man." Anger, defiance, low self-esteem, and even self-hate can overwhelm the drive to succeed. This racial outlook is particularly strong among the young, and is reflected in such youthful conventions as the use of the "revisionist self-denigrating" term "nigga," or "thug life."[66] Disaffected young blacks "take the racism they feel and use it to soothe their pain. Not only criminal behavior, but defiance and disruption in the classroom, irresponsible sex, and even the word "nigga" (perhaps the worst racial insult possible), all become self-identifying features of an authentic 'blackness' for these young [blacks]."[67] These behaviors and attitudes are certainly self-destructive, yet they are merely *reactive* to white-on-black oppression. If one could only walk for a day in the shoes of these young Americans—young black males, in particular— one would instantly understand this.[68]

While it will take some doing to manage dueling emotions, the government's apology and reparations will give slave descendants a much greater investment in America than they now have. With a genuine sense of belonging to the American family, slave descendants should begin to see themselves not as limited by skin color as they once were, and even less limited by racial anger, preatonement. The atonement trust fund will give them the financial and human capital needed to overcome many of the lingering effects of slavery and Jim Crow, including low-performing public schools and meager family resources to sustain a college education. If the trust fund does its job, slave descendants should have no felt need to soothe their despair in drugs and street crime or attempt to wield these pernicious elements as misguided forms of protests. In a postatonement America, slave descendants should feel secure enough in their investment as citizens to overlook everyday sources of racial friction—such as the sales clerk's dirty look or the carload of whites who yell racial slurs as they speed by. There should also be more of a willingness to submit to industrial discipline fully— playing by the rules of the workplace—as the primary reason to hold back— silent protest against a racially unjust America—will have faded.

None of this means slave descendants will be free from all racism in postatonement America. Atonement will not obviate the need for ongoing civil rights reforms. Slave descendants will have to continue to use our civil rights laws to fight racial discrimination wherever it occurs. Atonement only means that slave descendants now have reason to begin to trust the government's commitment to racial justice.

I find the experience of Lawrence Mugin, a Harvard-educated lawyer, who by his own admission made a conscious effort to be "the good black," most instructive as I ponder the knotty question of how slave descendants might proceed toward racial reconciliation in postatonement America. Paul Barrett writes about his former Harvard classmates with both insight and sensitivity in *The Good Black:*

> Despite his alienation from his past and membership in the contemporary version of DuBois' talented tenth, Mungin wasn't immune to infuriating stereotypes in middle-class white circles. When he returned from work dressed in a suit, he got friendly nods from neighbors in his apartment complex in Alexandria, Virginia. Later the same evening, however, wearing sweat clothes on his way to the gym, he found that the same neighbors would visibly tense up. On the elevator, some women would punch the

control panel and get off at the next floor, or clutch their handbag to their chest, as if Mungin were about to rip it away from them.

"I understand what's going through their minds, but how do you think that makes me feel?" Mungin asked angrily. "I'm black, so they think I'm going to rob or rape them. But I'm the same person who walks in with the Armani suit. Don't they see me? The answer is no. They see a black man. *I* am the one who is robbed. I am robbed of my reputation because of the color of my skin."

Race had crept up on Mungin and forced its way into his life. In his youth, he had avoided the issue—amazingly—and had few *visible* racial scars from that period. But he encountered isolated examples of hostility as soon as he arrived at Harvard. As a rule, he didn't react outwardly; he walked away. But by the time he reached his mid-30s, he had accumulated enough unhappy experiences that it was becoming difficult to contain his building anger. The effort made him weary. It left him confused about his black identity. He couldn't ignore it anymore, as was illustrated by his asking the question at his job interview about the number of black [attorneys] in Katten Muchin's Washington office. Being the sole black attorney worried him, but he didn't want to make a stink about it. When some of the black secretaries at Katten Muchin went out of their way to strike up conversations with him, and he learned that they had various grievances tied to race, he did nothing to investigate or come to their aid. Indeed, he speculated in conversation with his brother, Kenneth, that the secretaries were using race as an excuse, that they might be cooking up an unjustified lawsuit. Larry sounded to Kenneth as if "he was the big company man—just work hard, everything will be fine, no complaining," Kenneth told me later. In retrospect, Larry felt chagrined that he had dismissed the secretaries' complaints so quickly. "I didn't go into the place looking for discrimination," he said.[69]

Not so ironically, Mungin would later sue his employer, the Katten Muchin law firm, for employment discrimination in denying him a much-deserved partnership.

The lesson I draw from this story is that even "the good black" can expect an uneasy existence as she achieves worldly success in postatonement America. For those who think this assessment is too bleak, I cite the sobering story of the white New Orleans judge who attended a 2003 Halloween party costumed in blackface makeup, an afro wig, and a prison jumpsuit with shackles around his wrists and ankles. That and countless similar stories middle-class blacks tell in private strongly suggest that even well-educated, well-mannered slave descendants will have to continue to be on guard against racial discrimination.[70] Indeed, such continuing racism will make it very difficult for slave descendants to see themselves as unblack. Yet, atonement—the government's demonstrated commitment to racial justice—will give slave descendants the internal resolve and external means to overcome much of that racism and, hence, that instinctive sense of hopelessness that can result from racial subordination.

EPILOGUE

> My nation's journey toward justice has not been easy
> and it is not over. The racial bigotry fed by slavery did
> not end with slavery or with segregation, and many of
> the issues that still trouble America have roots in that
> bitter experience of other times.
>
> PRESIDENT GEORGE WALKER BUSH *(June 2003)*

With these words, spoken at the site of the infamous Goree Island in Dakar, Senegal, which served as a point of departure for the millions of Africans sent through the middle passage to America, President Bush came closer than any other American president to tendering an apology for slavery. We are, indeed, moving closer to the day when such an apology and reparations will become a reality. I would hope that President Bush would be the first president to initiate the atonement process. Not only does he have political pedigree as head of the party of Lincoln to move in this direction, but he also has an understanding of the need and power of redemption, which he gets through his deep religious faith.

Yet the president's statement at Goree Island stops short of the apology that is needed to begin the process of atonement and racial reconciliation for which I have argued in this book. Thus the question Susan Sontag poses in *Regarding the Pain of Others*,[1] still rings true: "[W]hy is there not already, in the nation's capital, which happens to be a city whose population is over-whelmingly African-American, a Museum of the History of Slavery?" After noting that the existing "Holocaust Memorial Museum and the future Armenian Genocide Museum and Memorial are about what didn't happen in America," Sontag answers her own question: "To have a museum chronicling the great crime that was African slavery in the United States of America would be to acknowledge that the evil was *here*. Americans prefer to picture the evil that was *there,* and from which the United States—a unique nation, one without any certifiable wicked leaders throughout its entire history—is exempt."[2] Given the reality of slavery and Jim Crow, the logic and fairness of the atonement syllogism (see Preface), and the necessity and morality of racial reconciliation, no American should feel proud of such shortsightedness, and no government—especially a representative democracy so dependant on political *leadership*[3]—should give comfort to it.

What is needed most from our government today is moral leadership on what is arguably the most important race question since the end of the civil rights movement. The government can begin to demonstrate such moral leadership by laying the foundation for its atonement. Much in the way Presidents Kennedy and Johnson educated the American people about the need for civil rights, President Bush should talk to the American people about the necessity for the government's atonement for slavery and Jim Crow. President Bush should say here in an address to the nation what he said in Africa, including his helpful reminder that, "At every turn, the struggle for equality was resisted by many of the powerful." Laying the foundation for atonement also means that the president must tell the American people that, as in the case of slavery and Jim Crow, they are going to have to look beyond their limited experiences and knowledge about the black experience to a broader reality, and that, most of all, they are going to have to stop being afraid and, instead, permit their moral instincts to overwhelm their fear of the future or otherness.

This will not be an easy task. Many Americans, including the powerful and sympathetic like former President Clinton, whose support of black Americans was so strong that he was sometimes referred to as the first "black" president in American history, believe that the reparations issue is racially divisive and thus should be avoided. Indeed, it was largely upon this basis that President Clinton refused to offer a formal apology for slavery during his presidency.[4] But that is precisely how our political leaders, as well as most white Americans, felt about the civil rights movement in its early stages. It may seem fatuous when we think about it today, but the movement for equal rights was at one time in the not-too-distant past judged too dangerous, too radical, too much of a threat to social stability and racial tranquility for the American people and the government to embrace. Few politicians had the moral courage to lead. Instead, they sought shelter behind public opinion polls.

Comparing the black redress movement to the early stage of the civil rights movement can prepare the American mind-set for atonement, as well as encourage proponents of reparations, in yet another way. Not unlike the black redress movement today, the civil rights movement did not seem to have much chance of success during the 1950s. Even after the Supreme Court overturned racially segregated public schools in 1954 in *Brown v. Board of Education,* the pace of public acceptance of the idea of equal rights was slow at best. The pace quickened dramatically, however, owing to five major events that took place in 1963.

The first watershed event took place in April of that year: Martin Luther King wrote his famous "Letter from Birmingham City Jail" in response to a published statement by eight white clergymen from Birmingham criticizing the use of nonviolent civil rights protests as "unwise and untimely." Reacting to the public upheaval caused by southern police officers' and white activists attacks' on peaceful civil rights demonstrators, these clergymen were, in effect, blaming the victim—the demonstrators who were being assaulted with sticks, rocks, dogs, and fire hoses. These ugly scenes made their way into the evening news and, hence, into the homes of people, not only in the United States, but all over the world. The Supreme Court had outlawed protest marches, but that did not stop black Americans from marching, especially after the Birmingham church bombing, which will be discussed in a moment. Civil disobedience was the call of the day. King himself was serving time in jail for having violated a court injunction against protest marches in Birmingham.[5]

The second momentous event that took place in 1963 came at the highest level of government: unable to continue to ignore the civil rights issue after Reverend King's powerful act of civil disobedience, and after the United States's international image began to be tarnished by the government's often violent responses to the protest marches, President John F. Kennedy gave a famous televised address to the nation in June. His subject was civil rights. In that speech, President Kennedy articulated what can be called the "acid test," and he did so in a most eloquent way:

If an American, because his skin is dark, cannot eat lunch in a restaurant open to the public, if he cannot send his children to the best public school available, if he cannot vote for the public officials who represent him, if, in short, he cannot enjoy the full and free life which all of us want, then who among us would be content to have the color of his skin changed and stand in his place? Who among us would then be content with the counsels of patience and delay?[6]

Two months after Kennedy's inspiring speech, King delivered his famous "I Have a Dream" speech at the largest civil rights demonstration in U.S. history—the national March on Washington. That speech, made on the steps of the Lincoln Memorial, so galvanized the nation, and so continues to inspire, that its words and delivery have become sacred images in our society.

The next earth-shattering event was the bombing of the Sixteenth Street Baptist Church in Birmingham, Alabama, on September 15, 1963. This cowardly act killed four black girls, ages ten to fourteen, who were in the church at the time of the bombing: Addie Mae Collins; Denise McNair; Carol Robertson; and Cynthia Wesley. So vile was this act that it drew an emotional response from many whites who were otherwise unsympathetic or indifferent to the plight of African Americans. Significant numbers of white citizens began to give the civil rights movement a closer look and, liking what they saw, began to turn against the segregationists.

The final earth-shattering event came just two months later: President Kennedy was assassinated in Dallas, Texas. The confluence of this tragedy with the other events of 1963 changed the public and political landscape regarding the civil rights movement, with which President Kennedy had by now become identified. These milestones made 1963 a pivotal year in the struggle for equal rights. Together, they propelled the civil rights movement into its successful orbit. Thus, the civil rights legislation President Kennedy had supported, but that had stalled in Congress, was passed into law in early 1964, sustained by more demonstrations and protest marches. The momentum continued through the end of the 1960s and into the early 1970s, with Congress passing a voting rights law in 1965, a fair housing law in 1968, and a 1972 amendment significantly expanding Title VII of the 1964 law. No one foresaw this kind of success at the inception of the civil rights movement in the 1950s.[7]

Like the pre-1964 civil rights movement, the modern black redress movement, which began with the introduction of H.R. 40 in 1989, is in its nascent stage. Thus, it is premature, to say the least, to see the movement as a madcap adventure. It would help if blacks stop talking about money and begin talking about atonement. Indeed, Americans on both sides of the color line must refocus. They must begin to see the modern black redress movement for what it truly is—an expression of the post-Holocaust vision of heightened morality, identity between victim and perpetrator, egalitarianism, and restorative justice—and for what it potentially offers—racial reconciliation.

SELECTED LIST OF OTHER ATROCITIES

Brazilian slave trade (1500–1888): Brazil imported more black slaves than any other nation in the western hemisphere. In 1996, the president of Brazil drafted policies aimed at compensating Afro-Brazilians.

Oppression of the Chiapas Indians in Mexico (1519–present): Beginning with the Spanish Conquest in the early sixteenth century, Indians in the Mexican state of Chiapas have been murdered, forced into labor or indentured servitude, and had their property seized. Beginning in 1986, Amnesty International has documented the torture, killing, and disappearance of these indigenous people. In 1994, the Chiapas Indians staged an unsuccessful revolt against the Mexican government. Atrocities continue today, and the Chiapas Indians continue to seek self-government and control of their land.

The expulsion of the Acadians by order of the British Government (1755): In 1713, the British took over a French colony known as Acadia and renamed it Nova Scotia. The British government exiled all Acadians from this region in 1755 because of the Acadian loyalty to France. Nearly half the Acadians died in the deportation. Many were exiled to Louisiana, where they are now known as Cajuns. The British government has issued no apology, and the exile continues to this day.

Removal of aboriginal children from their original families by the Australian government and the Catholic Church (1850–1967): Australian state and federal policies encouraged the removal of as many as 100,000 Aboriginal children from their families. The Catholic Church's assimilation policy was aimed at eliminating the spiritual and cultural identities of Aborigines. Children were placed in "welfare" camps or church-run orphanages. While under government care, many of the children were physically and sexually abused, or forced to work as unpaid laborers. The Catholic Church issued an apology in 1996.

New Zealand race wars (1863): British-initiated bloody race wars stripped New Zealand's Maoris of their tribal lands. Queen Elizabeth issued a formal apology and reparations in 1993. New Zealand issued an apology and reparations in 1996.

Overthrow of the sovereign kingdom of Hawaii (1893): The United States aided in the illegal overthrow of the sovereign kingdom of Hawaii. An apology was issued in 1993.

Turkish genocide of Armenians (1914–15): At least 1,000,000 Armenians were driven into the desert, beaten, starved to death, or forced into labor camps following official orders of the central government of Turkey.

Amritsar massacre (1919): British soldiers opened fire on a crowd of unarmed Indians protesting the extension of World War I detention laws. Between 400 and 1,000 were killed. Queen Elizabeth paid her respects at the scene of the massacre in 1997.

Soviet massacre of Polish officers (1940): In the spring of 1940, the Soviet secret police massacred almost 15,000 Poles—most of them military officers and other members of the Polish elite—and buried their bodies in mass graves (see www.vho.org/GB/Journals/JHR/1/1/FitzGibbon31–42.html). Boris Yeltsin supposedly issued an apology in 1993, but the Russian Communist leader Gennadi Zyuganov is quoted as having said in January 18, 2002, that Moscow should not bow to Poland's desire for an apology for the massacre of Poles by Soviet agents at Katyn during World War II. So whether Yeltsin actually apologized is in doubt.

Japanese Occupation of Guam (1941–44): The Japanese occupied Guam for thirty-one months during World War II. The Guamanian people were subjected to death, injury, forced labor, and internment. Stores and homes were looted, and it was made a crime to speak English, their official language. In 1944, the United States reclaimed control of Guam, and in 2001, Congress set up the War Claims Review Commission and allotted $500,000 to study the claims for restitution made by the Guamanian people. The Commission developed a two-page questionnaire that requires victims to explain how they were tortured or forced to work under the Japanese occupation of Guam during World War II. At the time of this writing, the questionnaires are still being filled out.

My Lai massacre (1968): On March 16, 1968, U.S. troops massacred 504 unarmed Vietnamese women, children, and old men at a hamlet called My
Lai, located in central Vietnam.

Chilean dictatorship (1973–90): Thousands of Chileans were tortured, murdered, or exiled by General Augusto Pinochet after he seized power and
declared himself president of Chile.

The Khmer Rouge's reign of terror (1975–79): An estimated 2,000,000 Cambo-
dians were starved, worked to death, or executed by the communist leader
Pol Pot, in what was later termed "the killing fields."

Argentine persecution of suspected leftist dissidents in the "Dirty War" (1976–83):
At least 9,000 suspected leftist dissidents were arrested, tortured, and many
of them murdered in Argentina during what was called the "Dirty War."

Gendarmerie terrorization in Senegal (1983–present): The Gendarmerie national
sénégalaise is responsible for the arbitrary arrest, brutal mutilation, and torture of people in Casamance, a region in southern Senegal. Crimes alleged
include obtaining forced confessions from suspects, torture in front of
family members, and unlawful executions, followed by possible interment
in mass graves.

Massacre in Iraq (1988): Iraqi president Saddam Hussein launched a campaign
against the Kurds resulting in as many as 200,000 being killed, primarily by
chemical weapons. Hundreds of villages were destroyed, and over a million
Kurds fled to bordering countries where many died from exposure. In 1991,
the United States and its Gulf War allies carried out "Operation Provide
Comfort" in an attempt to create a safe haven for Kurds in Northern Iraq.

Tienanmen Square massacre (1989): Hundreds of lives were lost in a bloodbath
in Beijing, China, when the People's Liberation Army (PLA) killed protest-
ers, many of them unarmed students and workers who were run over by
tanks and other military vehicles.

Indian oppression of Kashmiris (1989–present): Thousands of people have been
raped, tortured, and murdered by Indian forces occupying the disputed
region of Kashmir.

Massacres in Bosnia (1992–95): Bosnian Serbs killed as many as 7,000 Muslims
in a rural area outside Srebrenica in what has been called the worst war
crime in Bosnian history. This massacre was just one of many that occurred
during the war. Others include the forced removal of 150,000 to 200,000
Serbs, who were driven from their homes in the Krajina region of the
Republic of Serb Krajina (RSK) when the Croatian military launched
"Operation Storm" on August 4, 1995. One of the most horrific acts of

ethnic cleansing by Bosnian Serbs occurred in an April 1993 attack on the central Bosnian village of Ahmici. This brutal attack on approximately 116 Muslim men, women, and children was led by Vladimir Santic, commander of the notorious special-purpose military police unit known as the Jokers. Whole families were gunned down, and some victims were burned alive. Muslim houses and mosques were destroyed, but Croat buildings were left standing. In 2000, Santic and four other Bosnian Croats were found guilty and sentenced to long prison terms for the murders. They were tried by the International Criminal Tribunal for the former Yugoslavia (ICTY), established at the Hague by the United Nations in 1993 to prosecute war crimes growing out the Bosnian war. The ICTY is not the only tribunal that can prosecute Bosnian war criminals. In 1997 and then again in 2001, the Bosnian Serb ringleader Radovan Karadzic was convicted in absentia in an American court for masterminding a genocidal rape strategy that involved approximately 20,000 victims. This verdict has only symbolic significance, however, because it can only be enforced if Karadzic enters the United States. The ICTY convicted Momir Nikolic in 2003, and President Slobodan Milosevic is being tried at the Hague as of this writing. The ICTY is scheduled to complete its work by 2008, but without the United States and the European Union pressuring Balkan governments to cooperate with the tribunal in locating criminals, it is doubtful whether all the prosecutions will be completed or even begun by then.

Taliban oppression of the Afghan people (1992–present): Taliban leaders and militia have tortured and killed thousands of civilians in Afghanistan during their struggle for power.

Rwandan genocide (1994): In 100 days of terror in 1994, 800,000 Rwandans, most of whom were the Tutsis, were hacked to death by the smaller Hutus, who outnumbered the taller Tutsis. Seven out of ten Tutsis were killed in the massacre, which the United Nations, as well as the United States, Canada, and other countries, failed to prevent, even though forewarned by the Canadian UN commander, Maj. Gen. Romeo Dallaire. Shortly after the killings, the United Nations set up the International Criminal Tribunal for Rwanda (ICTR). The slow pace of convictions (only about twenty as of this writing) is overshadowed by the larger moral question: why did the international community fail to act to prevent the atrocity? In March of 2002, UN Secretary-General Kofi Annan apologized for the Security Council's failure to act to prevent the atrocity.

Croatian Army forces Serbian exile (1995): Approximately 150,000 Serbs who lived in the Krajina region were forced to flee their homes to Bosnia and Serbia by the Croatian Army.

Shan state atrocities in Myanmar (1996–98): Hundreds of the Shan ethnic minority have been tortured and killed by the Burmese army. Approximately 300,000 were also forced to leave their homes.

Rebel killings in Sierra Leone (1996–present): Hundreds of unarmed civilians are being brutally killed and mutilated by members of the Armed Forces Revolutionary Council (AFRC) and the armed Revolutionary United Front (RUF). The war of terror waged by the rebel alliance against Sierra Leone citizens has also resulted in the rape, enslavement, and abduction of civilians, as well as in the wanton amputation of limbs to terrorize the civilian population.

Ethnic riots in Indonesia (1998): Brutal riots resulted in the death of at least 1,000 people in Jakarta alone. In addition, approximately 150 women, mostly of the Chinese minority, were raped, and thousands of shops and vehicles were set on fire.

SUMMARY OF THE NEGOTIATIONS THAT
LED TO GERMANY'S FOUNDATION LAW

The negotiations leading up to the historic German Foundation Law, as well as other key features of the law, were summarized by the court in *In re Nazi Era Cases against German Defendants Litigation*, 198 F.R.D. 429 (D.N.J. 2000), at 431–37:

> The negotiations which culminated with the creation of the Foundation [Law] began in the Fall of 1998, when the German Government asked Stuart E. Eizenstat to help facilitate a resolution of the numerous class action law suits pending in the United States against German companies who utilized slave and forced labor, and committed other wrongs, during the Nazi era. . . .
>
> Over a year and a half, Eizenstat co-chaired a series of formal and informal discussions among lawyers for both Plaintiffs and Defendants and the German Government on a "proposed initiative to establish a foundation to make payments to victims of slave and forced labor and all others who suffered at the hands of German companies during the Nazi era.". . . Also participating in these discussions were the State of Israel, the governments of Belarus, the Czech Republic, Poland, Russia, and Ukraine, and the Conference on Jewish Material Claims Against Germany, which is an umbrella organization representing numerous international Jewish non-governmental organizations. . . . Through these numerous participants—which included interested parties on both sides of the litigation before the Court, as well as

legally disinterested third parties—the interests of victims were "broadly and vigorously" represented, as were the interests of Defendant corporations. . . .

According to Plaintiffs' attorneys who participated in the bulk of the meetings and conferences, the negotiations were intensive, lengthy, hard-fought, and conducted at arm's length. . . . The negotiations began with the parties far apart on virtually every issue, "ranging from the total amount of money, to its allocation among various types of claims, to the extent of coverage.". . .

The quasi-formal initiative which had been ongoing since February, 1998, was publicly announced by German Chancellor Gerhard Schroeder, as well as a group of German companies, on February 16, 1999. . . . After the public announcement, twelve formal conferences chaired by representatives of the United States and German Governments were held to discuss the initiative. . . . As a result of these conferences, and following the personal involvement of U.S. President Clinton and German Chancellor Schroeder, in December, 1999, it was agreed that a foundation would be established, in exchange for which plaintiffs would dismiss their claims against German defendants. . . .

After "extremely difficult" negotiations, the precise terms of funding for the foundation and of how those funds would be allocated were reached. . . . These negotiations were only successful after compromises were made by "all parties," . . . and were the result of "vigorous arm's length bargaining" between all present. . . .

In July, 2000, almost two and a half years after negotiations began, the German Parliament passed a law creating the Foundation "Remembrance, Responsibility and the Future," which closely embodied the detailed agreements reached by the parties to the negotiations. . . . The parties gathered in Berlin on July 17, 2000, to sign a Joint Statement concluding the negotiations, and expressing their support for the Foundation. The Governments of the United States of America and the Federal Republic of Germany simultaneously signed an Executive Agreement, which memorialized the specific commitments of the two Governments to the Foundation. . . .

Unlike typical international agreements, the Agreement between the Governments of the Federal Republic of Germany and the United States of America concerning the Foundation "Remembrance, Responsibility and the Future" is not a government-to-government claims settlement agreement. . . . Rather than extinguishing the legal claims of its nationals or anyone else, the United States merely helped facilitate an agreement between victims, German Industry, and the German Government. . . . By acting in this manner, the United States' goal was to "bring expeditious justice to the widest possible population of survivors, and to help facilitate legal peace.". . .

In keeping with this, the United States agreed to, via the filing of a Statement of Interest in all pending cases, "advise U.S. courts of its foreign policy interests . . . in the Foundation [Law] being treated as the exclusive remedy for World War II and Nazi era claims against German companies, and, concomitantly, in current and future litigation being dismissed.". . .

As previously mentioned, while the Foundation [Law] is not properly a "settlement" in the legal sense, German Industry and the German Government have insisted on the dismissal of all pending litigation in the United States, as a pre-condition to allowing the Foundation to make payments to victims. . . . The rationale is that, given the substantial contribution (a planned DM 5 Billion) of German Industry, they should not be asked or expected to contribute again for any wrong arising from the Nazi era. . . .

The Foundation [Law] administration is up and running, according to Prof. Burt Neuborne, who is both an attorney for a number of Plaintiffs and who holds the seat allocated to an American lawyer for the plaintiffs on the Foundation Board of Trustees. The first meeting of the Foundation Board of Trustees took place in Berlin on August 31, 2000. . . . The Board of Trustees is chaired by Dr. Dieter Kastrup, Germany's Permanent Representative to the United Nations. . . . The Board of Trustees functions as the policy-making and ultimate governance organ of the Foundation [Law]. . . .

Lastly, the Foundation [Law] has become economically viable. The German Government has already made its initial payment of DM 2.5 Billion . . . , and is scheduled to make its second payment by the end of f2000. German Industry is also publicly committed to making its payment of DM 5 Billion, with appropriate interest, as soon as the cases still pending in America are dismissed.

NOTES

PREFACE

1. *Grutter v. Bollinger*, 123 S. Ct. 2325, 2347 (2003) (Justice Ginsburg, with whom Justice Breyer joins, concurring).

2. For a rudimentary formulation of this argument within an international context, see *When Sorry Isn't Enough: The Controversy over Apologies and Reparations for Human Injustice*, ed. Roy L. Brooks (New York: New York University Press, 1999).

3. On the restorative powers of apology and forgiveness for community life, see Nicholas Tavuchis, *Mea Culpa: A Sociology of Apology and Reconciliation* (Stanford, Calif.: Stanford University Press, 1991).

4. That is the great disappointment I have with much of the extant American scholarship on redress, both legal, see, e.g., Eric A. Posner and Adrian Vermeule, "Reparations for Slavery and Other Historical Injustices," *Columbia Law Review* 103 (2003): 689–747, and nonlegal, see, e.g., Randall Robinson, *The Debt: What America Owes to Blacks* (New York: Dutton, 2000).

5. See Ruti G. Teitel, *Transitional Justice* (New York: Oxford University Press, 2000). For more on this theme, see, e.g., *Politics and the Past: On Repairing Historical Injustices*, ed. John Torpey (Lanham, Md.: Rowman & Littlefield, 2003); Elazar Barkan, *The Guilt of Nations: Restitution and Negotiating Historical Injustices* (New York: Norton, 2000); and Mark Gibney and Erik Roxstrom, "The Status of State Apologies," *Human Rights Quarterly* 23 (2001): 911.

6. For a discussion of civic republicanism, see Roy L. Brooks, *Structures of Judicial Decision-Making from Legal Formalism to Critical Theory* (Durham, N.C.:

Carolina Academic Press, 2002), 40–44 (additional sources cited therein). Missing from Turner's "frontier thesis" is the fact that Americans have supported a government that indulged white privilege for some 325 years and the fact that American Indians played a significant role in the settlement of the "frontier." See Frederick Jackson Turner, *Rereading Frederick Jackson Turner: "The Significance of the Frontier in American History" and Other Essays*, commentary by John Mack Faragher (New York: Holt, 1994). For an assessment of Turner's view of the frontier, see, e.g., Andro Linklater, *Measuring America: How an Untamed Wilderness Shaped the United States and Fulfilled the Promise of Democracy* (New York: Walker, 2002).

7. It may be that a full arsenal of weapons will have to be deployed in the struggle for slave redress. The atonement model is one of those weapons. To that extent, there is even room for the tort model, although I would not embrace that approach without first giving the atonement model an opportunity to succeed.

8. See U.S. Commission on Wartime Relocation and Internment of Civilians, *Personal Justice Denied* (Washington, D.C.: Government Printing Office, 1982) (Japanese Americans); U.S. Department of Justice, *Report to the Congress of the United States: A Review of the Restrictions on Persons of Italian Ancestry during World War II* (Washington, D.C.: Government Printing Office, 2001) (Italian Americans). See, generally, *When Sorry Isn't Enough*, ed. Brooks, pt. 4.

9. One of the best of these is George Hicks's *The Comfort Women: Japan's Brutal Regime of Enforced Prostitution in the Second World War* (New York: Norton, 1995).

10. Chronicled in Iris Chang, *The Rape of Nanking: The Forgotten Holocaust of World War II* (New York: Basic Books, 1997).

11. See "Lipinski Resolution," in *When Sorry Isn't Enough*, ed. Brooks, 149–50.

12. See Roy L. Brooks, "The Age of Apology," in ibid., 3. For a collection of atrocities see "Appendix: Selected List of Other Human Injustices," in ibid., 511. See also *Politics and the Past: On Repairing Historical Injustices*, ed. John Torpey (Lanham, Md.: Rowman & Littlefield, 2003); *Race, Rights and Reparation: Law and the Japanese American Internment*, ed. Eric K. Yamamoto et al. (Gaithersburg, Md.: Aspen Law & Business, 2001); Susanne Jonas, *Of Centaurs and Doves: Guatemala's Peace Process* (Boulder, Colo.: Westview Press, 2000); John A. Berry and Carol Pott Berry, *Genocide in Rwanda: A Collective Memory* (Washington, D.C.: Howard University Press, 1999); Mitchell T. Maki, Harry H. L. Kitano, and S. Megan Berthold, *Achieving the Impossible Dream: How Japanese Americans Obtained Redress* (Urbana: University of Illinois Press, 1999); Martha Minow, *Between Vengeance and Forgiveness* (Boston: Beacon Press, 1998).

13. Brooks, "Age of Apology," 3–4.

14. John Maynard Keynes, *The Economic Consequences of the Peace* (1919; reprint, New York: Walker, 2002).

15. See, e.g., Margaret MacMillan, *Paris 1919: Six Months That Changed the World* (New York: Random House, 2002).

16. This quotation is taken from a report by the U.S. Department of Justice Foreign Claims Settlement Commission, titled "German Compensation for National Socialist Crimes," reprinted in *When Sorry Isn't Enough,* ed. Brooks, 61; emphasis added.

17. For an engaging discussion, see, e.g., Norbert Frei, *Adenauer's Germany and the Nazi Past: The Politics of Amnesty and Integration,* trans. Joel Golb (New York: Columbia University Press, 2002).

18. *In re Nazi Era Cases against German Defendants Litigation,* 198 F.R.D. 429, 431 n. 4 (D.C.N.J. 2000) (citing UN sources).

19. Nell Jessup Newton, "Indian Claims for Reparations, Compensation, and Restitution in the United States Legal System," in *When Sorry Isn't Enough,* ed. Brooks, 262 (emphasis supplied). The Indian Claims Commission no longer exists. Most settled claims have involved monetary relief, but Congress has also restored at least 540,000 acres of public domain lands to various Indian tribes since the 1970s. See ibid., 266.

20. See *Grutter v. Bollinger,* 123 S. Ct. 2325 (2003) (upholding a university's narrowly tailored use of race in an admissions policy designed to achieve a diverse student body); *Gratz v. Bollinger,* 123 S. Ct. 2411 (2003) (upholding in principle race-conscious admissions policies similar to the one in *Grutter*).

I. THE PURPOSE AND THE HISTORY OF THE BLACK REDRESS MOVEMENT

1. After the Reconstruction Period (1865–77), former slaveholders regained control of southern legislatures and systematically stripped blacks of their status as first-class citizens with the enactment of Jim Crow laws that mandated racial segregation and sanctioned racial discrimination. The "First Reconstruction," as it is commonly called, ended with the infamous congressional compromise of the disputed presidential election of 1876. This compromise permitted the Republicans to retain the presidency in exchange for the pullout of federal troops that were stationed in the South to protect blacks from their former slave masters. Jim Crow officially ended with the passage of the Equal Employment Opportunities Act of 1972, which prohibited employment discrimination by federal, state, and local governments. "Racial discrimination by public employers was not made illegal under Title VII until March 24, 1972" (*Hazelwood School District v. United*

States, 433 U.S. 299, 309 [1977]). See Roy L. Brooks, "Use of the Civil Rights Acts of 1866 and 1871 to Redress Employment Discrimination," *Cornell Law Review* 62 (1977): 258, 259, 283.

2. See *Plessy v. Ferguson,* 163 U.S. 537 (1896). This case turned upon the constitutionality of a Louisiana law, passed in 1890, providing for separate railway carriages for the whites and blacks.

3. Philip B. Kunhardt Jr., Philip B. Kunhardt III, and Peter W. Kunhardt, *The American President* (New York: Riverhead Books, 1999), 28.

4. See *Hazelwood School District v. United States,* 309; Roy L. Brooks, "Use of the Civil Rights Acts of 1866 and 1871 to Redress Employment Discrimination," *Cornell Law Review* 62 (1977): 258, 259, 283.

5. For further discussion about Hall's collection, see Jeffrey Ghannam, "Repairing the Past," *American Bar Association Journal,* November 2000, 39.

6. Randall Robinson, *The Debt: What America Owes to Blacks* (New York: Dutton, 2000), 74.

7. For a more detailed discussion, see *When Sorry Isn't Enough,* ed. Brooks, pt. 6. For a discussion of the civil rights theories of Marcus Garvey, Martin Luther King, Louis Farrakhan, and other civil rights leaders, see Roy L. Brooks, *Integration or Separation? A Strategy for Racial Equality* (Cambridge, Mass.: Harvard University Press, 1996), 125–88, 283–84.

8. John Hope Franklin, *From Slavery to Freedom: A History of Negro Americans* (1947), 3d ed. (New York: Vintage Books, 1969), 159.

9. Robert Johnson Jr., "Repatriation as Reparations for Slavery and Jim-Crowism," in *When Sorry Isn't Enough,* ed. Brooks, 428–29.

10. Thomas Jefferson, *Notes on the State of Virginia* (1781–82), in *Writings* (New York: Library of America, 1984), 264.

11. Johnson, "Repatriation as Reparations," in *When Sorry Isn't Enough,* ed. Brooks, 429. For further discussion of the ACS and the abolitionists' criticism, see, e.g., Franklin, *From Slavery to Freedom,* 238–41.

12. Franklin, *From Slavery to Freedom,* 241.

13. For a discussion of the history of the return-to-Africa movement in Liberia, see Brooks, *Integration or Separation?* 156–67.

14. James Grahame, "Why the North and South Should Have Apologized," in *When Sorry Isn't Enough,* ed. Brooks, 349.

15. Robinson, *Debt,* 240–41.

16. *Berry,* 1994 WL 374537, at 1 (citing § 4 of the act of March 3, 1865, ch. 90, 13 Stat. 507).

17. See "Special Field Order No. 15," reprinted in *When Sorry Isn't Enough,* ed. Brooks, 365.

18. Judge Paul L. Friedman in *Pigford v. Glickman,* 185 F.R.D. 82, 85 (D.C.D.C.,

1999). See Deadria C. Farmer-Paellmann, "Excerpt from *Black Exodus: The Ex-Slave Pension Movement Reader*" in *Should America Pay? Slavery and the Raging Debate on Reparations,* ed. Raymond A. Winbush (New York: Amistad, 2003), 25.

19. Friedman in *Pigford v. Glickman,* 85–86 (emphasis supplied).

20. For a discussion of the Homestead Act, see, e.g., John Hope Franklin and Alfred A. Moss Jr., *From Slavery to Freedom: A History of Negro Americans,* 6th ed. (New York: Knopf, 1988), 214.

21. See, e.g., David W. Blight, "If You Don't Tell It Like It Was, It Can Never Be as It Ought to Be" (keynote talk delivered at Conference on Yale and Slavery, September 27, 2002, available at www.yale.edu/glc/events/memory.htm), 9–10.

22. Farmer-Paellmann, "Excerpt from *Black Exodus,*" in *Should America Pay?* ed. Winbush, 37.

23. Ibid., 27. See Blight, "If You Don't Tell It Like It Was," 9–10.

24. *Johnson v. McAdoo,* 45 App. D.C. 440 (1917).

25. Blight, "If You Don't Tell It Like It Was," 10.

26. This case is discussed in greater detail with more recent cases in chapter 4.

27. Blight, "If You Don't Tell It Like It Was," 10.

28. See H.R. 3491, 108th Cong., 1st sess. (November 17, 2003). For a more detailed discussion of the legislation, see Renwick McLean, "Congress Backs New Museum on Black History and Culture," *New York Times,* November 23, 2003, § 1 (main), 18.

29. See, e.g., Joe R. Feagin and Eileen O'Brien, "The Growing Movement for Reparations," in *When Sorry Isn't Enough,* ed. Brooks, 341–42. The "Black Manifesto," officially titled, "Manifesto," was adopted by the National Black Economic Development Conference in Detroit, Michigan, on April 26, 1969. The "Manifesto" is reproduced in its entirety as Appendix A in Boris I. Bitker's seminal work on slave redress, *The Case for Black Reparations* (New York: Random House, 1973).

30. "Commission to Study Reparations Proposals," H.R. 40, 101st Cong., 1st sess., in *Congressional Record* 135, E 4007 (Nov. 21, 1989).

31. www.kbabooks.com/reparations1.htm (available November 2002).

32. See, e.g., Feagin and O'Brien, "Growing Movement for Reparations," in *When Sorry Isn't Enough,* ed. Brooks, 342. See also N'COBRA's website, www.ncobra.com.

33. Congressman Hall's resolution is published in *When Sorry Isn't Enough,* ed. Brooks, 350.

34. See, e.g., Tom Campbell, "Tax Preparer Can Keep Working; But Judge Says Foster Must No Longer Claim 'Slavery Reparations,'" *Richmond Times-Dispatch,* October 26, 2002, B7.

35. Kenneth Nunn, "Rosewood," in *When Sorry Isn't Enough,* ed. Brooks, 435.

36. See California Legislature, 2000, Senate Bill 2199.

37. Ibid.

38. See Ghannam, "Repairing the Past," 43.

39. See Tamar Lewin, "Slave Reparation Movement Begins Gaining Momentum," *San Diego Union-Tribune,* June 8, 2001, E6.

40. Margot Roosevelt, "A New War over Slavery," *Time,* June 9, 2003, 20.

41. See, e.g., "Vatican Recommends Reparations to Atone for Slavery," *San Diego Union-Tribune,* August 30, 2001, A20.

42. For reports of the views expressed by Rice and Powell, see, e.g., "Rice against Reparations for Slavery," *San Diego Union-Tribune,* September 10, 2001, A9; "How Powell Decided to Shun Conference," *New York Times,* September 4, 2001, A8.

43. See United Nations, "Third Committee Approves Five-Part Draft Resolution Calling for Action to Counter Racism and Intolerance, as It Concludes Current Session" (press release, www.unhchr.ch/huricane/huricane . . . opendocume, available November 27, 2002), and "Report of the World Conference against Racism, Racial Discrimination, Xenophobia, and Related Intolerance, Durban, South Africa, August 8–September 7, 2001" (www.un.org/WCAR/aconf189_12 .pdf, available June 20, 2003).

44. "Down in Durban," *Wall Street Journal,* September 5, 2001, A26.

45. Ellis Cose, "The Solidarity of Self-Interest," *Newsweek,* August 27, 2001, 25.

46. "Down in Durban."

2. HARMS TO SLAVES AND FREE BLACKS

1. Orlando Patterson refers to the domesticated animal as "Sambo" and David Brion Davis describes the practice as "the effort to bestialize human beings." See David Brion Davis, *In the Image of God: Religion, Moral Values, and Our Heritage of Slavery* (New Haven, Conn.: Yale University Press, 2001), 134–35; Orlando Patterson, *Slavery and Social Death: A Comparative Study* (Cambridge, Mass.: Harvard University Press, 1982), 96.

2. Franklin and Moss, *From Slavery to Freedom,* 53.

3. See Roy L. Brooks, *Rethinking the American Race Problem* (Berkeley: University of California Press, 1990), 7 (sources cited).

4. Davis, *In the Image of God,* 133.

5. See "Ancient Slavery versus American Slavery" in chapter 6 for further discussion.

6. See, generally, Glenn C. Loury, "A Dynamic Theory of Racial Income Differences," in *Women, Minorities and Employment Discrimination,* ed. P. A. Wallace and A. Lamond (Lexington, Mass.: Lexington Books, 1977); id., *The Anatomy of Racial Inequality* (Cambridge, Mass.: Harvard University Press, 2002).

7. *Dred Scott v. Sandford*, 60 U.S. (19 How.) 393, 408 (1857).

8. Frederick Douglass, *Life and Times of Frederick Douglass* (1845; rev. ed., 1892; New York: Collier Books, 1962), 293.

9. See, generally, A. Leon Higginbotham Jr., *In the Matter of Color: The Colonial Period* (New York: Oxford University Press, 1978), 58, 98–99, 252–55, 262–63.

10. William W. Hening, ed., *The Statutes at Large . . . of Virginia* (Richmond, Va., 1809–23), 3: 537–40, chs. 16, 17 (1710); 4: 126–34, ch. 4 (1723); 4: 169–175, ch. 4 (1726); 4: 222–28, ch. 15 (1727); 4: 317–21, ch. 3 (1732); 4: 324–25, ch. 6 (1732); 4: 325–26, ch. 7 (1732); 5: 244, ch. 12 (1744); 5: 244–45, ch. 13 (1744); 6: 31, ch. 32 (1748); 5: 432–39, ch. 2 (1748); 5: 547–58, ch. 14 (1748); 5: 38, ch. 21 (1748); 6: 121–23, ch. 41 (1748); 6: 104–12, ch. 38 (1748); 6: 356–57, ch. 7 (1753); 8: 133–37, ch. 24 (1765); 8: 137–39, ch. 26 (1765); 8: 374–77, ch. 27 (1769); 8: 393, ch. 37 (1769); 8: 358–61, ch. 19 (1769); 9: 471–72, ch. 1 (1778); 11: 39–40, ch. 21 (1782); 11: 59, ch. 32 (1782); 12: 184, ch. 78 (1785); 12: 345, ch. 78 (1786); 12: 505, ch. 22 (1787); 12: 531, ch. 37 (1787); 13: 62, ch. 45 (1789).

11. Hening, ed., *Statutes at Large*, 4: 131.

12. Ibid., 9: 358.

13. Ibid.

14. See, e.g., Allen D. Candler, ed., *Colonial Records of Georgia*, vol. 18 (Atlanta: Franklin Printing and Publishing Co., 1904), 132–33.

15. Higginbotham, *In the Matter of Color*, 71, 98.

16. See, e.g., Earl Maltz, "Slavery, Federalism, and the Structure of the Constitution," *American Journal of Legal History* 36 (1992): 468, arguing that the Constitution did nothing to slavery, which was left to exist as it had prior to 1787, and that federal respect for comity dictated this result.

17. Paul Finkelman, *Slavery and the Founders: Race and Liberty in the Age of Jefferson* (Armonk, N.Y.: M. E. Sharpe, 1996), 6, quoting William Paterson.

18. Ibid., quoting James Iredell.

19. Ibid.

20. For a general discussion of the Articles of Confederation, see Merrill Jensen, *The New Nation: A History of the United States during the Confederation, 1781–1789* (New York: Knopf, 1950). See also Merrill Jensen, *The Articles of Confederation: An Interpretation of the Social-Constitutional History of the American Revolution* (Madison: University of Wisconsin Press, 1948), 146–48.

21. See Finkelman, *Slavery and the Founders*, 7–9.

22. Ibid., 3.

23. Don E. Fehrenbacher, *The Slaveholding Republic: An Account of the United States Government's Relations to Slavery*, ed. Ward M. McAfee (New York: Oxford University Press, 2001).

24. Davis, *In the Image of God*, 134.

25. Finkelman, *Slavery and the Founders*, 5, quoting Wendell Phillips, *The Constitution: A Pro-Slavery Compact; or Selections from the Madison Papers*, 2d ed. (New York: American Anti-Slavery Society, 1845), v–vi.

26. Finkelman, *Slavery and the Founders*, 3, quoting and citing several sources.

27. Paul Johnson, *A History of the American People* (New York: HarperCollins, 1998), 471.

28. William J. Bennett, ed., *The Book of Virtues* (New York: Simon & Schuster, 1993), 256. See, generally, Douglass, *Life and Times*.

29. Julius Lester, *To Be a Slave* (New York: Dial Press, 1968), 20–21.

30. Charles Ball, *A Narrative of the Life and Adventures of Charles Ball, a Black Man*, 3d ed. (Pittsburgh: John T. Shryock, 1854), 158–59.

31. Howard W. French, "The Atlantic Slave Trade: On Both Sides, Reason for Remorse," *New York Times*, April 15, 1998, sec. 4 (Week in Review), 1. See also Franklin and Moss, *From Slavery to Freedom*, 36–39 (estimating a high of 9.5 million); Lester, *To Be a Slave*, 26–27 (estimating a high of 50 million). For a general discussion of slavery, see Ira Berlin, *Generations of Captivity: A History of African-American Slaves* (Cambridge, Mass.: Belknap Press of Harvard University Press, 2003).

32. *Evidence on the Slave Trade* (Cincinnati: American Reform Tract and Book Society, 1855), 47.

33. Ball, *Narrative*, 159–60.

34. *Slave Narratives: A Folk History of Slavery in the United States from Interviews with Former Slaves*, prepared by the Federal Writers Project, 1936–38 (assembled by the Library of Congress, 1941).

35. Ibid.

36. Charles H. Nichols, *Many Thousand Gone: The Ex-Slaves' Account of Their Bondage and Freedom* (Leiden, Neth.: Brill, 1963), 20.

37. Lester, *To Be a Slave*, 28.

38. *Slave Narratives*.

39. Ibid.

40. Ibid.

41. Ibid.

42. Ira Berlin, "North of Slavery: Black People in a Slaveholding Republic" (paper given at the Conference on Yale, New Haven, and American Slavery, Yale University, September 27, 2002), 2, 9, 18.

43. Ibid., 4–6.

44. James Grahame, *Who Is to Blame? Or Cursory Review of "American Apology for American Accession to Negro Slavery"* (London: Smith, Elder, 1842), 52–53 (emphasis in original); Alexis de Tocqueville, *Democracy in America* (1835–39), and Lafayette quoted on p. 53.

45. Winthrop D. Jordan, *White over Black: American Attitudes toward the Negro, 1550–1812* (1968; reprint, Baltimore: Penguin Books, 1969), 134.

46. Clayton E. Cramer, *Black Demographic Data, 1790–1860: A Sourcebook* (Westport, Conn: Greenwood Press, 1997), 43.

47. Grahame, *Who Is to Blame?* 51–52.

48. Ibid., 57.

3. HARMS TO DESCENDANTS

1. Roy L. Brooks, *Integration or Separation? A Strategy for Racial Equality* (Cambridge, Mass.: Harvard University Press, 1996), ix.

2. See chapter 1, n. 1.

3. Dalton Conley, "The Cost of Slavery," *New York Times,* February 15, 2003. See *Grutter v. Bollinger.*

4. Conley, "Cost of Slavery" (referring to the economist Edward Wolff).

5. My focus on access to elite schools is driven by pragmatic considerations. Princeton, Yale, Stanford, and other prestigious institutions of higher education are "feeder" schools for the "centers of power" in American society—the highest-paying jobs and positions of power and influence.

6. Harry S. Ashmore, *Hearts and Minds: The Anatomy of Racism from Roosevelt to Reagan* (New York: McGraw-Hill, 1982), 44, quoting *Encyclopedia Britannica* (1910 ed.).

7. Ibid., 138.

8. See Stephan Thernstrom and Abigail Thernstrom, *America in Black and White: One Nation, Indivisible* (New York: Simon & Schuster, 1997), 493–529; Dinesh D'Souza, *What's So Great about America* (Washington, D.C.: Regnery, 2002), 101–2, 119.

9. D'Souza, *What's So Great about America,* 101–2.

10. "Whole Lott of Trouble," abcNews.com (Washington, December 11, 2002).

11. Andrew Hacker, "Andrew Hacker on George Fredrickson's Racism," *Journal of Blacks in Higher Education* [henceforth cited as *JBHE*] 38 (Winter 2002–3), 101; See also Joe R. Feagin, *Racist America: Roots, Current Realities, and Future Reparations* (New York: Routledge, 2000), 123–29.

12. *Grutter v. Bollinger.* (See also Linda Krieger, "Civil Rights Perestroika: Intergroup Relations after Affirmative Action," *California Law Review* 86 (1998): 1251, 1276–91, 1303.

13. Bonnie Harris, "Making a Case for Reparations," *Indianapolis Star,* October 17, 2002, 3B, quoting Indiana University's Professor John H. Stanfield II.

14. Shana Levin, "Social Psychological Evidence on Race and Racism," ch. 3 of *A Report of the AERA Panel on Racial Dynamics in Colleges and Universities,* ed.

Mitchell Chang et al. (Stanford, Calif.: Center for the Comparative Studies on Race and Ethnicity, 1999) (prepublication draft advance copy), 2.

15. For example, a police study of traffic stops made between July and November of 2002 showed "that of all those people whose cars were pulled over, . . . 22 percent [of] blacks were asked to exit their vehicles, compared with 7 percent of whites." "Blacks, Hispanics Are Searched More," *San Diego Union-Tribune,* January 7, 2003, A5. Lawsuits have been filed in recent years against large retail establishments such as Macy's, Dillard's, and J. C. Penney by black Americans who allege that these stores profile on the basis of race. Similar lawsuits have also been filed against Denny's and other restaurant chains alleging that they made blacks prepay for meals. For a general discussion, see Deborah Kong, "More Consumers File Complaints of Retail Stores' Racial Profiling," *San Diego Union-Tribune,* June 9, 2003, A46.

16. Glenn C. Loury, *The Anatomy of Racial Inequality* (Cambridge, Mass.: Harvard University Press, 2002), 23.

17. See Brooks, *Integration or Separation?* 104.

18. Watson Branch, "Reparations for Slavery: A Dream Deferred," *San Diego International Law Journal* 3 (2002): 177, 182, quoting James Baldwin, "Many Thousands Gone," in id., *Notes of a Native Son* (Boston: Beacon Press, 1984), 24.

19. See Marcella Bombardieri, "Theory Links Slavery, Stress Disorder: Proponents Make Case for a New Diagnosis," *Boston Globe,* November 12, 2002, B1. See also Alvin F. Poussaint and Amy Alexander, *Lay My Burden Down: Suicide and the Mental Health Crisis among African-Americans* (Boston: Beacon Press, 2000).

20. See Bombardieri, "Theory Links Slavery, Stress Disorder."

21. See, generally, Glenn C. Loury, "A Dynamic Theory of Racial Income Differences," in *Women, Minorities and Employment Discrimination,* ed. P. A. Wallace and A. Lamond (Lexington, Mass.: Lexington Books, 1977).

22. See, e.g., Jason Mazzone, "The Social Capital Argument for Federalism," *Southern California Interdisciplinary Law Journal* 27 (Winter 2001): 27.

23. See also Loury, *Anatomy of Racial Inequality.*

24. Stuart Henry and Dragan Milovanovic, *Constitutive Criminology: Beyond Postmodernism* (London: Sage, 1996), 103.

25. See Dragan Milovanovic and Katheryn K. Russell, *Petit Apartheid in the U.S. Criminal Justice System: The Dark Figure of Racism* (Durham N.C.: Carolina Academic Press, 2001), xvi.

26. Feagin, *Racist America,* 26.

27. See Thernstrom & Thernstrom, *America in Black and White,* 493–529; D'Souza, *What's So Great about America,* 101–2, 119.

28. Armstrong Williams, "Presumed Victims," in *Should America Pay? Slavery and the Raging Debate on Reparations,* ed. Raymond A. Winbush (New York: Amistad, 2003), 165.

29. John McWhorter, "Against Reparations," in ibid., 180.

30. Shelby Steele, ". . . Or a Childish Illusion of Justice? Reparations Enshrine Victimhood, Dishonoring Our Ancestors," in ibid., 197. See also id., *The Content of Our Character: A New Vision of Race in America* (New York: St. Martin's Press, 1990).

31. On the internal causes of the black enrollment deficiency in higher education, see the sections further on in this chapter titled "From the Colonial Era to the Civil War" and "From the Postbellum Era (1865–95) to *Brown v. Board of Education* (1954)."

32. Bombardieri, "Theory Links Slavery, Stress Disorder."

33. These statistics are taken from the American Council on Education's website under the title "Students of Color Make Enrollment and Graduation Gains," www.acenet.edu. (available September 23, 2002). These and other statistics are discussed later in this chapter.

34. Indeed, the protracted fight for school desegregation culminating in *Brown v. Board of Education* is clear evidence of the long-standing interest blacks have had in education. See, generally, Richard Kluger, *Simple Justice: The History of* Brown v. Board of Education *and Black America's Struggle for Equality* (New York: Knopf, 1976).

35. "Affirmative Action: History and Rationale," www.whitehouse.gov/WH/EOP/OP/html/aa02.html (available June 22, 1999).

36. In 2000, 31.4 percent of black families earned $50,000 or more, compared to 51.4 percent of whites. See U.S. Census Bureau, *2001 Statistical Abstract of the United States* (Washington, D.C.: Government Printing Office, 2002), 41 (table 38).

37. The short answer is that racial barriers still exist. It is just that some blacks have been luckier than other blacks. Without these racial barriers, some of which are discussed in this chapter, the pace of racial progress would be faster. See, generally, Roy L. Brooks, *Rethinking the American Race Problem* (Berkeley: University of California Press, 1990).

38. The study can be found at Dartmouth College's website, http://www.dartmouth.edu (available November 11, 2002). For discussion of the study, see Lance Kramer, "Study: Slavery's Effects Lasted Just 2 Generations," Dartmouth University via U-Wire, University Wire, www.lexis.com (available November 6, 2002).

39. Jason L. Riley, "Black, Successful—and Typical," *Wall Street Journal,* May 13, 2002, A16.

40. Civil Rights Act of 1866, 42 U.S.C. § 1981.

41. *Jones v. Alfred H. Mayer Co.,* 392 U.S. 409, 445 (1968).

42. Ronald Takaki, "Aesculapius Was a White Man: Antebellum Racism and Male Chauvinism at Harvard Medical School," *Phylon* 39, no. 2 (1978): 128–34, quotations at 128, 132, 129–30. For a discussion of the life of Martin Delany, see,

e.g., Robert S. Levine, *Martin Delany, Frederick Douglass, and the Politics of Representative Identity* (Chapel Hill: University of North Carolina Press, 1997). There is disagreement over whether Delany did in fact receive a medical degree from Harvard. See, e.g., Theodore Draper, "The Father of American Black Nationalism," *New York Review of Books,* March 12, 1970; id., "Writing Black History," ibid., July 2, 1970.

43. Walter George Robinson Jr., "Blacks in Higher Education in the United States before 1865" (diss., Southern Illinois University, 1976; Ann Arbor: University Microfilms International, 1979), 4. See also Carter G. Woodson, *African Heroes and Heroines* (Washington, D.C.: Associated Publishers, 1939), 25–47.

44. Robinson, "Blacks in Higher Education," 5. See also, however, www .historychannel.com/classroom/unesco/timbuktu.html (accessed February 5, 2004), according to which a Tuareg woman named Buktu originally settled Timbuktu (literally, Buktu's well) as a seasonal camp around 1100.

45. Ibid. See also J. C. DeGraft-Johnson, *African Glory: The Story of Vanished Negro Civilizations* (New York: Walker, 1954), 98, 105.

46. DeGraft-Johnson, *African Glory,* 105.

47. Robinson, "Blacks in Higher Education," 5. See DeGraft-Johnson, *African Glory,* 105; Franklin, *From Slavery to Freedom,* 14–19.

48. "Autobiography of Omar ibn Seid, Slave in North Carolina, 1831," *American Historical Review* 30 (July 1925): 791–95. See George E. Callcott, "Omar ibn Seid, a Slave Who Wrote an Autobiography in Arabic," *Journal of Negro History* 39 (January 1954): 58.

49. See, e.g., Marilyn J. Ross, *Success Factors of Young African-American Males at a Historically Black College* (Westport, Conn.: Bergin & Garvey, 1998), 16, 17; Julian B. Roebuck and Komanduri S. Murty, *Historically Black Colleges and Universities: Their Place in American Higher Education* (Westport, Conn.: Praeger, 1993), 22; Ellen N. Lawson and Marlene Merrill, "The Antebellum 'Talented Thousandth': Black College Students at Oberlin before the Civil War," *Journal of Negro Education* 52 (Spring 1983): 142–55; www.wilberforce.edu/opencms/ export/bulldog/welcome/history.html (accessed February 5, 2004), 50. See, e.g., Robinson, "Blacks in Higher Education," 11–13 (sources cited therein); Timothy Reese Cain, "African American Higher Education in Ohio: The Nineteenth Century," *Education Policy and Leadership at Ohio State University,* November 24, 1998, published at www.coe.ohio-state.edu/EDPL/Gordon/courses/863/cain.htm (available June 5, 2002).

51. Cain, "African-American Higher Education in Ohio," 3.

52. Ibid., 2.

53. Carter G. Woodson, *The Education of the Negro Prior to 1861* (Washington, D.C.: Associated Publishers, 1919), 276.

54. See Henry Allen Bullock, *A History of Negro Education in the South: From 1619 to Present* (Cambridge, Mass.: Harvard University Press, 1967), 12, 91, 97, 103.

55. See, e.g., Franklin, *From Slavery to Freedom*, 231; Woodson, *Education of the Negro Prior to 1861*, 279–82.

56. Franklin, *From Slavery to Freedom*, 231.

57. One of the first scholars to cite this figure was Charles S. Johnson in *The Negro College Graduate* (College Park, Md.: McGrath, 1938), 7. See also Frank Hamilton Bowles and Frank A. DeCosta, *Between Two Worlds: A Profile of Negro Higher Education* (New York: McGraw Hill, 1971), 25–26; Roebuck and Murty, *Historically Black Colleges and Universities*, 22; Robinson, "Blacks in Higher Education," 11.

58. See Lawson and Merrill, "Antebellum 'Talented Thousandth,'" 151–52 (table 1).

59. Clayton E. Cramer, *Black Demographic Data, 1790–1960: A Sourcebook* (Westport, Conn.: Greenwood Press, 1997), 1. The pre-1790 population studies typically provided no more information than the number of black men, women, and children in free black or white households. See, e.g., A. Leon Higginbotham Jr., *In the Matter of Color: The Colonial Period* (New York: Oxford University Press, 1978), 202.

60. Berlin, "North of Slavery," 2. See, e.g., Don E. Fehrenbacher, *The Slaveholding Republic: An Account of the United States Government's Relations to Slavery*, ed. Ward M. McAfee (New York: Oxford University Press, 2001). The compromise that brought the republic of the United States into formal existence granted the slaveholder distinct privileges and protections for his slave property, in return for which the North received certain commercial concessions. Historians have long concluded that "the Nation at large was fully aware of this bargain at the time, and entered into it willingly and with open eyes." Paul Finkelman, *Slavery and the Founders: Race and Liberty in the Age of Jefferson*, 2d ed. (Armonk, N.Y.: M. E. Sharpe, 2001), 5 (quoting sources).

61. Cramer, *Black Demographic Data*, 2.

62. Ibid.

63. Ira Berlin, *Slaves without Masters: The Free Negro in the Antebellum South* (New York: Pantheon Books, 1974), 49, 145, 175. See also Marina Wikramanayke, *A World in Shadow: The Free Black in Antebellum South Carolina* (Columbia, S.C.: University of South Carolina Press, 1973), 39–42.

64. Cramer, *Black Demographic Data*, 3.

65. Ross, *Success Factors of Young African-American Males.*, 15.

66. U.S. Department of Commerce, Bureau of the Census, *Negro Population, 1790–1915* (1918; reprint, New York: Kraus, 1969). See, e.g., Roebuck and Murty, *Historically Black Colleges and Universities*, 21; Franklin, *From Slavery to Freedom*, 144, 185–86.

67. Franklin, *From Slavery to Freedom,* 230.

68. Henry Louis Gates Jr., "The Perception of Black Literature as a Necessary Road to Membership in the Human Community," *JBHE* (Winter 1998–99), 108 (emphasis in original).

69. Jordan, *White over Black,* 134.

70. Ibid., vii, viii.

71. Cramer, *Black Demographic Data,* 43.

72. *Roberts v. City of Boston,* 5 Cush. (59 Mass.) 198 (1849), is the most important pre–Civil War school desegregation case. In this case, the highest court in Massachusetts rejected the plaintiff's challenge to the state's regime of school segregation on the grounds that states have plenary power to "arrange, classify, and distribute pupils." The court also offered the view that the law cannot change racial prejudice. After the Civil War, Iowa and Kansas ruled that school segregation was illegal under state law. See *Clark v. Board of Education,* 24 Iowa 266 (1868); *Ottawa v. Tinnon,* 26 Kan. 1 (1881). Notwithstanding the Kansas Supreme Court's ruling, many Kansas schools remained segregated until the U.S. Supreme Court's 1954 decision in *Brown v. Board of Education,* which dealt specifically with the Topeka, Kansas, school district.

73. For a list of institutions that accepted blacks by 1852, see Woodson, *Education of the Negro Prior to 1861,* 277.

74. See, e.g., Higginbotham, *In the Matter of Color,* 258; Roebuck and Murty, *Historically Black Colleges and Universities,* 21.

75. Jordan, *White over Black,* 354.

76. Woodson, *Education of the Negro Prior to 1861,* 257.

77. Ibid., 256 n. 1 (quoting Garrison).

78. Ibid., 258. See also ibid., 266–68; Franklin, *From Slavery to Freedom,* 230–31; Robinson, "Blacks in Higher Education," 14.

79. See Brooks, *Integration or Separation?* 156–58; Takaki, "Aesculapius," 128; Woodson, *Education of the Negro Prior to 1861,* 263. See, generally, ibid., 256–82.

80. See, e.g., Robinson, "Blacks in Higher Education," 14; Woodson, *Education of the Negro Prior to 1861,* 265.

81. Olivia Mancini, "Vassar's First Black Graduate: She Passed for White," *JBHE* 34 (Winter 2001–2), 108.

82. Juan Williams, "The Higher Education of Thurgood Marshall," *JBHE* 22 (Winter 1998–99), 82–88.

83. *McLaurin v. Oklahoma State Regents for Higher Education,* 339 U.S. 637, 640 (1950).

84. See U.S. Department of Commerce, Bureau of the Census, *Negro Population, 1790–1915,* 33; Preston Valien, "Desegregation in Higher Education: A Critical Summary," *Journal of Negro Education* 27, no. 3 (Summer 1958): 373, 374.

85. See U.S. Department of Commerce, Bureau of the Census, *The Social and Economic Status of the Black Population in the United States: A Historical View 1790–1978* (Washington, D.C.: Government Printing Office, 1980), 13.

86. See, e.g., W. J. Simmons, *Men of Mark: Eminent, Progressive and Rising* (Baltimore: Rewell, 1891), 236–37, 328–29, 1052; Bowles and DeCosta, *Between Two Worlds,* 33.

87. See W. E. B. Du Bois and A. G. Dill, *The College-Bred Negro American* (Atlanta: Atlanta University Press, 1910), 48–49.

88. See discussion of Lincoln and Wilberforce Universities earlier in this chapter.

89. Bowles and DeCosta, *Between Two Worlds,* 27–28. See also A. F. Beard, *A Crusade of Brotherhood* (Boston: Pilgrim Press, 1909), 121–41.

90. For a discussion of these distinctions, see, e.g., Carroll L. Miller, "Higher Education for Black Americans: Problems and Issues," *Journal of Negro Education* 50 (Summer 1981): 208.

91. See, e.g., Bowles and DeCosta, *Between Two Worlds,* 27–31; Charles S. Johnson, *The Negro in American Civilization* (London: Constable, 1931), 288; Woodson, *Education of the Negro Prior to 1861,* 271–74. The federal government's studies of HBCUs are published at, e.g., U.S. Department of Interior, Bureau of Education, *A Study of the Private and Higher Schools for Colored People in the United States* (Washington, D.C.: Government Printing Office, 1917) (the 1916 study); U.S. Department of Interior, Bureau of Education, *Survey of Negro Colleges and Universities,* by Arthur J. Klein, Division of Higher Education (1929; reprint, New York: Negro Universities Press, 1969) (the 1928 study); U.S. Department of Education, *The Traditionally Black Institutions of Higher Education, 1860 to 1982,* by Susan T. Hill, National Center for Education Statistics (NCES) 84308 (Washington, D.C.: Government Printing Office, 1985) (also discussing the 1947, or third government, study).

92. See, e.g., Johnson, *Negro College Graduate;* Jessie Parkhurst Guzman, *Negro Year Book, 1952* (New York: Wm. H. Wise, 1952); U.S. Department of Commerce, Bureau of the Census, *Characteristics of the Population, 1960* (Washington, D.C.: Government Printing Office, 1963); Henry Allen Bullock, *A History of Negro Education in the South: From 1619 to the Present* (Cambridge, Mass.: Harvard University Press, 1967).

93. See, e.g., U.S. Department of Interior, *Survey of Negro Colleges and Universities,* 5–32; U.S. Department of Education, *Traditionally Black Institutions of Higher Education, 1860 to 1982,* 1–3. "The black community lacked the financial resources to sustain major projects, and most of these schools were poor in quality and starved for funds." James M. McPherson, "White Liberals and Black Power in Negro Education, 1865–1915," *American Historical Review* 75, no. 5 (1970): 1357, 1359.

94. U.S. Department of Interior, *Survey of Negro Colleges and Universities*, 59. See, e.g., U.S. Department of Education, *Traditionally Black Institutions of Higher Education, 1860 to 1982*, 5; Johnson, *Negro in American Civilization*, 288; Bowles and DeCosta, *Between Two Worlds*, 43.

95. Dwight Oliver Wendell Holmes, *The Evolution of the Negro College* (College Park, Md.: McGrath, 1934), 69.

96. Felton G. Clark, "Negro Higher Education and Some Fundamental Issues Raised by World War II," *Journal of Negro Education* 11 (July 1942): 279, 280.

97. James D. Anderson, *The Education of Blacks in the South, 1860–1935* (Chapel Hill: University of North Carolina Press, 1988), 241.

98. Ibid. See *The General Education Board: An Account of Its Activities, 1902–1914* (New York: General Education Board, 1915); Erick Anderson and Alfred A. Moss Jr., *Dangerous Donations: Northern Philanthropy and Southern Education, 1902–1930* (Columbia: University of Missouri Press, 1999); J. M. Stephen Peeps, "Northern Philanthropy and the Emergence of Black Higher Education—Do-Gooders, Compromisers, or Co-conspirators?" *Journal of Negro Education* 50 (Summer 1981): 251.

99. Bowles and DeCosta, *Between Two Worlds*, 30. See also Du Bois and Dill, *College-Bred Negro American*, 14.

100. Bowles and DeCosta, *Between Two Worlds*, 53–54. See also, ibid., 48–49.

101. U.S. Department of Interior, *Survey of Negro Colleges and Universities*, 2.

102. Ibid., 33.

103. See William M. Kephart, "Minority Group Discrimination in Higher Education," *Journal of Educational Sociology* 23 (September 1949): 52, 54.

104. See Carroll L. Miller, "The Relative Educational Attainment of the Negro Population in the United States," *Journal of Negro Education* 22 (Summer 1953): 392–94, citing U.S. Department of Commerce, Bureau of the Census, *U.S. Census of Population: 1950, General Characteristics, U.S. Summary* (Washington, D.C.: Government Printing Office, 1952).

105. U.S. President's Commission on Higher Education, *Higher Education for Democracy*, vol. 1 (New York: Harper & Bros., 1950), 101.

106. See U.S. Department of Commerce, Bureau of the Census, *Negroes in the United States, 1920–1932* (Washington, D.C.: Government Printing Office, 1934), 241; id., *Negro Population in the United States, 1790–1915* (Washington, D.C.: Government Printing Office, 1918), 428. See also Bullock, *History of Negro Education in the South*, 171–72.

107. Bowles and DeCosta, *Between Two Worlds*, 30. See Du Bois and Dill, *College-Bred Negro American*, 14.

108. Booker T. Washington, *Up From Slavery* (1901; reprint, New York: Bantam Books, 1963), 155. Washington came to prominence in 1895, which, ironically,

was the year in which Frederick Douglass died. Until his death, Douglass, the famous black abolitionist, was the most important black person in America. Washington's home base was the Tuskegee Normal and Industrial Institute in Tuskegee, Alabama, which trained "teachers to stress the familiar experiences and skills of the farm and the Negro community." Harvey Wish, "Negro Education and the Progressive Movement," *Journal of Negro History* 49, no. 3 (July 1964): 184, 187. On Douglass's fascinating life, see his *Life and Times*.

109. Brooks, *Integration or Separation?* 129. See, e.g., Clark, "Negro Higher Education and Some Fundamental Issues Raised by World War II," 279. The closeness of Washington's and Du Bois's views on education is often overlooked. "After all," as Wish points out, "[Washington] sent his children to college. . . . He too knew the importance of what DuBois called 'The Talented Tenth.'" Wish, "Negro Education and the Progressive Movement," 187.

110. See Brooks, *Integration or Separation,* 129–30; August Meier and John H. Bracey Jr., "The NAACP as a Reform Movement, 1909–1965: 'They Reach the Conscience of America,'" *Journal of Southern History* 59 (February 1993): 3, 17. For a discussion of the history of the NAACP and school desegregation, see, generally, Kluger, *Simple Justice.*

111. Michael Fultz, "'The Morning Cometh:' African American Periodicals, Education, and the Black Middle Class, 1900–1930," *Journal of Negro History* 80, no. 3 (1995): 97, 102, 104.

112. Monroe H. Little, "The Extra-Curricular Activities of Black College Students, 1868–1940," *Journal of Negro History* 65 (Spring 1980): 135, 136–37 (original and secondary sources cited therein).

113. Wish, "Negro Education and the Progressive Movement," 186–87.

114. Anderson, *Education of Blacks in the South, 1860–1935,* 247.

115. Wish, "Negro Education and the Progressive Movement," 187.

116. Kunhardt et al., *American President,* 28.

117. See Nathaniel Weyl, *The Negro in American Civilization* (Washington, D.C.: Public Affairs Press, 1960), 87. See, generally, C. Vann Woodward, *The Strange Career of Jim Crow* (1955), 2d rev. ed. (New York: Oxford University Press, 1966); Louis R. Harlan, *Separate and Unequal Public School Campaigns and Racism in the Southern Seaboard States, 1901–1915* (Chapel Hill: University of North Carolina Press, 1958); Charles S. Mangum Jr., *The Legal Status of the Negro* (Chapel Hill: University of North Carolina Press, 1940).

118. Anson Phelps Stokes, "American Race Relations in War Time," *Journal of Negro Education* 14, no. 4 (Autumn 1945): 535, 548.

119. Ashmore, *Hearts and Minds,* 1982), 37. See, generally, John Hope Franklin, "History of Racial Segregation in the United States," *Annals of American Academy of Political & Social Scientists* 34 (March 1956): 1.

120. See *Berea College v. Kentucky,* 211 U.S. 45 (1908).

121. U.S. Department of the Interior, Bureau of Education, *Report of the Commissioner of Education, 1890–91,* vol. 1 (Washington, D.C.: Government Printing Office, 1894), 260. See Bowles and DeCosta, *Between Two Worlds,* 32. For further discussion of this discriminatory tradition, see, e.g., Chas H. Thomson, "Introduction: The Problem of Negro Higher Education," *Journal of Negro Education* 2, no. 3 (July 1933): 257; Henry J. McGuinn, "The Courts and Equality of Educational Opportunity," *Journal of Negro Education* 8 (April 1939): 150.

122. Marcia G. Synnott, "The Admission and Assimilation of Minority Students at Harvard, Yale, and Princeton, 1900–1970," *History of Education Quarterly* 19, no. 3 (Autumn 1979): 285, 295.

123. Ibid., 290–91, 295.

124. Ibid., 294–95.

125. Vicky Bouloubasis, "Blue & White Online—The Roots of Race Relations: Peeling Back the Layers of Integration," www.uncoedu/student/orgs/bw/thematic __01/uncroots.html (available June 11, 2002).

126. *Brown v. Board of Education,* 347 U.S. 483, 495 (1954).

127. *Brown v. Board of Education,* 349 U.S. 294, 301 (1955).

128. *Gayle v. Browder,* 352 U.S. 903 (1956).

129. *State of Florida, ex rel Hawkins v. Board of Control,* 350 U.S. 413, 414 (1956).

130. Alex M. Johnson Jr., "Bid Whist, Tonk, and *United States v. Fordice*: Why Integration Fails African-Americans Again," *California Law Review* 81 (1993): 1401, 1443–46. See, e.g., Wendy Brown-Scott, "Race Consciousness in Higher Education: Does 'Sound Educational Policy' Support the Continued Existence of Historically Black Colleges?" *Emory Law Journal* 43 (1994): 48; Gil Kujovich, "Equal Opportunity in Higher Education and the Black Public College: The Era of Separate But Equal," *Minnesota Law Review* 72 (1987): 29.

131. See, e.g., *Adams v. Richardson,* 351 F. Supp. 636 (D.C. 1972), modified and affirmed, 480 F.2d 1159 (D.C. Cir. 1973).

132. *United States v. Fordice,* 505 U.S. 717 (1992), 729, 748 (emphasis in original).

133. *Missouri v. Jenkins,* 515 U.S. 70, 114 (1995) *(Jenkins III)* (Thomas, J., concurring).

134. The Court's decision denying certiorari in the case is reported in an article written by Peter Applebone, "Equal Entry Standards May Hurt Black Students in Mississippi," *San Diego Union-Tribune,* April 24, 1996, A10.

135. Anson Phelps Stokes, "American Race Relations in War Time," *Journal of Negro Education* 14, no. 4 (Autumn 1945): 535, 538, 550. See also Daniel Kryder, *Divided Arsenal: Race and the American State during World War II* (Cambridge: Cambridge University Press, 2000).

136. Stokes, "American Race Relations in War Time," 550.

137. See Roy L. Brooks, *Structures of Judicial Decision-Making from Legal Formalism to Critical Theory* (Durham, N.C.: Carolina Academic Press, 2002), 284.

138. For a discussion of the civil rights movement, see, e.g., *Civil Rights since 1787: A Reader on the Black Struggle,* ed. Jonathan Birnbaum and Clarence Taylor (New York: New York University Press, 2000); Kluger, *Simple Justice.*

139. Bouloubasis, "Blue & White Online."

140. Valien, "Desegregation in Higher Education," 373, 378.

141. Thernstrom and Thernstrom, *America in Black and White,* 390.

142. U.S. Department of Education, *Traditionally Black Institutions of Higher Education, 1860 to 1982,* 44. See also ibid., xvi.

143. These college participation rates are consistent with studies of other age cohorts. See Deborah Carter and Reginald Wilson, *Twelfth Annual Status Report on Minorities in Higher Education* (Washington, D.C.: American Council on Education, 1993), 44–45, table 1. See also Brooks, *Rethinking the American Race Problem,* 81; *A Common Destiny: Blacks and American Society,* ed. Gerald J. Jaynes and Robin M. Williams Jr. (Washington, D.C.: National Academy Press, 1989), 339–40.

144. Synnott, "Admission and Assimilation of Minority Students at Harvard, Yale, and Princeton, 1900–1970," 297.

145. See David Karen, "The Politics of Class, Race and Gender: Access to Higher Education in the United States, 1960–1986," *American Journal of Education* 99 (1991): 208, 217.

146. See, e.g., U.S. Department of Education, *Traditionally Black Institutions of Higher Education, 1860 to 1982,* 43. In 1965, Congress created several programs, including grants-in-aid, work study, and loans, to reduce the financial barriers to college for low-income students. Also, in 1972, Congress established what is now called the Pell Grant Program, which has become "the major source of financial aid for low-income students." Ibid.

147. *Regents of the University of California v. Bakke,* 438 U.S. 265 (1978). See also *Grutter v. Bollinger;* Ronnie Bernard Tucker, *Affirmative Action, the Supreme Court, and Political Power in the Old Confederacy* (Lanham, Md..: University Press of America, 2000), 78–85, 231; Jeanne B. Fisher, "Bakke Case: Part I—The Issues," *Journal of College Student Personnel* 19 (March 1978): 174; Jeanne B. Fisher, "Bakke Case: Part II—An Analysis and Implications," *Journal of College Student Personnel* 20 (May 1979): 264. And see, too, Thernstrom and Thernstrom, *America in Black and White,* 401, 413–20.

148. See U.S. Department of Education, *Youth Indicators, 1996: Trends in the Well-Being of American Youth,* NCES 96–027 (Washington, D.C.: Government Printing Office, 1996), 70.

149. Howard K. Cameron, "Nonintellectual Correlates of Academic Achievement," *Journal of Negro Education* 37 (Summer 1968): 252, 254 (citing a study conducted by Kenneth Clark and another scholar).

150. See, generally, Joel Campbell, *Testing of Culturally Different Groups* (Princeton, N.J.: Educational Testing Service, 1964).

151. For discussion of the SAT during this time frame, see, e.g., David Owen, *None of the Above: Behind the Myth of Scholastic Aptitude* (Boston: Houghton Mifflin, 1985), 216; Winton H. Manning, "The Measurement of Intellectual Capacity and Performance," *Journal of Negro Education* 37 (Summer 1968): 258, 262 n. 11 (sources cited therein). Gail E. Thomas, "College Characteristics and Black Students' Four-Year College Graduation," *Journal of Negro Education* 50 (Summer 1981): 328, 329 (sources cited therein).

152. For a discussion of these studies, see, e.g., Brooks, *Integration or Separation,* 36–39.

153. Thernstrom and Thernstrom, *America in Black and White,* 406. See ibid., 397–401 (summary of studies on the SAT racial gap), 401–3, esp. n. 34 (discussing studies correlating SAT scores to college GPA).

154. Thomas, "College Characteristics and Black Students' Four-Year College Graduation," 331.

155. Jay Mathews, "The 100 Best High Schools in America," *Newsweek,* June 2, 2003, 53.

156. Thomas, "College Characteristics and Black Students' Four-Year College Graduation," 330–43 (sources cited therein). For a discussion of other factors, see, generally, *Recruitment and Retention of Black Students in Higher Education,* ed. Johnson N. Niba and Regina Norman (Lanham, Md.: University Press of America, 1989).

157. Carroll L. Miller, "Higher Education for Black Americans: Problems and Issues," *Journal of Negro Education* 50 (Summer 1981): 208, 212.

158. Kenneth B. Clark, "Black S.A.T. Scores," *New York Times,* October 12, 1982. What this suggests, then, is the following:

> If SAT scores reflect the fundamental inequality of American society . . . , then admission decisions based on them do, too. The SAT is much more than a thermometer if it serves to maintain the unfairness it allegedly exposes. And it is much less than a social equalizer if it functions to reproduce the status quo.
>
> The crime of the SAT is not that it conveys an unwelcome "message" about the level of education American society provides for the underprivileged; the crime of the SAT is that it disguises this inequality as a morally neutral difference in "aptitude." Wealthy whites don't see SAT results as

proof that the poor are mistreated. Like the *Fortune* editor quoted earlier, they see them as proof that mistreatment of the poor is fair. (Owen, *None of the Above,* 227)

159. See Alvin F. Poussaint and Carolyn O. Atkinson, "Negro Youth and Psychological Motivation," *Journal of Negro Education* 37 (Summer 1968): 241. "There is a substantial difference between 'interest in going to college' and 'planning to attend college.'" Miller, "Higher Education for African Americans," 212.

160. See James A. Anderson, "Cognitive Styles and Multicultural Populations," in *Recruitment and Retention of Black Students in Higher Education,* ed. Niba and Norma, 29–51. See also Janice E. Hale-Benson, *Black Children: Their Roots, Culture, and Learning Styles* (Baltimore: John Hopkins University Press, 1986), 15–16.

161. This story is taken from Sari Horowitz, "An African American Graduate Looks Out from the Ivy League," *JBHE* 24 (Summer 1999): 126.

162. See "Vital Signs: The Statistics That Describe the Present and Suggest the Future of African Americans in Higher Education," *JBHE* 2 (Winter 1993–94): 31, 39 (relying on data from the Department of Education and the American Council on Education).

163. See U.S. Department of Education, "Degree-Granting Postsecondary: Enrollment," www.nces.ed.gov, 264, 267, tables 221 and 223 (available June 14, 2002). See also U.S. Department of Education, *Traditionally Black Institutions of Higher Education, 1860 to 1982,* 44.

164. See "The Progress of Black Students Matriculations at the Nation's Highest-Ranked Colleges and Universities," *JBHE* 29 (Autumn 2000): 17; Synnott, "Admission and Assimilation of Minority Students at Harvard, Yale, and Princeton, 1900–1970," 297; Karen, "Politics of Class, Race and Gender," 208, 217.

165. It is also useful to note that while the number of black applications to four-year public and private colleges increased from about 72,000 to 117,000 and from about 35,000 to 42,000, respectively, between 1985 and 1999 (compared to a *decline* in white applications from about 643,000 to 609,000 and about 473,000 to 359,0000, respectively), the rate of acceptance for black applicants decreased, especially after 1996, from 65 percent to 47 percent and from 61 percent to 50 percent, respectively, during this period (compared to a decrease in white acceptance at public colleges, from 72 percent to 70 percent, and an increase in white acceptance at private colleges, from 60 percent to 63 percent). See Hunter Breland et al., "Trends in College Admission 2000: A Report of a Survey of Undergraduate Admissions Policies, Practices, and Procedures" (sponsored by the College Board, Educational Testing Service, and several other educational organizations), www.nces.ed.gov, tables 2.3 and 2.4 (available June 14, 2002).

166. See "Black-White Higher Education Equality Index," *JBHE* 34 (Winter 2001–2): 78; Deborah J. Wilds, *Minorities in Higher Education,* Seventeenth Annual Status Report (Washington, D.C.: American Council on Education, 2000), 69–70, table 1; Carter and Wilson, *Twelfth Annual Status Report on Minorities in Higher Education,* 44–45, table 1.

167. In a subsequent report, the American Council on Education shows declining enrollment for both black and white students at 39.4 percent and 43.2 percent, respectively, for 2000. See www.acenet.edu (available October 22, 2002).

168. See U.S. Department of Education, "Degree-Granting Postsecondary: Enrollment," www.nces.ed.gov/programs/digest/d01/dt208.asp, 243, table 208, "Total Fall Enrollment in Degree-Granting Institutions, by Level of Study, Sex, and Race/Ethnicity of Student: 1976 to 1999" (available December 3, 2003). See also Robert Bruce Slater, "The Growing Gender Gap in Black Higher Education," *JBHE* 3 (Spring 1994): 53.

169. Researchers at the *JBHE* report that:

In 1999, the latest year for which complete data is available, there were 603,000 African-American men enrolled in higher education in the United States. This was up 24 percent during the decade of the 1990s. At the same time, in 1999, there were 757,000 black men incarcerated in federal, state, and local prisons. Therefore there were 25 percent more black men in prison in the United States than were enrolled in institutions of higher education. During the 1990s the gap between higher education enrollments and prison inmates grew substantially. In 1990 there were 485,000 black men enrolled in higher education and 508,800 black men in jail. In 1990 the gap was less than 5 percent. ("Weekly Bulletin," *JBHE,* June 26, 2003, www.jbhe.com)

See also Fox Butterfield, "Study Finds Big Increase in Black Men as Inmates since 1980," *New York Times,* August 28, 2002, A14.

170. Slater, "Growing Gender Gap," 58, 59. See Andrew Hacker, *Mismatch: The Growing Gulf between Men and Women* (New York: Scriber, 2003).

171. Valora Washington and Joanna Newman, "Setting Our Own Agenda: Exploring the Meaning of Gender Disparities among Blacks in Higher Education," *Journal of Negro Education* 60 (Winter 1991): 19, 23 (sources discussed therein).

172. See Brooks, *Integration or Separation?* 30 (sources cited therein).

173. Washington and Newman, "Setting Our Own Agenda," 19, 23.

174. See Thomas Kochman, *Black and White Styles in Conflict* (Chicago: University of Chicago Press, 1981).

175. Alexander Aleinikoff, "A Case for Race Consciousness," *Columbia Law Review* 91 (1991): 1060, 1109.

176. Davis, *In the Image of God*, 134.

177. Ibid., 28.

178. "Education Secretary Issues Final Policy Guidance on Minority Scholarships," *Civil Rights Monitor* (Winter 1994): 4–5.

179. 78 F.3d 932 (5th Cir. 1996), cert. den. sub nom. *Texas v. Hopwood*, 518 U.S. 1033 (1996). *Hopwood* was reversed in *Grutter v. Bollinger*, holding that race could be used in a narrowly tailored admissions program designed to achieve a diverse student body.

180. "Diversity in Medical Schools on Decline," *San Diego Union-Tribune*, August, 23, 2002, A7. Much of this information can be found in governmental sources pulled together by the editors of the *JBHE:* see Theodore Cross and Robert Bruce Slater, "How Bans on Race-Sensitive Admissions Severely Cut Black Enrollments at Flagship State Universities," ibid., 38 (Winter 2002–3): 93; "The California Ban on Affirmative Action Is Causing Severe Damage to Black Opportunities in the Nation's Largest System of Higher Education," ibid., www.jbhe.com/latest/35_california_ban.html (June 19, 2002); "The Academics Who Are Screening Racial Quotas Need to Recheck Their Arithmetic," ibid. 35 (Spring 2002): 72; "Look What Happens When Affirmative Action Is Banned: Black Students Are Pushed Down into Second- and Third-Tier Institutions of Higher Education," ibid. 34 (Winter 2001–2): 82–94; "The Progress of Black Students Matriculations at the Nation's Highest-Ranked Colleges and Universities," ibid. 29 (Autumn 2000): 17. See also Andrea Guerrero, *Silence at Boalt Hall: The Dismantling of Affirmative Action* (Berkeley: University of California Press, 2002). See, generally, Daniel Koretz, Michael Russell, Chingwei David Shin, Cathy Horn, and Kelly Shasby, "Testing and Diversity in Postsecondary Education: The Case of California," in *Education Policy Analysis Archives,* vol. 10, ed. Gene V. Glass (January 7, 2000), epaa.asu.edu/epaa/v10n1 (available June 10, 2002).

181. For a more detailed discussion, see Roy L. Brooks, Gilbert Paul Carrasco, and Michael Selmi, *Civil Rights Litigation: Cases and Perspectives,* 2d ed. (Durham, N.C.: Carolina Academic Press, 2000), 498–99 (sources cited therein).

182. See www.ucop.edu/acadadv/datamgmt/lawmed/law-enrolls-eth2.html. See also Andrea Guerrero, *Silence at Boalt Hall: The Dismantling of Affirmative Action* (Berkeley: University of California Press, 2002), 110, 172, table 9.

183. The Twenty-fourth Amendment, ratified on January 23, 1964, abolished the poll tax, which required voters to pay a tax before they could vote. When the poll tax began to appear in the South after Reconstruction, it often had a "grandfather" provision that exempted a voter from paying the tax if his grandfather had had the right to vote. This facially neutral provision worked an additional dis-

crimination on blacks throughout the years, because blacks were not permitted to vote during slavery. For further discussion of the "freeze" theory, see Brooks, Carrrasco, and Selmi, *Civil Rights Litigation*, 573–81 (discussing cases). See also the "poker game" story at the beginning of this chapter.

184. See Roy L. Brooks, "The Affirmative Action Issue: Law, Policy, and Morality," *Connecticut Law Review* 22 (1990): 323, 360–61.

185. See Thernstrom and Thernstrom, *America in Black and White*, 401–2.

186. See William G. Bowen and Derek Bok, *The Shape of the River: Long-Term Consequences of Considering Race in College and University Admissions* (Princeton, N.J.: Princeton University Press, 1998).

187. Ibid., 61.

188. Ibid., 18–23, 56, 58, 68, 77–85, 93–94, 99–100, 112–14, 157, 160–62, 167–68, 186–87, 191; "Perpetuating the Falsehood That Affirmative Action Students Will Have a Lower Dropout Rate If They Attend Less Selective Colleges," *JBHE* 36 (Summer 2002): 50; "The Soft Bigotry of Low Expectations: Self-Esteem and the SAT," ibid., 29 (Autumn 2000): 104. "Diversity in Medical Schools on Decline," *San Diego Union-Tribune*, August, 23, 2002, A7. The average grade point average of blacks at elite schools in the Bowen and Bok study, which is an older study, is lower than the average grade point average for whites (2.16 versus 3.15). Bowen and Bok, *Shape of the River,* 72.

189. For a discussion, see, e.g., Jess Bravin, "Law School Admission Council Aims to Quash Overreliance on LSAT," *Wall Street Journal,* March 29, 2001, B1.

190. See Thernstrom and Thernstrom, *America in Black and White*, 395, 406; "The Worsening of the Racial Gap in SAT Scores," *JBHE* 33 (Autumn 2001): 22–23; David Grissmer, Ann Flanagan, and Stephanie Williamson, "Why Did the Black-White Score Gap Narrow in the 1970s and 1980s?" in *The Black-White Test Score Gap*, ed. Christopher Jencks and Meredith Phillips (Washington, D.C.: Brookings Institution Press, 1998), 182–226; Christopher Jencks and Meredith Phillips, "The Black-White Test Gap: An Introduction," in ibid., 1–8.

191. Jencks and Phillips, "Black-White Test Gap: An Introduction," 13. See also Christopher Jencks, "Racial Bias in Testing," in *Black-White Test Score Gap,* ed. id. and Phillips, 66–69.

192. Jencks and Phillips, "Black-White Test Gap: An Introduction," 14. See also Jencks, "Racial Bias in Testing," 69–71.

193. Jencks and Phillips, "The Black-White Test Gap: An Introduction," 14 (emphasis in original). See also Jencks, "Racial Bias in Testing," 71–73.

194. Jencks, "Racial Bias in Testing," 65.

195. Claude Steele, "Understanding the Performance Gap," in *Who's Quantified,* ed. Lani Guinier and Susan Sturm (Boston: Beacon Press, 2001), 64.

196. Eric Hoover, "College Board Approves Major Changes for the SAT," *Chronicle of Higher Education,* June 28, 2002.

197. On de facto segregated schools, see Brooks, *Integration or Separation?* 24–28 (sources cited therein). Racial segregation in schools is on the rise. See "Weekly Bulletin," *JBHE,* February 1, 2003, www.jbhe.com (discussing report from the Civil Rights Project at Harvard University).

198. See Richard Herrnstein and Charles Murray, *The Bell Curve: Intelligence and Class Structure in American Life* (New York: Free Press, 1994).

199. See, e.g., Richard E. Nisbett, "Race, Genetics, and IQ," in *Black-White Test Score Gap,* ed. Jencks and Phillips, 89.

200. Both studies are reported in "The Worsening of the Racial Gap in SAT Scores," *JBHE* 33 (Autumn 2001): 22–16.

201. *Grutter v. Bollinger,* citing Erica Frankenberg, Chungmei Lee, and Gary Orfield, *A Multiracial Society with Segregated Schools: Are We Losing the Dream?* (Cambridge, Mass.: The Civil Rights Project, Harvard University, 2003), 4, 11, www.civilrightsproject.harvard.edu/research/reseg03/AreWeLosingtheDream .pdf (as visited June 16, 2003, and available in Clerk of Court's case file); Brief for National Urban League et al. as *Amici Curiae* 11–12, citing General Accounting Office, *Per-Pupil Spending Differences between Selected Inner City and Suburban Schools Varied by Metropolitan Area* (Washington, D.C.: Government Printing Office, 2002), 17; Peter D. Hart and Robert M. Teeter, "A National Priority: Americans Speak on Teacher Quality" (June 2002), 2, 11 (public opinion research conducted for Educational Testing Service); The No Child Left Behind Act of 2001, Pub. L. 107–110, 115 Stat. 1425, 20 U.S.C. A. § 7231 (2003 Supp. Pamphlet).

202. Brooks, *Integration or Separation?* 5–6.

203. Meredith Phillips et al. "Family Background, Parenting Practices, and the Black-White Test Score Gap," in *Black-White Test Score Gap,* ed. Jencks and Phillips, 138.

204. Ibid. See also Bowen and Bok, *Shape of the River,* 80; Wayne J. Camara and Amy Elizabeth Schmidt, *Group Differences in Standardized Testing and Social Stratification* (New York: College Entrance Examination Board, 1999), 1, 4–13.

205. John U. Ogbu, *Black American Students in an Affluent Suburb: A Study of Academic Disengagement* (Mahwah, N.J.: Lawrence Erlbaum Associates, 2003).

206. See ibid.

207. I know of two poor white families, one a female-headed household, who have done nothing but make a pest of themselves at their children's schools, and who have hounded me for information and opportunities for their children. Their children attended Harvard, Berkeley, and NYU.

208. "The Test Score Gap," PBS, *Frontline,* www.pbs.org/wgbh/pages/frontline/

shows/sats/ (available June 14, 2002) (emphasis added). See also Phillips et al., "Family Background, Parenting Practices, and the Black-White Test Score Gap," 103–45.

209. Ogbu unfortunately does not indicate whether this factor was present in his study *Black American Students in an Affluent Suburb.*

210. For a discussion of the racial problems middle-class blacks face, see, e.g., Joe R. Feagin and Melvin P. Sikes, *Living with Racism: The Black Middle-Class Experience* (Boston: Beacon Press, 1994); Ellis Cose, *The Race of a Privileged Class: Why Are Middle-Class Blacks Angry? Why Should America Care?* (New York: HarperCollins Publishers, 1993).

211. See, e.g., Claude Steele, "Understanding the Performance Gap," in *Who's Quantified,* 60–67; id., "A Threat in the Air: How Stereotypes Shape Intellectual Identity and Performance," in *Promise and Dilemma: Perspectives on Racial Diversity and Higher Education,* ed. Eugene Y. Lowe Jr. (Princeton, N.J.: Princeton University Press, 1999), 92–123; Jennifer Crocker, Brenda Major, and Claude Steele, "Social Stigma," in *The Handbook of Social Psychology* (New York: McGraw-Hill, 1998), 2: 504–38.

212. "The Soft Bigotry of Low Expectations: Self-Esteem and the SAT," *JBHE* 29 (Autumn 2000): 104. See also Toni Schmader, Brenda Major, and Richard H. Gramzow, "How African-American College Students Protect Their Self-Esteem," *JBHE* 35 (Spring 2002): 116–19. Excerpted from "Coping with Ethnic Stereotypes in the Academic Domain: Perceived Injustice and Psychological Disengagement," *Journal of Social Issues* 57, no. 1 (Spring 2001): 93–111.

213. Steele, "Understanding the Performance Gap," 62.

214. This controversy is played out on the pages of *Psychological Bulletin.* Several articles on both sides of the issue are presented in the May 2002 issue (128, no. 3).

215. See U.S. Bureau of Census, *Educational Attainment in the United States (Update): March 2000,* Current Population Reports, P20–536 (Washington, D.C.: Government Printing Office, 2000), 4, 7. U.S. Department of Education, *Youth Indicators, 1996,* 70.

216. See "Perpetuating a Falsehood: Affirmative Action and the Black Student Dropout Rate," *JBHE* 35 (Spring 2002): 10; Wilds, *Minorities in Higher Education,* 76, table 3.

217. See U.S. Department of Education, National Center for Education Statistics, *Descriptive Summary of 1995–96 Beginning Postsecondary Students: Six Years Later,* NCES 2003–151, by Lutz Berkner, Shirley He, and Emily Forrest Cataldi, Project Officer: Paula Knepper (Washington, D.C.: Government Printing Office, December 2002), table B; "Special Report: African-American College Graduation Rates: Intolerably Low, and Not Catching Up to Whites," *JBHE* 37 (Autumn 2002): 89; Theodore Cross, "The Thernstrom Fallacy: Why Affirmative Action

Is Not Responsible for High Dropout Rates of African-American Students," *JBHE* 20 (Summer 1998): 91. For historical analyses, see, e.g., Mel Elfin and Sarah Burke, "Race on Campus," *U.S. News & World Report,* April 19, 1993, 55; "Vital Signs: The Statistics That Describe the Present and Suggest the Future of African Americans in Higher Education," *JBHE* 3 (Spring 1994): 43. See U.S. Department of Education, National Center for Education Statistics, *Persistence and Attainment in Postsecondary Education for Beginning AY 1980–90 Studies as of Spring 1992,* NCES 94–477 (Washington, D.C.: Office of Educational Research and Improvement, November 1993).

218. Thernstrom and Thernstrom, *America in Black and White,* 395, 406.

219. See Cross, "Thernstrom Fallacy," 91–96.

220. Brooks, *Rethinking the American Race Problem,* 99. See Slater, "Growing Gender Gap," 57; U.S. Department of Education, National Center for Education Statistics, *Descriptive Summary of 1995–96 Beginning Postsecondary Students,* 9.

221. Cross, "Thernstrom Fallacy," 96 (emphasis deleted).

222. For a discussion of the Federal Reserve report, see "Widening Racial Wealth Gap Is a Serious Barrier to Higher Education," *JBHE* 39 (Spring 2003): 48–49. See also Melvin L. Oliver and Thomas M. Shapiro, *Black Wealth/White Wealth: A New Perspective on Racial Inequality* (New York: Routledge, 1996).

223. Dalton Conley, "The Cost of Slavery," *New York Times,* February 15, 2003 (www.nytimes.com).

224. Gerry Braun, "The Gospel According to George: Molded by His Childhood and a Preacher's Worldview, This Circumspect Activist Leaves a Singular Legacy," *San Diego Union-Tribune,* December 24, 2000, E1.

225. Ibid.

226. Ibid.

227. "The Sudden Decline in the Nationwide Number of Black Faculty," *JBHE* 35 (Spring 2002): 12–13. See, e.g., Martin Anderson, "Why the Shortage of Black Professors?" ibid. 1 (Autumn 1993): 26.

228. See, e.g., Walter R. Allen, "College in Black and White: Black Student Experiences on Black and White Campuses," in *In Pursuit of Equality in Higher Education,* ed. Eileen Ostermann (Dix Hills, N.Y.: General Hall, 1987), 135–37.

229. Nathan McCall, *Makes Me Wanna Holler: A Young Black Man in America* (New York: Random House, 1994), 290.

230. Joe R. Feagin, *The Continuing Significance of Racism: U.S. Colleges and Universities* (Washington, D.C.: American Council on Education, 2002), 24.

231. Ibid., quoting a former Stanford professor.

232. Ibid., quoting a black respondent to a national study.

233. David Glenn, "Scholars Present Data in Hopes of Bolstering Legal Defense of Affirmative Action," *Chronicle of Higher Education,* August 20, 2002, 1.

234. See Roy L. Brooks, "Life after Tenure: Can Minority Law Professors Avoid the Clyde Ferguson Syndrome," *University of San Francisco Law Review* 20 (1986): 419, 420–22.

235. See Haynes Johnson, "Racism Still Smolders on Campus," *USA Today,* May 10, 1988; Dinesh D'Souza, *Illiberal Education: The Politics of Race and Sex on Campus* (New York: Vintage Books, 1992), 125.

236. See Elfin, "Race on Campus," 53.

237. These incidents are collected in every issue of the *JBHE* from the summer of 2000 to the spring of 2002; see also Anthony R. DeAugelli and Scott L. Heisberger, "African American Undergraduates on a Predominantly White Campus: Academic Factors, Social Networks, and Campus Climate," *Journal of Negro Education* 62 (Winter 1993): 67, 75–78.

238. "Weekly Bulletin," *JBHE,* February 1, 2003 (www.jbha.com, available February 1, 2003).

239. Michele Collison, "For Many Freshmen, Orientation Now Includes Efforts to Promote Racial Understanding," *Chronicle of Higher Education,* September 7, 1988, A29.

240. Alvin P. Sanoff and Scott Minerbrook, "Students Talk About Race," *U.S. News & World Report,* April 19, 1993, 57; Ken Emerson, "Only Correct," *New Republic,* February 18, 1991, 18; Jeff Rosen, "Hate Mail," ibid., 19; Elfin, "Race on Campus," 53. Each issue of the *JBHE* contains a record of the most recent racial incidents on college campus.

241. Ibid., 58, 64.

242. Thomas Sowell, *Inside American Education: The Decline, the Deception, the Dogmas* (New York: Free Press, 1993), 133.

243. James Earl Davis, "College in Black and White: Campus Environment and Academic Achievement of African American Males," *Journal of Negro Education* 63 (Autumn 1994): 620, 622.

244. Ibid., 120, 121.

245. Racial differentials alone may not constitute a race problem, but they do, at the very least, raise a rebuttable presumption that one exists. As the Supreme Court has said, "absent explanation, it is ordinarily to be expected that nondiscriminatory hiring practices will in time result in a work force more or less representative of the racial and ethnic composition of the population in the community from which employees are hired." *Teamsters v. United States,* 431 U.S. 324, 339 n. 20 (1977). Hence, it is conceivable that some racial differentials, some capital deficiencies, are the product of merit rather than racial harms. Under this view, merit-produced racial differentials would be acceptable.

This leads to perhaps a most difficult question: can we as a society live with permanent racial differentials, even if merit-based? Can we tolerate racial stratification—images of Jim Crow—in higher education, in jobs, in housing, in health care, in the administration of justice, and so on? Thankfully, we are not presented with such a situation today. For, as I have attempted to demonstrate in this chapter, significant racial differentials are primarily produced by racial harms. We are faced with a race problem, pure and simple, one that requires the ministrations of the central government.

4. THE TORT MODEL

1. See, e.g., Robinson, *Debt*; Posner and Vermeule, "Reparations," 689; Robert Westley, "Many Billions Gone: Is It Time to Reconsider the Case for Black Reparations?" *Boston College Law Review* 40 (1998): 429; Vicene Verdum, "If the Shoe Fits, Wear It: An Analysis of Reparations to African Americans," *Tulane Law Review* 67 (1993): 597; Charles Krauthammer, "Reparations for Black Americans," *Time,* December 31, 1990, 18. Although Posner and Vermeule attempt to raise moral questions beyond the realm of litigation, they miss many of the important conceptualizations worked out in chapter 5 and in such works as *Politics and the Past: On Repairing Historical Injustices,* ed. John Torpey (Lanham, Md.: Rowman & Littlefield, 2003); Elazar Barkan, *The Guilt of Nations: Restitution and Negotiating Historical Injustices* (New York: Norton, 2000); and Mark Gibney and Erik Roxstrom, "The Status of State Apologies," *Human Rights Quarterly* 23 (2001): 911.

2. A legislative illustration of the tort model can be found in the Rosewood Compensation Act of 1994, discussed in chapter 1. Like all expressions of the tort model, this legislation emphasizes victim compensation.

3. For a more detailed discussion, see "Deficiencies of Tort Model" at the end of this chapter.

4. See Krauthammer, "Reparations for Black Americans," 18.

5. Corporations as well as individuals held slaves. Several "private actions" discussed later in this chapter are being brought against some of these corporations.

6. See, e.g., *In re Nazi Era Cases against German Defendants Litigation,* 198 F.R.D. 429 (D.N.J., 2000); *Princz v. Federal Republic of Germany,* 26 F.3d 1166 (D.C. Cir. 1994); *Burger-Fischer v. Degussa AG,* 65 F. Supp. 2d 248 (D.N.J. 1999); *Iwanowa v. Ford Motor Co.,* 67 F. Supp. 2d 424 (D.C.N.J. 1999); *Fishel v. BASF Group,* 175 F.R.D. 525 (S.D. Iowa, 1997); *In re World War II Era Japanese Forced Labor Litigation,* 164 F. Supp. 2d 1160 (N.D. Cal. 2001); *Joo v. Japan,* 172 F. Supp. 2d 52 (D.D.C. 2001).

7. *Marta v. Nepa,* 385 A.2d 727, 730 (Del. 1978).

8. *United States v. Snider,* 779 F.2d 1151, 1159 (6th Cir. 1985); *Tustin Elevator & Lumber Co. v. Ryno,* 373 Mich. 322, 129 N.W. 2d 409, 414 (Mich. 1964). Most jurisdictions require that circumstances must show that "the recipient of the benefit

[was put] on notice that she (plaintiff) expected to be paid for her services." *Bellanca Corp. v. Bellanca,* 53 Del. 378, 169 A.2d 620, 623 (Del. 1961); *Iwanowa v. Ford Motor Co.,* at 471.

9. "Restitution of Implied Contracts," *American Jurisprudence,* 2d ed., vol. 66 (St. Paul, Minn.: West, 1973), 945. See, e.g., *Iwanowa v. Ford Motor Co.,* at 471 (cases cited therein).

10. *Iwanowa v. Ford Motor Co.,* at 471. See, e.g., *Cantor Fitzgerald v. Cantor,* 724 A.2d 571, 585 (Del. Ch. 1998) (adopting the limited rule); *Dumas v. Auto Club Ins. Ass'n,* 437 Mich. 521, 473 N.W.2d 652, 663 (Mich. 1991) (adopting the liberal rule).

11. "The American Law Institute notes in its proposed draft of the Restatement Third, Restitution that the term 'unjust enrichment' is a term of art, and that the substantive part of the law of restitution is concerned with identifying those forms of enrichment that the law treats as 'unjust' for the purpose of imposing liability. . . . [T]he term ['unjust enrichment'] refers to . . . enrichment that lacks an adequate legal basis." *American Jurisprudence,* § 9.

12. See, e.g., *Fleer Corp. v. Topps Chewing Gum, Inc.,* 539 A.2d 1060, 1063 (Del. 1988).

13. *Black's Law Dictionary,* ed. William S. Anderson, 3d ed. (San Francisco: Bancroft-Whitney, 1969), 1320.

14. *Kammer Asphalt Paving Co., Inc. v. East China Township Schools,* 443 Mich. 176, 504 N.W. 2d 635, 640 (Mich. 1993).

15. Feagin, *Racist America,* p.18.

16. Patricia J. Williams, *The Alchemy of Race and Rights* (Cambridge, Mass.: Harvard University Press, 1991), 101.

17. Feagin, *Racist America,* 18 (sources cited therein).

18. *In re World War II Era Japanese Forced Labor Litigation* (2001), at 1182.

19. Ibid.

20. *Marbury v. Madison,* 5 U.S. (1 Cranch) 137, 169, 2 L.Ed. 60 (1803).

21. California Code of Civil Procedure § 354.6(b).

22. *In re World War II Era Japanese Forced Labor Litigation* (2001), at 1168.

23. *In re World War II Era Japanese Forced Labor Litigation,* 114 F. Supp. 2d 939, 942 (N.D. Cal. 2000).

24. See *In re World War II Era Japanese Forced Labor Litigation* (2001), at 1163–68.

25. See *Taiheiyo Cement Corporation v. Superior Court,* 129 Cal Rptr. 2d 451 (Cal. Ct. App. 2003) (holding that § 354.6 did not violate the political question doctrine and was not preempted by the peace treaty, because Korea was not a signatory and plaintiff is Korean).

26. Alien Torts Claims Act, 28 U.S.C. § 1350.

27. *Kadic v. Karadzic,* 70 F.3d 232, 236 (2d Cir. 1995).

28. 28 U.S.C. § 1350 nn. The Torture Victim Protection Act was enacted in 1991 as a statutory note to the Alien Torts Claims Act.

29. See *In re World War II Era Japanese Forced Labor Litigation* (2001), at 1179–82.

30. Ibid., 1178.

31. Ibid. (cases cited therein); *Iwanowa v. Ford Motor Co.,* at 439 (cases cited therein).

32. Ibid., 440, (citing Robert Jackson, the Nuremberg prosecutor, in his final report to President Truman).

33. See, e.g., Max du Plessis, "Reparations and International Law: How Are Reparations to Be Determined (Past Wrongs or Current Effects), Against Whom, and What Form Should They Take?" (paper delivered at 2003 CLEA Conference on "Reparations: Theory, Practice and Legal Education," held at University of Windsor Faculty of Law, Windsor, Ontario, Canada, June 12–14, 2003), 10–11 and n. 15.

34. Ibid., 26 n. 19.

35. Ibid., 5, quoting Article 13.

36. Ibid., 6, quoting sources.

37. Genocide was only outlawed in international law after World War II. The Nazis war criminals were not convicted of genocide during the Nuremberg trials. They were convicted of committing "crimes against humanity," a generic *jus cogens* concept, which incorporates genocide after World War II. See ibid., 27 n. 21 (courses cited).

38. See Foreign Sovereign Immunity Act of 1976, 28 U.S.C. §§ 1605–7. See also *Argentine Republic v. Amerado Hess Shipping,* 488 U.S. 428 (1989).

39. *Princz v. Federal Republic of Germany,* 26 F.3d 1166 (D.C.C. 1994).

40. Ibid., 1168.

41. *In re Nazi Era Cases against German Defendants Litigation,* 431 n. 4 (citing UN sources).

42. *Princz v. Federal Republic of Germany* (1994), at 1168.

43. Ibid.

44. *Princz v. Federal Republic of Germany,* 813 F. Supp. 22, 26 (D.D.C. 1992).

45. *Princz v. Federal Republic of Germany* (1994), at 1169, 1176. Federal diversity jurisdiction is provided for on a number bases in 28 U.S.C. § 1332.

46. See ibid., 432–33 (citing Foundation Law and several court filings, including statement of Secretary of State Madeleine K. Albright and declaration of Stuart E. Eizenstat, the Clinton administration's deputy secretary of the treasury and special representative of the president and the undersecretary of state on Holocaust issues).

47. Forced labor claims brought under the Alien Tort Claims Act are, for

example, subject to a ten-year limitation period borrowed from the Torture Victim Protection Act. See *In re World War II Era Japanese Forced Labor Litigation* (2001), at 1180.

48. California Insurance Code §§ 13800–13807.

49. See *American Insurance Association v. Garamendi,* 123 S. Ct. 2374 (2003).

50. For a captivating account of these negotiations, see Stuart E. Eizenstat, *Imperfect Justice: Looted Assets, Slave Labor, and the Unfinished Business of World War II* (New York: Public Affairs, 2003).

51. For a summary of the negotiations leading up to the German Foundation Law, see Appendix 2.

52. President, Proclamation, Executive Order 9102, *Federal Register* 7, no. 2165 (March 20, 1942). President, Proclamation, Executive Order 9066, *Federal Register* 7, no. 1407 (February 25, 1942).

53. *Hohri v. United States,* 586 F. Supp. 769, 775 (D.D.C. 1984).

54. Ibid., 776–77, quoting DeWitt report.

55. See, e.g., Morton Grodzins, *Americans Betrayed: Politics and the Japanese Evacuation* (Chicago: University of Chicago Press, 1949), 291.

56. *Hohri v. United States,* 586 F. Supp., at 778 (sources cited therein).

57. Ibid. (sources cited therein).

58. For a collection of these lawsuits, see ibid., 779 n. 12.

59. *Hirabayashi v. United States,* 320 U.S. 81 (1943).

60. *Yasui v. United States,* 320 U.S. 115 (1943).

61. *Korematu v. United States,* 323 U.S. 214 (1944).

62. Evacuation Claims Act of 1948, 50 App. U.S.C. § 1981.

63. *Race, Rights and Reparation,* ed. Yamamoto et al., 427.

64. *Hohri v. United States,* 847 F.2d 779 (Fed. Cir. 1988) (*per curiam* opinion), affirming 586 F. Supp. 769 (D.D.C. 1984) (holding appellants' claims were barred by statute of limitations and sovereign immunity); *United States v. Hohri,* 482 U.S. 64 (1987) (holding that Federal Circuit rather than the appropriate region court of appeals has jurisdiction in this case); *Hohri v. United States,* 793 F.2d 304 (D.C. Cir. 1986) (*per curiam* opinion) (request for rehearing *en banc* denied).

65. See Federal Rule of Civil Procedure 60(b) abolishing various common law writs. See also *United States v. Morgan,* 346 U.S. 502 (1954).

66. For an excellent discussion of the *curam nobis* litigation, see Peter Irons, *Justice at War: The Story of the Japanese Internment Cases* (1983; Berkeley: University of California Press, 1993); and id., ed., *Justice Delayed: The Record of the Japanese American Internment Cases,* ed. Peter Irons (Middletown, Conn.: Wesleyan University Press, 1989).

67. Leon Friedman, "Introduction," in *Southern Justice,* ed. id. (New York: Pantheon Books, 1965), 7.

68. Ibid., 7–8. Articles in the volume include "A Busy Spring in the Magnolia State," "Municipal Ordinances, Mississippi Style," "Sociology and the Law: A Field Trip to Montgomery, Alabama," "Louisiana Underlaw," "The Case of the Disappearing Docket," "Clarksdale Customs," "Clinton, Louisiana," "The Abdication of the Southern Bar," "Southern Appellate Courts: A Dead End," and "Segregated Justice."

69. Ibid., 8–9. See also Ramsey Clark, *Crime in America: Observations on Its Nature, Causes, Prevention and Control* (New York: Simon & Schuster, 1970); Victor S. Navasky, *Kennedy Justice* (New York: Atheneum, 1971); Jack Bass, *Unlikely Heroes: The Dramatic Story of the Southern Judges of the Fifth Circuit Who Translated the Supreme Court's* Brown *Decision into a Revolution for Equality* (New York: Simon & Schuster, 1981).

70. *Race, Rights and Reparation,* ed. Yamamoto et al., 319. See *Hirabayashi v. United States,* 828 F.2d 591 (9th Cir. 1987).

71. Judge Belloni's order is reprinted in *Race, Rights and Reparations,* ed. Yamamoto et al., 318.

72. See n. 64 above.

73. *Hohri v. United States,* 586 F. Supp., at 786, quoting 28 U.S.C. § 2401(a) and citing cases.

74. Ibid., 791.

75. See Federal Tort Claims Act, 28 U.S.C. §§ 1346(b), 2401(b), 2671–80.

76. See *Hohri v. United States,* 586 F. Supp., at 791–94, citing 28 U.S.C. § 2401(b).

77. See *United States v. Hohri,* 482 U.S. 64 (1987); *Hohri v. United States,* 793 F.2d 304 (D.C. Cir. 1986).

78. Jurisdiction arises under the "Little Tucker Act," 28 U.S.C. § 1346(a)(2).

79. *Hohri v. United States,* 847 F.2d 779 (Fed. Cir. 1988).

80. See Civil Liberties Act of 1988, 50 U.S.C. Appx. § 1989b.

81. For a thorough discussion, see *When Sorry Isn't Enough,* ed. Brooks, 171–200.

82. *Pigford v. Glickman,* 182 F.R.D. 341 (D.D.C. 1998), consent decree approved and entered, 185 F.R.D. 82 (1999), reversing district court's order, inter alia, extending filing deadlines under consent decree, 292 F.3d 918 (D.C. Cir. 2002).

83. See *Pigford v. Glickman,* 185 F.R.D., at 104.

84. *Johnson v. MacAdoo,* 45 U.S. App. D.C. 440 (1917).

85. *Berry v. United States,* 1994 WL 374537 (N.D. Cal.). The official federal supplement citation is not available.

86. Ibid., at 1, citing § 4 of the act of March 3, 1865, ch. 90, 13 Stat. 507.

87. See "Special Field Order No. 15," reprinted in *When Sorry Isn't Enough,* ed. Brooks, 365–66.

88. See discussion of the Good Faith Purchaser Doctrine later in this chapter.

89. See Greg Steinmetz, "One Family's Battle for Ancestral Land Poses Hard Questions," *Wall Street Journal,* November 11, 1996, A1. The more usual remedy is not specific performance but damages. See Neal E. Boudette, "Seeking Reparation: A Holocaust Claim Cuts to the Heart of the New Germany," ibid., March 29, 2002, A1. The traditional maxim in American law is that specific performance is an "extraordinary" remedy and thus will only be awarded when no money damages are adequate. See, e.g., Abraham Chayes, "The Role of the Judge in Public Law Litigation," *Harvard Law Review* 89 (1976): 1281, 1282–1302.

90. See Warren Freedman, "The Restitution of Land Rights in South Africa" (paper delivered at 2003 CLEA Conference on "Reparations: Theory, Practice and Legal Education," held at University of Windsor Faculty of Law, Windsor, Ontario, Canada, June 12–14, 2003).

91. For example, in March 2002, Secretary of the Interior Gale Norton stated the federal government's willingness to return 692,000 acres of public land to the Klamath Tribes of Oregon: "Klamath Tribes have property rights that must be honored. . . ." "Klamath Tribes May Get Land Back," *San Diego Union-Tribune,* March 20, 2002, A6.

92. 28 U.S.C. §§ 1346(a)(2), 1491(a)(2).

93. *Berry v. United States,* at 2, quoting 28 U.S.C. § 1346(a)(2).

94. Ibid., 2–3.

95. Ibid., 3, citing 28 U.S.C. § 2401(a).

96. Quiet Title Act, 28 U.S.C. § 2409a.

97. Tucker Act, 28 U.S.C. § 1346(f).

98. See Quiet Title Act, 28 U.S.C. §§ 2409a(a) (exempting Tucker Act claims).

99. Ibid., § 2409a(f).

100. *Berry v. United States,* at 3.

101. Ibid.

102. See the "Gold Train" case, *Rosner v. United States,* 231 F. Supp. 2d 1202 (S.D. Fla. 2002) (tolling the statute of limitations on these grounds in a class action brought by Hungarian Jews against the United States to recover personal property stolen by pro-Nazi Hungarian government during World War II and subsequently seized and sold by the United States).

103. *Berry v. United States,* at 2–3 (cases cited therein).

104. See *Bivens v. Six Unknown Named Agents of the Federal Bureau of Narcotics,* 403 U.S. 388 (1971).

105. *Berry v. United States,* at 3 n. 4.

106. *Cato v. United States,* 70 F.3d 1103 (9th Cir. 1995).

107. Ibid., 1106.

108. Ibid., 1110.

109. Ibid., 1109.

110. See *Bolling v. Sharpe,* 347 U.S. 497 (1954), dealing with federal law mandating school segregation in Washington, D.C. For a discussion of the current historical perspective on the Constitution and the constitutional provisions that recognized the institution of slavery, see, e.g., Paul Finkelman, *Slavery and the Founders: Race and Liberty in the Age of Jefferson,* 2d ed. (Armonk, N.Y.: M. E. Sharpe, 2001), 3–36, and Berlin, "North of Slavery."

111. *Cato v. United States,* citing 28 U.S.C. §§ 1346(b) (FTCA) and 2401(b) (applicable statute of limitations).

112. Ibid., 1110–11.

113. Ibid., 1111, citing 5 U.S.C. § 702.

114. Ibid., 1105.

115. See *Bell v. United States,* 2001 U.S. Dist. LEXIS 14812 (N.D. Tex. 2001) *(pro se* complaint of incarcerated plaintiff seeking reparations dismissed pursuant to *Cato v. United States)*; *Obadele v. United States,* 52 Fed. Cl. 432 (2002) (black plaintiffs not entitled to relief under Civil Liberties Act, which applies to Japanese-American internees).

116. This case has a number of opinions reported at: 182 F.R.D. 341 (D.D.C. 1998) (class certification granted); 185 F.R.D. 82 (D.D.C. 1999) (consent decree approved and entered). Other cases dealing with post-consent decree issues, primarily the misconduct of class counsel "bordering on legal malpractice" to meet critical consent decree deadlines, are reported under the title *Pigford v. Veneman* at 143 F. Supp. 2d 28 (D.D.C. 2001) (imposing fines on class counsel); 148 F. Supp. 2d 31 (D.D.C. 2001) (questioning class counsel's fidelity to their clients); 182 F. Supp. 2d 50 (D.D.C. 2002) (granting pro bono counsel's "motion to endow," giving arbitrary discretion to extend deadlines established under original consent decree "so long as justice requires") reversed and remanded 292 F.3d 918 (D.C.Cir. 2002). The named defendants in these actions, Dan Glickman and Ann Veneman, held the office of secretary of agriculture under Presidents Clinton and George W. Bush, respectively.

117. Equal Credit Opportunity Act, 15 U.S.C. § 1691.

118. See *Pigford v. Glickman,* 185 F.R.D. at 86.

119. See Equal Credit Opportunity Act, e(f).

120. *Pigford v. Glickman,* 185 F.R.D. at 88.

121. Ibid., quoting the report.

122. *United States v. Sioux Nation of Indians,* 448 U.S. 371, 397–98 (1980).

123. See Agricultural, Rural Development, Food and Drug Administration, and Related Agencies Appropriations Act, 1999, Pub. L. No. 105–277, 122 Stat. 2681 (codified as 7 U.S.C. § 2297, nn.).

124. *Pigford v. Glickman,* 185 F.R.D. at 92.

125. See ibid., at 88, 89.

126. Ibid., 103–4.

127. *Alexander v. Governor of the State of Oklahoma,* Docket No. 03cv00133 (N.D. Okl.), filed February 24, 2003.

128. Under the terms of the court-approved settlement, farmers were given two options, known as Track A and Track B. Track A required the farmer to provide something more than a "mere scintilla" of proof that he applied for and been denied USDA credit assistance or other benefits between 1981 and 1996. The minimal standard of proof was in recognition of the fact that most class members "had little in the way of documentation or proof" of discriminatory treatment or damages. Track A awards were capped at $50,000 plus forgiveness of certain USDA loans. Although most of the farmers opted for Track A, as of July 2002, "just under 13,000 farmers have been approved for Track A payments, and about 8,500 have had their claims rejected." Allen G. Breed, "Black Farmers Still Fighting for Settlement 4 Years Ago: The Government Has Rejected 40% of the Claims," *Telegraph Herald* (Dubuque, Iowa), September 1, 2002, A7. Track B imposed no cap on damages, but required farmers, after limited discovery, to prove their claims (that they were treated differently from a "similarly situated" white farmer), by a preponderance of evidence in one-day mini-trials before an arbitrator. Track B imposes strict time frames for filing, processing, trying, and reviewing claims. As of July 2002, the USDA has settled fifty-eight Track B claims. Awards were given in thirty-five cases, of which thirty-one were appealed by the government. The highest amount paid to a Track B claimant was $780,000. The lowest amount was $7,500. Attorneys for the farmers estimate that as of July 2002, the government has paid out "more than $1 billion to Track A and B claimants, plus fees for lawyers and administrators and other costs." Ibid.

129. *Pigford v. Glickman,* 292 F.3d at 921.

130. Ibid., 921–23.

131. Ibid., 927.

132. Allen G. Breed, "Black Farmers Still Fighting for Settlement," *Telegraph Herald* (Dubuque, Iowa), September 1, 2002, A7. See Neely Tucker, "A Long Road of Broken Promises for Black Farmers; USDA Fights Claims after Landmark Deal," *Washington Post,* August 13, 2002, A10.

133. See, e.g., *Saylor v. Lindsley,* 456 F.2d 896 (2d Cir. 1972); Lester Brickman, *Anatomy of a Madison County (Illinois) Class Action: A Study of Pathology,* Civil Justice Report No. 6 (New York: Center for Legal Policy at the Manhattan Institute, 2002).

134. *Alexander v. Governor of the State of Oklahoma,* Docket No. 03cv00133 (N.D. Okl.), filed February 24, 2003.

135. See, e.g., Alfred Brophy, *Reconstructing the Dreamland: The Tulsa Riot of*

1921 (New York: Oxford University Press, 2002); Brooks, *Integration or Separation?* 270–73.

136. *Alexander v. Governor of the State of Oklahoma,* para. 192.

137. Civil Rights Act of April 20, 1871, 42 U.S.C. §1981

138. In particular, 28 U.S.C. §§ 1331, 1343, and 1367.

139. *Alexander v. Governor of the State of Oklahoma,* para. 147j.

140. See, e.g., *Farmer-Paellmann v. FleetBoston Financial Corporation, Aetna, Inc., CSX,* C.A. No. 1:02–1862 (E.D.N.Y., 2002); *In re African-American Slave Descendants Litigation,* 231 F. Supp. 2d 1357 (2002); *Hurdle v. Fleetboston Financial Corporation, et al.,* Case No. CGC-02–412388 (San Francisco Superior Court, 2002).

141. *Farmer-Paellmann v. FleetBoston Financial Corporation, Aetna, Inc., CSX,,* Complaint, paras. 25 and 26. Jury trial demanded.

142. *Hurdle v. FleetBoston Financial Corporation, et al.,* CGC-02–412388 (Superior Court, County of San Francisco, September 9, 2002).

143. See Federal Diversity Jurisdiction, 28 U.S.C. § 1332(a).

144. The best discussion I have seen of the status of slavery per se as a violation of customary international law as opposed to a violation of natural law, which at times was equated with the notion of *jus gentium* (or law of nations), is an unnamed student note. See "American Slavery and the Conflicts of Laws," *Columbia Law Review* 71 (1971): 74.

145. *Dred Scott v. Sanford,* 60 U.S. (19 How.) 393, 408 (1857).

146. A. E. Keir Nash, "A More Equitable Past? Southern Supreme Courts and the Protection of the Antebellum Negro," *North Carolina Law Review* 48 (1970): 197, 201.

147. See ibid. for a detailed discussion.

148. Ibid., 202.

149. Ibid., 208. The reference is to Justice Marshall's signature opinion in *Marbury v. Madison,* 1 Cranch 137, 2 L.Ed. 60 (1803), in which, through clever legal footwork, he discovers the doctrine of judicial review in the Constitution.

150. See *State v. Reed,* 9 N.C. (2 Hawks) 454 (1823).

151. Ibid., at 456. For a different reading of the opinion, see Nash, "A More Equitable Past?" 209.

152. See *State v. Hale,* 9 N.C (2 Hawks) 582 (1823).

153. See Anthony J. Sebok, "Prosaic Justice," *Legal Affairs,* September–October 2002, 51. See also id., "The Brooklyn Slavery Class Action: More Than Just a Political Gambit," www.writ.news.findlaw.com/sebok/20020409.html (available April 9, 2002).

154. *Moses v. MacFarlen,* 97 Eng. Rep. 676 (K.B. 1760).

155. Ibid., 681.

156. Hanoch Dagan, "The Law and Ethics of Restitution" (unpublished chapter, draft of December 30, 2002), 42.

157. Ibid., 41 (quoting Sebok).

158. See Brooks, "Age of Apology," in *When Sorry Isn't Enough,* ed. id., 6.

159. Dagan, "Law and Ethics of Restitution," 43.

160. Ibid., 43.

161. Ibid., 46 (sources cited).

162. Ibid., 48–49.

163. Ibid., 51.

164. Ibid., 47, 50.

165. See Sebok, "Prosaic Justice," 51. The new technology allegation is contained in many private-action complaints. See, e.g., Complaint in *Farmer-Paellmann v. FleetBoston Financial Corporation, Aetna, Inc., CSX,* at 45 and 46.

166. Dagan, "Law and Ethics of Restitution," 47 and n. 162. Dagan cites as a possible precedent in support of plaintiffs, *Bonder v. Banque Paribas,* 114 F. Supp. 2d 117, 134–35 (E.D.N.Y. 2000).

167. Carl A. Auerbach, "The Relation of Legal Systems to Social Change," *Wisconsin Law Review* 1980 (1980): 1227, 1227.

168. I am not opposed to the use of litigation as a backup to failed legislation. That is precisely what happened in *Alexander v. Governor of the State of Oklahoma,* a slave-redress case in which I personally participated.

169. For a more detailed discussion and for references to more sources, see Jay Tidmarsh and Roger H. Trangsrud, *Complex Litigation: Problems in Advanced Civil Procedure* (New York: Foundation Press, 2002), 3.

170. Apology in the context of litigation can be pursued through the revival of several ancient writs. For example, the Roman and Roman-Dutch civil law (called "common law" in Anglo-American law) remedy of *amende honorable* (which means a retraction or apology) could be invoked to redress an infringement of a person's dignity or reputation. Although it was declared abrogated by reason of disuse in 1910—see J. R. Midgley, "Retraction, Apology and Right of Reply," *Tydskrif vir Hedendaagse Romeins-Hollandse Reg* [THR-HR] 58 (1995): 288—this remedy could be revised under the new South African Constitution. See David McQuoid-Mason, "Invasion of Privacy: Common Law v. Constitutionalize Delict," *ACTA Juridica* 2000 (2000): 227, 234. South Africa has a civil law remedy for infringement of dignity under the Roman-Dutch law of *actio injuriarum.* Technically, this law provides a remedy for intentional invasions of personality rights. Should American courts decide to adopt these Dutch-Roman Law remedies, as I hope they do, I would not find that sufficient. The apologies that would arise under these ancient laws would necessarily be coercive and hence cannot produce the requisite remorse that is needed for racial reconciliation and

repair of the perpetrator's wounded moral character, more about which in the next chapter. I am extremely grateful, however, to David McQuoid-Mason of the Faculty of Law at the University of Natal in Durban, South Africa, for bringing these ancient remedies to my attention.

171. Watson Branch, "Reparations for Slavery: A Dream Deferred," *San Diego International Law Journal* 3 (2002): 177, 196 (citing sources).

172. Ibid.

173. Notwithstanding the doctrine of *res judicata,* which is supposed to prevent inconsistent judicial determinations of the same set of facts, inconsistency does occur. See, e.g., *State Farm Fire and Casualty Co. v. Century Home Components,* 275 Or. 97, 550 P. 2d 1185 (Or. 1976).

174. See relevant discussion in the Preface. See, generally, *When Sorry Isn't Enough,* ed. Brooks.

5. THE ATONEMENT MODEL

EPIGRAPH: Ronald Reagan, Remarks at the Site of the Future United States Holocaust Memorial Museum, October 5, 1988, www.library.ushmm.org/faqs .htm.

1. Ruti G. Teitel, *Transitional Justice* (New York: Oxford University Press, 2000), has a nice discussion of the forward-looking potential of reparations.

2. Gene C. Johnson Jr., "L.A.'s Slavery Ordinance Is All about 'Due Respect,'" *San Diego Voice & Viewpoint,* June 5, 2003, A1.

3. Brooks, "Age of Apology," in *When Sorry Isn't Enough,* ed. id., 7, quoting Article 55(c) of the UN Charter.

4. Willy Brandt, *My Life in Politics* (London: Hamish Hamilton, 1992), 200.

5. Ian Fisher, "At Site of Massacre, Polish Leader Asks Jews for Forgiveness," *New York Times,* July 11, 2001, A1 (emphasis added).

6. This is not to say, however, that timing is irrelevant. Obviously, the closer the apology to the atrocity the more virtuous it is, because the perpetrator is now in a position to do something immediately about the consequences of the atrocity instead of allowing these negative effects to linger on for generations, if not centuries. Also, in terms of political considerations, the close proximity of the atrocity in time and space plus the fact that victims are alive would probably make it easier to pitch the idea of apology to the perpetrator than if the atrocity is ancient and the victims are all dead. But one can also argue that, as a strictly moral matter, a tender of apology when memories of the atrocity have long faded is more virtuous because the perpetrator is under no external pressure to issue it and, hence, it serves no self-interest, other than the fact that it retires the perpetrator's moral duty. When, as in the case of slavery, the atrocity's lingering effects create tangible

disadvantage for an identifiable group in society, these additional external pressures may make it not only virtuous, but also necessary (or "affordable") for the government to act virtuously—that is, to do the right thing. This seems especially so if the disadvantaged group is able to exert substantial political pressure on the government either through electoral politics or acts of civil disobedience. Notwithstanding these considerations as to the most advantageous time in which to pitch apology, my fundamental point still holds—namely, the imposition of a statute of limitations on the moral duty to apologize is improperly legalistic.

7. See, e.g., George Hicks, "The Comfort Women Redress Movement," in *When Sorry Isn't Enough,* ed. Brooks, 113

8. Louis E. Newman, "The Quality of Mercy: On the Duty to Forgive in the Judaic Tradition," *Journal of Religious Ethics* 15 (Fall 1987): 155.

9. Roger Cohen, "Wiesel Urges Germany to Ask Forgiveness," *New York Times,* January 28, 2000, A3.

10. See Mark Gibney and Erik Roxstrom, "The Status of State Apologies," *Human Rights Quarterly* 23 (2001): 911, 931.

11. Wilhelm Verwoerd, "Justice after Apartheid? Reflections on the South African TRC," in *When Sorry Isn't Enough,* ed. Brooks, 479, 480–82.

12. Elazar Barkan, *The Guilt of Nations: Restitution and Negotiating Historical Injustices* (New York: Norton, 2000), xx n.

13. See, e.g., Jürgen Habermas, *Justification and Application: Remarks on Discourse Ethics,* trans. Ciaran Cronin (Cambridge: Polity Press, 1993).

14. Donald W. Shriver Jr., *An Ethic for Enemies: Forgiveness in Politics* (New York: Oxford University Press, 1995), 91.

15. Davis, *In the Image of God,* 168–69 (italics added). ·

16. David W. Blight, *Race and Reunion: The Civil War in American Memory* (Cambridge, Mass.: Harvard University Press, 2001).

17. Mark Alden Branch, "The Slavery Legacy," *Yale Alumni Magazine,* February 2002, 34 (quoting Davies).

18. Davis, *In the Image of God,* 168. See Ulrich Bonnell Phillips, *American Negro Slavery: A Survey of the Supply, Employment and Control of Negro Labor as Determined by the Plantation Régime.* (New York: D. Appleton, 1918).

19. Ibid., 167.

20. See ibid., 14 n. 12. See also ibid., 6–7, 166–68; Branch, "Slavery Legacy," 34–37.

21. Issacs D. Balbus, "The Psycho-Dynamics of Racial Reparations" (unpublished paper delivered at Conference on "Apologies: Mourning the Past and Ameliorating the Present," Claremont Graduate University, February 7–10, 2002), 2.

22. Ibid., 3.

23. Ibid., 41 n. 4 (citing works co-authored with Melanie Klein).

24. Williams, *Alchemy of Race and Rights,* 101.

25. John Torpey, "'Making Whole What Has Been Smashed': Reflections on Reparations," *Journal of Modern History* 73 (2001): 333, 351 (quoting Lukas Meyer, "Inheriting Public Goods and Public Evils" (MS, University of Bremen, June 1999, 15).

26. Ibid., quoting Tyler Cowen, "How Far Back Should We Go?" (MS, George Mason University, July 1999).

27. Michael Henderson, *Forgiveness: Breaking the Chain of Hate* (Wilsonville, Or.: Book Partners, 1999), 39.

28. Ibid., 33, 34.

29. Ibid., 25, quoting Sir William Deane, governor-general of Australia.

30. See Barkan, *Guilt of Nations.*

31. For a more detailed discussion of the international reparations movement, see, e.g., Priscilla B. Hayner, *Unspeakable Truths: Facing the Challenge of Truth Commissions* (New York: Routledge, 2002); Barkan, *Guilt of Nations;* Desmond Tutu, *No Future without Forgiveness* (New York: Doubleday, 1999); Martha Minow, *Between Vengeance and Forgiveness: Facing History after Genocide and Mass Violence* (Boston: Beacon Press, 1998); Watson Branch, "Reparations for Slavery: A Dream Deferred," *San Diego International Law Journal* 3 (2002): 177, 178–82. See, generally, *When Sorry Isn't Enough,* ed. Brooks. On other reparations movements in the United States, see also *Race, Rights and Reparation,* ed. Yamamoto et al., and Arnold Krammer, *Undue Process: The Untold Story of America's German Alien Internees* (Lanham, Md.: Rowman & Littlefield, 1997).

32. See Brooks, "Age of Apology," in *When Sorry Isn't Enough,* ed. id., 9.

33. In January 2002, for example, West Georgia College, which is a small college located in Georgia, apologized for rejecting every black applicant from the town's all-black high school in 1955 and 1956. To solidify that apology, the college established through an anonymous donor a scholarship fund for the descendants of the sixty or seventy students who were denied admissions some fifty years ago. See "Scholarship Is Apology for Bias," *San Diego Union-Tribune,* January 18, 2002, Nation Update, A20.

34. The Rosewood Compensation Act, for example, provided, inter alia, scholarship funds for minority students who were not direct descendants of the Rosewood families who suffered in the 1923 race riot. See Brooks, "Age of Apology," in *When Sorry Isn't Enough,* ed. id, 10.

35. In *Grutter v. Bollinger,* the Supreme Court upheld the University of Michigan Law School's race-based affirmative action program designed to achieve a diverse student body, saying: "We expect that 25 years from now, the use of racial preferences will no longer be necessary to further the interest approved today." Twenty-five years is a generation as well as the period of time in which the Court

last visited this particular affirmative-action question. See *Regents of Univ. of Cal. v. Bakke*, 438 U.S. 265 (1978).

36. For example, as Justice Harlan noted in *Plessy v. Ferguson*, which constitutionalized the separate-but-equal doctrine, or Jim Crow, an Asian "can ride in the same passenger coach with white citizens of the United States, while citizens of the black race . . . [cannot]." 163 U.S. 537, 560 (1896).

37. Census data for 2000 show 22 percent of blacks below the poverty line, compared to 21 percent of Hispanics, 10 percent of Asians/Pacific Islanders, and 9 percent of whites. The Hispanic poverty rate would be lower if it did not include undocumented workers who are typically unskilled and seek low-paying jobs. Median black family income for 2000 was $34,192, compared to $35,054 for Hispanics, $53,256 for whites, and $61,511 for Asians/Pacific Islanders. The latter figure is skewed by the fact that South Asian countries like India and Pakistan export mainly highly skilled workers. For example, none of India's 160 million "Untouchables," the lowest Hindu castes, emigrate to the United States. It is just the opposite with Hispanics—it is mainly the poor and unskilled coming across the U.S.-Mexican border. Hispanic income would be higher if it did not include undocumented workers. See U.S. Department of Commerce, Bureau of the Census, *Statistical Abstract of the United States: 2002*, 122d ed. (Washington, D.C.: Government Printing Office, 2002), 436 (table 658), 441 (table 668). Native Americans, of course, have the asset of sovereignty, which has brought what Native Americans refer to as the "new buffalo economy"—such as casinos and mining—to their lands. See Brooks, *Integration or Separation?* 251–52.

Some Asians would go so far as to say that they experience virtually no racism today. As Dinesh D'Souza declares, "I am constantly surprised by how much I hear racism talked about and how little I actually see it. (Even fewer are the incidents in which I have experienced it directly)." D'Souza, *What's So Great about America* (Washington, D.C.: Regnery, 2002), 118. Frank Wu suggests, however, that Asians experience more racism than the "model minority myth" would seem to suggest. He points, as an example, to a major study conducted in May 2001 of highly educated individuals in New York City, Los Angeles, and Chicago in which one-third of those responding believed that "Chinese Americans probably have too much influence in high technology and are more loyal to China than the United States." Wu, *Yellow: Race in America beyond Black and White* (New York: Basic Books, 2002), 12. In a 2003 report on the first-ever national study of housing discrimination against Asians conducted by the Department of Housing and Urban Development (HUD), Asian Americans renters experienced more housing discrimination than blacks and Latinos, and Asian American home buyers experienced about the same level of discrimination as Latinos but more than blacks. This information requires further study, however, because the forms of housing discrimination were not all the same. In the national home-buying study, for example, blacks were the victims of "steering"—being recommended and shown housing in predominantly minority neighborhoods—but Asians and Latinos were not. Generally, blacks experienced different and more forms of discrimination than either Asians or Latinos. See Department of Housing and Urban Development, "Discrimination in Metropolitan Housing Markets: National Results from Phase 1 and Phase 2 of the Housing Discrimination Study (HDS)," www.huduser.org/publications/hsgfin/hsgfin/hds.html (available July 2, 2003). What this may mean is that Chinese and other Asians are experiencing uneven assimilation into the nation's culture. See Iris Chang, *The Chinese in America: A Narrative History* (New York: Viking Press, 2003).

38. See Feagin, *Racist America,* ch. 7; Feagin, "White Supremacy and Mexican Americans: Rethinking the Black-White Paradigm," *Rutgers Law Review* 54 (Summer 2002): 959–87. See also sources cited in previous note.

39. Mireya Navarro, "Census Reflects Hispanic Identity That Is Hardly Black and White," *New York Times,* § 1 (main), November 9, 2003, 1.

40. Boris I. Bittker, *The Case for Black Reparations* (New York: Random House, 1973), 131.

41. Darrell L. Pugh, "Collective Rehabilitation," in *When Sorry Isn't Enough,* ed. Brooks, 372.

42. Ibid.

43. See, e.g., John Tierney, "Life: The Cost-Benefit Analysis," *New York Times,* § 4 (Week in Review), May 18, 2003, 14.

44. J. H. P. Pafford, "Shakespearean Romance; The Heart's Forest. A Study of Shakespeare's Pastoral Plays," *Renaissance Quarterly* 27 (Spring 1974): 105, 106, agreeing with Howard Felperin, *Shakespearean Romance* (Princeton, N.J.: Princeton University Press, 1972).

45. William Shakespeare, "The Merchant of Venice," in *The Complete Works of Shakespeare* Cambridge Text (Garden City, N.Y.: Doubleday, Inc., 1936), 469 (4.1.178–224).

46. Jeanne Moskal, *Blake, Ethics, and Forgiveness* (Tuscaloosa: University of Alabama Press, 1994), 12.

47. See, e.g., Henderson, *Forgiveness: Breaking the Chains of Hate,* 4–5; Newman, "Quality of Mercy," 155. See also Eugene B. Borowitz and Frances Weinman Schwartz, *The Jewish Moral Virtues* (Philadelphia: Jewish Publication Society, 1999); Dietrich Von Hildebrand, *Christian Ethics* (New York: David McKay, 1953); Karen S. Peterson, "Mending Our Broken Hearts," www.usatoday.com, December 10, 2001 (available July 15, 2002).

48. See Paul A. Newberry, "Joseph Butler on Forgiveness: A Presupposed Theory of Emotion," *Journal of the History of Ideas* 62, no. 2 (2001): 233. See also

Shriver, *Ethic for Enemies;* Kathleen Dean Moor, *Pardons: Justice, Mercy and the Public Interest* (New York: Oxford University Press, 1989); Jeffrie G. Murphy and Jean Hampton, *Forgiveness and Mercy* (New York: Cambridge University Press, 1988); A. C. Ewing, *The Morality of Punishment with Some Suggestions for a General Theory of Ethics* (Montclair, N.J.: Patterson Smith, 1970); Norvin Richards, "Forgiveness," *Ethics* 99 (October 1988): 77; R. S. Downie, "Forgiveness," *Philosophical Quarterly* 15, no. 59 (1965): 128. Joseph Butler's sermons were first published in 1726, and have been republished in *Butler's Fifteen Sermons Preached at the Rolls Chapel; and, A Dissertation of the Nature of Virtue,* ed. T. A. Roberts (London: Society for Promoting Christian Knowledge, 1970).

49. Paul Lauritzen, "Forgiveness: Moral Prerogative or Religious Duty?" *Journal of Religious Ethics* 15 (Fall 1987): 141, 150.

50. Henderson, *Forgiveness,* 4 (quoting Huston Smith).

51. Lauritzen, "Forgiveness," 143.

52. Lorna McGregor, "Individual Accountability in South Africa: Cultural Optimum or Political Facade?" *American Journal of International Law* 95 (January 2001): 32, 37.

53. See Tutu, *No Future without Forgiveness.*

54. Downie, "Forgiveness," 128, 133.

55. Downie also posits that "the forgivee may refuse to accept forgiveness." Ibid.

56. Ibid., 134.

57. Ibid., 128.

58. "Forgiveness," in *Encyclopedia of Ethics,* ed. Lawrence C. Becker (New York: Garland, 1992), 381.

59. Newman, "Quality of Mercy," 155.

60. Ibid.

61. "Forgiveness" in *Encyclopedia of Ethics,* 381.

62. Peterson, "Mending Our Broken Hearts." See Trudy Govier, "The Ethics of Forgiveness," *Interaction* 6 (Fall 1994): 10 (citing Downie and Hesburg).

63. Peterson, "Mending Our Broken Hearts," 2, quoting David Heim, executive editor of *Christian Century,* an ecumenical journal of theological commentary.

64. Lauritzen, "Forgiveness," 148.

65. Ibid., 150.

66. For a discussion of Digeser's interesting proposal, see Peter Digeser, "Forgiveness and Politics: Dirty Hands and Imperfect Procedures," *Political Theory* 26 (October 1998): 700–724; quotations, 703, 705.

67. Dick Morris, *Power Plays: Win or Lose—How History's Great Political Leaders Play the Game* (New York: HarperCollins, 2002).

68. See ibid.

69. See, e. g., Martha Minow, *Between Vengeance and Forgiveness: Facing His-*

tory after Genocide and Class Violence (Boston: Beacon Press, 1998); Shriver, *Ethic of Enemies.*

70. Torpey, "'Making Whole What Has Been Smashed,'" 354.

71. Ibid., 356.

72. *Brown v. Board of Education,* 347 U.S. 483 (1954).

73. *Cooper v. Aaron,* 358 U.S. 1, 16 (1958).

74. See, e.g., *Adarand Constructors, Inc. v. Pena,* 518 U.S. 200 (1995) (race); *United States v. Virginia,* 518 U.S. 515 (1996) (gender); *City of Cleburne v. Cleburne Living Center, Inc.,* 473 U.S. 432 (1985) (discussing various standards of judicial review). See, generally, Erwin Chemerinsky, *Constitutional Law: Principles and Policies* (New York: Aspen Law & Business, 1997), 638–746; William W. Van Alstyne, "The Demise of the Right-Privilege Distinction in Constitutional Law," *Harvard Law Review* 81 (1968): 1439.

75. *Slaughter-House Cases,* 83 U.S. 36, 81 (1872).

76. See, e.g., *Mississippi University for Women v. Hogan,* 538 U.S. 718 (1982) (applying the Fourteenth Amendment to gender-based discrimination); *City of Richmond v. J. A. Croson, Co.,* 488 U.S. 469 (1989) (striking down race-based affirmative action).

77. Cf., e.g., *Plessy v. Ferguson* (1896), 559; *Brown v. Board of Education* (1954), at 4.

78. Brooks, *Integration or Separation?* 208, 210–11 (citations omitted).

79. *Plessy v. Ferguson,* at 558 (Harlan, J., dissenting).

80. For a discussion of these cases, see, e.g., Roy L. Brooks, Gilbert P. Carrasco, and Gordon A. Martin, *Civil Rights Litigation: Cases and Perspectives* (Durham, N.C.: Carolina Academic Press, 1995), ch. 10; Jed Rubenfeld, "Affirmative Action," *Yale Law Journal* 107 (1997): 427.

81. *Adarand Constructors, Inc. v. Peña,* 515 U.S. 200 (1995).

82. See *Adarand Constructors, Inc. v. Peña,* and, generally, Brooks, *Rethinking the American Race Problem,* 51–52.

83. See *Grutter v. Bollinger.*

84. See, e.g., *United States v. Virginia; Craig v. Boren,* 429 U.S. 191 (1976).

85. *City of Richmond v. J. A. Croson Co.,* 488 U.S. 469 (1989).

86. Ibid., 486–94 (pt. 2 of Justice O'Connor's opinion, in which Chief Justice Rehnquist and Justice White joined).

87. *Metro Broadcasting, Inc. v. FCC,* 497 U.S. 547 (1990).

88. Ibid., 564–65.

89. *Adarand Constructors, Inc. v. Peña,* at 227.

90. *Jacobs v. Barr,* 959 F.2d 313 (D.C. Cir. 1992), *cert. denied* 506 U.S. 831 (1992).

91. Civil Liberties Act of 1988, 50 App. U.S.C., §§ 1989(a)–(d).

92. This finding would seem to be refuted by the U.S. Department of Justice's

Review of the Restrictions on Persons of Italian Ancestry during World War II (2001), which shows that Italian Americans faced many of the same deprivations as Japanese Americans.

93. *Jacobs v. Barr,* at 322.

94. See, e.g., *Fullilove v. Klutznick,* 448 U.S. 448, 478 (1980) (Congress had "evidence of a long history of marked disparity in the percentage of public contracts awarded to minority business enterprises").

95. Civil Rights Act of 1964, 42 U.S.C, §§ 2000(e)–2005(g).

96. *Congressional Record* 118 (1972): 7168.

97. *Local 28, Sheet Metal Workers' International Association v. Equal Employment Opportunity Commission,* 478 U.S. 421, 424, 446–47 (1986); *Local Number 93, International Association of Firefighters v. City of Cleveland,* 478 U.S. 501, 516 (1986).

98. *Sheet Metal Workers' International Association v. Equal Employment Opportunity Commission,* at 474 n. 46.

99. See ibid., 474.

100. Ibid.

6. OPPOSING ARGUMENTS

1. After writing this chapter, I received a copy of "Justice and Greed: Black and White Support for Reparations" (MS, 2003) by Professor Michael Dawson of Harvard University and Professor Rovana Popoff of the University of Chicago. Many of the points raised in this excellent paper are presented in this chapter. Nonetheless, I believe the paper is worth reading, as is Charles J. Ogletree, "Repairing the Past: New Efforts in the Reparations Debate in America," *Harvard Civil Rights–Civil Liberties Law Review* 38 (2003): 279.

2. Christopher Hitchens, "Who's Sorry Now," *Nation,* May 29, 2000, 9. See, e.g., Walter Rodney, *How Europe Underdeveloped Africa* (London: Bogle-L'Ouverture Publications, 1972).

3. Davis, *In the Image of God,* 134–35. See Orlando Patterson, *Slavery and Social Death: A Comparative Study* (Cambridge, Mass.: Harvard University Press, 1982), 96.

4. These remarks are taken from a speech discussed in the Epilogue.

5. Howard W. French, "The Atlantic Slave Trade: On Both Sides, Reason for Remorse," in *When Sorry Isn't Enough,* ed. Brooks, 355, 357 (interviewing Basil Davidson).

6. Ibid.

7. Alexis de Tocqueville, *Democracy in America* (1835–39), ed. and trans. Har-

vey C. Mansfield and Delba Winthrop (Chicago: University of Chicago Press, 2000), 327.

8. Davis, *In the Image of God,* 130–31 n. 1. See also, Nathaniel Weyl, *The Negro in American Civilization* (Washington, D.C.: Public Affairs Press, 1960), 9–10; Carleton S. Coon, *The Story of Man: From the First Human to Primitive Culture and Beyond* (New York: Knopf, 1954), 211 ff.

9. A precise estimate of the number of slaves taken to the Americas is hard to come by because of the absence of careful or uniform record keeping. For a discussion of the problem, see, e.g., Franklin and Moss, *From Slavery to Freedom,* 39; Weyl, *Negro in American Civilization,* 9.

10. Davis, *In the Image of God,* 130.

11. Ibid., 135 n. 9, citing Robert W. Harms, *River of Wealth, River of Sorrow: The Central Zaire Basin in the Era of the Slave and Ivory Trade, 1500–1891* (New Haven, Conn.: Yale University Press, 1981).

12. See Claude Meillassoux, *The Anthropology of Slavery: The Womb of Iron and Gold,* trans. Alide Dasnois (Chicago: University of Chicago Press, 1991).

13. Scott McLemee, "The Slave History You Don't Know: A Scholar's Startling Study of the Southwest Wins Unprecedented Acclaim," *Chronicle of Higher Education,* May 16, 2003, p A14 (quotations from interview with James F. Brooks). See James F. Brooks, *Captives and Cousins: Slavery, Kinship, and Community in the Southwest Borderlands* (Chapel Hill: University of North Carolina Press, 2002).

14. Aristotle, *Works,* trans. W. D. Ross, in *Great Books of the Western World,* ed. Robert Maynard Hutchins, vol. 9 (Chicago: Encyclopedia Britannica, 1952), 2: 448–49, *Politics* 1.1255a [5]–[35]. See also Davis, *In the Image of God,* 128–30.

15. *The Oxford Encyclopedia of Ancient Egypt,* vol. 3, Donald B. Redford, editor in chief (New York: Oxford University Press, 2001), 294.

16. Weyl, *Negro in American Civilization,* 5. See William E. H. Lecky, *History of European Morals from Augustus to Charlemagne* (1869; reprint, New York: G. Braziller, 1955), 327 (arguing that "the slave code of Imperial Rome compares not unfavorably with those of some Christian nations").

17. Weyl, *Negro in American Civilization,* 6. It has also been suggested that the Christian churches believed that "slavery would not be permitted in an ideal world of perfect justice, but was simply a fact of life that symbolized the compromises that must be made in the sinful world of reality." Davis, *In the Image of God,* 130. On Greek and Roman slavery, see, generally, Wiedemann, *Greek and Roman Slavery.*

18. Weyl, *Negro in American Civilization,* 5.

19. Tocqueville, *Democracy in America,* 327 ff.

20. Weyl, *Negro in American Civilization,* 3–4, 5. See Ludwig Friedlaender,

Roman Life and Manners under the Early Empire (London: Routledge, 1928), 1, 33–70.

21. *Dred Scott v. Sandford,* at 408. See chapter 2 for a clarification of the Court's infamous characterization of black rights.

22. Tocqueville, *Democracy in America,* 327.

23. Weyl, *Negro in American Civilization,* 10.

24. Davis, *In the Image of God,* 133.

25. The Cynics, Stoics, and other Greek philosophers objected to wide acceptance of human bondage in Greek society. While not evidence of a change in Greek thinking about slavery, these dissenting voices do indicate that support for slavery in Greek society was hardly unanimous. See Davis, *In the Image of God,* 129. For a general discussion of slavery in Greek society, see Thomas Wiedemann, *Greek and Roman Slavery* (Baltimore: Johns Hopkins University Press, 1981).

26. Weyl, *Negro in American Civilization,* 5.

27. Ibid., 6.

28. Ibid., 8. The Justinian Code, which codified the law and custom of the Roman Empire, exhibited an "extraordinarily humane attitude" toward the slaves. For example, it permitted a free woman to marry a slave upon the consent of the slave's master.

29. Ibid.

30. See Robert C. H. Shell, *Children of Bondage: A Social History of the Slave Society at the Cape of Good Hope, 1652–1813* (Middletown, Conn.: Wesleyan University Press, 1994), 332–70.

31. Davis, *In the Image of God,* 131 n. 1. "This eruption of antislavery thought," Davis points out, "cannot be explained by economic interest. The Atlantic slave system, far from being in decay, had never appeared so prosperous, so secure, or so full of promise." Ibid. It was just that "[b]y the 1730s, arguments in favor of slavery, including the one that equated it with war, were beginning to appear absurd to a generation of English and French writers who had learned from Locke and others to take an irreverent view of past authority and to subject all questions to the test of reason. . . . [Ironically,] John Locke, the great enemy of all absolute and arbitrary power, had been the last major philosopher to seek a justification for absolute and perpetual slavery." Ibid., 132–33.

32. See Shell, *Children of Bondage,* 332–70.

33. David McCullough, *John Adams* (New York: Simon & Schuster, 2001), 131.

34. See, e.g., Feagin, *Racist America,* 15.

35. These words appear in the opening lines of the Declaration itself. See, e.g., *The U.S. Constitution and Fascinating Facts About It,* 6th ed., supplemental text by Robert F. Tedeschi Jr. (Naperville, Ill.: Oak Hill Publishing, 1996), 45.

36. McCullough, *John Adams,* 131. See also ibid., 131–33. Vermont's constitution outlawed slavery in 1777. See, e.g., Davis, *In the Image of God,* 134.

37. See, e.g., Camille Paglia, "Ask Camille: Camille Paglia's Online Advice for the Culturally Disgruntled," in *When Sorry Isn't Enough,* ed. Brooks, 353–54; *Should America Pay? Slavery and the Raging Debate on Reparations,* ed. Raymond A. Winbush (New York: Amistad, 2003), pt. 3 ("Voices for and against Reparations").

38. Brooks, *Structures of Judicial Decision-Making,* 209–10 (sources cited therein).

39. Richard Delgado, "Linking Arms: Recent Books on Interracial Coalition as an Avenue of Social Reform," *Cornell Law Review* 88 (2003): 855, 870 (citations omitted). See Cheryl I. Harris, "Whiteness as Property," *Harvard Law Review* 106 (1993): 1709.

40. See Feagin, *Racist America.*

41. Robert S. McElvaine, "They Didn't March to Free the Slaves," in *When Sorry Isn't Enough,* ed. Brooks, 358, 359.

42. Vivian B. Martin, "Everyone Stands to Gain from Reparations Debate," *Hartford Courant,* November 7, 2002, A17.

43. Wu, *Yellow,* 18.

44. Jennifer Fleischner, "Remembering Slavery," in *When Sorry Isn't Enough,* ed. Brooks, 333, 334.

45. *Local 28, Sheet Metal Workers' International Association v. Equal Employment Opportunity Commission,* 474.

46. U.S. Constitution, Amend. 14, sec. 1.

47. Civil Rights Act of 1964, 42 U.S.C. 2000e-2(a)(1).

48. Voting Rights Act of 1965, 42 U.S.C. 1971(a)(1).

49. See, generally, Roy L. Brooks, Gilbert Paul Carrasco, and Michael Selmi, *Civil Rights Litigation: Cases and Perspectives,* 2d ed. (Durham, N.C.: Carolina Academic Press, 2000), ch. 10.

50. See *Jacobs v. Barr,* 959 F.2d 313 (D.C. Cir. 1992), cert. denied, 506 U.S. 831 (1992).

51. See James M. McPherson, *For Cause & Comrades: Why Men Fought in the Civil War* (New York: Oxford University Press, 1997), 117–30.

52. D'Souza, *What's So Great about America?* 59. Connerly's remarks were made in a debate on reparations between the two of us that aired on MSNBC in March 2002.

53. William Darity and Dania Frank, "The Economics of Reparations," *Political Economy of Ending Racism and the WCAR,* 93, no. 2 (May 2003): 326, 328.

54. See Diana B. Henriques, "Concern Growing as Families Bypass 9/11 Victims' Fund," *New York Times,* main section, August 31, 2003, 1. Some victims have chosen litigation over the federal payout. See Larry Neumeister, "Ruling Opens Door for 9/11 Lawsuits," *San Diego Union-Tribune,* September 10, 2003, A6.

55. D'Souza, *What's So Great about America?* 28.

56. Ibid., at 133.

57. Ibid., quoting Salman Rushdie.

58. Ibid., at 189–90.

59. Ibid., 101–2.

60. Ibid., 172.

61. See chapter 3. For much of the past dozen years, I have attempted to document and argue that race matters. See, e.g., Brooks, *Rethinking the American Race Problem*; id., *Integration or Separation;* Brooks, Carrasco, and Selmi, *Civil Rights Litigation.*

62. Brian M. Carney, "Bookshelf: What Machiavelli Can Still Teach Us, Even in a Democracy," *Wall Street Journal,* August 21, 2003, D8.

63. See Joe Feagin and Eileen O'Brien, *White Men on Race: Power, Privilege, and the Shaping of Cultural Consciousness* (Boston: Beacon Press, 2003).

64. Michael Eric Dyson, *Holler If You Hear Me: Searching for Tupac Shakur* (New York: Basic Civitas Books, 2001), 153, quoting the rap artist Tupac Shakur.

65. Peter Rowe, "Peace Officer: Refugee Brings Sense of Justice to Little Mogadishu," *San Diego Union-Tribune,* November 9, 2003, E1.

66. See Dyson, *Holler If You Hear Me,* 144. Rap artist Tupac Sakur, who died a violent death at the age of 25 in September, 1996, coined the expression "thug life" in an attempt to rescue the hip-hop term "nigga," or "nigger," "by redefining it" to stand for an "underdog" who is "never ignorant [and] get[s] goals accomplished" (ibid.). Yet, the absurdity of this misadventure is irrefutably demonstrated by the fact that "historically astute and racially sensitive whites have rarely attempted to use the term, even with black friends. When these whites stepped out of bounds, black friends or colleagues readily set them straight" (ibid., 145.). If the revisionism were successful, blacks rappers would feel pride rather than pain when their savvy white friends used their invention. The hip-hop generation is not the first generation of blacks to use the derogatory "N" word as a form of civil rights protest. The black comedian Dick Gregory, for example, used the term in this manner in the 1960s. See Dick Gregory, *Nigger: An Autobiography* (New York: Dutton, 1964). See generally Randall Kennedy, *Nigger: The Strange Career of a Troublesome Word* (New York: Pantheon Books, 2002).

67. Brooks et al., *Civil Rights Litigation,* 684.

68. It took his own drug addiction for the controversial, conservative talk-show host Rush Limbaugh to understand the extent to which an individual can be "powerless to overcome his addiction." See "Limbaugh Returns to Radio after Rehab for Painkillers," *San Diego Union-Tribune,* November 18, 2003, A8. Prior to being caught purchasing drugs illegally, Limbaugh stated these harsh words, "Too many whites are getting away with drug use. Find the ones who are getting

away with it . . . and send them up the river" (Evan Thomas, "Cover Story: Rush Limbaugh's World of Pain," *Newsweek,* October 20, 2003, 45).

69. Paul M. Barrett, *The Good Black: A True Story of Race in America* (New York: Dutton, 1999), 42–43.

70. See "La. Judge Ripped for Halloween Costume," *San Diego Union-Tribune,* November 11, 2003, A6.

EPILOGUE

1. Susan Sontag, *Regarding the Pain of Others* (New York: Farrar, Straus & Giroux, 2003) (emphasis in original).

2. Ibid., 87–88.

3. Our founders eschewed a direct democracy in favor of a representative democracy to temper the passions of the people. A representative democracy imposes an obligation on its political leaders to shape rather than merely follow public opinion. For a more detailed discussion, see Carnes Lord, *The Modern Prince: What Leaders Need to Know Now* (New Haven, Conn.: Yale University Press, 2003).

4. See "Clinton Opposes Slavery Apology," in *When Sorry Isn't Enough,* ed. Brooks, 352.

5. See Martin Luther King Jr., "Letter from Birmingham City Jail," in *The American Civil Rights Movement: Readings and Interpretations,* ed. Raymond D'Angelo (New York: McGraw-Hill/Dushkin, 2001), 320.

6. *Civil Rights since 1787: A Reader on the Black Struggle,* ed. Jonathan Birnbaum and Clarence Taylor (New York: New York University Press, 2000), 491.

7. For a detailed discussion of these civil rights laws, see Brooks et al., *Civil Rights Litigation.*

SELECTED BIBLIOGRAPHY

"The Academics Who Are Screaming Racial Quotas Need to Recheck Their Arithmetic." *Journal of Blacks in Higher Education* 35 (Spring 2002): 72.

ACE News Net. www.acenet.edu (available October 22, 2002).

"Affirmative Action: History and Rationale." www.whitehouse.gov/WH/EOP/OP/html/aa02.html (available June 22, 1999).

Ainsworth, Bill. "Perot Defends Company's Ethics." *San Diego Union-Tribune,* July 12, 2001.

Aleinikoff, Alexander. "A Case for Race Consciousness." *Columbia Law Review* 91 (1991): 1060–25.

Allen, Walter R. "College in Black and White: Black Student Experiences on Black and White Campuses." In *In Pursuit of Equality in Higher Education,* edited by Anne S. Pruitt, 132–45. Dix Hills, N.Y.: General Hall, 1987.

American Council on Education. "Students of Color Make Enrollment and Graduation Gains." www.acenet.edu (available September 23, 2002).

American Jurisprudence. Vol. 66. 2d ed. St. Paul, Minn.: West Group, 2002.

"American Slavery and the Conflicts of Laws." *Columbia Law Review* 71 (1971): 74–99.

Anderson, Eric, and Alfred A. Moss Jr. *Dangerous Donations: Northern Philanthropy and Southern Education, 1902–1930.* Columbia: University of Missouri Press, 1999.

Anderson, James A. "Cognitive Styles and Multicultural Populations." In *Recruit-*

ment and Retention of Black Students in Higher Education, edited by Johnson N. Niba and Regina Norman. Lanham, Md.: University Press of America, 1989.

Anderson, James D. The Education of Blacks in the South, 1860–1935. Chapel Hill: University of North Carolina Press, 1988.

Anderson, Martin, et al. "Why the Shortage of Black Professors?" Journal of Blacks in Higher Education 1 (Autumn 1993): 25–34.

Applebone, Peter. "Equal Entry Standards May Hurt Black Students in Mississippi." San Diego Union-Tribune, April 24, 1996.

Aristotle. Works. Vol. 2. Translated by W. D. Ross. In Great Books of the Western World, edited by Robert Maynard Hutchins, vol. 9. Chicago: Encyclopedia Britannica, 1952.

Ashmore, Harry S. Hearts and Minds: The Anatomy of Racism from Roosevelt to Reagan. New York: McGraw-Hill, 1982.

Auerbach, Carl A. "The Relation of Legal Systems to Social Change." Wisconsin Law Review 1980 (1980): 1227–1340.

"Autobiography of Omar ibn Seid, Slave in North Carolina, 1831." American Historical Review 30, no. 4 (July 1925): 787–95.

Balbus, Issacs D. "The Psycho-Dynamics of Racial Reparations." Unpublished paper delivered at Claremont Graduate University, Conference on Apologies: Mourning the Past and Ameliorating the Present, February 7–10, 2002. Author's files.

Ball, Charles. A Narrative of the Life and Adventures of Charles Ball, a Black Man. 3d ed. Pittsburgh: John T. Shryock, 1854.

Ball, Edward. Slaves in the Family. New York: Farrar, Straus & Giroux, 1998.

Barkan, Elazar. The Guilt of Nations: Restitution and Negotiating Historical Injustices. New York: Norton, 2000.

Barrett, Paul M. The Good Black: A True Story of Race in America. New York: Dutton, 1999.

Bass, Jack. Unlikely Heroes: The Dramatic Story of the Southern Judges of the Fifth Circuit Who Translated the Supreme Court's Brown Decision into a Revolution for Equality. New York: Simon & Schuster, 1981.

Beard, A. F. A Crusade of Brotherhood. Boston: Pilgrim Press, 1909.

"Beat the Odds Graduation Stories." www.oprah.com (available June 7, 2002).

Bennett, William J., ed. The Book of Virtues: A Treasury of Great Moral Stories. New York: Simon & Schuster, 1993.

Berlin, Ira. Generations of Captivity: A History of African-American Slaves. Cambridge, Mass.: Belknap Press of Harvard University Press, 2003.

———. "North of Slavery: Black People in a Slaveholding Republic." Paper delivered at the Conference on Yale, New Haven, and American Slavery, Yale University, September 27, 2002. Author's files.

———. *Slaves without Masters: The Free Negro in the Antebellum South.* New York: Pantheon Books, 1974.

Berry, John A., and Carol Pott Berry. *Genocide in Rwanda: A Collective Memory.* Washington, D.C.: Howard University Press, 1999.

Bittker, Boris I. *The Case for Black Reparations.* New York: Random House, 1973. Reprint. Boston: Beacon Press, 2003.

"Blacks, Hispanics Are Searched More." *San Diego Union-Tribune,* January 7, 2003.

Blacks Law Dictionary. 3d ed. Edited by William S. Anderson. San Francisco: Bancroft-Whitney, 1969.

"Black-White Higher Education Equality Index." *Journal of Blacks in Higher Education* 34 (Winter 2001–2): 78.

The Black-White Test Score Gap. Edited by Christopher Jencks and Meredith Phillips. Washington, D.C.: Brookings Institute, 1998.

Blight, David W. "If You Don't Tell It Like It Was, It Can Never Be as It Ought to Be." Keynote Speech, delivered at Conference on Yale and American Slavery. www.yale.edu/glc/events/memory.htm (available September 27, 2002).

———. *Race and Reunion: The Civil War in American Memory.* Cambridge, Mass.: Harvard University Press, 2001.

Bombardieri, Marcella. "Theory Links Slavery, Stress Disorder: Proponents Make Case for a New Diagnosis." *Boston Globe,* November 12, 2002.

Borowitz, Eugene, and Frances Weinman Schwartz. *The Jewish Moral Virtues.* Philadelphia: Jewish Publication Society, 1999.

Boudette, Neal E. "Seeking Reparation: A Holocaust Claim Cuts to the Heart of the New Germany." *Wall Street Journal,* March 29, 2002.

Bouloubasis, Vicky. "Blue & White Online—The Roots of Race Relations: Peeling Back the Layers of Integration." www.unco.edu/student/orgs/bw/thematic_01/uncroots.html (available June 11, 2002).

Bowen, William G., and Derek Bok. *The Shape of the River: Long-Term Consequences of Considering Race in College and University Admissions.* Princeton, N.J.: Princeton University Press, 1998.

Bowles, Frank Hamilton, and Frank A. DeCosta. *Between Two Worlds: A Profile of Negro Higher Education.* New York: McGraw-Hill, 1971.

Branch, Mark Alden. "The Slavery Legacy." *Yale Alumni Magazine,* February 2002, 34–37.

Branch, Watson. "Reparations for Slavery: A Dream Deferred." *San Diego International Law Journal* 3 (2002): 177–206.

Brandt, Willy. *My Life in Politics.* London: Hamish Hamilton, 1992.

Braun, Gerry. "The Gospel According to George: Molded by This Childhood and a Preacher's Worldview, This Circumspect Act Must Leave a Singular Legacy." *San Diego Union-Tribune,* December 24, 2000.

Bravin, Jess. "Law School Admission Council Aims to Quash Overreliance on LSAT." *Wall Street Journal,* March 29, 2001.

Breed, Allen G. "Black Farmers Still Fighting for Settlement 4 Years Ago: The Government Has Rejected 40% of the Claims." *Telegraph Herald* (Dubuque, Iowa), September 1, 2002.

Breland, Hunter, et al. "Trends in College Admission 2000: A Report of a Survey of Undergraduate Admissions, Policies, Practices and Procedures." www.nces.ed.gov (available June 14, 2002).

Brickman, Lester. *Anatomy of a Madison County (Illinois) Class Action: A Study of Pathology.* Civil Justice Report No. 6. New York: Center for Legal Policy at the Manhattan Institute, 2002.

Brooks, James F. *Captives and Cousins: Slavery, Kinship and Community in the Southwest Borderlands.* Chapel Hill: University of North Carolina Press, 2002.

Brooks, Roy L. "The Affirmative Action Issue: Law, Policy, and Morality." *Connecticut Law Review* 22 (1990): 323–71.

———. "The Age of Apology." In *When Sorry Isn't Enough: The Controversy over Apologies and Reparations for Human Injustice,* edited by Roy L. Brooks, 3–11. New York: New York University Press, 1999.

———. *Integration or Separation? A Strategy for Racial Equality.* Cambridge, Mass.: Harvard University Press, 1996.

———. "Life after Tenure: Can Minority Law Professors Avoid the Clyde Ferguson Syndrome." Symposium. *University of San Francisco Law Review* 20 (1985–86): 419–27.

———. *Rethinking the American Race Problem.* Berkeley: University of California Press, 1990.

———. *Structures of Judicial Decision Making from Legal Formalism to Critical Theory.* Durham, N.C.: Carolina Academic Press, 2002.

———. "Use of Civil Rights Acts of 1866 and 1871 to Redress Employment Discrimination." *Cornell Law Review* 62 (1976–77): 258–88.

———, ed. *When Sorry Isn't Enough: The Controversy over Apologies and Reparations for Human Injustice.* New York: New York University Press, 1999.

Brooks, Roy L., Gilbert Paul Carrasco, and Gordon A. Martin. *Civil Rights Litigation: Cases and Perspectives.* Durham, N.C.: Carolina Academic Press, 1995.

Brooks, Roy L., Gilbert Paul Carrasco, and Michael Selmi. *Civil Rights Litigation: Cases and Perspectives.* 2d ed. Durham, N.C.: Carolina Academic Press, 2000.

Brophy, Alfred. *Reconstructing the Dreamland: The Tulsa Riot of 1921.* New York: Oxford University Press, 2002.

Brown-Scott, Wendy. "Race Consciousness in Higher Education: Does 'Sound Educational Policy' Support the Continued Existence of Historically Black Colleges?" *Emory Law Journal* 43 (1994): 1–81.

Bullock, Henry Allen. *A History of Negro Education in the South: From 1619 to the Present.* Cambridge, Mass.: Harvard University Press, 1967.

Butler, Joseph. *Butler's Fifteen Sermons Preached at the Rolls Chapel; and, A Dissertation of the Nature of Virtue.* Edited by T. A. Roberts. London: Society for Promoting Christian Knowledge, 1970.

Butterfield, Fox. "Study Finds Big Increase in Black Men as Inmates since 1980." *New York Times,* August 28, 2002.

Cain, Timothy Reese. "African American Higher Education in Ohio: The Nineteenth Century." *Education Policy and Leadership at Ohio State University,* November 24, 1998. www.coe.ohio-state.edu/EDPL/Gordon/courses/863/cain .htm (available June 5, 2002).

"The California Ban on Affirmative Action Is Causing Severe Damage to Black Opportunities in the Nation's Largest System of Higher Education." *Journal of Blacks in Higher Education.* www.jbhe.com/latest/35_california_ban.html (available June 19, 2002).

Callcott, George H. "Omar ibn Seid, a Slave Who Wrote an Autobiography in Arabic." *Journal of Negro History* 39, no. 1 (January 1954): 58–63.

Camara, Wayne J., and Amy Elizabeth Schmidt. *Group Differences in Standardized Testing and Social Stratification.* New York: College Entrance Examination Board, 1999.

Cameron, Howard K. "Nonintellectual Correlates of Academic Achievement." *Journal of Negro Education* 37, no. 3 (Summer 1968): 252–57.

Campbell, Joel. *Testing of Culturally Different Groups.* Princeton, N.J.: Educational Testing Service, 1964.

Campbell, Tom. "Tax Preparer Can Keep Working; But Judge Says Foster Must No Longer Claim 'Slavery Reparations.'" *Richmond Times-Dispatch,* October 26, 2002.

Candler, Allen D., ed. *Colonial Records of Georgia.* Vol. 18. Atlanta: Franklin Printing and Publishing Co., 1904.

Carter, Deborah, and Reginald Wilson. *Twelfth Annual Status Report on Minorities in Higher Education.* Washington, D.C.: American Council on Education, 1993.

Chang, Iris. *The Chinese in America: A Narrative History.* New York: Viking Press, 2003.

———. *The Rape of Nanking: The Forgotten Holocaust of World War II.* New York: Basic Books, 1997.

Chayes, Abraham. "The Role of the Judge in Public Law Litigation." *Harvard Law Review* 89 (1976): 1281–1302.

Chemerinsky, Erwin. *Constitutional Law: Principles and Policies.* New York: Aspen Law & Business, 1997.

Civil Rights since 1787: A Reader on the Black Struggle. Edited by Jonathan Birnbaum and Clarence Taylor. New York: New York University Press, 2000.

Clark, Felton G. "Negro Higher Education and Some Fundamental Issues Raised by World War II." *Journal of Negro Education* 11, no. 3 (July 1942): 279–91.

Clark, Kenneth B. "Blacks' SAT Scores." *New York Times,* October 12, 1982.

Clark, Ramsey. *Crime in America: Observations on Its Nature, Cause, Prevention and Control.* New York: Simon & Schuster, 1970.

"Clinton Opposes Slavery Apology." In *When Sorry Isn't Enough: The Controversy over Apologies and Reparations for Human Injustice,* edited by Roy L. Brooks, 352. New York: New York University Press, 1999.

Cohen, Roger. "Wiesel Urges Germany to Ask Forgiveness." *New York Times,* January 28, 2000.

Collison, Michele. "For Many Freshmen, Orientation Now Includes Efforts to Promote Racial Understanding." *Chronicle of Higher Education,* September 7, 1988.

A Common Destiny: Blacks and American Society. Edited by Gerald David Jaynes and Robin M. Williams Jr. Washington, D.C.: National Academy Press, 1989.

Conley, Dalton. "The Cost of Slavery." *New York Times,* February 15, 2003.

The Constitution: A Pro-Slavery Compact; Or Extracts from the Madison Papers. 2d ed. Selected by Wendell Phillips. New York: American Anti-Slavery Society, 1845.

Coon, Carleton S. *The Story of Man: From the First Human to Primitive Culture and Beyond.* New York: Knopf, 1954.

Cose, Ellis. *The Rage of a Privileged Class: Why Are Middle-Class Blacks Angry? Why Should America Care?* New York: HarperCollins, 1993.

———. "The Solidarity of Self-Interest." *Newsweek,* August 27, 2001, 25.

Cramer, Clayton E. *Black Demographic Data, 1790–1860: A Sourcebook.* Westport, Conn.: Greenwood Press, 1997.

Crocker, Jennifer, Brenda Major, and Claude Steele. "Social Stigma." In *The Handbook of Social Psychology,* 4th ed., edited by Daniel T. Gilbert and Susan T. Fiske, 2: 504–53. New York: McGraw-Hill, 1998.

Cross, Theodore. "The Thernstrom Fallacy: Why Affirmative Action Is Not Responsible for High Dropout Rates in African-American Students." *Journal of Blacks in Higher Education* 20 (Summer 1998): 90–98.

Cross, Theodore, and Robert Bruce Slater. "How Bans on Race-Sensitive Admissions Severely Cut Black Enrollments at Flagship State Universities." *Journal of Blacks in Higher Education* 38 (Winter 2002–3): 93–99.

Cummings, Jeanne, Jacob M. Schlesinger, and Michael Schroeder. "Securities Threat: Bush Crackdown on Business Fraud Signals New Era." *Wall Street Journal,* July 10, 2002.

D'Augelli, Anthony R., and Scott L. Hershberger. "African American Undergraduates on a Predominantly White Campus: Academic Factors, Social Networks, and Campus Climate." *Journal of Negro Education* 62, no. 1 (Winter 1993): 67–81.

D'Souza, Dinesh. *Illiberal Education: The Politics of Race and Sex on Campus.* New York: Vintage Books, 1992.

———. *What's So Great about America?* Washington, D.C.: Regnery, 2002.

Dagan, Hanoch. "The Law and Ethics of Restitution." Unpublished draft of December 30, 2002. Author's files..

Davis, David Brion. *In the Image of God: Religion, Moral Values, and Our Heritage of Slavery.* New Haven, Conn.: Yale University Press, 2001.

Davis, James Earl. "College in Black and White: Campus Environment and Academic Achievement of African American Males." *Journal of Negro Education* 63, no. 4 (Autumn 1994): 620–33.

Dawson, Michael, and Rovana Popoff. "Justice and Greed: Black and White Support for Reparations." Unpublished article, 2003.

DeGraft-Johnson, J. C. *African Glory: The Story of Vanished Negro Civilizations.* New York: Walker, 1954.

Delgado, Richard. "Linking Arms: Recent Books on Interracial Coalition as an Avenue of Social Reform." *Cornell Law Review* 88 (2003): 855–84.

Department of Housing and Urban Development. "Discrimination in Metropolitan Housing Markets: National Results from Phase 1 and Phase 2 of the Housing Discrimination Study (HDS)." www.huduser.org/publications/hsgfin/hsgfin/hds.html (available July 2, 2003).

Digeser, Peter. "Forgiveness and Politics: Dirty Hands and Imperfect Procedures." *Political Theory* 26, no. 5 (October 1998): 700–724.

"Diversity in Medical Schools on Decline." *San Diego Union-Tribune,* August 23, 2002.

Douglass, Frederick. *Life and Times of Frederick Douglass: His Early Life as a Slave, His Escape from Bondage, and His Complete History, Written by Himself.* New York: Collier Books, 1962. Originally published in 1845 as *Narrative of the Life of Frederick Douglass, an American Slave, Written by Himself.* The revised edition on which the Collier Books edition is based appeared in 1892.

"Down in Durban." *Wall Street Journal,* September 5, 2001.

Downie, R. S. "Forgiveness." *Philosophical Quarterly* 15, no. 59 (April 1965): 128–34.

Draper, Theodore H. "The Father of American Black Nationalism." *New York Review of Books,* March 12, 1970.

———. Reply to "Writing Black History," by Dorothy Sterling. *New York Review of Books,* July 2, 1970.

Du Bois, W. E. B., and A. G. Dill, eds. *The College-Bred Negro American.* Atlanta, Ga.: Atlanta University Press, 1910.

Du Plessis, Max. "Reparations and International Law: How Are Reparations to Be Determined (Past Wrongs or Current Effects), against Whom, and What Form Should They Take?" Paper delivered at the 2003 CLEA Conference on "Reparations: Theory, Practice and Legal Education," held at University of Windsor, Faculty of Law, in Windsor, Ontario, Canada, June 12–14, 2003. Author's files.

Dyson, Michael Eric. *Holler If You Hear Me: Searching for Tupac Shakur.* New York: Basic Civitas Books, 2001.

"Education Secretary Issues Final Policy Guidance on Minority Scholarships." *Civil Rights Monitor,* Winter 1994.

Eizenstat, Stuart E. *Imperfect Justice: Looted Assets, Slave Labor, and the Unfinished Business of World War II.* New York: Public Affairs, 2003.

Elfin, Mel, and Sarah Burke. "Race on Campus." *U.S. News & World Report,* April 19, 1993, 52–53, 55–56.

Emerson, Ken. "Only Correct." *New Republic,* February 18, 1991, 18–19.

Evidence on the Slave Trade. Cincinnati: American Reform Tract and Book Society, 1855.

Ewing, A. C. *The Morality of Punishment with Some Suggestions for a General Theory of Ethics.* Montclair, N.J.: Patterson Smith, 1970.

Farmer-Paellmann, Deadria C. "Excerpt from Black Exodus: The Ex-Slave Pension Movement Reader." In *Should America Pay? Slavery and the Raging Debate on Reparations,* edited by Raymond A. Winbush, 22–31. New York: Amistad, 2003.

Feagin, Joe R. *The Continuing Significance of Racism: U.S. Colleges and Universities.* Washington, D.C.: American Council on Education, 2002

——. *Racist America: Roots, Current Realities, and Future Reparations.* New York: Routledge, 2000.

——. "White Supremacy and Mexican Americans: 'Rethinking the Black-White Paradigm.'" *Rutgers Law Review* 54 (2002): 959–87.

Feagin, Joe R., and Eileen O'Brien. "The Growing Movement for Reparations." In *When Sorry Isn't Enough: The Controversy over Apologies and Reparations for Human Injustice,* edited by Roy L. Brooks, 341–44. New York: New York University Press, 1999.

Feagin, Joe R., and Melvin P. Sikes. *Living with Racism: The Black Middle-Class Experience.* Boston: Beacon Press, 1994.

Fehrenbacher, Don E. *The Slaveholding Republic: An Account of the United States Government's Relations to Slavery,* completed and edited by Ward M. McAfee. New York: Oxford University Press, 2001.

Felperin, Howard. *Shakespearean Romance.* Princeton, N.J.: Princeton University Press, 1972.

Finkelman, Paul. "The Founders and Slavery: Little Ventured, Little Gained." *Yale Journal of Law and the Humanities* 13 (2001): 413–49.

——. *Slavery and the Founders: Race and Liberty in the Age of Jefferson.* Armonk, N.Y.: M. E. Sharpe, 1996.

——. *Slavery and the Founders: Race and Liberty in the Age of Jefferson.* 2d ed. Armonk, N.Y.: M.E. Sharpe, 2001.

Fisher, Ian. "At Site of Massacre, Polish Leader Asks Jews for Forgiveness." *New York Times,* July 11, 2001.

Fisher, Jeanne B. "Bakke Case: Part I—The Issues." *Journal of College Student Personnel* 19 (1978): 174–79.

——. "Bakke Case: Part II—An Analysis and Implications." *Journal of College Student Personnel* 20 (1979): 264.

Fleischner, Jennifer. "Remembering Slavery." In *When Sorry Isn't Enough: The Controversy over Apologies and Reparations for Human Injustice,* edited by Roy L. Brooks, 333–35. New York: New York University Press, 1999.

"Forgiveness." In *Encyclopedia of Ethics,* edited by Lawrence C. Becker. New York: Garland, 1992.

Forman, James. "The Black Manifesto." Appendix A in *The Case for Black Reparations,* by Boris I. Bitker. New York: Random House, 1973.

Frankenberg, Erica, Chungmei Lee, and Gary Orfield. *A Multiracial Society with Segregated Schools: Are We Losing the Dream?* Cambridge, Mass.: The Civil Rights Project, Harvard University, 2003.

Franklin, John Hope. *From Slavery to Freedom: A History of Negro Americans.* 1947. 3d ed. New York: Vintage Books, 1969.

———. "History of Racial Segregation in the United States." *Annals of American Academy of Political & Social Scientists* 34 (March 1956): 1–9.

Franklin, John Hope, and Alfred A. Moss Jr. *From Slavery to Freedom: A History of Negro Americans.* 6th ed. New York: Knopf, 1988.

Freedman, Warren. "The Restitution of Land Rights in South Africa." Paper delivered at the 2003 CLEA Conference on "Reparations: Theory, Practice and Legal Education," held at University of Windsor, Faculty of Law, in Windsor, Ontario, Canada, June 12–14, 2003. Author's files.

Frei, Norbert. *Adenauer's Germany and the Nazi Past: The Politics of Amnesty and Integration.* Translated by Joel Golb. New York: Columbia University Press, 2002.

French, Howard W. "The Atlantic Slave Trade: On Both Sides, Reason for Remorse." *New York Times,* April 15, 1998.

Friedlaender, Ludwig. *Roman Life and Manners under the Early Empire,* vol. 1. London: Routledge, 1928.

Friedman, Leon, ed. *Southern Justice.* New York: Pantheon Books, 1965.

Fultz, Michael. "'The Morning Cometh': African American Periodicals, Education, and the Black Middle Class, 1900–1930." *Journal of Negro History* 80, no. 3 (1995): 97–112.

Gates, Henry Louis Jr. "The Perception of Black Literature as a Necessary Road to Membership in the Human Community." *Journal of Blacks in Higher Education* 22 (Winter 1998–99): 108–9.

The General Education Board: An Account of Its Activities, 1902–1914. New York: General Education Board, 1915.

Ghannam, Jeffrey. "Repairing the Past." *American Bar Association Journal* 86 (November 2000): 39–43, 70.

Gibney, Mark, and Erik Roxstrom. "The Status of State Apologies." *Human Rights Quarterly* 23 (2001): 911–39.

Glenn, David. "Scholars Present Data in Hopes of Bolstering Legal Defense of Affirmative Action." *Chronicle of Higher Education,* August 20, 2002.

Govier, Trudy. "The Ethics of Forgiveness." *Interaction* 6, no. 3 (Fall 1994): 10.

Grahame, James. *Who Is to Blame? Or Cursory Review of "American Apology for American Accession to Negro Slavery."* London: Smith, Elder, 1842.

———. "Why the North and South Should Have Apologized." In *When Sorry Isn't Enough: The Controversy over Apologies and Reparations for Human Injustice,* edited by Roy L. Brooks, 347–49. New York: New York University Press, 1999.

Gregory, Dick. *Nigger, An Autobiography.* New York: Dutton, 1964.

Grissmer, David, Ann Flanagan, and Stephanie Williamson. "Why Did the Black-White Score Gap Narrow in the 1970s and 1980s?" In *The Black-White Test Score Gap,* edited by Christopher Jencks and Meredith Phillips, 182–226. Washington D.C.: Brookings Institute, 1998.

Grodzins, Morton. *Americans Betrayed: Politics and the Japanese Evacuation.* Chicago: University of Chicago Press, 1949.

Guerrero, Andrea. *Silence at Boalt Hall: The Dismantling of Affirmative Action.* Berkeley: University of California Press, 2002.

Guzman, Jessie Parkhurst. *Negro Year Book, 1952.* New York: Wm. H. Wise, 1952.

Hacker, Andrew. "Andrew Hacker on George Fredrickson's Racism." *Journal of Blacks in Higher Education* 38 (Winter 2002–3): 100–101.

———. *Mismatch: The Growing Gulf between Men and Women.* New York: Scribner, 2003.

Hale-Benson, Janice E. *Black Children: Their Roots, Culture and Learning Styles.* Baltimore: Johns Hopkins University Press, 1986.

Haley, Alex. *Roots.* Garden City, N.Y.: Doubleday, 1976.

Hall, Tony P. "Defense of Congressional Resolution Apologizing for Slavery." In *When Sorry Isn't Enough: The Controversy over Apologies and Reparations for Human Injustice,* edited by Roy L. Brooks, 350–51. New York: New York University Press, 1999.

Harlan, Louis R. *Separate and Unequal Public School Campaigns and Racism in the Southern Seaboard States, 1901–1915.* Chapel Hill: University of North Carolina Press, 1958.

Harris, Bonnie. "Making a Case for Reparations." *Indianapolis Star,* October 17, 2002.

Harris, Cheryl I. "Whiteness as Property." *Harvard Law Review* 106 (1993): 1709–91.

Hayner, Priscilla B. *Unspeakable Truths: Facing the Challenge of Truth Commissions.* New York: Routledge, 2002.

Herrnstein, Richard J., and Charles Murray. *The Bell Curve: Intelligence and Class Structure in American Life.* New York: Free Press, 1994.

Henderson, Michael. *Forgiveness: Breaking the Chain of Hate.* Wilsonville, Or.: BookPartners, 1999.

Hening, William W., ed. *The Statutes at Large: Being a Collection of All the Laws of Virginia, from the First Session of the Legislature, in the Year 1619: Published Pursuant to an Act of the General Assembly of Virginia, Passed on the Fifth Day of February One Thousand Eight Hundred And Eight.* 13 vols. Richmond, Va., 1809–23.

Henry, Stuart, and Dragan Milovanovic. *Constitutive Criminology: Beyond Postmodernism.* London: Sage, 1996.

Hicks, George. *The Comfort Women: Japan's Brutal Regime of Enforced Prostitution in the Second World War.* New York: Norton, 1995.

———. "The Comfort Women Redress Movement." In *When Sorry Isn't Enough: The Controversy over Apologies and Reparations for Human Injustice,* edited by Roy L. Brooks, 113–25. New York: New York University Press, 1999.

Higginbotham, A. Leon, Jr. *In the Matter of Color: The Colonial Period.* New York: Oxford University Press, 1978.

Hitchens, Christopher. "Who's Sorry Now." *Nation,* May 29, 2000.

Holmes, Dwight Oliver Wendell. *The Evolution of the Negro College.* College Park, Md.: McGrath, 1934.

Hoover, Eric. "College Board Approves Major Changes for the SAT." *Chronicle of Higher Education,* July 5, 2002.

Horowitz, Sari. "An African American Graduate Looks Out from the Ivy League." *Journal of Blacks in Higher Education* 24 (Summer 1999): 126–27.

"How Powell Decided to Shun Conference." *New York Times,* September 4, 2001. www.kbabooks.com/reparations1.htm (available November 2002).

Irons, Peter. *Justice at War: The Story of the Japanese Internment Cases.* 1983. Berkeley: University of California Press, 1993.

———, ed. *Justice Delayed: The Record of the Japanese American Internment Cases.* Middletown, Conn.: Wesleyan University Press, 1989.

Jefferson, Thomas. *Notes on the State of Virginia.* 1781–82. In *Writings.* New York: Library of America, 1984.

Jencks, Christopher. "Racial Bias in Testing." In *The Black-White Test Score Gap,* edited by Christopher Jencks and Meredith Phillips, 55–85. Washington D.C.: Brookings Institute, 1998.

Jencks, Christopher, and Meredith Phillips. "The Black-White Test Gap: An Introduction." In *The Black-White Test Score Gap,* edited by Christopher Jencks and Meredith Phillips, 1–51. Washington D.C.: Brookings Institution Press, 1998.

Jensen, Merrill. *The Articles of Confederation: An Interpretation of the Social-Constitutional History of the American Revolution.* Madison: University of Wisconsin Press, 1948.

———. *The New Nation: A History of the United States during the Confederation, 1781–1789.* New York: Knopf, 1950.

Johnson, Alex M., Jr. "Bid Whist, Tonk, and United States v. Fordice: Why Integration Fails African-Americans Again." *California Law Review* 81 (1993): 1401–70.

Johnson, Charles S. *The Negro College Graduate.* College Park, Md.: McGrath, 1938.

———. *The Negro in American Civilization.* London: Constable, 1931.

Johnson, Gene C., Jr. "L.A.'s Slavery Ordinance Is All About 'Due Respect.'" *San Diego Voice & Viewpoint,* June 5, 2003.

Johnson, Haynes. "Racism Still Smolders on Campus." *USA Today,* May 10, 1988.

Johnson, Paul. *A History of the American People.* New York: HarperCollins, 1998.

Johnson, Robert, Jr. "Repatriation as Reparations for Slavery and Jim-Crowism." In *When Sorry Isn't Enough: The Controversy over Apologies and Reparations for Human Injustice,* edited by Roy L. Brooks, 428–29. New York: New York University Press, 1999.

Jonas, Susanne. *Of Centaurs and Doves: Guatemala's Peace Process.* Boulder, Colo.: Westview Press, 2000.

Jordan, Winthrop D. *White over Black: American Attitudes toward the Negro, 1550–1812.* 1968. Reprint. Baltimore: Penguin Books, 1969.

Karen, David. "The Politics of Class, Race and Gender: Access to Higher Education in the United States, 1960–1986." *American Journal of Education* 99 (1991): 208–37.

Kennedy, Randall. *Nigger: The Strange Career of a Troublesome Word.* New York: Pantheon Books, 2002.

Kephart, William M. "Minority Group Discrimination in Higher Education." *Journal of Educational Sociology* 23 (September 1949): 52–57.

Keynes, John Maynard. *The Economic Consequences of the Peace.* 1919. New York: Walker, 2002.

King, Martin Luther, Jr. "Letter from Birmingham City Jail." In *The American Civil Rights Movement: Readings and Interpretations,* edited by Raymond D'Angelo, 320. New York: McGraw-Hill/Dushkin, 2001.

"Klamath Tribes May Get Land Back." *San Diego Union-Tribune,* March 20, 2002.

Kluger, Richard. *Simple Justice: The History of* Brown v. Board of Education *and Black America's Struggle for Equality*. New York: Knopf, 1976.

Kochman, Thomas. *Black and White Styles in Conflict*. Chicago: University of Chicago Press, 1981.

Kong, Deborah. "More Consumers File Complaints of Retail Stores' Racial Profiling." *San Diego Union-Tribune,* June 9, 2003.

Koretz, Daniel, et al. "Testing and Diversity in Postsecondary Education: The Case of California." *Education Policy Analysis Archives*. epaa.asu.edu/epaa/v10n1 (available June 10, 2002).

Kramer, Lance. "Study: Slavery's Effects Lasted Just 2 Generations." *Dartmouth University* via U-wire, University wire. www.lexis.com (available November 6, 2002).

Krammer, Arnold. *Undue Process: The Untold Story of America's German Alien Internees*. Lanham, Md.: Rowman & Littlefield, 1997.

Krauthammer, Charles. "Reparations for Black Americans." *Time,* December 31, 1990, 18.

Krieger, Linda H. "Civil Rights Perestroika: Intergroup Relations after Affirmative Action." *California Law Review* 86 (1998): 1251–1333.

Kryder, Daniel. *Divided Arsenal: Race and the American State during World War II*. Cambridge: Cambridge University Press, 2000.

Kujovich, Gil. "Equal Opportunity in Higher Education and the Black Public College: The Era of Separate but Equal." *Minnesota Law Review* 72 (1987): 29–114.

Kunhardt, Philip B., Jr., Philip B. Kunhardt III, and Peter W. Kunhardt. *The American President*. New York: Riverhead Books, 1999.

"La. Judge Ripped for Halloween Costume." *San Diego Union-Tribune,* November 11, 2003, A6.

Lauritzen, Paul. "Forgiveness: Moral Prerogative or Religious Duty?" *Journal of Religious Ethics* 15 (1987): 141.

Lawson, Ellen N., and Marlene Merrill. "The Antebellum 'Talented Thousandth': Black College Students at Oberlin before the Civil War." *Journal of Negro Education* 52, no. 2 (Spring 1983): 142–55.

Lecky, William E. H. *History of European Morals from Augustus to Charlemagne*. Vol. 1. 1869. Reprint. New York: G. Braziller, 1955.

Leo, John. "Enslaved to the Past." *U.S. News & World Report,* April 15, 2002, 39.

Lester, Julius. *To Be a Slave*. New York: Dial Press, 1968.

Levin, Shana. "Social Psychological Evidence on Race and Racism." In *A Report of the AERA Panel on Racial Dynamics in Colleges and Universities,* edited by Mitchell Chang, Daria Witt, James Jones, and Kenji Hakuta, ch. 3, 1–20. Stanford, Calif.: Center for the Comparative Studies on Race and Ethnicity, 1999. Prepublication draft advance copy.

Levine, Robert S. *Martin Delany, Frederick Douglass, and the Politics of Representative Identity.* Chapel Hill: University of North Carolina Press, 1997.

Lewin, Tamar. "Slave Reparation Movement Begins Gaining Momentum." *San Diego Union-Tribune,* June 8, 2001.

"Limbaugh Returns to Radio after Rehab for Painkillers." *San Diego Union-Tribune,* November 18, 2003, A8.

Linklater, Andro. *Measuring America: How an Untamed Wilderness Shaped the United States and Fulfilled the Promise of Democracy.* New York: Walker, 2002.

"Lipinski Resolution." In *When Sorry Isn't Enough: The Controversy over Apologies and Reparations for Human Injustice,* edited by Roy L. Brooks, 149–50. New York: New York University Press, 1999.

Little, Monroe H. "The Extra-Curricular Activities of Black College Students, 1868–1940." *Journal of Negro History* 65, no. 2 (Spring 1980): 135–48.

"Look What Happens When Affirmative Action Is Banned: Black Students Are Pushed Down into Second- and Third-Tier Institutions of Higher Education." *Journal of Blacks in Higher Education* 34 (Winter 2001–2): 82–94.

Lord, Carnes. *The Modern Prince: What Leaders Need to Know Now.* New Haven, Conn.: Yale University Press, 2003.

Loury, Glenn C. "A Dynamic Theory of Racial Income Differences." In *Women, Minorities and Employment Discrimination,* edited by P. A. Wallace and A. Lamond, ch. 8. Lexington, Mass.: Lexington Books, 1977.

———. *The Anatomy of Racial Inequality.* Cambridge, Mass.: Harvard University Press, 2002.

MacMillan, Margaret. *Paris 1919: Six Months That Changed the World.* New York: Random House, 2002.

Maki, Mitchell T., Harry H. L. Kitano, and S. Megan Berthold. *Achieving the Impossible Dream: How Japanese Americans Obtained Redress.* Urbana: University of Illinois Press, 1999.

Maltz, Earl. "Slavery, Federalism, and the Structure of the Constitution." *American Journal of Legal History* 36 (1992): 468.

Mancini, Olivia. "Vassar's First Black Graduate: She Passed for White." *Journal of Blacks in Higher Education* 34 (Winter 2001–2): 108–9.

Mangum, Charles S., Jr. *The Legal Status of the Negro.* Chapel Hill: University of North Carolina Press, 1940.

Manning, Winton H. "The Measurement of Intellectual Capacity and Performance." *Journal of Negro Education* 37, no. 3 (Summer 1968): 258–67.

Martin, Vivian B. "Everyone Stands to Gain from Reparations Debate." *Hartford Courant,* November 7, 2002.

Mathews, Jay. "The 100 Best High Schools in America." *Newsweek,* June 2, 2003, 48.

Mazzone, Jason. "The Social Capital Argument for Federalism." *Southern California Interdisciplinary Law Journal* 27 (Winter 2001): 27–62.

McCall, Nathan. *Makes Me Wanna Holler: A Young Black Man in America.* New York: Random House, 1994.

McCullough, David. *John Adams.* New York: Simon & Schuster, 2001.

McElvaine, Robert S. "They Didn't March to Free the Slaves." In *When Sorry Isn't Enough: The Controversy over Apologies and Reparations for Human Injustice,* edited by Roy L. Brooks, 358–59. New York: New York University Press, 1999.

McGregor, Lorna. "Individual Accountability in South Africa: Cultural Optimum or Political Façade?" *American Journal of International Law* 95 (2001): 32–45.

McGuinn, Henry J. "The Courts and Equality of Educational Opportunity." *Journal of Negro Education* 8, no. 2 (April 1939): 150–63.

McLean, Renwick. "Congress Backs New Museum on Black History and Culture." *New York Times,* November 23, 2003, § 1 (main), 18.

McLemee, Scott. "The Slave History You Don't Know: A Scholar's Startling Study of the Southwest Wins Unprecedented Acclaim." *Chronicle of Higher Education,* May 16, 2003.

McPherson, James M. *For Cause & Comrades: Why Men Fought in the Civil War.* New York: Oxford University Press, 1997.

———. "White Liberals and Black Power in Negro Education, 1865–1915." *American Historical Review* 75, no. 5 (1970): 1357–86.

McQuoid-Mason, David. "Invasion of Privacy: Common Law v. Constitutionalize Delict." *ACTA Juridica* 2000 (2000): 227.

McWhorter, John. "Against Reparations." In *Should America Pay? Slavery and the Raging Debate on Reparations,* edited by Raymond A. Winbush, 136–37. New York: Amistad, 2003.

Meier, August, and John H. Bracey Jr. "The NAACP as a Reform Movement, 1909–1965: 'They Reach the Conscience of America.'" *Journal of Southern History* 59 (February 1993): 3–30.

Meillassoux, Claude. *The Anthropology of Slavery: The Womb of Iron and Gold.* Translated by Alide Dasnois. Chicago: University of Chicago Press, 1991. Originally published as *Anthropologie de l'esclavage: Le Ventre de fer et d'argent* (Paris: Presses universitaires de France, 1986).

Midgley, J. R. "Retraction, Apology and Right of Reply." *Tydskrif vir Hedendaagsc Romeins-Hollandse Reg* [THR-HR] 58 (1995): 288.

Miller, Carroll L. "Higher Education for Black Americans: Problems and Issues." *Journal of Negro Education* 50, no. 3 (Summer 1981): 208–23.

———. "The Relative Educational Attainment of the Negro Population in the United States." *Journal of Negro Education* 22, no. 3 (Summer 1953): 388–404.

Milovanovic, Dragan, and Katheryn K. Russell, eds. *Petit Apartheid in the U.S. Criminal Justice System: The Dark Figure of Racism.* Durham, N.C.: Carolina Academic Press, 2001.

Minow, Martha. *Between Vengeance and Forgiveness: Facing History after Genocide and Mass Violence.* Boston: Beacon Press, 1998.

Moore, Kathleen Dean. *Pardons: Justice, Mercy and the Public Interest.* New York: Oxford University Press, 1989.

Morris, Dick. *Power Plays: Win or Lose—How History's Great Political Leaders Play the Game.* New York: HarperCollins, 2002.

Moskal, Jeanne. *Blake, Ethics, and Forgiveness.* Tuscaloosa: University of Alabama Press, 1994.

Murphy, Jeffrie G., and Jean Hampton. *Forgiveness and Mercy.* New York: Cambridge University Press, 1988.

Myrdal, Gunnar. *An American Dilemma: The Negro Problem and Modern Democracy.* New York: Harper and Bros., 1944.

Nash, A. E. Keir. "A More Equitable Past? Southern Supreme Court and the Protection of the Antebellum Negro." *North Carolina Law Review* 48 (1970): 197–242.

National Coalition of Blacks for Reparations in America. www.ncobra.com (available June 2, 2003).

Navarro, Mireya. "Census Reflects Hispanic Identity That Is Hardly Black and White." *New York Times,* § 1 (main), November 9, 2003, 1.

Navasky, Victor S. *Kennedy Justice.* New York: Antheneum, 1971.

Newberry, Paul A. "Joseph Butler on Forgiveness: A Presupposed Theory of Emotion." *Journal of the History of Ideas* 62, no. 2 (April 2001): 233–44.

Newman, Louis E. "The Quality of Mercy: On the Duty to Forgive in the Judaic Tradition." *Journal of Religious Ethics* 15, no. 2 (Fall 1987): 155–72.

Newton, Nell Jessup. "Indian Claims for Reparations, Compensation, and Restitution in the United States Legal System." In *When Sorry Isn't Enough: The*

Controversy over Apologies and Reparations for Human Injustice, edited by Roy L. Brooks, 261–69. New York: New York University Press, 1999.

Nichols, Charles H. *Many Thousand Gone: The Ex-Slaves' Account of Their Bondage and Freedom.* Leiden, Neth.: Brill, 1963.

Nisbett, Richard E. "Race, Genetics and I.Q." In *The Black-White Test Score Gap,* edited by Christopher Jencks and Meredith Phillips, 86–102. Washington, D.C.: Brookings Institution Press, 1998.

Nunn, Kenneth. "Rosewood." In *When Sorry Isn't Enough: The Controversy over Apologies and Reparations for Human Injustice,* edited by Roy L. Brooks, 435–37. New York: New York University Press, 1999.

Ogbu, John U. *Black American Students in an Affluent Suburb: A Study of Academic Disengagement.* Mahwah, N.J.: Lawrence Erlbaum Associates, 2003.

Ogletree, Charles J. "Repairing the Past: New Efforts in the Reparations Debate in America." *Harvard Civil Rights–Civil Liberties Law Review* 38 (2003): 279.

Oliver, Melvin L., and Thomas M. Shapiro. *Black Wealth/White Wealth: A New Perspective on Racial Inequality.* New York: Routledge, 1995.

Owen, David. *None of the Above: Behind the Myth of Scholastic Aptitude.* Boston: Houghton Mifflin, 1985.

The Oxford Encyclopedia of Ancient Egypt. Vol. 3. Edited by Donald B. Redford. New York: Oxford University Press, 2001.

Pafford, J. H. P. Review of *Shakespearean Romance,* by Howard Felperin, and *The Heart's Forest. A Study of Shakespeare's Pastoral Plays,* by David Young. *Renaissance Quarterly* 27, no. 1 (Spring 1974): 105–7.

Paglia, Camille. "Ask Camille: Camille Paglia's Online Advice for the Culturally Disgruntled." In *When Sorry Isn't Enough: The Controversy over Apologies and Reparations for Human Injustice,* edited by Roy L. Brooks, 353–54. New York: New York University Press, 1999.

Patterson, Orlando. *Slavery and Social Death: A Comparative Study.* Cambridge, Mass.: Harvard University Press, 1982.

Peeps, J. M. Stephen. "Northern Philanthropy and the Emergence of Black Higher Education—Do-Gooders, Compromisers, or Co-Conspirators?" *Journal of Negro Education* 50, no. 3 (Summer 1981): 251–69.

"Perpetuating a Falsehood: Affirmative Action and the Black Student Dropout Rate," *Journal of Blacks in Higher Education* 35 (Spring 2002): 10.

"Perpetuating the Falsehood That Affirmative Action Students Will Have a Lower Dropout Rate If They Attend Less Selective Colleges." *Journal of Blacks in Higher Education* 36 (Summer 2002): 50.

Peterson, Karen S. "Mending Our Broken Hearts; Can Terrorists Ever Be Forgiven?" *USA Today,* December 10, 2001.

Phillips, Meredith, Jeanne Brooks-Gunn, Greg J. Duncan, Pamela Klebanov, and Jonathan Crane. "Family Background, Parenting Policies, and the Black-White Test Score Gap." In *The Black-White Test Score Gap,* edited by Christopher Jencks and Meredith Phillips, 103–45. Washington, D.C.: Brookings Institution Press, 1998.

Phillips, Ulrich Bonnell. *American Negro Slavery: A Survey of the Supply, Employment and Control of Negro Labor as Determined by the Plantation Régime.* New York: D. Appleton, 1918. Reprint. Baton Rouge: Louisiana State University Press, 1969.

Politics and the Past: On Repairing Historical Injustices. Edited by John Torpey. Lanham, Md.: Rowman & Littlefield, 2003.

Posner, Eric A., and Adrian Vermeule. "Reparations for Slavery and Other Historical Injustices." *Columbia Law Review* 103 (2003): 689–747.

Poussaint, Alvin F., and Amy Alexander. *Lay My Burden Down: Suicide and the Mental Health Crisis among African-Americans.* Boston: Beacon Press, 2000.

Poussaint, Alvin F., and Carolyn O. Atkinson. "Negro Youth and Psychological Motivation." *Journal of Negro Education* 37, no. 3 (Summer 1968): 241–51

"The Progress of Black Student Matriculations at the Nation's Highest-Ranked Colleges and Universities." *Journal of Blacks in Higher Education* 29 (Autumn 2000): 16.

Pugh, Darrell L. "Collective Rehabilitation." In *When Sorry Isn't Enough: The Controversy over Apologies and Reparations for Human Injustice,* edited by Roy L. Brooks, 372–73. New York: New York University Press, 1999.

Race, Rights and Reparation: Law and the Japanese American Internment. Edited by Erik K. Yamamoto, Margaret Chon, Carol L. Izumi, Jerry King, and Frank H. Wu. Gaithersburg, Md.: Aspen Law & Business, 2001.

Reagan, Ronald. Remarks at the Site of the Future United States Holocaust Memorial Museum, October 5, 1988. www.library.ushmm.org/faqs.htm (available July 2002).

Recruitment and Retention of Black Students in Higher Education. Edited by Johnson N. Niba and Regina Norman. Lanham, Md.: University Press of America, 1989.

"Restitution and Implied Contracts." *American Jurisprudence.* 2d ed. Vol. 66. St. Paul, Minn.: West Group, 2002.

"Rice against Reparations for Slavery." *San Diego Union-Tribune,* September 10, 2001.

Richards, Norvin. "Forgiveness." *Ethics* 99 (October 1988): 77–97.

Riley, Jason L. "Black, Successful—and Typical." *Wall Street Journal,* May 13, 2002.

Robinson, Randall. *The Debt: What America Owes to Blacks.* New York: Dutton, 2000.

Robinson, Walter George, Jr. "Blacks in Higher Education in the United States before 1865." Diss., Southern Illinois University, 1976. Ann Arbor: University Microfilms International, 1979.

Rodney, Walter. *How Europe Underdeveloped Africa.* London: Bogle-L'Ouverture Publications, 1972.

Roebuck, Julian B., and Komanduri S. Murty. *Historically Black Colleges and Universities: Their Place in American Higher Education.* Westport, Conn.: Praeger, 1993.

Roosevelt, Margot. "A New War over Slavery." *Time,* June 9, 2003, 20.

Rosen, Jeff. "Hate Mail." *New Republic,* February 18, 1991, 19–21.

Ross, Marilyn J. *Success Factors of Young African-American Males at a Historically Black College.* Westport, Conn.: Bergin & Garvey, 1998.

Rowe, Peter. "Peace Officer: Refugee Brings Sense of Justice to Little Mogadishu." *San Diego Union-Tribune,* November 9, 2003, E1.

Rubenfeld, Jed. "Affirmative Action." *Yale Law Journal* 107 (1997): 427–72.

Sacerdote, Bruce. "Slavery and the Intergenerational Transmission of Human Capital." www.dartmouth.edu/~bsacerdo/wpapers/Slavery3.pdf (available November 11, 2002).

Sanoff, Alvin P., et al. "Students Talk about Race." *U.S. News & World Report,* April 19, 1993, 57–58, 61–64.

Schmader, Toni, Brenda Major, and Richard H. Gramzow. "How African-American College Students Protect Their Self Esteem." *Journal of Blacks in Higher Education* 35 (Spring 2002): 116–19. Excerpted from "Coping with Ethnic Stereotypes in the Academic Domain: Perceived Injustice and Psychological Disengagement." *Journal of Social Issues* 57, no. 1 (Spring 2001): 93–111.

"Scholarship Is Apology for Bias." *San Diego Union-Tribune,* January 18, 2002.

Sebok, Anthony J. "The Brooklyn Slavery Class Action: More Than Just a Political Gambit." writ.news.findlaw.com/sebok/20020409.html (available April 9, 2002).

———. "Prosaic Justice." *Legal Affairs,* September/October 2002, 51–53.

Shakespeare, William. *The Merchant of Venice.* In *Complete Works of Shakespeare.* Cambridge text. Garden City, N.Y.: Doubleday, 1936.

Shell, Robert C. H. *Children of Bondage: A Social History of the Slave Society at the*

Cape of Good Hope, 1652–1838. Middletown, Conn.: Wesleyan University Press, 1994.

Sherman, William T. "Special Field Order No. 15: 'Forty Acres and a Mule.'" In *When Sorry Isn't Enough: The Controversy over Apologies and Reparations for Human Injustice,* edited by Roy L. Brooks, 365–66. New York: New York University Press, 1999.

Should America Pay? Slavery and the Raging Debate on Reparations. Edited by Raymond A. Winbush. New York: Amistad, 2003.

Shriver, Donald W., Jr. *An Ethic for Enemies: Forgiveness in Politics.* New York: Oxford University Press, 1995.

Simmons, William J. *Men of Mark: Eminent, Progressive and Rising.* Baltimore: Rewell, 1891.

Slater, Robert Bruce. "The Growing Gender Gap in Black Higher Education." *Journal of Blacks in Higher Education* 3 (Spring 1994): 52–59.

Slave Narratives: A Folk History of Slavery in the United States from Interviews with Former Slaves. Prepared by the Federal Writers' Project, 1936–38. Assembled by the Library of Congress, Washington, D.C., 1941.

"The Soft Bigotry of Low Expectations: Self-Esteem and the SAT." *Journal of Blacks in Higher Education* 29 (Autumn 2000): 104–5.

Sontag, Susan. *Regarding the Pain of Others.* New York: Farrar, Straus & Giroux, 2003.

Sowell, Thomas. *Inside American Tradition: The Decline, the Deception, the Dogmas.* New York: Free Press, 1993.

"Special Field Order No. 15: 'Forty Acres and a Mule.'" In *When Sorry Isn't Enough: The Controversy over Apologies for Human Injustice,* edited by Roy L. Brooks, 365–66. New York: New York University Press, 1999.

"Special Report: African-American College Graduation Rates: Intolerably Low and Not Catching Up to Whites." *Journal of Blacks in Higher Education* 37 (Autumn 2002): 89–102.

Steele, Claude M. "A Threat in the Air: How Stereotypes Shape Intellectual Identity and Performance." In *Promise and Dilemma: Perspectives on Racial Diversity and Higher Education,* edited by Eugene Y. Lowe Jr., 92–129. Princeton, N.J.: Princeton University Press, 1999.

———. "Understanding the Performance Gap." In *Who's Qualified?* edited by Lani Guinier and Susan Sturm, 60–67. Boston: Beacon Press, 2001.

Steele, Shelby. *The Content of Our Character: A New Vision of Race in America.* New York: St. Martin's Press, 1990.

———. ". . . Or a Childish Illusion of Justice? Reparations Enshrine Victimhood, Dishonoring Our Ancestors." In *Should America Pay? Slavery and the Raging Debate on Reparations,* edited by Raymond A. Winbush, 197–99. New York: Amistad, 2003.

Steinmetz, Greg. "One Family's Battle for Ancestral Land Poses Hard Questions." *Wall Street Journal,* November 12, 1996.

Stokes, Anson Phelps. "American Race Relations in War Time." *Journal of Negro Education* 14, no. 4 (Autumn 1945): 535–51.

"The Sudden Decline in the Nationwide Number of Black Faculty." *Journal of Blacks in Higher Education* 35 (Spring 2002): 12–13.

Synnott, Marcia G. "The Admission and Assimilation of Minority Students at Harvard, Yale, and Princeton, 1900–1970." *History of Education Quarterly* 19, no. 3 (Autumn 1979): 285–304.

Takaki, Ronald. "Aesculapius Was a White Man: Antebellum Racism and Male Chauvinism at Harvard Medical School." *Phylon* 39, no. 2 (1978): 128–34.

Tavuchis, Nicholas. *Mea Culpa: A Sociology of Apology and Reconciliation.* Stanford, Calif.: Stanford University Press, 1991.

Teitel, Ruti G. *Transitional Justice.* New York: Oxford University Press, 2000.

"The Test Score Gap." PBS, *Frontline,* www.pbs.org/wgbh/pages/frontline/shows/sats/ (available June 14, 2002).

Thernstrom, Stephan, and Abigail Thernstrom. *America in Black and White: One Nation, Indivisible.* New York: Simon & Schuster, 1997.

Thomas, Evan. "Cover Story: Rush Limbaugh's World of Pain." *Newsweek,* October 20, 2003, 45.

Thomas, Gail E. "College Characteristics and Black Students' Four-Year College Graduation." *Journal of Negro Education* 50, no. 3 (Summer 1981): 328–45.

Thomson, Chas H. "Introduction: The Problem of Negro Higher Education." *Journal of Negro Education* 2, no. 3 (July 1933): 257–71.

Tidmarsh, Jay, and Roger H. Trangsrud. *Complex Litigation: Problems in Advanced Civil Procedure.* New York: Foundation Press, 2002.

Tierney, John. "Life: The Cost-Benefit Analysis." *New York Times,* May 18, 2003.

Tocqueville, Alexis de. *Democracy in America.* 1835–39. Translated and edited by Harvey C. Mansfield and Delba Winthrop. Chicago: University of Chicago Press, 2000.

Torpey, John. " 'Making Whole What Has Been Smashed': Reflections on Reparations." *Journal of Modern History* 73, no. 2 (June 2001): 333–58.

Tutu, Desmond. *No Future without Forgiveness.* New York: Doubleday, 1999.

Tucker, Neely. "A Long Road of Broken Promises for Black Farmers; USDA Fights Claims after Landmark Deal." *Washington Post,* August 13, 2002.

Tucker, Ronnie Bernard. *Affirmative Action, the Supreme Court and Political Power in the Old Confederacy.* Lanham, Md.: University Press of America, 2000.

Turner, Frederick Jackson. *Rereading Frederick Jackson Turner: "The Significance of the Frontier in American History" and Other Essays.* Commentary by John Mack Faragher. New York: Holt, 1994.

United Nations. "Report of the World Conference against Racism, Racial Discrimination, Xenophobia, and Related Intolerance, Durban, South Africa, August 8–September 7, 2001." www.un.org/WCAR/aconf189_12.pdf (available June 20, 2003).

———. "Third Committee Approves Five-Part Draft Resolution Calling for Action to Counter Racism and Intolerance, as It Concludes Current Session." www.unhcr.ch/huricane/huricane . . . opendocume. (press release, available November 27, 2002).

United States. Commission on Wartime Relocation and Internment of Civilians. *Personal Justice Denied.* Washington, D.C.: Government Printing Office, 1983.

———. Department of Commerce, Bureau of the Census. *Characteristics of the Population, 1960.* Washington, D.C.: Government Printing Office, 1963.

———. *Educational Attainment in the United States (Update): March 2000.* Current Population Reports, P20–536. Washington, D.C.: Government Printing Office, 2000.

———. *Negroes in the United States, 1920–1932.* Washington, D.C.: Government Printing Office, 1934.

———. *Negro Population, 1790–1915.* Washington, D.C.: Government Printing Office, 1918. Reprint. New York: Kraus, 1969.

———. *The Social and Economic Status of the Black Population in the United States: A Historic View, 1790–1978.* Washington, D.C.: Government Printing Office, 1980.

———. *Statistical Abstract of the United States: 2002.* 122d ed. Washington, D.C.: Government Printing Office, 2002.

———. *2001 Statistical Abstract of the United States.* Washington, D.C.: Government Printing Office, 2002.

———. *U.S. Census of Population: 1950, General Characteristics, U.S. Summary.* Washington, D.C.: Government Printing Office, 1952.

———. Department of Education, National Center for Education Statistics. *Descriptive Summary of 1995–96 Beginning Students: Six Years Later.* Washington, D.C.: Government Printing Office, December 2002.

——. *Persistence and Attainment in Post-Secondary Education for Beginning AY 1980–90 Studies as of Spring 1992.* Washington, D.C.: Office of Educational Research and Improvement, November 1993.

——. "Degree-Granting Post-Secondary: Enrollment." www.nces.ed.gov (available June 14, 2002).

——. *Youth Indicators, 1996: Trends in the Well-Being of American Youth.* Washington, D.C.: Government Printing Office, 1996.

——. Office of Educational Research and Improvement. *The Traditionally Black Institutions of Higher Education, 1860 to 1982,* by Susan T. Hill, National Center for Education Statistics (NCES) 84308. Washington, D.C.: Government Printing Office, 1985.

——. Department of Interior, Bureau of Education. *A Study of the Private and Higher Schools for Colored People in the United States.* Washington, D.C.: Government Printing Office, 1917.

——. *Survey of Negro Colleges and Universities,* by Arthur C. Klien, Division of Higher Education. Washington, D.C.: Government Printing Office, 1929; reprinted, New York: Negro University Press, 1969.

——. Department of Justice. "German Compensation for National Socialist Crimes." In *When Sorry Isn't Enough: The Controversy over Apologies for Human Injustice,* edited by Roy L. Brooks, 61–67. New York: New York University Press, 1999.

——. *Report to the Congress of the United States: A Review of the Restrictions on Persons of Italian Ancestry during World War II.* Washington, D.C.: Government Printing Office, 2001.

——. President's Commission on Higher Education. *Higher Education for Democracy.* Vol. 1. New York: Harper & Bros., 1950.

The U.S. Constitution and Fascinating Facts about It. 6th ed. Supplemental text by Robert F. Tedeschi Jr. Naperville, Ill.: Oak Hill, 1996.

Valien, Preston. "Desegregation in Higher Education: A Critical Summary." *Journal of Negro Education* 27, no. 3 (Summer 1958): 373–80.

Van Alstyne, William W. "The Demise of the Right-Privilege Distinction in Constitutional Law." *Harvard Law Review* 81 (1968): 1439–64.

"Vatican Recommends Reparations to Atone for Slavery." *San Diego Union-Tribune,* August 30, 2001.

Verdun, Vincene. "If the Shoe Fits, Wear It: An Analysis of Reparations to African Americans." *Tulane Law Review* 67 (1993): 597–668.

Verwoerd, Wilhelm. "Justice after Apartheid? Reflections on the South African TRC." In *When Sorry Isn't Enough: The Controversy over Apologies and Repara-*

tions for Human Injustice, edited by Roy L. Brooks, 479–86. New York: New York University Press, 1999.

"Vital Signs: The Statistics That Describe the Present and Suggest the Future of African Americans in Higher Education." *Journal of Blacks in Higher Education* 1 (Autumn 1993): 15–24; 2 (Winter 1993–94): 33–43; 3 (Spring 1994): 29–39.

Von Hildebrand, Dietrich. *Christian Ethics.* New York: David McKay, 1953.

Washington, Booker T. *Up from Slavery.* 1901. Reprint. New York: Bantam Books, 1963.

Washington, Valora, and Joanna Newman. "Setting Our Own Agenda: Exploring the Meaning of Gender Disparities among Blacks in Higher Education." *Journal of Negro Education* 60, no. 1 (Winter 1991): 19–35.

"Weekly Bulletin." February 1, 2003. www.jbhe.com (available February 1, 2003).

Westley, Robert. "Many Billions Gone: Is It Time to Reconsider the Case for Black Reparations?" *Boston College Law Review* 40 (1998): 429–76.

Weyl, Nathaniel. *The Negro in American Civilization.* Washington, D.C.: Public Affairs Press, 1960.

"Whole Lott of Trouble." abcnews.com (available December 11, 2002).

"Widening Racial Wealth Gap Is a Serious Barrier to Higher Education." *Journal of Blacks in Higher Education* 39 (Spring 2003): 48–49.

Wiedemann, Thomas. *Greek and Roman Slavery.* Baltimore: Johns Hopkins University Press, 1981.

Wikramanayake, Marina. *A World in Shadow: The Free Black in Antebellum South Carolina.* Columbia, S.C.: University of South Carolina Press, 1973.

Wilds, Deborah J. *Minorities in Higher Education.* Seventeenth Annual Status Report. Washington, D.C.: American Council on Education, 2000.

Williams, Armstrong. "Presumed Victims." In *Should America Pay? Slavery and the Raging Debate on Reparations,* edited by Raymond A. Winbush, 165–71. New York: Amistad, 2003.

Williams, Juan. "The Higher Education of Thurgood Marshall." *Journal of Blacks in Higher Education* 22 (Winter 1998–99): 82–88.

Williams, Patricia J. *The Alchemy of Race and Rights.* Cambridge, Mass.: Harvard University Press, 1991.

Wish, Harvey. "Negro Education and the Progressive Movement." *Journal of Negro History* 49, no. 3 (July 1964): 184–200.

Woodson, Carter G. *African Heroes and Heroines.* Washington, D.C.: Associated Publishers, 1939.

———. *The Education of the Negro Prior to 1961.* Washington, D.C.: Association for the Study of Negro Life and History / Associated Publishers, 1919.

Woodward, C. Vann. *The Strange Career of Jim Crow.* 1955. 2d rev. ed. New York: Oxford University Press, 1966.

"The Worsening of the Racial Gap in SAT Scores." *Journal of Blacks in Higher Education* 33 (Autumn 2001): 22–26.

Wu, Frank. *Yellow: Race in America beyond Black and White.* New York: Basic Books, 2002.

CASES

Adams v. Richardson, 351 F. Supp. 636 (D.D.C. 1972), modified and aff'd, 480 F.2d 1159 (D.C. Cir. 1973)

Adarand Constructors, Inc. v. Pena, 515 U.S. 200 (1995)

Alexander v. Governor of the State of Oklahoma, Docket No. 03cv00133 (N.D. Okl.) filed February 24, 2003

American Insurance Association v. Garamendi, 123 S. Ct. 2374 (2003)

Argentine Republic v. Amerada Hess Shipping Corp., 488 U.S. 428 (1989)

Bell v. United States, 2001 WL 1041792, 2001 U.S. Dist. LEXIS 14812 (N.D. Tex. 2001)

Bellanca Corp. v. Bellanca, 169 A.2d 620 (Del. 1961)

Berea College v. Kentucky, 211 U.S. 45 (1908)

Berry v. United States, 1994 WL 374537, 1994 U.S. Dist. LEXIS 9665 (N.D. Cal. 1994)

Bivens v. Six Unknown Named Agents of Federal Bureau of Narcotics, 403 U.S. 388 (1971)

Bodner v. Banque Paribas, 114 F. Supp. 2d 117 (E.D.N.Y. 2000)

Bolling v. Sharpe, 347 U.S. 497 (1954)

Brown v. Board of Education [Brown I], 347 U.S. 483 (1954)

Brown v. Board of Education [Brown II], 349 U.S. 294 (1955)

Burger-Fischer v. Degussa AG, 65 F. Supp. 2d 248 (D.N.J. 1999)

Cantor Fitzgerald L.P. v. Cantor, 724 A.2d 571 (Del. Ch. 1998)

Cato v. United States, 70 F.3d 1103 (9th Cir. 1995)

City of... [see name of city]

Cleburne, City of, v. Cleburne Living Center, Inc., 473 U.S. 432 (1985)

Clark v. Board of Education, 24 Iowa 266 (1868)

Cooper v. Aaron, 358 U.S. 1 (1958)

Craig v. Boren, 429 U.S. 190 (1976)

Dred Scott v. Sandford, 60 U.S. (19 How.) 393 (1857)

Dumas v. Auto Club Insurance Association, 473 N.W.2d 652 (Mich. 1991)

Farmer-Paellmann v. FleetBoston Financial Corp., Aetna, Inc., CSX, C.A. No. 1:02–1862 (E.D.N.Y. 2002)

Fishel v. BASF Group, 175 F.R.D. 525 (S.D. Iowa 1997)

Fleer Corp. v. Topps Chewing Gum, Inc., 539 A.2d 1060 (Del. 1988)

Florida ex rel. Hawkins v. Board of Control, 350 U.S. 413 (1956)

Fordice, United States v., 505 U.S. 717 (1992)

Fullilove v. Klutznich, 448 U.S. 448 (1980)

Gayle v. Browder, 352 U.S. 903 (1956)

Gratz v. Bollinger, 123 S. Ct. 2411 (2003)

Grutter v. Bollinger, 123 S. Ct. 2325 (2003)

Hale, State v., 9 N.C. (2 Hawks) 582 (1823)

Hazelwood School District v. United States, 433 U.S. 299 (1977)

Hirabayashi v. United States, 320 U.S. 81 (1943), writ of error *coram nobis* granted 828 F.2d 591 (9th Cir. 1987)

Hohri v. United States, 793 F.2d 304 (D.C. Cir. 1986)

Hohri v. United States, 847 F.2d 779 (Fed. Cir. 1988), aff'g 586 F. Supp. 769 (D.D.C. 1984)

Hohri v. United States, 482 U.S. 64 (1987)

Hopwood v. State of Texas, 78 F.3d 932 (5th Cir. 1996), cert. denied *sub nom.*, 518 U.S. 1033 (1996), rev'd *Grutter v. Bollinger*, 2003 WL 21433492, 2003 U.S. LEXIS 4800 (June 23, 2003)

Hurdle v. FleetBoston Financial Corporation, et al., CGC-02–412388 (Superior Court, County of San Francisco, September 9, 2002)

In re African-American Slave Descendants Litigation, 231 F. Supp. 2d 1357 (2002)

In re Nazi Era Cases against German Defendants Litigation, 198 F.R.D. 429 (D.N.J. 2000)

In re World War II Era Japanese Forced Labor Litigation, 114 F. Supp. 2d 939 (N.D. Cal. 2000)

In re World War II Era Japanese Forced Labor Litigation, 164 F. Supp. 2d 1160 (N.D. Cal. 2001)

Iwanowa v. Ford Motor Co., 67 F. Supp. 2d 424 (D.N.J. 1999)

Jacobs v. Barr, 959 F.2d. 313 (D.C. Cir. 1992), cert. denied, 506 U.S. 831 (1992)

Johnson v. McAdoo, 45 App. D.C. 440 (1917)

Jones v. Alfred H. Mayer Co., 392 U.S. 409 (1968)

Joo v. Japan, 172 F. Supp. 2d 52 (D.D.C. 2001)

Kadic v. Karadzic, 70 F.3d 232 (2d Cir. 1995)

Kammer Asphalt Paving Co., Inc. v. East China Township Schools, 504 N.W.2d 635 (Mich. 1993)

Korematsu v. United States, 323 U.S. 214 (1944)

Local 28, Sheet Metal Workers' International Association v. Equal Employment Opportunity Commission, 478 U.S. 421 (1986)

Local No. 93, International Association of Firefighters v. City of Cleveland, 478 U.S. 501 (1986)

Marbury v. Madison, 5 U.S. (1 Cranch) 137 (1803)

Marta v. Nepa, 385 A.2d 727 (Del. 1978)

McLaurin v. Oklahoma State Regents for Higher Education, 339 U.S. 637 (1950)

Metro Broadcasting, Inc. v. FCC, 497 U.S. 547 (1990)

Mississippi University for Women v. Hogan, 458 U.S. 718 (1982)

Missouri v. Jenkins, 515 U.S. 70 (1995) (Jenkins III)

Morgan, United States v., 346 U.S. 502 (1954)

Moses v. MacFarlen, 97 Eng. Rep. 676 (K.B. 1760)

Obadele v. United States, 52 Fed. Cl. 432 (2002)

Ottawa v. Tinnon, 26 Kan. 1 (1881)

Pigford v. Glickman, 182 F.R.D. 341 (D.D.C. 1998), 185 F.R.D. 82 (D.D.C. 1999)

Pigford v. Veneman, 143 F. Supp. 2d 28 (D.D.C. 2001); 148 F. Supp. 2d 31 (D.D.C. 2001); 182 F. Supp. 2d 50 (D.D.C. 2002) rev'd and remanded by 292 F.3d 918 (D.C. Cir. 2002)

Plessy v. Ferguson, 163 U.S. 537 (1896)

Princz v. Federal Republic of Germany, 813 F. Supp. 22 (D.D.C. 1992), rev'd by 26 F.3d 1166 (D.C. Cir. 1994)

Reed, State v., 9 N.C. (2 Hawks) 454 (1823)

Regents of the University of California v. Bakke, 438 U.S. 265 (1978)

Richmond, City of, v. J. A. Croson Co., 488 U.S. 469 (1989)

Roberts v. City of Boston, 5 Cush. (59 Mass.) 198 (1849)

Rosner v. United States, 231 F. Supp. 2d 1202 (S.D. Fla. 2002)

Saylor v. Lindsley, 456 F.2d 896 (2d Cir. 1972)

Sioux Nation of Indians, United States v., 448 U.S. 371 (1980)

Slaughter-House Cases, 83 U.S. 36 (1872)

Snider, United States v., 779 F.2d 1151 (6th Cir. 1985)

State Farm Fire and Casualty Co. v. Century Home Components, Inc., 550 P.2d 1185 (Or. 1976)

State v. . . . [see under name of opposing party]

Taiheiyo Cement Corp. v. Superior Court, 129 Cal. Rptr. 2d 451 (Cal. Ct. App. 2003)

Teamsters v. United States, 431 U.S. 324 (1977)

Tustin Elevator & Lumber Co. v. Ryno, 129 N.W.2d 409 (Mich. 1964)

United States v. . . . [see under name of opposing party]

Virginia, United States v., 518 U.S. 515 (1996)

Yasui v. United States, 320 U.S. 115 (1943)

STATUTES

U.S. Constitution

Amend. XIII (Slavery and Involuntary Servitude)
Amend. XIV (Equal Protection and Due Process)
Amend. XV (Voting)

Federal Codes

5 U.S.C.

§ 702 (Administrative Procedure Act, Right of Review)

7 U.S.C.

§ 2297 (Agricultural and Related Agencies Appropriations Act)

15 U.S.C.

§ 1691 (Equal Credit Opportunity Act)

28 U.S.C.

§ 1331 (Federal Question Jurisdiction)
§ 1332 (Federal Diversity Jurisdiction)
§ 1343 (Civil Rights Jurisdiction)
§ 1346(a)(2) (Little Tucker Act)
§ 1346(b) (Federal Tort Claims Act)

§1346(f)

§ 1350 (Alien Tort Claims Act)

§ 1367 (Federal Supplemental Jurisdiction)

§ 1491(a)(1) (Tucker Act)

§ 1491(a)(2)

§ 1605–7 (Foreign Sovereign Immunity Act)

§ 2401(b) (Federal Tort Claims Act Statute of Limitations)

§ 2409a (Quiet Title Act)

§§ 2671–80 (Federal Tort Claims Act)

42 U.S.C.

§ 1971 (Voting Rights Act of 1965)

§ 1981 (Civil Rights Act of 1866)

§§ 2000e-2(a)(1) and 2000e-5(g) (Civil Rights Act of 1964, Title VII)

50 U.S.C.

§ 1989b (Civil Liberties Act of 1988)

50 App. U.S.C.

§ 1981 (Evacuation Claims Act of 1948)

§§ 1989(a)–(d) (Civil Liberties Act of 1988)

Executive Orders

9066 (February 19, 1942) (World War II Removal and Internment)

9102 (March 20, 1942) (World War II Removal and Internment)

Federal Rules of Civil Procedure

60(b)

California Codes

CAL. CIV. PRO. CODE §§ 354.6(a)–(c) (World War II Slave Labor Victim Act)

CAL. INS. CODE §§ 13800–13807 (Holocaust Victim Insurance Relief Act of 1999
[HVIRA])

Congressional Bills

"Commission to Study Reparation Proposals," HR 40, 101st Cong., 1st sess. (Nov. 21, 1989)

EEO Act of 1972 (Pub. L. 92–261), §§ 4(a)–8(c) [codified at 42 U.S.C. §§ 2000e-5(a) to 2000e-9(c)]

California Legislative Bills

California Legislature, 2000, Senate Bill 2199

INDEX

ABC News, 38, 40
abolitionists, 5, 25–26, 32–33, 55–56, 58,
    63, 170, 194
accounting, 14, 101
Acheson, Dean, 69
ACS (American Colonization Society), 5,
    55
acting white, 85–86
Adams, John, 181
Adams, John Quincy, 181
Adarand Constructors, Inc. v. Peña, 174,
    176, 179
Adenauer, Konrad, xv
Administrative Procedures Act, 124
admissions policies, 65–66, 68–69, 71–
    73, 79–81, 238n134, 240–41n158,
    243n179
Aesop, 184
Aetna Insurance Company, 15
affirmative action, xvi, 71–72, 75, 79–82,
    90, 172, 175–79, 192–93, 223n20, 261–
    62n35
Africa, repatriation to, 4–5, 56, 224n13
African governments, 18, 180

African Methodist Episcopal (A.M.E.)
    Church, 50, 59
African slavery, 181–82, 185, 188, 207–8
agape, 165
Age of Apology, xiii–xiv
Age of Jackson, xii
Alabama State University, 90
Albright, Madeleine, 110, 251n46
Aleuts, xiii, 177
Alexander's Magazine, 63
*Alexander v. Governor of the State of Okla-
    homa,* 127, 130–31, 258n168
Alienikoff, Alexander, 78
Alien Tort Claims Act (ATCA), 99, 104–
    6, 110, 251–52n47
Allen, Walter, 94
Allen, William G., 51
Allied Forces, xiv–xv, 100, 103
Alpha Phi Alpha, 56
alternative-life argument, 46
American Colonization Society (ACS), 5,
    55
American Council on Education, 93
American Dream, 41

American Jews, 18, 107–12, 194
American Negro Slavery (Phillips), 149
American Revolution, 21, 32, 85, 96, 133,
    185
American Sociological Association, 94
Amherst College, 50, 82, 89
amnesia, 165, 167, 192; collective, 141, 150
amnesty, 147
Anderson, Jourdon, 6
Anderson, P. H., 6
Andrew Johnson and Reconstruction
    (McKitrick), 150
anti-affirmative action, 79–81
anti-discrimination laws, 70–71
anti-Israel forces, 16–18
AP (Advanced Placement) exams, 73, 84,
    86
apartheid: in Jim Crow era, ix, 44, 69,
    124; in South Africa, xiii, xvi, 35, 140,
    147
apology: African governments and, 180;
    atonement model and, ix–x, xii–xvii,
    143–54, 156–63, 259–60n6, 261n33;
    black redress movement and, 10–15,
    201; Federal Republic of Germany
    and, xv, 107, 143–44; forced labor liti-
    gation and, 112; Japanese American
    removal and internment and, 118;
    slave-redress litigation and, 123, 138–
    39, 258–59n170; tort model and, 100;
    U.S. government and, ix–x, 141–43,
    156, 169–70, 181, 185, 188, 201
Aristotle, 183
Articles of Confederation, 2, 24, 227n20
Ashmore, Harry, 37–38
Asians, 87, 160–61, 190–91, 262–63n37.
    See also names of Asian ethnic groups
Askia the Great, 49
assault and battery, 101, 108, 134
asymmetrical social measures, 155, 172,
    177, 193, 195–96
ATCA (Alien Torts Claims Act), 99,
    104–6, 110, 251–52n47

Atlanta University, 60, 63
atonement: forgiveness and, 143, 166, 168;
    racial reconciliation and, ix–x, 194,
    201, 202–6, 221n2; rhetoric of, 19 *(see
    also* post-Holocaust vision of redress);
    tort model and, 99, 112, 139–40
atonement model, x, xii, xvi–xvii, 3, 6,
    10–12, 141–79, 222n7; apology, anat-
    omy of, 143–54, 188; forgiveness, anat-
    omy of, 163–69; political implications
    of, xii–xiii, 169–71, 201–2, 208; repa-
    rations, anatomy of, 155–63, 191–93;
    reparations, constitutionality of, 171–
    79
atonement money, xvii, 140, 156
atonement syllogism, x, 208
atonement trust fund, xi, 157, 159–63,
    169, 172–79, 191, 198–99, 202, 204
atrocities, xii–xvii, 213–17, 222n12;
    atonement model and, ix–xii, 11,
    141–47, 153, 155–56, 165, 195–96,
    259–60n6; tort model and, 114,
    116, 140. *See also* Jim Crow; slavery
attrition rates, black, 72–74, 89–95
Auerbach, Carl, xiv
Australian aborigines, xiii, 12, 153
Ayres, Ian, 102

backlash, white, 79, 171
*Bakke, Regents of the University of Califor-
    nia v.,* 71, 79, 174
Balbus, Ike, 150–51
Ball, Charles, 27–29
Ball, Edward, 3
banks. *See* financial institutions
Banks, Tanya, 160
Banneker, Benjamin, 4
Barkan, Elazar, 148, 155
Barr, Jacobs v., 176–77
Barrett, Paul, 204–5
BASF corporation, 108
basic capital, 2–3, 21
Bayer corporation, 108

"racially neutral" justifications, 62, 81,
243–44n183
racial preferences, 2, 71, 79–80, 90, 174,
192–93, 243n179, 261–62n35
racial profiling, 40, 42, 230n15
racial progress, 45–47, 51, 159, 169, 171,
231n37
racial reconciliation: atonement model
and, ix–x, xii, xvi–xvii, 141–43, 157,
163–64, 168–69, 171; black redress
movement and, 194–95, 202–6; in
South Africa, 147; tort model and,
99–100, 139, 258–59n170
racial slavery, 20–21, 23, 148–49, 157,
180, 182–83, 187–88
racism: atonement model and, 171, 200–
201, 204, 270n61; free blacks and, 33;
higher education and, 50, 54–56, 73–
74, 93–96, 240–41nn158,159, 248n237;
as justification for racial slavery, 183–
85, 188; psychology of slavery and, 38–
40; socioeconomics of slavery and, 46;
Zionism and, 16–18
racist heritage, 190
racist rhetoric, 37, 54, 87
railroad cars, 67, 173, 224n2
rappers, 86, 202–3, 270n66
Reagan, Ronald, xii, xiii, 39, 79, 118
Reason, Charles L., 51
received traditions, 37–48; psychology
of slavery, 37–41; socioeconomics of
slavery, 41–48
Reconstruction, 2, 7–8, 44, 70, 120–22,
149–50, 169, 194, 223–24n1, 243–
44n183
Red Cross, 107
reduction, harms of, 42, 44
Regarding the Pain of Others (Sontag), 207
Rehabilitation Act (1973), 71
rehabilitative reparations, 156–57, 198
Rehnquist, William, 175, 265n86
Reid, Omar, 41
remorse, xiv, 142–43, 166, 258–59n170

Renaissance, 186
"Repairing the Past: New Efforts in
the Reparations Debate in America"
(Ogletree), 266n1
reparations: in atonement model, ix–x,
xiii–xiv, xvii, 142–43, 155–63, 171–79;
black redress movement and, 11–19,
197–99; Federal Republic of Germany
and, xv, 107–8, 188; Japanese American removal and internment and, 118,
176–77; tort model and, 139; U.S.
government and, 142–43, 169–71, 208
Reparations Coordinating Committee,
130
repatriation to Africa, 4–5, 33, 56, 224n13
representative democracy, xii, 152, 202,
208, 271n3
repression, harms of, 42, 44, 53
resentment, overcoming of, 164–65,
167–69, 264n66
responsibility: civic, 143, 152, 154; moral,
156; personal, 138, 144
restitutionary law, 99, 101, 135–37
restorative justice, xv–xvi, 6, 11, 19, 141,
147–48, 195–96, 211
retention rates, black, 72–73
retributive justice, 147
Rice, Condoleeza, 17, 226n42
Rice University, 80
Richmond Theological Seminary, 58
rights of action, 99, 132–37. *See also*
common-law rights of action
Riley, Jason, 45
Riley, Richard W., 79
Ringle, Kenneth D., 113
Riverside Church (New York City), 11
Robertson, Carol, 210
Roberts v. City of Boston, 234n72
Robinson, Randall, 14
Rodriguez, Patricia, 161
role models, 77, 86, 92
Roman slavery, 184, 186, 267n16, 268n28
Roosevelt, Franklin, xiii, 10, 112

U.S. Constitution: atonement model and, 171–79; slavery and, 2, 21, 24–25, 34, 52, 117, 124, 187, 227n16, 233n60, 255n110; tort model and, 99. *See also titles of court cases*

U.S. Department of Agriculture, 7–8, 125–29, 256n128

U.S. Department of Education, 81

U.S. Department of State, 108, 113

U.S. Environmental Protection Agency, 163

U.S. government: atonement and, ix–x, 141–42, 148–49, 151–54, 156–63, 169–70, 181, 185, 188, 201; black redress movement and, ix–xiii, xvi, 2–18; constitutional or statutory law, 100, 104–6, 109, 121–24; free blacks and, 32, 34; higher education and, 60–61, 65, 70–71, 239n146; Indians and, xvi, 12; slave-redress litigation against, 99–100, 119–30, 255nn110,115; slavery and, 21, 138

U.S. Internal Revenue Service, 13–14

U.S. Supreme Court: atonement model and, 159, 171–79; higher education and, 65, 248–49n245; Japanese American removal and internment and, 113–15, 118; psychology of slavery and, 40; tort model and, 110–11. *See also titles of court cases*

U.S. Treasury Department, 9

Valien, Preston, 69

Vashon, George B., 51

Vassa, Gustavus, 4

Vassar College, 56, 82, 89–90

Vatican, 16

Vaughan, Walter, 9

venture capital funds, 162

Versailles, Treaty of, xiv

Verwoerd, Wilhelm, 147

veterans: black, 10, 69, 130; white, 100, 103, 194

victim groups, 17–18

victimhood, 188, 191

"victimization by self-fulfilling prophecy," 73

victimology, black, xvii, 41, 43

victim-perpetrator identification: atonement model and, xv–xvii, 141–47, 156, 163–70, 177–79, 195, 201, 259–60n6; lack of, 34–35; post-Holocaust vision of, 11, 19, 141, 148, 211; tort model and, x, 100

violence, racial, 14, 44, 46, 64, 94, 130–31, 142, 171

Virginia slave code, 22–23

virtue, 200–201

Voice of the Negro (magazine), 63

Voting Rights Act (1965), 193

Wall Street Journal, 17–18, 38, 45

War Relocation Authority, 112

Warsaw Ghetto, 143

Washington, Booker T., 62, 236–37nn108,109

Washington, Bushrod, 5

Washington, George, 5, 21, 187

Washington, Valora, 78

Washington Post, 92

wealth: higher education and, 74, 91, 92–93, 96, 240–41n158; psychology of slavery and, 40; redistributed, 102; socioeconomics of slavery and, 42–43, 47

wealthy black families, 162

wealthy white families, 3, 99, 137

Webster, Daniel, 5

welfare, xvii, 142, 155, 196

Wesley, Cynthia, 210

West Georgia College, 261n33

Weyl, Nathaniel, 184, 186

What's Great about America (D'Souza), 199

Wheatley, Phillis, 4, 63

whipping, 30–31

White, Byron, 175, 265n86

white Americans: free blacks and, 32; innocence of, 151–54, 188–92; psychology of slavery and, 38–40; slave redress and, xi–xii, 148–54, 196, 201–2; tort model and, 3, 6, 98

white guilt, 98, 150–51

white-on-black oppression, 161, 196, 203

White over Black: American Attitudes toward the Negro, 1550–1812 (Jordan), 54

white Southerners, 2, 9, 190

white supremacy, 38

Wiesel, Elie, 146–47

Wiggins, Edith, 95

Wilberforce, William, 181

Wilberforce University (Ohio), 50, 56, 59, 60

Wilkens, Roy, 69

Williams, Armstrong, 43, 188

Williams, Nancy, 29–30

Williams, Patricia, 102, 152

Williams, Vanessa, 160

Williams College, 89

Williamson, Joel, 66

Wilson, Ella, 31

Wilson, Henry, xiv

Wilson, Woodrow, 170

Winfrey, Oprah, 148

Winthrop, Governor, 23

Woods, Tiger, 148

Woodson, Carter G., 51

World Conference against Racism, Racial Discrimination, Xenophobia and Related Intolerance (Durban, S.A.), 16–18, 226n42

World War I, xiv, 44, 130

World War II, xiii, xvi, 44, 68–69, 100–112, 254n102. *See also* Holocaust; Japanese American removal and internment

wrongful death, 131, 134

Wu, Frank, 191, 262–63n37

Yale Alumni Magazine, 149

Yale University, 65, 70, 75–76, 82, 89, 95, 162

Yasui, Minoru, 114, 116

Yasui v. United States, 114, 139

Young, Whitney, 69

Zionism, 16–18

Compositor:	BookMatters, Berkeley
Indexer:	Sharon Sweeney
Text:	11/14 Adobe Garamond
Display:	Adobe Garamond / Gill Sans Book
Printer and binder:	Sheridan Books, Inc.